See You in the Piazza

See You in the Piazza

❀

New Places to Discover in Italy

F R A N C E S   M A Y E S

CROWN
NEW YORK

Copyright © 2019 by Frances Mayes

All rights reserved.
Published in the United States by Crown, an imprint of the Crown
Publishing Group, a division of Penguin Random House LLC, New York.
crownpublishing.com

CROWN and the Crown colophon are registered trademarks of Penguin
Random House LLC.

Library of Congress Cataloging-in-Publication data is available upon request.

ISBN 978-0-451-49769-7
Ebook ISBN 978-0-451-49771-0

Printed in the United States of America

Book design by Elina Nudelman
Map and p. 124 illustration by Meredith Hamilton
Jacket design by Elena Giavaldi and Alane Gianetti
Jacket photograph: Paolo Tralli/Shutterstock

10 9 8 7 6 5 4 3 2 1

First Edition

FOR EDWARD

Italy

Valle D'Aosta

Trentino-Alto Adige

Friuli Venezia Giulia

Milano

Lombardy

Veneto

Venezia

Piemonte

Emilia-Romagna

Liguria

Firenze

Toscana

Marche

Umbria

Lazio

Abruzzo

Roma

Molise

Campania

Puglia

Napoli

Basilicata

Sardegna

Calabria

Sicilia

Contents

Le Marche

Lazio

Puglia

Sardegna

Sicilia

Epilogue

Italy, the endless surprise. The places I've chosen for this book are *for example,* because if you travel adventurously, you will find many others that draw you close and let you see why you ventured so far, and what you will take with you when you leave. Will it be a swim in the October-cold sea at Carloforte on Isola di San Pietro in Sardegna, a dip that jolted you out of summer doldrums and propelled you with great energy into the fall? Or a plate of arugula dressed with lemon juice and fresh olive oil in Sorrento, when the taste wedded to the heady scents of citrus blossoms from trees layered in ascending terraces all around you? That became the way you wanted to eat for the rest of your life. The regal cardinal striding into the Vatican. So pompous, you're thinking, but then you catch a glimpse of his robe caught in his rear end, proving that the divine is human. The mad woman performing Aïda arias in the fountain of Rome's Campo de' Fiori; lanterns' shadows flickering on stone when you looked out over the deserted Piazza Navona at three in the morning, hearing only the splash of the outlandish fountains below. And then a man starts playing Vivaldi on his flute. Your Rome, all in a day. The private moments, the little bursts of secret meaning that travel can give, the ancient light through the Greek columns at Selinunte, grazing the face of your child, casting her into the long historical span of time. Places give us such gifts, if we are ready to receive them.

I DIVIDE MY time between Italy and the United States. My home in Tuscany, Bramasole, became second nature to me and now is the place I've lived the longest of anywhere in my life. Do I know Italy well? No. Not because I haven't traveled, cooked, observed, gazed at a million paintings, and read the convoluted history. To know Italy takes ten lifetimes. Each time I return, I feel the same excitement I knew in the first years of living here. So much to learn, and what luck, I'll have five weeks or six days or three months—surely I will begin to feel I've a grasp on the place. But Italy remains elusive. Just beyond that hilltop castle, there's a valley of olive trees, then another town where the stony streets are pale gold instead of gray. The pasta is different there—made with half bread crumbs—the dialect is unintelligible, the local duomo's frescoes are painted in apricots and chalky blues with sublime faces you later see in the local bar while you sip your Negroni. You were in Bevagna; now you're a few kilometers away in Montefalco, a new world. Infinite differences—all packed into a country about the size of Arizona.

HUNGERING FOR MORE—MORE understanding, more exposure, more pasta—my husband, Ed, and I suddenly pack our little white Alfa Romeo and hit the road. Sometimes we are joined by William, our grandson; sometimes we are joined by friends, for an hour or for a week. Our wanderlust awakened: For a year and a half, we seek unique places hidden in plain sight, and also cities such as Genova and Parma—the names known, but who has lingered there? Italy. Infinite.

BECAUSE PASTA IS the national anthem, I'm searching for quintessential tastes of each place, though instead of pasta I might fall for *sbrisolona,* the crumbly, nutty dessert that turns divine when dipped in zabaglione. That swim in Carloforte? Followed by robust *paccheri,* a large hollow pasta with a talent for soaking up tomato and eggplant sauce. A fritto misto followed, fish just pulled from the water, crisply fried and succulent. That lusty dinner *became* Carloforte! And impossible to forget the pitcher of fruity red wine and the salad of wild greens picked that morning from the earth. The score of our adventure is the music of many corks popping.

Travel is a journey into one's own ignorance. Nothing proves this more quickly than dipping into Italian wine varieties. In every region, there are grapes—*nisiola, teroldego, nerello mascalese*—I've never known existed, as well as particular winemaking methods, such as the revival of aging in clay amphoras lined with beeswax. The Greeks and Romans, who seem to have known everything, also buried their *giare*. In effect, they're planting the wine into the earth.

SUCH PASSION EVERYWHERE for food. Even a two-year-old has an adventurous palate! More snails! He bangs with his spoon. More! We share the zeal. On arrival in every town, Ed begins plotting. How many lunches? How many dinners can we enjoy in this exceptional place? And markets! Each town retains the tradition of weekly go-to-market day. What's freshest, what's ready to plant, who has the truffles, who has the best porchetta, are the little violet artichokes in yet? I try to plan to be in a town on market day. There, you pick up a recipe for *topinambur,* Jerusalem artichokes, or you're offered a taste of the *annurca* apple (*an-nurche,* plural), an ancient variety that is picked green and ripened to winey sweetness on straw beds. (The grower will brag that Italy has a thousand five hundred varieties of apple, while the French have only fifteen. A suspect figure, but I admire his passion, *molto italiano*.) Vendors sometimes still hawk their wares, their high croaking voices hearkening back to the Middle Ages, when in these same streets men sold their honey and chickpeas.

THE MOST VIVID pleasures of Italy are the simple ones. You're installed at a table on a sun-drenched piazza. You have your notebook and the whole day. There's nothing you must do except let that sundial cast its shadow on the next hour, let the apricot façade of a renaissance palazzo reflect on the faces of those around you, let the memories of what brought you here rise and facet in your mind, let the waiter bring that second cappuccino before you set forth into the day.

FRESH MEMORIES: GREEK-WHITE villages of Puglia clinging to cliffs above the sea, the siren call of the Lazio coast, knotty medieval streets of Genova, vast underground Roman cisterns in Fermo, green hikes and hot chocolate in the Dolomiti, the trail of Frederick II's Puglian Romanesque churches, afternoons on the golden Tuscan beaches, the atmospheric Torino coffee bars where Cesare Pavese would write . . . Endless, yes.

See You in the Piazza is arranged geographically, north to south, instead of in the chronological trajectory of my travels. Since there's no thread of continuity, you may choose to read the sections randomly, though I suggest reading about whole regions together, as travels within them are usually contiguous.

Finding unexpected places to travel in Italy couldn't be easier. Just veer off any road. Several websites often lead me in surprising directions: The Touring Club Italiano produces good guides, extensive travel services, trips, and maps to all of Italy—and has for over 120 years. Their Bandiere Arancioni (orange banner) site, http://www .bandierearancioni.it, identifies more than two hundred small towns of particular beauty and cultural significance. I visited many for this book: In Piemonte: Neive, Cherasco, La Morra, Barolo, Orta San Giulio. In Trentino–Alto Adige: Campo Tures, Vipiteno. In Veneto: Asolo, Montagnana, Arquà Petrarca. In Friuli Venezia Giulia: Cividale del Friuli. In Liguria: Varese Ligure. In Toscana: Massa Marittima. In Umbria: Montefalco, Bevagna. In Le Marche: Mercatello sul Metauro. In Puglia: Troia, Orsara, Alberobello.

I Borghi più belli d'Italia, http://borghipiubelliditalia.it/borghi/, lists the most beautiful small towns of Italy. Not an exhaustive list but still useful.

Also helpful: various sites list Blue Flag beaches, those determined by the Foundation for Environmental Education to have the cleanest water and environmentally sound coasts.

I'm enthusiastic about the government-sponsored program of *agriturismi,* farm stays. These vary from boutique hotel standard to the simplest room. The advantage of either is that you meet local people who are usually hospitable and helpful. You may make a friend, or at least get to pet a goat. Often the *agriturismo* family will offer cheese-making or cooking classes. Check out the farms at https://www.agriturismo.it/en/.

If you like staying in historic inns, and sometimes castles, Dimore d'Epoca, http://www.dimoredepoca.it/en/, provides many romantic and characteristic listings.

For wine and restaurants, I rely on finding a local *enoteca* to learn about the area's vineyards. There are numerous useful apps and, prior to travel, I recommend downloading several. We especially like *Gambero Rosso*'s yearly wine and restaurant guides. Even though they're in Italian, the guides are symbol-oriented and easy to understand. While you're in an *enoteca,* a bar, bookstore, or produce stand, it's a good moment to ask, "Where do you eat for a special occasion?" You're likely to be told of a good local place with atmosphere.

I'M THRILLED TO include recipes from some of our favorite restaurants. Chefs have been enthusiastic, generous, and happy to share their talents. In translating their sometimes elusive notes, I've tried to keep the chef's tone—and to preserve the Italian way of presenting a recipe, which often leaves room for your own creativity. I've left the notation *QB, quanto basta,* meaning "how much is enough," or "to taste." Seasonings are almost always *QB* in an Italian recipe. No "¼ teaspoon of salt" or "6 leaves of basil"! Usually, too, the chef has left quantities of broth or wine open to common sense; I have sometimes inserted quantities when the amount didn't seem obvious, as when "a glass of white wine" is called for. What size glass might that be? When ingredients may be hard to obtain, such as a particular cheese, or wild game such as hare, I've suggested substitutes, although almost everything is available via Internet sources. Some recipes are challenging! I think they represent the new directions I'm finding in restaurants all over Italy, where chefs are suddenly improvising, taking traditions and running with them. Not to worry—there will always be *tagliatelle al ragù.* While testing, I learned new techniques and usages that I now carry over into other recipes. I hope you have fun trying these recipes that chefs have chosen as representative of their kitchens.

When looking for apartments and villas: Buyer beware. I've rented probably a hundred and still can make a mistake, although most have been pleasant and well located. Ask yourself what they're *not* showing in the photographs, then ask to see that omitted bathroom or kitchen. Tiny box showers, furniture covered with throws, bad art, dark rooms—all send up warning flags. While bad reviews can't always be trusted—some people are cranks—lots of iffy reviews certainly cause me to return to search. Look up the address on Google Earth to ascertain that the location is not beside a major road or in an inconvenient neighborhood.

Trains are a fantastic option. Italy has many fast trains, some with business class ambiance and friendly service of drinks, sandwiches, and snacks. The train trip often seems too short! Consult http://www.trenitalia.com and look for the Freccia (arrow) line: Frecciargento, Frecciarossa, and Frecciabianca. Italo, a private high-speed line, is another fabulous option: https://www.italotreno.it/en. The normal intercity trains are great, too.

Luggage is a burden. Best advice: Travel light.

Piemonte

Torino

The waiter slides toward me a clear little glass layered with cream, chocolate, and coffee. Sip the layers and you taste Torino. The *bicerin*—dialect for small glass—has come to be synonymous with the many atmospheric cafés that are the city's life blood. Torino is flush with regal boulevards and piazzas ringed with these delicious haunts. I'm at the wood-paneled Caffè Al Bicerin, intimate, with candles on tiny marble tables. In this very place, someone in 1763 first concocted the *bicerin,* a wickedly sumptuous drink. I like a place that remembers a coffee drink invented 256 years ago.

I've slipped into other historic cafés to sample their *bicerin* or lemonade or cappuccino. Bliss. There's Caffè Torino under the grand arcades, where the great Cesare Pavese, who lived nearby, used to meet other writers; Caffè Mulassano, with a marble bar and bentwood chairs, said to have the best espresso in town; Baratti e Milano, more chocolate- and confection-oriented than the others but with an old-world air; and Caffè San Carlo, all gilt and columns and statues.

In late afternoon, the cafés serve *aperitivi*. No surprise: Campari and vermouths such as Punt e Mes were all invented in Torino. Order a drink and you're welcome to a lavish buffet of *stuzzichini*—crostini, olives, chips, focaccia, prosciutto, slices of omelet, and *grissini,* bread sticks (also invented in Torino). This interlude previews dinner. Which is glorious to anticipate. Torino restaurants are up there with the best in Italy.

LATE MORNING, ED and William, who've been out walking, meet me under the arcades at Caffè Torino. They are impressed by its bodacious chandeliers, smooth waitstaff, and medallion of a rampant bull inlaid in the flagstones outside the door. This is a perfect perch for watching the human parade. We order cappuccino, then *tramezzini,* the triangular half sandwiches made of trimmed, soft white bread—the kind of air bread we usually scorn. "These were invented in Torino," I tell them. "At Caffè Mulassano. The weird poet D'Annunzio made up the name . . ." Mine is ham and cheese.

"*Tramezzo,* a divider. Across the middle," Ed says. "The *-ino* or *-ini* is the diminutive."

"Across the middle of the morning or across the corners of the bread?" William asks.

"Who knows? It was easier to say than the popular 'English tea sandwich.'"

"Everything was invented in Torino?" William concludes.

Unlike *panini,* the *tramezzini* usually have mayonnaise. Almost all bars, train stations, and cafés serve a variety. Ed took to them right away, especially the tuna and olive for a mid-morning snack.

Spread out on the table, our books on Piemonte and the poems of Pavese. Never much of a café sitter, I could while away the morning like this. A well-dressed businessman grinds his foot over the balls of the gold bull. Not sure how that brings the good luck it's reputed to.

We stroll along Via Garibaldi and Via Roma, checking out the designer shops (oh, no! William is attracted to Louis Vuitton belts). Torino has eighteen kilometers of covered walkways, a reminder that inclement weather can pour in from the Alps. The chic shops are punctuated by more appealing cafés in glass-roofed Galleria San Federico, where we happen upon Cinema Lux, an Art Nouveau theater. In smaller streets we find Libreria Internazionale Luxemburg, a vintage British bookstore and a cool contemporary café and art space.

Where are the tourists? we wonder. They're all in Florence. We came to Torino last summer with William and loved every minute of the four days we spent blessedly free from mobs. We all agreed—we needed more time here. As we begin a trip into Piemonte, we decided to light here again.

What a fantastic place to bring a child or young adult! Highlights from our first visit:

WE TOOK A TAXI OUT TO THE MUSEO NAZIONALE DELL'AUTOMOBILE. Even if you're not a car fan, you have to swoon at the design genius on display. The emphasis is on vintage Fiat, Lancia, and Alfa Romeo, though there are Bugattis, Ferraris, and others. A long-time *Alfista* (one who adores Alfas), Ed examined each.

EATALY: the Italian food emporium near the car museum. We walked there from the car museum to have lunch and to look at the amazing range of olive oil, pasta, honey, jam, wine, and other products, all from this country.

MUSEO EGIZIO: after Cairo, the largest Egyptian museum in the world. Torino began collecting in 1630, and now displays 6,500 items (with another 26,000 in storage). The museum is located right in the *centro*.

MUSEO NAZIONALE DEL CINEMA IN THE MOLE ANTONELLIANA, where on the ground floor you can watch movie clips in lounge chairs with head-phones. You spiral up to three floors of changing displays; many are interactive, demonstrating the history of photography and film. It's a lively tour. The glass-walled elevator takes you to the tower for a view over Torino and the Alps in the distance. I didn't go; it looked claus-trophobic and harrowing. Ed and William did, and they reported it was claustrophobic and harrowing.

VIA PO: Stroll along this grand boulevard lined with *palazzi* and arrive at the Po River. The rarefied French influence of the House of Savoy, which ruled Italy from 1861 to 1946, is everywhere in Torino. A gaily lit string of cafés beckons as evening falls. A moment to time-travel to nineteenth-century Paris.

WE ARE STAYING at the home of Pavese! By chance, I came across a listing for a B & B called La Luna e i Falò (*The Moon and the Bonfires* is the title of one of Pavese's novels). I was shocked to see that the B & B had been his home. With awe, I reserved two of its three rooms. His own copies of his paperbacks lie on the hall table. His small writing room (or was it his dining room?) is now the guests' sitting room. Our bedroom, furnished with antiques, blue toile fabrics, a table in front of a window, looks out at the graceful balconies that festoon the elegant houses across the street.

I open the window and look at what Pavese looked at. Where he smoked and smoked, and wrote and wrote. Where he sipped Campari and left his slippers by the chair. The current dining room, where we're served afternoon tea and breakfast at round tables with flowers and silver, must have been his living room. There would have been books and paintings. If he appeared today, what would he think? Yes, the young woman who checked us in says, yes, he lived here in 1950 when he committed suicide. "Not at home," she adds quickly. "He locked this door for the last time and checked into Hotel Roma near the train station. Overdose of sleeping pills. He was two weeks shy of forty-two."

All that passion and romance and darkness and profundity and work silenced by a handful of pills. There's an undercurrent of loss running through his poems but a swifter stream of longing and acute love for people. I tried this translation of his poem "La Casa":

THE HOUSE

The man alone listens to the calm voice
with eyes half-closed, almost a breath
blowing on the face, a friendly breath
that rises, incredibly, from a time gone.

The man alone listens to the ancient voice
that his fathers, in their time, have heard, clear

and absorbed, a voice that like the green
of the ponds and the hills darkens at evening.

The man alone knows a shadow voice,
caressing, that rises in the calm tones
of a secret spring: he drinks it attentively,
eyes closed, and it doesn't seem past.

And the voice that one day stopped the father
of his father, and everyone of dead blood.
A woman's voice that sings secretly
At the threshold of the house, to the falling dark.

I like his poem. He is trying to express something that cannot really be said. Translating feels like pouring water through a sieve. Two lines don't go happily into English. Perhaps aren't that happy in Italian, either. That's okay. Pavese has pulled me into an intensely private moment. A woman sings. The song has been heard by his father and his father's father before. The threshold—now and then, life and death, love and loss. The song spirals in his DNA. A lullaby, a love song, a dirge.

I LIKE HIS house, too. There's a squeak to a floorboard, a panel of sunlight falling in at an angle, a gray quietness where something might happen. And it did. Beginning with Walt Whitman, Pavese worked vigorously on translations, in addition to his own novels and poetry. *Moby-Dick!* From this small room, he brought contemporary American fiction to Italy: Sinclair Lewis, John Dos Passos, Sherwood Anderson, William Faulkner, Gertrude Stein. Nights of work. Then he would take long walks in the rain.

AT LUNCH WE stop at Pepino on Piazza Carignano and sit outside for quick vegetable salads. William notices an old, wheeled ice cream cart parked near the door and people at the next table ordering what we called "nuggets" when I was growing up. We find out that the *Pinguino,* penguin, the original chocolate-dipped ice cream on a stick, was invented here in 1939. Pepino has been making gelato since 1884. "That list of Torino inventions is getting longer," William remarks. I think for years *invented in Torino* will be a family saying.

ALL OF PIEMONTE is known for the pleasures of the table but Torino particularly so. Those Savoy royals brought from France the tradition of fabulous desserts, not always, or even usually, a given in Italy (except for gelato). The wine region just to the north, the irresistible cheeses, the ever-present taste of hazelnut, the coveted beef of Piemontese Fassone cows, and *sopratutto,* above all—chocolate. Not only plain chocolate but *gianduia,* chocolate with roasted hazelnuts, one of those genius mother-of-necessity inventions at a time when chocolate was scarce and roasted hazelnuts were incorporated to stretch the quantity. *Gianduia* probably was named after a *commedia dell'arte* character. A foil-wrapped *gianduia* in the shape of Gianduia's hat is called *giannuiotto.* The plump triangles melt in your mouth and on your fingers.

Several superb chocolate makers reign in Torino. Our good friends in Tuscany, Aurora and Fulvio, grew up here. With the gift of a lavish box that could have held a limited-edition art book, they introduced us to Guido Gobino chocolates. Last year, we visited the jewel-box shop at via Giuseppe Luigi Lagrange, 1. Now, we retrace those steps. *Gianduia,* check, fruit *gelatine* (jellies), check. Also the jellies of pear, lemon, myrtle covered with milk chocolate. But this time we go for the ganache, flavored with Barolo, candied lemon, orange and almond, lemon and cloves, vermouth. William selects our box for the road. After being offered several delectable tastes, we can't even try a chocolate granita or a cold summer *bicerin.*

I so want to write about food! Where to begin? I could write an entire book about Torino. We were wild about every restaurant we tried on our trip last year, beginning with the classic Tre Galline and the inventive bio-aware Consorzio. Before the Savoys entered with their fancy ways, Torinese were feasting on goose, rabbit, venison, boar, snails, goat, and—oh, yes—donkey. Never scorned: *il quanto quarto,* the fifth part, meaning offal. Modern chefs are still inventing around these ingredients, which endure in temples of gastronomy dusted with Michelin stars.

We each had our favorite restaurants. Mine was:

Del Cambio. The long mirrors sending back the sparkle of chandeliers; the tables, drawn up to claret velvet banquettes and laden with polished cutlery and hothouse flowers; the atmosphere of friendly hauteur. I wished I'd worn a black dress and very high heels, but the printed silk shirt and linen pants had to do. I imagined all the occasions that Torinesi families have celebrated here.

Since 1757, Del Cambio has served the locally beloved *finanziera,* a stew our friend Fulvio always raves about anytime he returns to Torino for a visit. The hallowed dish earned its name from what was on the backs of bankers who dined at this very restaurant; they wore coats called *finanziere,* financiers. The recipe is sometimes called *finanziera Cavour,* for the prime minister—statesman who frequented the restaurant. The ingredients include brains and veins, veal, bone marrow, calf and/ or rooster testicles, cockscomb, wattle, mushrooms, Marsala or Barolo, parsley, garlic, and bay leaves. *Finanziera's* popularity in Torino reveals something essential about the local palate: Anything that moves or grows is fair game. Were we brave enough to try this signature dish?

I'm afraid, in summer, we tended toward lighter fare. Pretty shapes of melon on ice; gossamer fried slices of vegetables; *plin* (pinched ravioli) with *lardo;* lemon, and mackerel; *vitello tonnato* (a Piemontese favorite, veal with a creamy tuna sauce); sea bass in sea lettuce. William is served a small amount of wine. He wore a fitted gray sport coat and white shirt. He was wide-eyed with pleasure. I had a glimpse of the man he will be, someday sitting with someone he loves.

Service is cordial. If you get up from the table, the waiter doesn't just refold your napkin. He brings a fresh one. This lighting makes everyone look glamorous. I'm intrigued by a bejeweled older woman next to us (an aged-out high-class prostitute?), sitting beside her ancient, coiffed, and silent mother. There's a story there, as there's a story everywhere.

Dessert arrived. A *gianduia* expanse topped with blackberries and, on top of William's, a chocolate model of the Mole Antonelliana, the tower he ascended. The tower is toppled and we all had a bite.

ED'S FAVORITE: CIRCOLO DEI LETTORI, formerly a private literary club that now hosts publishing events and book clubs in its reading room, but also serves lunch and dinner in hushed, clubby rooms lined with paintings of artists. What a special lunch, watched by the faces of Torino's artists.

William's favorite, and a topic of conversation all year: **Combal.Zero,** a long taxi ride outside town to Rivoli, one of the royal palaces, and now Museo d'Arte Contemporanea. By the time we arrived, the museum was long closed. We had to ring at a gate, where a hip-looking guy escorted us to the long, glass-walled restaurant of Chef Davide Scabin. Only two other tables were occupied. (This really is too far from town for a spontaneous visit.) William was immediately stunned when they presented a water menu, listing an array from all over Europe with their mineral contents. He and Ed proceeded with the extravagant tasting menu, far too experimental for my tame palate. Ed selected the wine pairings and William was offered pairings as well, various fruit, water, and tea preparations. The courses began to roll out. This, clearly, is play. The chef is having fun. We had fun, too. The waiters hovered, enjoying William's awe and delight. It's a party.

TORINO: FORTY MUSEUMS. Sixty markets. Churches, more cafés, contemporary galleries—we must come back. Again, and again. We cannot, we agree, leave without visiting the Musei Reali complex, the residences and collections of the Savoy rulers, and the gardens designed by André Le Nôtre. The scale of the city complex is daunting. We tour the royals' personal quarters, which are so gilded and frescoed and sumptuous that we emerge feeling that we must be gold-leafed ourselves. I like the neoclassical ballroom best—the gold rosettes on the coffered ceiling with allegorical dancers representing Time frolicking around Apollo and the Muses. The Armeria, a grand room of armorial dress, is surprisingly interesting because the heavy plates often are decorated or personalized. Fashion was as important as protection.

The painting and sculpture of the Galleria Sabauda occupies a light-filled wing with rooms off a long statue-lined hall. There are works to love—Fra Angelico's *Madonna and Child,* Veronese's *Supper in the House of Simon the Pharisee,* a fascinating painting of a sixteenth-century outdoor market by Jacopo Bassano, an evocative Annunciation by an unknown painter—but overall, the collection weighs numbingly, toward dark religious scenes.

What we three love is the Biblioteca Reale, an expansive library and archive with arched ceilings and parquet floors worn to a honeyed patina by the steps of decades of readers. The shelves hold leather and vellum texts with antique ladders strategically placed for reaching high volumes. A metal balustrade runs around the catwalk for the second level; on the first are inviting tables. The self-portrait of Leonardo da Vinci lives here but isn't on view right now. We only glimpse the garden, as rain has begun to come down at a hard slant. We're thankful for the shield provided by all the arcaded streets.

BY LUCK, FULVIO and Aurora are in town visiting Gaetano, Fulvio's father. We confer about where to meet and they suggest Camilla's Kitchen off via Po. Although the world is in jeans and T-shirts, Torino diners still dress. Aurora always looks as if she stepped off a runway. It's fun to see friends in new contexts; memories are made this way. In the intimate restaurant, we're seated at a round table with velvet chairs and an attentive waitstaff, who appear immediately with prosecco.

I'm proud when the waiter assumes William will be ordering in English, then breaks into a smile when he flawlessly chooses *capesante arrosto* in Italian. The roasted scallops are served with *topinambur,* Jerusalem artichokes, and a cream of anchovies with smoked salt. (I have to remember to tell William later about the word *topinambur.*) Ed seconds that motion and the rest of us order the risotto *Acquerello* with shrimp and saffron. How did *arborio* rice ever get to be the recommended one for risotto? *Carnaroli* is much less viscous and, as I see with the first taste, *Acquerello* sends that prized variety up a few notches. *Acquerello,* from Vercelli in Piemonte, is *carnaroli* aged for eighteen months or longer. This hardens the kernels, rendering proteins and starch less water soluble. Hence, less sticky. I remind myself to take some cans home for winter risottos.

I'm curious to see if Fulvio will order the *finanziera,* soul food to him, but—like groups of Italians often do—we all order the same *secondo: brasato di Piemontese alla sabauda con patate ratte.* Delicious. Beef in the style of the Savoys: braised with Barolo (formerly Marsala was used), garlic, black truffles, and butter. *Patate ratte,* similar to fingerlings, are slender yellow potatoes, originally from France, with the thin skin left unpeeled. Aurora selects the wine: Pelissero 2014, a *nebbiolo* from just north in Langhe. The ruby-red brings together all the flavors of the *brasato*. We order a second bottle, which smells of rose petals. An evening of warmth and rich tastes with old friends in an old city.

BACK AT PAVESE'S house, I can't stop thinking of him. I'm reading *Family Lexicon,* a memoir by the novelist Natalia Ginzburg, his intimate friend in Torino during the difficult fascist years. They both were sent into exile to the south for their antifascist activities. They worked for Einaudi, the great publisher in Torino. Ginzburg's memoir, impossible to put down, is structured around family sayings. We all have them. Her family's are absurd and funny and crop up in different contexts, all of which illuminate vibrant, tangled relationships. Though she writes obliquely about herself, she approaches Pavese dead-on, capturing his wicked smile, and the loss she felt when her friend took his life "one summer in Torino when none of us were there." Her own sorrows are so strangely withheld (her husband was tortured and killed by Nazis) that the ellipses are even more poignant than if she had written them out. She does as Emily Dickinson advises: "tell the truth but tell it slant."

EARLY, I WALK around the neighborhood, which probably has changed little from when Pavese lived here. *Tranquillo.* A nearby park. Torino! City of writers, fighters of tyranny, vintage tram cars, elegant pastry shops, city of a million trees.

BEFORE DRIVING NORTH to explore Piemonte, we stop at Porta Palazzo, Europe's largest open-air market. It fills a covered iron-and-glass arena and spills into surrounding lots and streets. Tented like a souk, rowdy and colorful! Every vegetable, herb, flower possible. What asparagus! I wish I could buy the *trombette,* the long zucchini of Albenga, the *cicoriette*, baby chicory, and a sack of multicolored peppers. *Costine?* A mix of ribbed vegetables. *Catalogna?* A chicory originating in Catalan. Sliced watermelons shine under a red awning, casting color on everyone's faces as they pass by. We do buy luscious cherries. Ed is stopped by the egg seller's red-checked table, covered with tiny blue eggs, quail eggs, eggs *da bere,* for drinking. Duck eggs. Eggs in colors I'd like to paint on walls— teal, malt, sand, and cream. *Buonissime,* the sign says. Really good!

William takes many photos of faces and fruit. Ed is looking for an espresso for the road. Time to leave. The car is baking. "*Topinambur,*" I explain, "got its name from a Brazilian tribe visiting the Vatican at the same moment this New World tuber, Jerusalem artichoke, was on display. Through some mix-up, the sunchoke plant got the tribe's name."

"Franny, are you making this up? And could you crank up the air?"

"No! And the Jerusalem part came from Italian immigrants in America, who called it *girasole,* sunflower, and *girasole* sounded to Americans like *Jerusalem.*"

We take several wrong turns exiting the city.

We don't want to go. Oops! We forgot to see the Shroud of Turin.

NOTES:

A food historian writes about *finanziera.* http://www.francinesegan.com /art_finanziera.php

Links to some of Cesare Pavese's poems, translated by Geoffrey Brock and published by Copper Canyon. https://www.poetryfoundation.org /poems/49939/passion-for-solitude

Family Lexicon, Natalia Ginzburg, brilliantly translated by Jenny McPhee and published by the New York Review of Books.

Riso Cavour

RICE CAVOUR, SERVES 4

I'm fascinated by Chef Matteo Baronetto's elegant and highly unusual recipe featuring two kinds of rice. *Venere*, a black rice raised in the Po Valley, is whole-grain, fragrant, and healthy. In this recipe, since the *venere* dries for a long time in the oven, it's best to complete that step the day before. *Carnaroli*, a long-grain, high-starch rice, is my favorite for risotto. The tomatoes, also, can be prepared ahead. I suggest roasting a whole pan of tomatoes; extras will be easy to use in other dishes. This recipe assumes that you have some beef ragù on hand—always a good plan.

FOR THE TOMATO CONFIT
16 cherry tomatoes
Salt and pepper, *QB*
3 tablespoons extra-virgin olive oil
Thyme sprigs
1 clove garlic, minced

Prepare the tomato confit. Cut a small cross on the lower part of each tomato, blanch them in boiling water for about 20 seconds, cool in ice water, and then peel them. Season with salt and pepper, 2 tablespoons of the olive oil, sprigs of thyme, and the garlic; arrange in a single layer on a baking sheet and roast in the oven at 175°F for about 4 hours. Moisten with the rest of the olive oil and refrigerate.

FOR THE FIRST RICE
¾ cup *venere* rice
3 tablespoons sunflower oil

Boil the *venere* rice in plenty of salted water (as you would cook pasta) for 25 to 30 minutes, drain, and spread onto a baking sheet lined with parchment. Let the rice dry in the oven for 8 hours at 150°F. Once dry, fry it in small quantities and very quickly in hot sunflower oil in a nonstick skillet. The rice should be crispy.

FOR THE SECOND RICE

1 onion, studded with whole cloves

Extra-virgin olive oil, *QB*

4 cups water

Coarse salt

1 cup *carnaroli* rice

6 tablespoons butter

In a large pot, sauté the onion in a little olive oil until browned, about 6 minutes. Remove from the heat and add the water, salt, and rice all at once, watching out for spatters. Return to the heat and bring the water to a boil. Boil the *carnaroli* rice over a medium-high flame, uncovered, for about 15 minutes, stirring frequently. Discard the onion and any stray cloves. Drain the rice and place in a bowl, moistening lightly with oil to prevent the grains from sticking.

Sauté the *carnaroli* rice in a nonstick pan over lively heat with a tablespoon of oil and the butter until the grains are dry, and slightly crisp, about 10 minutes. In 3–4 more, they become *croccante,* crisp. Keep warm.

TO FINISH:

4 large eggs

Ragù, *QB*

Celery leaves

Poach the eggs in boiling water for 3 minutes. Warm the already prepared ragù.

Arrange each egg in the middle of a warm plate, season lightly with coarse salt. Spoon the *carnaroli* over the egg and arrange 3 or 4 tomatoes around the edge with tufts of celery leaves. Finish the dish with a dollop of ragù and the *venere* rice.

Del Cambio, Torino, Piemonte

Orta San Giulio

The bride's father rowed her from the **Orta San Giulio** landing to the Municipio dock where the wedding would take place. Wearing fairy-tale white, she stood in the middle of the wooden boat, looking as though she would break into an aria and swan dive into the lapis-blue water. A short distance away lay the island of San Giulio with its castle and blur of trees forming an ethereal backdrop. The boat rocked slightly when it came abreast of the landing. The bride held out her bouquet for balance and stepped forward into the outstretched hands of the groom. We applauded. I'd never before seen a boat rowed by someone in top hat, cutaway morning coat, and tails.

Lago d'Orta put a big, glorious kiss on a memorable day. That night at the dinner, the bride and her father danced. He had choreographed the complicated movements for weeks, and there had been a minor tiff over the amount of practice. No matter now—they dipped and twirled and she maintained her grace, even in high heels. We guests sat at round tables under the stars, listening to the lake water's lapping. We who'd traveled many miles to share candlelight, music, and the moon luminous through a veil of silver clouds. Heartfelt toasts, winded toasts, the cutting of the cake: So they were wed.

THE BRIDAL COUPLE, now happy with their baby girl, may dream of the night swim when the lake turned ink-dark, the drifts of flowers on every table, or the wretched flight delay out of Milano. Ed and I best remember suffused blue evening air and the fortuitous position of the long, squared U-shaped piazza, the fourth side being the water, its greensward edge lined with boats ready to take you to the island. Surely one of the most felicitous town plans in Italy.

We've returned to explore what we had no time for during the wedding. William, with us for all of Piemonte, is joined by his bulky tripod, lenses, and cameras, and thus so are we. I'd fantasized about staying at Villa Crespi, a Moorish extravaganza and a member of the reliably luxe Relais & Châteaux group. All booked! Never mind. Piemonte isn't short of fantastic places to sleep and eat. We discover Hotel Castello Dal Pozzo in nearby **Oleggio Castello**. A castle and a grand villa, gardens, terraces, and a refined restaurant, Le Fief. From our room, we see the blue splotch of Lago Maggiore in the distance.

We arrive in time for lunch. Is this strange? That I find formal restaurants relaxing? The crisp table linens, good cutlery and crystal, understated flowers, the little stool for my handbag, the attentive waitstaff, the quiet so conducive to conversation—all testify *for this hour or two we will be superbly fed and charmed.* No matter that we are in tennis shoes and wrinkled linen. William is the "young gentleman." And what would he prefer to drink? Not a blink when he requests a Coke with his pasta. I order salad with green and red tomatoes and big pink shrimp. Ed's choice is the most interesting. His salad is topped with a peeled soft-boiled egg that has been dipped in bread crumbs and deep fried, a golden ball. Cut into it and out slips the sun. (Light-years from a Scotch egg!) Slivers of summer truffle elevate the concept. After all this and a glass of local white wine, we're ready to explore.

• • •

HOW PROFOUNDLY CHANGED a place becomes without cars. In Orta San Giulio, you easily slip into a lost-in-time state of mind. The human scale returns. Low cafés and shops, all pastel and frescoed, face the tree-lined space along the water. Birds twittering and the slosh of wake are predominant sounds, and what's growing indicates a lucky micro-climate: palms, oleanders, and tea olive. William photographs the in-candescent glow inside a large white morning glory.

The main industry seems to be the production of gelato; there's a shop every few steps. Am I constantly asking William if he'd like a cup or cone? Why do I feel a twinge of disappointment when he declines? I'm too fond of the two-scoop cup of pistachio and chocolate. Since, traditionally, gelato isn't made in the winter in Italy, this must be a ghost town in January. At that point, locals must repair to the Enoteca Al Boeuc for some sustaining *vino rosso*. In June, what's most attractive is the Orta Beach Club, where you can swim and rent kayaks. Lake swim-ming is the best: no fear of sharks cruising below you. In such water, limpid and fresh, I even like to get my hair wet.

Along the promenade, boatmen stand around chatting in groups. It's easy and cheap to hire a Chris-Craft–type boat to take you to Isola San Giulio, which is so close you could swim if you weren't liable to be drowned by one of the speeding launches. It's also easy to arrange lon-ger boat trips around this smallest of the famed northern lakes.

WHAT'S ON THIS small island? A few villas, a square bell tower, a castle, a restaurant with a view, and a cloistered group of Benedictine nuns, who while away the hours mending vestments or baking commu-nion wafers and a bread called *pane di San Giulio*. They dwell in silence. All over the island are the abbess's signs extolling the merits of quiet and meditation. The twelfth-century basilica was built over an earlier one that probably dates from the fifth or sixth century. Though not impressive from outside, the interior is extraordinary. Frescoes every-where. The earliest date from 1421. On a column, I find a graphic San Lorenzo, martyr and patron saint of cooks. Two men with long forks appear to be about to rotate him on the grill while—wide-eyed and hands in prayer—Lorenzo approaches medium-well done.

Elsewhere on the wall of the basilica, Giulio sails from Greece to the island on his outspread cloak, steering with his staff. Yes! With one wave of his hand he frees the island from a besieging serpent-like dragon. We're at an intersection of faith and fairy tale. Two stairways lead down to a crypt where San Giulio lies in a silver mask and robes.

Intent on the paintings, I almost missed the *ambo*. A new word for me, it's the raised pulpit many old churches have for speaking or reading the gospels to upturned faces. San Giulio's serpentine *ambo,* of dark green serpentine marble, is carved with mythological beasts struggling with animals. One of the birds resembles a monster pigeon. A griffin fights a crocodile, a deer is attacked by a ferocious centaur. A good versus evil lesson, no doubt. There are the Evangelists' symbols: Luke's winged ox, John's eagle, Mark's lion (looks more like a pussycat), and Matthew's angel. Amid them stands Guglielmo da Volpiano, a revered holy person of the island in the tenth century.

A SMALL FERRY runs about the lake, stopping at villages. On Thursday, many locals take the trip to **Omegna** for market day. We drive the eight kilometers and stroll around the lively town. The lake ends here and close mountains cast reflections in the water. A spate of six- and seven-story apartment buildings follows the curve of the shore. Not pretty but they must offer fabulous views. A stream runs through the old town, with more picturesque houses built along the banks.

Ravenous, we stop at busy Pomodoro, a simple local café that specializes in *sfilatini,* pizzas rolled in the shape of baguettes. The fillings are endless: Gorgonzola and apple, pesto and *lardo, fontina* and potato, truffle and porcini, squid and shrimp. William orders the grilled vegetable one and it arrives, long as a celery stalk. Ed tries the fried perch from the lake. I should have chosen the *sfilatini,* but ordered *crespelle* with fresh tomatoes instead; they were bland. William shared.

. . .

WILLIAM HAS SELECTED Pàscia in nearby Invorio for dinner. We've always had great fun introducing him to food. At two months, he squirmed and shook his fists when Ed placed his espresso or a clove of garlic under his nose. "Here's a strawberry," Ed would say, "you're really going to like these." Last year in Venice, he got wind of something called the tasting menu and he has never looked back. This has become expensive. It's also enormously pleasurable to see him open up to unfamiliar foods, to listen to his responses. Picky myself, I love seeing him take on Ed's philosophy: Try it.

Paolo Gatta, the chef, is thirty. As I've seen in many places on my Italian tours, he trained elsewhere then brought home what he learned. His restaurant is in a converted house whose pastels and glass look kin to mid-century Miami. We're seated in a curved room lined with windows. Paolo comes to the table to discuss what's up today. Because his *orto* is flourishing, we will have a vegetable meal. His favored oil is extracted daily from sesame seeds. "We're in your hands," Ed tells him, "and, yes, we'll have the wine pairings." For William, there will be a procession of inventive fruit-based drinks.

So it begins—and doesn't end for a long time. Raw, tiny spinach in a savory broth; Jerusalem artichokes marinated for two weeks, a miniature caprese, a spoon of puréed apple, carrot, parsley. A taco with Japanese prunes. A confident chef improvising from his garden. The wines—generous pours—come forth: a Franciacorta, a Ligurian white, another white from the Dolomiti, and a big local *nebbiolo*. An interruption for a palate cleanser of sparkling water with basil. Everything on small plates. Paolo's surprises keep everyone talking. A dessert finale: saffron wafers over vanilla gelato, various delectable biscotti, and apricot soup with pea shoots. "Are you sure those are peas?" William asks.

A FEW KILOMETERS away, **Stresa** on Lago Maggiore looks immediately familiar. It was the setting for a videotape Italian course I took years ago. I almost expect to see milling about the people who taught me to order coffee. Lined along the water are the Art Nouveau hotels, Villa e Palazzo Aminta and the Grand Hotel des Isles Boromees, where Hemingway wrote part of *A Farewell to Arms*. These flower-festooned confections call up a gentle nostalgia for tea in the afternoons and voile sundresses with inherited jewelry, and perhaps a game of whist. Hydrangeas are blooming. Not just tidy shrubs with baby-face-sized flowers, these mound and spread and climb, smears of blue and pink growing out of stone walls and tumbling down in a cascade of flowers. After Orta, this lake feels enormous. At sixty-nine kilometers long, Maggiore is the second-largest northern Italian lake. Dotting the flat azure expanse are the fabled Borromean Islands—Isola Bella, Isola Madre, Isola dei Pescatori, and Isola San Giovanni. There's much to be said for islands in lakes; every one must have a compelling story—a mystery or a romance to guard.

Along the shore, boat rentals are easy. And there's gelato at the quay. Balancing our hazelnut and peach cones, we hop on board and take off for an hour's spin on the calm waters ringed with mountains. The Borromeo family began building *palazzi* and fabulous gardens in 1632; in the Italian way, the dynasty still owns and lives part-time in their magic kingdoms. We debark on Isola Bella and take a quick walk around but do not visit the famous palazzo with a many-terraced pyramidal garden, home to white peacocks. Edith Wharton in *Italian Villas and Their Gardens* quotes a Bishop Burnet writing in 1685:

> *There lies here two Islands called the* Borromean *Islands, that are certainly the loveliest spots of ground in the World, there is nothing in all Italy that can be compared to them.*

I buy a flouncy, smocked sundress for our neighbor Chiara's little daughter. Ed calls her from the market stand. Bad connection. "What size dress for Adele?" Chiara and her mother, Fiorella, are on the beach with the children in Forte dei Marmi. We're trying to show her the dress on the phone. Static. It's starting to rain. "Eighteen months. Perfect." Many ciao-ciaos while the market vendor waits. We rush back to our sleek boat and view the other islands through a scrim of rain. Invigorating, out on the water, full throttle.

WE'RE HUNGRY FOR a truly local dining experience with traditional cuisine. I call Pinocchio in Borgomanero. A storm hits as we're leaving. We wait it out in the hotel's castle wine bar, relaxing on the covered loggia with a Campari soda and a view of the wet lawns. Even the rain seems green.

At the restaurant, we're greeted by a collection of carved Pinocchios, a passion of the chef-owner. His daughter, a dignified signora, greets us warmly, as if we're old friends. After last night's extravaganza, we resist the elaborate *degustazione* menu. Still the antipasti plates begin to roll. Fried frog legs, as well as *batsoà,* an ancient preparation of pig trotters boiled for hours then deboned (labor!), bathed in vinegar, breaded, and fried. The name is ironic, from *bas de soie,* silk stockings, along the line of the silk purse from a sow's ear—and the humble feet *are* transformed. Another starter from deep in the tradition, *frittata rognosa,* is a flat frittata with cheese, sausage or *salume,* pancetta, onions, and lots of celery. What's the *rognosa*? Mangy? "Something lost in translation," Ed says. "I think it also means bumpy."

Following these delights, William only wants *agnolotti,* the ravioli-type pasta stuffed not with the usual spinach and ricotta but with three white meats: goose, chicken, and rabbit. Much to ponder on this traditional Piemontese menu. This is an inclusive cuisine—every part, no matter how interior, is utilized. The much-loved *finanziera* of Turin, William reminds me, includes everything from brains to testicles, even a rooster's comb.

The signora is happy to discuss the menu. Sliced goose liver scaloppine, little veal kidneys in Marsala with sweetbreads and hazelnut butter, and, to William's astonishment, *tapulone di asino.* Donkey in a mince preparation—*tapulone* comes from a dialect word meaning "chopped." The tough donkey meat must be long simmered in wine. This dish goes back, she tells us, to the founding of the town. A group of hungry pilgrims rested for the night and ate their own pack animal. Apparently, they woke the next morning in great clarity and decided to found Borgomanero on the spot.

We know the raunchy wild salad *puntarelle,* and here is the *catalogna* we saw in the Torino market—a lettuce with a dandelion-shaped leaf on a long white stalk. Ed selects *calamaretti,* little squid-shaped pasta, served with squid. I order a filet of beef. The white cows of Piemonte are famous as the best beef in Italy. The chef sears the filet on either side then finishes it in the oven on a bed of aromatic hay and under a cloud of meringue. The signora presents it with a big smile, knowing I will be amazed at the toasty mound of meringue.

"How does this work?" I ask.

"The beef becomes very tender." She rakes away the puffy cloud, just as you would the salt crust on a fish before serving. I'm intrigued although dubious that hay and egg white have great transformative powers, but it is the most meltingly tender beef I've ever tasted. Equally *eccellente:* the Cumot Nebbiolo d'Alba DOC, suggested by the signora, who knows a thing or two about wine.

We don't order dessert but it arrives anyway: a plate of little pastries, chocolates and meringues over vanilla gelato with a foamy zabaglione sauce. We manage. As we linger over coffee, we talk about the two extremes of local cooking we've experienced. Last night's experimental, high-concept vegetable dinner and tonight's deep-rooted presentation of papa-in-the-kitchen's grand traditions of the area. Ed sips an Averna. "Let's don't decide which we like better. Let's like both."

ONLY THE THIRD breakfast at Castello Dal Pozzo and already the friendly waiter knows that William will have hot chocolate and that my cappuccino should be decaffeinated. He seems genuinely disappointed that we're leaving. We are, too. Shouldn't we have taken a swim out to the island?

Le Langhe

LA MORRA, BAROLO, CASTIGLIONE FALLETTO,
SERRALUNGA D'ALBA, AND NOVELLO

I know all too well the Piemontese *gianduia,* the heavenly
marriage of chocolate and *nocciola*, hazelnut. We're at the
source—and what a lovely tree! Serrated heart-shaped
leaves, and the forming nut wears a wrinkled tutu. In
Barolo country, groves of hazelnut trees line the north faces
of hills, where vineyards are not allowed to be planted.
Grapes rule: Barolo is king.

As we drive into the Langhe, the rollicking knolls—
Langhe is dialect for hills—shine with brilliant green
vineyards, every twig and leaf well tended. On higher
hilltops, castle towns silhouette against the horizon.
Tiny villages nestle in the dips of valleys, surrounded by
regimented rows of *nebbiolo* grapes that will soon become
the legendary Barolo or Barbaresco wines. We're moving
through mile after mile of landscape paintings.

When guests arrive at my house bearing a bottle of
Barolo, I am hoping dinner lives up to the drink. Barolo
and its genteel first cousin, Barbaresco, are the crown jewels
of Piemonte. We chose the well-located village of **La Morra**

for exploring the area's numerous castle towns and the wine centers. Three days. We think that might be the limit of wine-focused travel with our grandson. But he's easy. Loves to explore, photograph, and, of course, eat. Three packed days, then we have a final night in Torino.

WE HAVE TO park outside town and roll in our bags to UVE Rooms and Wine Bar. Right away, the village entices us with small shops and *enotece*. You could hold the place in the palm of your hand. The main street rises to a park with panoramic views of the countryside. As we turn into the inn's courtyard, I spot across the street Paesi Tuoi, a bookstore also emblazoned with *La luna e i falò*—both titles of Cesare Pavese novels. Someone here loves him.

William checks into the floor below us. (I can't get used to him on his own at fifteen.) He quickly unpacks, plugging in umpteen devices. Our room upstairs is luxurious, with Barolo-colored armchairs and sheer draperies. Arches in the middle of the room divide the sitting area from the bedroom. Contemporary, with a hit of glam. Outside the window, the façade of a church with bells that ring in the hours. I like staying right in the middle of the village. You can pop out for a walk or a coffee, or for a jaunt to the bookstore. Base camp established in the Langhe.

OUTSIDE PAESI TUOI, there's a bench, with a couple of novels to read while you rest. Inside, I meet the owner and, of course, ask about the Pavese allusions: *The Moon and the Bonfires* and *Your Countries*. "Pavese was my uncle, the brother of my mother." Incredible! All his books are here, plus a good selection of others. Some wall space is devoted to framed drawings. How wonderful to own a store like this.

SINCE WE WILL be driving a lot, I'm thankful for the surprise upgrade Avis gave us in Torino. The big Audi sedan makes the backseat—my fate—quite easy, while the front accommodates the long legs of Ed and William. Guidance off, map in glove compartment: We're in ideal roaming country. *That* looks interesting; let's take a left. And distances are short between towns. We stop first at a chapel that William spotted in the guidebook. Cappella del Barolo, painted by Sol LeWitt and David Tremlett, startles the landscape. On the Brunate vineyard land, a modest brick chapel built in 1914 became a playground for the Barolo-loving American and English artists, who painted wild stripes and curves of drastic primary colors inside and out. The ruined farmhouse nearby fascinates me more. William soon turns to photographing surrounding hills with clouds' shadows racing across the glowing fields and a lilac scarf of fog at the horizon.

Barolo, smaller than I expected, has one thing on its mind. *Enotece* with tastings in progress line the cobbled streets, and the castle at the end houses an engaging wine museum. Down in the keep, you can sample the immense range of local wines. The museum could have been dull but the designers keep exhibits dynamic with active displays and a minimum of pedagogy. One is a facsimile of a typical country kitchen, complete with life-size videos of a young chef and a home-cooking *nonna* talking from opposite sides of the room: the two generations learning from each other. Dioramas, a formal dining room, winemaking equipment, a churn of galleries—all charm us.

Over a lunch at Rosso Barolo that is not as quick as we hoped— who's in a hurry in Barolo?—we plot the rest of the day: popping in and out of more of the castle towns. How many can we see?

The waiter recommends the *tajarin con verdure dell'orto e basilico.* We're introduced to the favorite Piemontese pasta: *tajarin* is dialect for tagliolini, "little cuts" of pasta resembling thin ribbons. Often served with the region's famous white truffles or with mushrooms, the pasta with garden vegetables and basil tastes like summer. *Tajarin* is yellow, rich, with many more eggs than the usual pasta, and very tender. We peruse the classic Piemontese menu of pastas, tongue, snails, beef tartare, and boar. Ed and William want the cream of zucchini soup with tomato sorbet and the roasted octopus with chickpea cream. First (but not last) glass: the big, mouthy Barolo del Comune di Barolo.

No dessert, but I can't wait another minute to try the renowned local cheeses, especially the goat-milk *robiola d'Alba.* I often serve a *robiola* rolled inside sliced bresaola for an antipasto platter. This one is young and gooey, very delicate. The sweet Gorgonzola, on home ground, is unctuous, thickly rich. *Castelmagno,* which we haven't had before, is a mostly cow's-milk cheese, aged for one to five months, and is the oldest cheese around—going back to 1277. Crumbly and a bit grainy, it has a strong presence and depth of flavor. I can see a happy pairing with fig jam, a handful of walnuts, and a dark honey.

Le Langhe invites wandering: Castiglione Falletto, Novello, Serralunga d'Alba.

Castiglione Falletto, with massive medieval brick walls cornered with turrets where Rapunzel might let down her golden hair. Tucked into a corner of the castle, there's an underground tasting room where local producers showcase their superb wines. From the church of San Lorenzo, long views of—what else?—vineyards spooling down the hills.

Serralunga d'Alba's castle silhouettes against the sky. Its three towers are all different: a graceful round, a short squat one, and a tall overlook. Rebuilt over an older castle, this one is late enough—fourteenth century—to show some Gothic influence. Frescoes and gardens inside. (Guided tours are available, but not today.) Colorful and well-kept houses line cobbled streets surrounding the castle. After lunch, when no one is out, the town seems to slip back into history.

Besides producing powerful, structured Barolos, Serralunga also is known for Barolo Chinato, especially the one made by Cappellano vineyard, where it was invented in the 1800s by Giuseppe Cappellano. He was a pharmacist by trade, and the wine may have some salubrious effect, since one ingredient is said to be macerated quinine from cinchona bark. The recipe remains a secret. Enjoy this version of Barolo as an after-dinner *digestivo,* but pour over ice as an *aperitivo* or mix in cocktails and spritzes. We like to serve an after-dinner sip around the winter holidays because of its bittersweet, spicy clove and cardamom taste. It's lovely with a little twist of orange peel and a plate of great chocolates from Piemonte.

NOVELLO—I LIKE ENTERING a town through a gated clock tower. Easy travel: Buzzing in and out of these villages, most with under a thousand inhabitants. Quick walk around, survey the views, onward. We're really just absorbing the terrain and way of life. Castle, *enoteca,* winding streets no wider than paths, a shared history of ownership by a powerful medieval family, some lasting six hundred years. Chimneys! I love the distinctive small brick temples that cap the chimneys. Even Barolo wasn't the least crowded; these lesser-known castle towns are uninterrupted by tourists.

Lively Novello's *castello* is the prettiest so far, though not nearly as old as most. Built over ruins of another, the neo-Gothic castle was only finished in 1880—yesterday, in Italian time—and the only one that looks livable. Most have no windows except at the highest level (higher than anyone could climb), but this late building was never in danger of marauders. It has a new life as Albergo Al Castello. I'd like to check in.

The Chiesa di San Michele Arcangelo, instead, is seventeenth century with a huge dome and impressive fresco cycle. "How did they have something so fancy in such a small place?" William wonders.

"Mystery of Italy," says Ed.

"Deep pockets and stranglehold of the Roman Catholic Church," I add.

EARLY JULY DAYS. We get to see sunset across the vineyard, the raked light changing from clear to honey to amber, and then streaks of rose and cerulean. We double back to Barolo for dinner at Winebar Barolo Friends: bare tables, the art and wine cases creating a casual atmosphere. Nothing casual about the wine list. We dither, and Ed finally chooses Cordero di Montezemolo Barolo Monfalletto '13, from a vineyard in La Morra. "It's from vines that are between fifteen and fifty years old, on a property dating from 1340."

"Sounds romantic enough." Still a bit young, the wine rims the glass with the characteristic clear brick color, while the body is deep garnet. Tannins, oh yes, but not harsh. If this wine were a man, he would not be slim, detached, and elegant. He would be a stocky powerhouse with a big laugh.

"IT'S AN ALL Barolo night," William says, sipping his fizzy water. We've all opted for the risotto made with *Acquerello* rice and Barolo, then the *stinco di vitello al Barolo*. *Acquerello* is *the* rice, toasted and aged. I always laugh at the word *stinco,* which doesn't sound good in English but means that tender cut of beef or pork, the shank.

Just breathing in the scents of the wine is almost enough. The risotto, creamy and subtle, must be soul food to the Piemontese. Fall-off-the-bone beef. They get to eat like this all the time!

Le Langhe

ALBA, CHERASCO, SANTO STEFANO BELBO, AND NEIVE

Alba, gentle word. Dawn. I've wanted to come here for many years. We've tried a couple of times to reserve for the divine October white truffle feasts but everything is always booked. Not today; hardly any tourists about. Alba, though only around thirty-two thousand inhabitants, seems like a real city, elegant brick, with open piazzas in the old *centro,* surrounded by cafés and blooming oleander. It's hot. We do what we seldom do, just sit with coffees and *merende* (mid-morning snacks). There are churches and museums to see but still we talk, watch people, spread out the morning. Alba must be a fabulous place to live. The best wine and food, and obviously enlightened people who keep their town impeccable.

I've read that the Saturday market branches into many streets. Even on Monday morning, bicycles stream by, women are intent on shopping, and aromas of pastry and bread exhale from open doorways. First, we visit the

Cattedrale di San Lorenzo, Romanesque, from the early 1100s, but re-modeled and shape-shifted a few times in the intervening years, includ-ing a front-and-center rose window opened in the nineteenth century. Added in 1512, fabulous marquetry choir stalls intrigue the three of us. Inlays of various woods tint the designs of plants, books, landscapes with villages, musical instruments, fruit baskets, and religious symbols. An awkward modern altar and throne chair and aggressive suspended lighting are intrusive and, to my eye, ugly.

We pass stylish wine-tasting rooms, Cignetti for chocolates and con-fections (since 1878), good-looking clothing stores, and Franco Fedele, a high-end carpenter's shop where I would want to have my bookcases made if I lived here. Just the way the tools are displayed in the window tells you a true artisan works inside. William buys a jar of Nutella, nos-talgic childhood treat of every Italian. He wants to see if it tastes differ-ent in Alba, where it was invented.

"Look up," we keep saying. Medieval towers everywhere. Arcades and umbrellas: shade is necessary in summer. I love the Chiesa della Maddalena, a fantasy of brickwork and a wild frescoed dome with winged priests frolicking among the *putti.* William is more enchanted with the portal of San Domenico. Rounded bricks—sage, rose, coral—stacked into rows of columns frame the entry.

Food dreamers come from everywhere to dine at Piazza Duomo. They're closed, and besides we didn't reserve months in advance. (Who does that?) Instead, we get to have lunch at La Piola, their more infor-mal place right on the duomo piazza. Airy and open, the café couldn't be more inviting. The name, in dialect, means "very local *osteria.*" The day's menu posted on a chalkboard says casual, plates designed by American artists say hip; and quirky: two fun chandeliers of curved wire and pic-tures of birds, made by Kiki Smith. We love everything—squash flower soup, *vitello tonnato, agnolotti* filled with *Castelmagno* cheese with black truffles and hazelnuts. We've neglected the white wines of Piemonte and rectify that with a glass of Ceretto Arneis, soft and soulful. The Ceretto vineyard family, art patrons and important winemakers, owns this restaurant as well as Piazza Duomo.

Finally, the classic local dessert, *bonèt* (little cap), similar to a flan, but made with cocoa and crumbled amaretti cookies. This treat was born in the thirteenth century, although cocoa, a relatively new accoutrement to the dish, was added after the discovery of the Americas. Italy is where you taste time.

A SHORT DRIVE to **Cherasco**—what a surprise. Deserted during the *pausa,* elements of the town remind me of renaissance paintings of an ideal city. There's also that strange emptiness of towns in cowboy movies— a place holding its breath—just before the bandits arrive. The one bird sounds like it's chirping into a megaphone. Why the grand triumphal arch at the end of the wide via Vittorio Emanuele II? And the row of seigniorial *palazzi* with beautiful doors, the arcaded sidewalks like those in Torino? Castle, yes, all local towns have one. Ed and William want to sit outside a bar and have a gelato. I dash off to see the slender, brick Madonna del Popolo. On one side, there's the Orto dei Padri Somaschi, a re-creation of a *hortus conclusus,* walled garden, of the Somaschi, a chari- table order. The wooden boxed beds look modern but planted in them are the same flowers, herbs, and shrubs that have graced this place for centuries. On the other side of the church, the magnificent monastery has been converted into the pleasant-looking four-star Hotel Somaschi.

BESIDE THE TRIUMPHAL arch stands the pretty blue-gray oratory of Sant'Agostino and a graceful bell tower. The arch, built between 1672 and 1677, looks as if it hasn't been touched since the last stone was laid. I photograph the *palazzi* doors: one is imposing, one painted the palest dove gray; another, the color of pistachio gelato. I have to run my hand over a dark walnut double door with huge nail heads and a knocker shaped like a woman's ringed hand.

San Pietro is the town's important thirteenth-century church. I get to see another garden, the re-created monks' garden of simples. Built concurrently with the founding of the city (1243), the church has been at the mercy of various interventions. It has a rather forlorn appearance, but I give it a closer look. The façade retains blocks of carved stone recycled from earlier buildings: spolia. I'm always curious to see these. Several show vegetal designs, two are of worn-down birds, and one ap- pears to be two horses. The walled garden is laid out in the shape of a cross. The four squares are divided again into four more, all planted with roses, aromatics, and vegetables known in Italy before the discovery of the Americas. (Imagine Italy without the tomato!) Four trees represent the seasons: holly, apple, medlar, pomegranate.

WILLIAM AND ED have not been idle over their gelato. "Did you know this place is known for snails? That's a local specialty. There's even a snail farm. I saw a recipe with snails, leeks, and apples. Not sure—sounds good but . . ." William is on his iPad. "And it's antique central. Several markets a year and shops. Too bad everything's closed, Franny." Heavy irony, since he would never allow himself to be dragged into an antique shop.

Ed adds, "One reason this place is so refined is that the Savoys escaped the plague of 1630 by setting up residence here. It was always a retreat from the city. That Palazzo Salmatoris we saw was where the shroud of Torino was hidden from the French."

"We should have come earlier when everything was open."

"Well, that's Italy. Sidewalks roll up in the afternoon. You've got to just live with that."

"Yes, years and years here and I am always surprised that the custom endures."

A lone man rides by on his bicycle. Someone backs a car out of a garage. Things may be about to stir, but we are done for the day.

JUST OUTSIDE LA MORRA, we get to dine at Bovio, outdoors on a summer night overlooking the hills. Obviously, we've happened upon a special-occasion kind of place. It's refined but not fussy, rooted but not rustic. We sit down among families and groups of friends and we know that we are going to eat well, drink well; the evening will be glorious. The menu showcases the territory. Hard to choose but we order quail salad with chestnuts and truffles, onions stuffed with sausage and *Taleggio,* duck cannelloni with spinach and truffles, veal filet with mushrooms, roasted kid with vegetables. As the wine list is voluminous, Ed confers with the waiter and chooses Barolo Arborina 2012, made by this restaurant's family vineyard, Gianfranco Bovio. We are sitting on the home turf.

Memorable, I know, as I snap a photo of William having his first sip of Barolo. He takes it seriously and wants to know if what he tastes is what we taste. The waiter has poured just a half-inch.

Blissful food, wine, blissful evening in La Morra.

I KNEW THAT Cesare Pavese was born in nearby **Santo Stefano Belbo**. Although a city person, he remained close to his earliest home, but never in a sentimental way. He valued the rural life's struggles, poignancy, fatalism, and the primal connection to the land. When the bookstore owner tells us about the foundation devoted to Pavese's work in his hometown, I have to go.

The director of the small museum, a welcoming woman, takes us around. Photographs, reproductions of his working notebook—page after page of fascinating lists of words—artwork framed with quotes from his books, and a brilliant portrait of him. She tells us how to find his villa and grave. We set off walking; it is farther than we thought but we find the house, still lived in except for the side where he was born. A faded peach-colored, two-story house in the shape of a U, paint flaking off its shutters: never grand, but with a sense of itself. A short distance away, we find the cemetery and his crumbling grave with his name and an epitaph: HO DATO POESIA AGLI UOMINI. I gave poetry to the people.

At Ape Wine Bar at lunch, the curly-haired waiter who looks as if he could be a tenor in an opera pauses to feed his baby a bottle. The mother is lunching with friends; he's serving. Pavese, I'm thinking, is part of their consciousness. Their parents may have known him. The waiter tells us that *The Moon and the Bonfires* is still celebrated on a night in spring when farmers cut back their vines and burn the old wood. That I would like to see. The baby, utterly content, falls into a milk doze. Ed and William attack their fried fish; I look out over the town, trying to imagine the child Pavese here and the grown writer returning. From *The Moon and the Bonfires:* "We need a country, if only for the pleasure of leaving it. Your own country means that you are not alone, that you know there is something of you in the people and the plants and the soil, that even when you are not there it waits to welcome you home." The waiter brings a bowl of perfect strawberries. And that's the last of the Pavese quest.

. . .

EN ROUTE BACK to La Morra, we swing by **Neive,** listed as one of *I Borghi più belli d'Italia,* the most beautiful small towns in Italy. Yes, it is. Two gates, an almost circular layout. Like other gems we've visited, Neive has the long history, the towers, churches, chapels, *palazzi.* All well preserved. "Can we go back to the hotel? I'm getting Stendhal Syndrome big time." Ed hardly ever flags.

"Me, too," William says. He's traveled enough to know what Stendhal Syndrome means.

Back in La Morra, they head upstairs and I go over to the bookstore to thank Maurizio and to say good-bye.

We stay in for dinner. UVE's courtyard is quiet and candlelit. Everyone on the staff here has been exceptionally friendly. We order pastas and yet another great Barolo. After dinner, we stroll around town. All quiet. The park at the end of the street looks over a swath of dark vineyards with a few lights in farmhouses and more glittering in the clear sky.

BACK IN TORINO, we turn in our car and walk. I pick up a few *tomini* cheeses and store them in the minibar at the hotel. I love these little white pillows; the delicate cheese is so good spread on bruschetta.

Turin Palace Hotel, right across from the train station, just underwent a makeover and is pitch-perfect. High ceilings, a terrace off our room, snowy duvets, and lots of space. We rest with books, have a drink on the rooftop bar, and an excellent dinner.

Early, we catch the Frecciargento, fast train to Florence, then the pokey train to Cortona. William is looking out the window. "Franny, do you think I could go to college in Torino?" That he even has the thought thrills me.

Damn, I left the cheeses in the minibar.

NOTES:

Three paintings of an ideal city were created in the 1480s at the court of the Duke of Montefeltro in Urbino in Le Marche. Attributed to several artists, such as Piero della Francesca, Fra Carnevale, or Francesco di Giorgio Martini, the panels remain a mystery. Ideal architecture was an interest of the duke. His palace reveals the extent, not only in its architecture but in various marquetry panels showing utopian visions of towns. The ideal city most associated with Piero della Francesca remains in Urbino. The other two hang in the Walters Art Museum in Baltimore and the Gemäldegalerie in Berlin.

Ape Wine Bar: In Italian, *ape* means bee.

Stendhal Syndrome: Travelers who are overwhelmed by too much beauty are in the grips of a state described in the nineteenth century by Stendhal (Marie-Henri Beyle), who wrote *The Red and the Black*. After contemplating a fresco in Florence, his character's sensations and passions collided: "I had palpitations . . . the life went out of me." Such travelers are in need of a break and a cold glass of water.

Cipolla Cotta al Forno Ripiena di Fonduta e Salsiccia di Bra

BAKED ONION STUFFED WITH FONDUE AND BRA SAUSAGE, SERVES 6

Chef Marco Boschiazzo's savory roasted onions travel well from lunch to antipasti to first course. The particular spreadable veal sausage from Bra probably will not be available, but do try it when traveling in Piemonte. I substitute a mix of ground veal and a small amount of pork fat. Not at all the same but rustic and savory. My friend Susan tried using sweet Italian sausage with happy results.

6 large yellow onions, unpeeled

1 cup fresh cream

½ cup whole milk

11 ounces Taleggio cheese, cut into small pieces

7 ounces Bra sausage, cut into small pieces (or sauté ¼ pound ground veal and 3 slices finely chopped pancetta)

Salt and pepper, *QB*

1 tablespoon butter

Preheat the oven to 250°F.

Roast the onions on a sheet pan in the oven for 2 hours. When they are cool enough to handle, cut off the first third. Scoop out most of the insides (reserving the outer shells), let drain in a colander, then chop the insides and set aside.

Increase the oven temperature to 350°F.

Pour the cream and milk in a medium saucepan, then bring almost to a boil. Lower the heat and add the Taleggio. Stir as the cheese melts. Remove the saucepan from the heat and continue stirring for about 1 minute.

Meanwhile, sauté the sausage or meat mixture in a hot pan until browned. Add the chopped onions and about two-thirds of the cheese fondue. Stir to combine, and season with salt and pepper.

Stuff the onions with the filling and dab them lightly with flakes of butter. Bake the onions in a 350°F oven for 15 minutes. Heat the rest of the fondue, then serve the onions on a warm fondue bed.

Ristorante Bovio, La Morra, Piemonte

Fiori di Zucca Ripieni di Ricotta, Verdure Piccole e Pomodori Freschi

PUMPKIN FLOWERS STUFFED WITH RICOTTA, SMALL VEGETABLES, AND FRESH TOMATOES, SERVES 4

Chef Dennis Panzeri's stuffed flowers bloom again on the plate, delicate and summery. Zucchini or squash flowers may be used—just pick the males, the ones not developing into a vegetable. To remove the pistil, I use tweezers. If the flowers are small, halve the recipe for the filling and sauce.

FOR THE STUFFED FLOWERS

1 carrot, diced

1 stalk celery, diced

1 small white onion, diced

2 to 3 tablespoons olive oil

1 zucchini, diced

4 button mushrooms, diced

1 clove garlic, minced

1 bay leaf

Salt and pepper, *QB*

2 cups whole-milk ricotta

3 ounces grated Parmigiano-Reggiano

4 basil leaves, torn

Nutmeg, a few grates

12 flowers, pistils and stems removed

1 tablespoon unsalted butter, cut in small pieces

FOR THE SAUCE

6 ripe tomatoes

Juice of a half orange

3 tablespoons extra-virgin olive oil

Salt and pepper, *QB*

1 tablespoon balsamic vinegar

Basil leaves, for garnish

Prepare the stuffed flowers:

In a medium skillet over medium heat, sauté the carrot, celery, and onion in 2 tablespoons of the oil until translucent, about 3 minutes, then add the zucchini, mushrooms, garlic, and bay leaf. Season with ¼ teaspoon salt and the pepper. Continue to sauté for 5 minutes. Transfer to a bowl. Discard the bay leaf. Gently stir in the ricotta, half the Parmigiano, the basil, and the nutmeg.

Fill the flowers and put them in an oiled baking dish, scatter the butter over them, and sprinkle with the remaining Parmigiano.

Prepare the sauce:

Cut the tomatoes in fourths and blend them to a very fine consistency in a food processor, then pass them through a sieve.

Put the tomato pulp again in the blender, add the orange juice, and whip with 1 tablespoon of the extra-virgin olive oil. Add salt, pepper, and the balsamic vinegar. Chill until ready to serve.

Bake the flowers in a 400°F oven for 15 minutes and serve them with the chilled tomato sauce. Garnish with basil leaves.

Ristorante La Piola, Alba, Piemonte

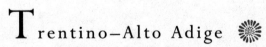
Trentino–Alto Adige

Trento

Let's all move to Trento. We'd never regret it. We'd be surrounded by the impressive towns of Merano, Bolzano, Rovereto, the marly green Adige river rushing through the countryside, easy drives to nature reserves, ski resorts, bicycle and hiking trails in the mountains, the great wines of the Alto Adige. The cheese, the food! Compact and walkable, but still big enough (with a population of around 117,000) to feel like a real city, Trento easily wins hearts and minds.

Its center is anchored by the weighty Castello Buonconsiglio and protected by a stretch of steep, machicolated stone walls. We're drawn first into the travel bookstore and emerge with a stack. William needs batteries and spots a camera store where he also buys a sensible bag for all his supplies. Although the center looks as though it could be preserved in amber, the vibe feels totally modern. The Pasticceria San Vigilio offers delicious juice extracts in fresh combinations: mint, ginger, apple, and lemon or pineapple, peach, and lemon. We order one melon-carrot-orange juice and one strawberry-pomegranate-carrot. Ed sticks to espresso. We leave with a bag of pastel macarons. More bookstores— irresistible!

GETTING HERE WAS less enjoyable. We left Cortona early, planning on reaching the Alto Adige by late morning. On the traffic-crazed au- tostrada north of Bologna, we had just pulled out of an Autogrill and gotten up to speed when the car lurched and made a screeching sound. "Blowout!" William shouted. Ed squeezed over two lanes, hazard light flashing. Not easy in hundred-mile-an-hour traffic. What luck—he reached a pull-out space just ahead. The front right tire wasn't just flat: it was shredded down to the wheel rim. Too hot to touch. Though val- iant, the two guys couldn't get the thing off. The space where we parked was littered with food wrappers, condoms (*who would have sex here?*), rot- ting fruit. On the phone, we tried to reach roadside assistance from Alfa Romeo. Hard to say exactly where we were, but William noticed a ki- lometer marker on the median. The phone kept cutting out. Finally, Ed got through. They would send a tow truck but warned that on Saturday, it would be hard to locate an open garage. Cars and mammoth trucks whooshed by. We drank water to survive the ninety-degree heat, and searched the Internet for any *gommista* in the area. The tow truck came. We were ratcheted up onto the back and the driver took off like the Formula One racer he must have once been. We swayed and bounced, trying not to look sideways when he took a curve. But he found an open garage; we were able to buy a used tire, the only one they had that fit with our others, and soon we were back on the mad autostrada. "Things have a way of working out in Italy," Ed reminded us.

AROUND A CORNER, we face the grand Piazza Duomo—one of the most harmonious squares in the country, ringed with handsome build- ings and centered on the playful fountain of Neptune. We scan the el- egant bishops' palace, the long north side of the Basilica Duomo di San Vigilio, and the eleventh-century bell tower with a crenellated top. All the domes are different—hexagonal, onion-shaped, square-topped. A fine rose window and rows of slender colonnades enliven the side of the church. Midway, a small porch juts out. The bishops at the Council of Trent entered here, it is said, and I imagine them passing through the rose-variegated columns supported by a pair of doleful lions. They would have looked out at the mountains rising in the background, peaks still sporting snow in mid-June.

The rest of the piazza looks secular, inviting. A four-story frescoed building with arcaded sidewalks and green awnings shelters a café. When I walk closer, I see that the paintings are of mythological scenes on the left, and on the right, allegorical scenes representing time, love, virtue, and other good things. My guidebook says the scenes form "a moral book inspired by renaissance culture." Other buildings of varying heights, painted soft apricot, Pompeian red, and butter yellow, contribute to the vital pulse of the piazza. And everywhere, umbrellas sheltering those sipping drinks, staring into phones, and visiting with friends. What more could you want? Well, another espresso for Ed. William is taking a million photos. Then we gelato along, happily.

Running off the piazza, via Rodolfo Belenzani, the most elegant street in town, is wider than other streets and lined with seignorial *palazzi*. Most are frescoed. Palazzo Quetta Alberti-Colico's sixteenth-century paintings show traces of fifteenth-century ones beneath. The designs in faded royal blues and reds echo the shapes of the windows. Other fanciful geometric touches resemble some sort of renaissance board game. During the Council of Trent meetings, which were convened in three sessions between 1545 and 1563, many of the visiting bishops stayed on this street. In similar washed-away colors, Palazzo Geremia's frescoes depict characters from history, a wheel of fortune, and people arranged in trompe-l'oeil windows beside real ones. The street ends with the church of San Francesco Saverio, where we see traces of an earlier structure on the façade.

This town is adorned with towers and other incredible *palazzi*. I especially admire Palazzo Larcher Fogazzaro on via Mazzini—a noble Baroque building with a marvelous tall, polished door, and a balcony held up by two carvings of Atlas. A woman is buzzing herself in while balancing a bag of groceries. I wish I could see her apartment, the life lived inside it.

· · ·

IN LATE AFTERNOON, we check into the oxblood-red Villa Madruzzo, a former grand home. There are newer rooms in another building, but we're in the old villa. Our big, old-fashioned and comfortable room is next to William's. He is old enough at fifteen to have his own room, but I still want him close by. We reach his favorite amenity—an indoor pool—by tunnel.

We didn't realize when we booked, but we signed up for half-board. This breakfast-and-dinner-included custom lingers in many traditional Italian hotels. I rather like sitting down among people who have their wine bottles, half-empty from last night, on the table and already know the waitstaff. The window-lined dining room reminds me of summers when I would go with my grandmother to White Springs, Florida. The grand white hotel was always full of regulars, who came frequently to sip the sulfur waters. The water tasted like the smell of Easter eggs I found in the bushes weeks after the hunt. In the grand dining room, or so I remember it, we ate butter beans, corn, ham, biscuits, peach turnovers—all the southern delights of summer.

At Villa Madruzzo, they're serving local German-influenced food. This tree-level dining room feels like a terrarium. The guests speak German. Trento citizens speak predominantly Italian; but north of here, German prevails. And in pockets, the ancient language Ladin, a mix of Latin and Friulian-Swiss dialects, still thrives.

William and I are up for the platter of herb dumplings poached in broth with sauerkraut, smoked pork, and potato pancakes. Very tasty, and nothing like anything I've ever eaten in Italy! Ed's choice on the set menu is another hearty serving of yellow mushrooms, veal meatballs, chard, and polenta.

BRILLIANT. EXHILARATING. MUSE: Muse delle Scienze. We are overwhelmed by the hard, soaring lines of the museum of science designed by Renzo Piano. Trento has brought to stunning success a languishing industrial area just a short walk from town. The whole complex is near the Adige. The museum, residences, parks, conference centers, and more give the impression that the space is a town unto itself. Alto Adige is one of the richest areas in the whole European Union. How enlightened—they're translating their success into artistic works.

The large and airy museum is like a giant, sharp-angled greenhouse, whose jutting, pointed shapes recall glaciers and the surrounding mountains. Pools reflect the glass panels, a watery mosaic. The initial visual impact primes us for a stupendous interior.

We start on the sixth floor, the top. The exhibits are built around a large atrium looking down all the way to the bottom floor. Here's the magic, what mesmerizes: Suspended by thin wires at different heights all the way to the ground floor are the birds and animals of the Dolomiti. As if in a dream, the animals float in midair. The taxidermy is superb— everything looks caught *right* now, in motion. This is the most fabulous science and natural history museum I've ever seen. (Many are gloomy.) We're interactive with all the smart exhibits—ecology, aquariums, history of the Dolomites, pendulums, extinction, avalanches, climate change, even a way to see how you'd look in the caveman era. MUSE floods the mind and senses.

We walk around the atrium as we descend, catching the creatures from different perspectives. When I was a child, my father told me that when pets died, they went to "happy hunting ground." I imagined meadows, not questioning if my rabbit and baby ducks still would be prey to his bird dogs. In MUSE, these suspended rabbits and foxes and wolves and deer all inhabit the air of a peaceable kingdom. Here, Daddy, is happy hunting ground.

Trento, a hard place to leave.

NOTES:

The languages Ladin and Ladino are often confused. Ladino, evolved from Spanish and Hebrew, is not spoken in this area. The local language, Ladin, has different forms and evolved from Latin roots, plus Swiss and Friulian dialects.

A description of MUSE: https://www.cultura.trentino.it/eng /Cultural-venues/All-cultural-venues/Museums-and-collections/Muse -Science-Museum-Trento

On Renzo Piano: http://www.archdaily.com/273403/happy -birthday-renzo-piano

Rovereto

On the way up to the Alto Adige, we bypassed Rovereto because of our blowout on the autostrada, which delayed us by three hours. We knew we would be too late arriving in Trento if we'd stopped. After visiting Trento, I feel torn. Ready to explore more of the Dolomiti north of here but also pulled to double back. There is something I want to see in Rovereto.

"Let's go," Ed says. "You'll just regret it if we don't." Back along the Adige—castles strategically positioned for outlooks, abbeys and church spires, the pleasure of the neat rows of grapes rolling down hillsides—an easy drive.

ROVERETO'S TREE-LINED AND broad main street has no curbs. The sidewalks slope gently down. What a good idea. Though it looks like a pleasant walking town, we drive straight to the object of this quest: MART, Museo di Arte Moderna e Contemporanea di Trento e Rovereto. This is another waving plume in the hat of this region. A stellar art collection housed in a building designed by Mario Botta. I remember well when his San Francisco Museum of Modern Art rocked the sensibilities of the Bay Area in 1994. After reading about his work since then, I am inspired to see what he accomplished in Rovereto.

COULD THIS BE the entrance, a narrow street between two *palazzi?* Unprepossessing, and no preparation for the surprise of stepping into a soaring atrium. The steel and Plexiglas dome resembles a spider web, with the center an open oculus like the Pantheon's. Rain and snow can fall into the fountain below. The slot and square windows in the lower walls also remind me of the Pantheon, although with a touch of rigor that recalls slits in castles for arrow shooting, and also the rationalist buildings beloved by the fascists.

The collection features the work of modernist Italian painters and of the Futurists, those bad boys. Although the Futurists' jarring work is better known, the other painters of the twentieth century, such as Giorgio Morandi, Massimo Campigli, Julius Evola, Achille Funi, Mario Sironi, and Manilo Rho, were more individualistic. Funi's *Ragazzo con le mele (Boy with an Apple)*, Rho's *Woman in Red,* and Campigli's *Donne sul terrazzo (Women on a Terrrace)*—which recalls both fresco technique and Etruscan tomb painting—are three favorites. And Alberto Burri! I am a longtime admirer of this painter from Città di Castello, near Cortona. While serving as a medical doctor in World War Two, he was captured and sent to a POW camp in Texas, where he began making art out of found items—cardboard, wire, and cellophane. Much of his work is displayed in his hometown, though he was influential worldwide to many artists, including Robert Rauschenberg.

And how fabulous—Fortunato Depero's *Movimento d'uccello (Movement of a Bird)*. Reading over the famous Marinetti manifesto of 1909, I laugh at the bombast. Down with libraries, museums, feminism, and morality! The artists of the movement are under thirty and expect to be extinct by forty. The century has turned, ushering in speed, machines, velocity, all manner of movement. Art must embrace disruption and industry. War is "hygienic." "A racing car . . . is more beautiful than the *Victory of Samothrace*." Down with Italy's past culture, even pasta!

A Futurist favorite of mine is Gino Severini, a Cortona boy who dropped his painting of religious subjects and took up fractured motions and wild colors. We get to see his *Ballerina* from 1913, and *Plastic Rhythm of 14 July*, and *Portrait of Madame MS*. He's good. A trattoria in Cortona displays a print of Severini's dancehall painting *La Danza del pan pan al Monico, Dance of the Pan Pan at the Monico*. The colors, angles, and rhythms of the dancers run to the edge of the canvas—no context of a room, just collective motion. How many evenings I've waited for my *ribollita* while admiring his joyous whirl and energy. In old age, Severini returned to Cortona. As his own motion slowed, the long DNA in every Italian painter's blood must have proven too strong to resist: He took up painting the Madonna once again. A couple of times a week, I walk up the path of his mosaic stations of the cross. All Futurist motion stalled.

We linger and linger. Lively contemporary exhibitions express the museum's architectural momentum. One is simply a doorway with music and talk seeping out. A collaboration between Turkish writer Orhan Pamuk and Grazia Toderi, *Words and Stars* combines imagined maps, celestial maps, and real visions of the lights of Istanbul, with prose that dwells on how our minds connect with the movement of light and stars. (Long gone now, but perhaps it will travel.) There's a drifty ambiguity: The words seem to dissolve as I try to read the handwriting of the earth—its oceans, lights, earth formations.

Botta's interior is *so* white. The airiness, the sculptural openings in walls, the monumental stairways, the turns—all take you on a journey. The excitement of the art communicated by its house. Imagine, in this small town. How did this miracle happen?

The Hotel Rovereto is something of a time warp with its plain furnishings and bleak light at the window. Sitting on the edge of the bed, I feel like the solitary figure in Edward Hopper's *Hotel Room*. Fortunately, the restaurant serves good local food. As we attack a big fish in salt crust, we ponder the wonders we have seen.

NOTE:

Orhan Pamuk's novel of a doomed romance, *The Museum of Innocence*, inspired him to create an eponymous museum in Istanbul. Not to be missed! Personal, intriguing, imaginative, the museum is an Ottoman house transformed into a cabinet of curiosities. Pamuk's project is obsessive: All objects named in the narrative of his book are displayed.

Merano

As we drive from Rovereto to Merano, William suggests
a detour. He's spotted Lago di Tovel on the map and
already knows he wants to see mountain lakes. We're on
a precipitous road. I'm unable to read because of endless
switchbacks. We climb and dip and climb and finally the
forest parts and we arrive.

The green, green water, fringed with conifers and
hardwood trees, is backed by the jagged gray peaks of the
Brenta Dolomites, some with white rock slopes that I first
think are covered with snow. We start to walk the lake path,
past a beach where a few people are sunning on towels. In
the shade, family picnics are in progress. Swimming isn't
allowed. How frustrating to lie in the sun, unable to splash
into this clear water to cool off. Planning only to go a little
way, we keep walking, drawn by the shifting scenery and
the water changing color as depths and shadows play. Soon
we're a third of the way around. Go back or continue?

We go on. An easy walk. Only a few others on the trail.
Most turn back. Why does this place seem different?

I've walked with pleasure around many lakes, but here, something else is happening—an exhilaration. Contact high. Is it the clarity of the air sharply defining where water meets trees, trees meet mountains, and the mountains, sky? I take off my sunglasses, thinking the lenses distort color. But, no. The scene is vibrant and super-real. Sunlight glints off the facets of the peaks, turning the stone angles pink and gray and violet. The air deeply fresh and the lake translucent, like a painting on a mirror. I sense how I would feel in the water, water clear as air, frigid, purifying water. Even imagining a plunge is renewing.

Halfway around, we come upon another beach where a few pale forms are stretched out on their towels. Others have ventured into the forbidden water. I take off my shoes and step in up to my ankles. Quick thrums of pain shoot up my legs. Forget swimming. The path turns craggy and uphill for a hundred yards or so, then smooths out onto a wider path covered with pine needles. Quiet. A crow caw splits the air. As afternoon lengthens the shadows, the water turns from emerald to inky blue, even turquoise where the sun hits. William stops to photograph a waterfall and stream rushing through ferns. We've walked only two hours, two memorable hours.

WHEN WE REACH Merano, it's late in the day. We're at Villa Adria, a pretty Belle Époque hotel that feels like someone's lovely summer house. We're greeted as though we're being welcomed back, although it's our first time here. Piero, who must have worked here forever, shows us the reading room, cozy with books, antiques, and Oriental rug. French doors open to a flowery terrace. William is enchanted by the 1914 wooden elevator, like a fanciful birdcage with upholstered benches. Our rooms look out over villas with terraces and gardens. Obviously, we're in a microclimate; this looks like Florida.

William is introduced to the austere style of making up the bed with an individual duvet. "I like a top sheet," he says. "This thing is heavy." Merano is full of "cure hotels" (medical), now rethought as spas (sybaritic). Villa Adria is a place where most guests check in for a week of relaxation and treatments, and some active trips organized by the hotel. Biking, hiking, golf, and excursions are listed for the following day. When I reserved, I was charmed by the website. Creative, original people and individuals, I read, are the most welcome. We hoped we qualified. Staff photos include all the housemaids and waiters. I like the attitude.

Piero brings us prosecco on the terrace and the reflection off the putty-colored building casts a sunny glow over everyone. *La vita è bella.* The dinner hour is earlier up in this area than in Tuscany. When we stroll into the yellow dining room at eight, our table is the only vacant one. The staff is welcoming and the buffet (not my preferred way to dine) lavish. The waiter has the good recommendation of a citrusy Ploner Sauvignon. "Do you all think hotels have moods?" I ask.

William gives a slight eye-roll but gamely answers, "Possibly. What's the mood here?"

"I think . . . optimistic."

Ed says, "Effervescent. The mood of someone about to sing an aria."

"I'm going to get some more pasta." William is smiling. Who knows what goes on in the head of someone fifteen traveling with grandparents? But I can imagine.

THE LUCKIEST TOWNS are those built along a river and if the river is the picturesque Passer, double luck. Were the surrounding mountains placed there simply to enhance the setting of this elegant town? Nineteenth-century Merano was where the Habsburg empress Elisabeth, affectionately called Sissi, came for her health, bringing in her wake family and an Austrian court entourage. Other nobles followed, enjoying the mild winter and participating in baths, drinking the waters, and promenading in gardens with fountains and pavilions. An outdoor treatment was "the terrain cure," which simply meant walking on slightly rising paths. No major exertion required, wrote a Professor M. J. Örtel of Munich, but a proven remedy for the heart, circulation, and muscles.

The genteel aura of an aristocratic spa town remains. The white and pale yellow neoclassical and Liberty (Art Nouveau) buildings, long paths along the river, and curated shopping streets would lure Sissi today. She might be taken aback by the egalitarian Merano thermal baths project. Designed by notable architect Matteo Thun, the complex right in town offers twenty-five different pools, plus saunas—one with a snow room to cool in—and massages and other treatments with local products such as hay, wool, and fruits. Besides various hot and cold pools, there's a salt pool, one for non-swimmers, another for children. Hotel Terme Merano stays open all year. I fancy sitting in a steaming pool surrounded by snowbanks.

I'm stunned at Thun's vision. A vast glass box, maybe fifteen meters high, placed like a cloche over pools that abut each other, with lounging platforms in between. You're in a paradisaical terrarium. I love bold architecture that isn't just for flash but embraces function in surprising ways. Thun's ancient colleague would be the architect of the baths of Caracalla in Rome.

I didn't expect to be stunned by this region's contemporary architecture. Renzo Piano's MUSE in Trento, Mario Botta's MART in Rovereto, now Matteo Thun. We will definitely come back to the Thun *terme* for a few days of escape. But now, we want to see the rest of Merano.

"Okay, Franny," Ed says, "do towns have moods—and if so, what's the tenor of Merano?" We're walking down the Corso Libertà, lined with upscale shops and trees, including the southern *magnolia grandiflora* with dinner-plate blooms. The parking area is crammed with bicycles.

"Light-hearted. I can imagine everyone listening to lyric opera and song cycles. Everyone's house is filled with flowers and bowls of fruit on the table. And hearty. Everyone skis and toboggans in winter. Hot chocolate and little fried pastries."

William points out shiny community bicycle pumps along the sidewalk. He sends off a photo to his parents, both dedicated cyclists, who are up and out early, and gets an immediate reply: *Sign of a superior civilization.*

I did say upscale. The supernal market, Pur, has wheeled wicker shopping carts, an espresso bar, jewel-box produce, artisan flours, local cheeses. Even the milk must come from the nicest cows. Ed starts a conversation, first with the barista, then with someone else over the merits of linden honey. William collects a few snacks for the car trip—fresh apple juice, chocolate, German pretzels, baby radishes like rubies. I'm lingering over a table of handcrafted wooden cutting boards and spoons. "But you're Italian," I overhear.

Ed answers, *"Magari. Sono Americano."* Meaning, would that I were. I'm American.

"But that's impossible, you speak perfectly the Italian." Music to Ed's ears. An Italian has mistaken him for a native. This happens everywhere. One reason is that Ed talks to the taxi driver, the desk clerk, the waiter. With anyone, he starts up immediately. William and I should. When I'm complimented on my Italian, that's because no one expects Americans to speak at all. And my southern accent invades. William is learning. This is his third summer studying with lovely Laura at Polymnia in Cortona, backed up in North Carolina by a weekly tutor. We both have that silly fear of making mistakes, whereas that doesn't stop Ed. He realized long ago that rhythm is the thing. If you've got that down, you're understood.

A little shop I like is Via Vai, at number 41, where only Italian wines and products are sold. Most of the town speaks German and sells German goods. Stefano Visintin, the owner, tells me he needed to make a stand. We're in Italy! He compliments *me* on my Italian, then Ed walks in and three sentences later, here we go: "But of course *you* were born in Italy . . ."

Even though we don't need anything, we buy rose hip tea, truffle potato chips, more chocolate—this time Italian—and plum jam. Ed, beaming. *Italiano.*

Both Ed and William are drawn to the sleek and fashionable mountain gear. Numerous shops lure them, and, although they are not rock climbing or taking strenuous hikes, they like the super-lightweight orange and crimson and navy jackets, the multicolored rope coils, nifty tools and backpacks. They don't buy as much as a water bottle but they're discussing how Prada and Dolce & Gabbana must have been influenced by mountain sports, by bicycling. Even I begin to want a cool red backpack. I drag them out to the other shops on via Portici, an arcaded street of painted houses with pretty oculus windows, and the branching of arcaded alleyways toward cafés and clothing boutiques. Most amazing is the *macelleria,* butcher, G. Siebenförcher—the paradigm meat market. Step into the chilly space, clean as an operating room, and see every type of *salumi,* speck, smoked meat, prosciutto, pancetta, sausage, plus beef, lamb, veal, fowl, pork in all cuts, venison, boar, hare, pheasant, and duck. Downstairs, cheese world.

Our trusty restaurant guides don't give much space to Merano. We walk into Bistro Sieben, which looks fine and is. I'm becoming addicted to the local *pane croccante di segale,* a crunchy rye bread with seeds. We order roasted vegetable strudel, the potato and cheese dumplings. All these dumplings! May I not turn into one myself, but they are good. We have salads, too, and soon are back out on the arcaded street.

What catches my eye most in the Duomo di San Nicolò are not the bone-thin columns splaying gracefully into the ceiling, nor the precious carved pews, nor the stained-glass windows that depict the miracles of San Nicolò. All arresting—but I am most delighted by the doors' artful ironwork. We walk all around the church, inside and out, examining this phenomenal part of the architecture and admiring the clever levers, locks, hinges, knobs, and cunningly wrought decorative flourishes. Touch them and you touch the hand of the artist.

Of the old cemetery that used to surround the Duomo, all that remains is a wall mounted with old tombstones, which leads to the octagonal Cappella di Santa Barbara, the chapel for funerals, a one-room church with round stained-glass windows with simple paisley designs, more Turkish than Austrian or Italian. Barbara, now removed from the official list of saints because of her mere legendary status, was a virgin martyr killed by her pagan father. After the deed, he was struck dead by lightning. Hence, she's the person to pray to in a storm. Why is she here? This area used to be active in silver mining and she's the saint for miners. Since Barbara is also the name of my older sister, I light a votive for her.

THE PUBLIC HERB garden, the walk of poets, the scent garden, the winter walk, the summer walk, castles, paths among cedars, oleanders, olives, pomegranates, more gardens. This is a genteel watering hole. One should light here for four or five days, at least, not rush through as we are. We lean on the lacy iron bridge looking down at the river rippling over rocks. A tightly groomed dog has escaped his leash and rolls in the mud. William calculates kilometers on his phone. We are anxious to get out into the mountains.

Monte San Vigilio/Lana

From Merano, it's only eleven kilometers to Lana, through vineyards and laden orchards. We could lean out of the window and grab an apple. On the edge of Lana, we leave the car in covered parking near the lift up to Vigilius Mountain Resort. None of us ever has been on a cable car. We load in our bags along with two brave souls and their coach, who are taking the lift up for paragliding. I'm scared, but once we begin, it seems that we're never too far above the ground. Like the birds, we skim through the larch forest. Up we go. And up, the town of Lana and the valley receding quickly.

Gripping the railing, I focus on the wide view and try not to imagine the cable snapping, sending us careening down the mountain. William smiles all the way up. Ed, of course, talks with the paragliders and their coach.

Soon we swing gently to a stop. There to meet us is a man, incongruously in a suit, from the hotel. He whisks our luggage onto a small vehicle. We walk—no cars allowed up here—the short distance to the hotel, a luxury monastic building designed by Matteo Thun, architect of Merano's thermal complex. The larch-wood exterior looks as though it was gathered from weathered old fences, though the sweep and shape of the design say that the place is contemporary. Instead of landscaping, there are purple and yellow wildflowers and swaying grasses. And views and views of blue-tinged mountains.

We get to stay three nights. Will I go stir-crazy? No car, no streets, no shops, the entire concrete world gone. What there is to do: Walk, read, swim, soak in a hot pool that is half inside and half outside in the trees. Eat, of course. The hotel has a casual restaurant in Tyrolian style, and, upstairs, Ristorante 1500—for 1,500 meters above sea level—which conjures the feel of a barn with its exposed wood and three-hundred-year-old beams.

An architect's make-the-best-of-it moment in designing a hotel must be the hallways. How to design that difficult space, other than with wallpaper and patterned rugs? At Vigilius the halls are not static. They're wide with smooth stone floors, and playful sculptures on pedestals punctuate the way. The sculpture exhibits change periodically. Our rooms have the Germanic folded duvet bedcovers—no top sheet—but also contemporary rosy velvet chairs facing the view. On a ledge, a book of short narratives, an annual publication written by guests, and a basket of Braeburn apples from a local farmer. The bathroom counters and tub surrounds are made of pale, smooth larch. By the tub, a jar of hay for a soaking bath.

All through this area, we've heard murmurs about climate change, and as many awards attest, our hotel is state-of-the-art eco. The dividing three-quarters-high wall between bedroom and bath is made of baked clay. It doubles as the heater for the room. I read an elaborate description of the hotel's biomass (wood chip) heating system, with such filtration that pollutants are minimal. Many excellent hotels in the region have no air-conditioning because they've never needed it. End of June. Hot. Now they do. At night on the ground floor, we can open the door in our glass wall for a breeze but I'm afraid of animals coming in. Lucky for William, he's on the second floor. Still, owls could fly in and settle on the bed.

· · ·

WE'VE ARRIVED FROM Merano late in the day. William is ready for the pool. At the entrance to the spa area, I see Greek words from Heraclitus etched on the glass wall.

πάντα ῥεῖ

The attendant doesn't know what it means, and neither do I. We have the indoor infinity pool to ourselves, the hot pool, too. Moving from the one pool to the other and back, we seem to float through the glass wall and into the view. Both pools are paved with white stone slabs. After, we feel energized. Is that because the water is slightly radioactive? Throughout the hotel this buzzy, prized water runs in all the pipes. It's highly regarded as therapeutic, and is sold as bottled water as well.

William is out for shots of the streaky purple sunset. We rest. Already the go-go-go of the last few days melts away in the peace of this place.

ALL GUESTS ARE invited to the living room for a prosecco before dinner. I adore the unlikely colors. Long sofa banquettes built along two walls are upholstered in burnt-ocher velvet with orange, plum, and red pillows, all the colors that dance in the fireplace. Beyond the glass wall, we drift out to the terrace for the *aperitivo*. All the other guests speak German. My German is limited to *es var einwal ein junger Bauer* (there was once a young farmer), and Ed's to *Frühstück* (breakfast) and *Einfahrt* and *Ausfahrt* (entrance and exit, which provoke laughs on the autostrada). We are exiled to our own company. William, the only child present, is brought a drink of mint and orange. Suddenly a downpour opens and we rush inside. A gray skein of mist covers the mountains and the larch forest darkens.

OUR FIRST NIGHT, we chose Stube Ida, the hotel's Tyrolian bistro. I don't know what home cooking is in these hills but, please, let it be like this. *Frico,* a fried potato crisp with guanciale and red onions; cabbage leaves stuffed with the great Piemontese Fassone beef, buckwheat, and sour cream butter; fried chicken with sour peppers and apple chutney; gnocchi with chanterelles and thyme; black bread soup; *tagliata* (sliced grilled steak) with rosemary and a sauce of *vino schiava,* a DOC grape of the area. Savory and comforting, like the restaurant's atmosphere: A huge tile stove remains from an earlier incarnation of the inn; wooden tables and mountain chairs with heart shapes carved out of the backs speak to the tradition but don't read as kitschy; and, of course, the mountain view. Hikers stop here at lunch and eat out on the terrace but it's different at night, when the coziness kicks in.

OUT EARLY, WE take the short walk to chair lifts for further adventures in higher meadows and forests. This time, I'm not afraid; the ride feels exhilarating, bobbing along over hikers and cows ringing their bells and lowing. Closed into the chair with a bar across pulls out fleetingly some lost primordial memory of being confined in a stroller. We take well-marked trails to a lake, but when we arrive, we find the lake has become a marsh. The trails are easy and tamed. No scrambling or tricky footing, just alpine air and gorgeous blue sky. We walk all morning and circle back to the chair lift in plenty of time for salads on the terrace, more pool time, and, for the men, an hour with kettle bells in the exercise room. I retire to read.

WE'RE FALLING INTO a routine of hikes, lounging with books by the pool twice a day, and photographing bees burrowing into flower faces. Ed studies Italian. I'm unable to put down my Jane Gardam novel. We're easily clocking seven or eight miles a day outdoors.

The last two nights we have long dinners at the more formal Restaurant 1500, where Chef Filippo Zoncato presides over the kitchen. We bond with a waiter from Sardinia who regales us with descriptions of Sardinian food while pouring tastes of Alto Adige white wines from the Cantina Terlano co-operative of twenty-four winemakers. Crisp and fresh as a local apple, their Terlano Chardonnay sets a standard. And here's my love, Sanct Valentin sauvignon from St. Michael-Eppan. All their whites are winsome and strong. We also fall hard for the Pinot Nero Sonnenberg, Cantina Burggräfler.

Some of our favorite tastes from the chef's brilliant locally sourced menu:

"Tacos" formed from celery root and filled with sweet and sour carrots, soft goat cheese, zucchini, and oregano.

Rice with asparagus, grated egg, and *luppolo selvatico,* wild hops.

Lamb with purée of fave and *agretti,* that bitter, grass-like green.

Suckling pig with kohlrabi, rye, roasted onions, and caraway.

Branzino, sea bass, with rhubarb, turnip greens, and toasted pine nuts.

Millefoglie with pistachio, hazelnut, and sorbet of *sambuco* (elder tree) flowers.

Yellow peach with cream of white chocolate and Champagne granita and basil.

After dinner, movies (usually in German) are shown in the library, or we can lie out in the wildflowers, looking up at the stars. They seem so close you could reach out and snatch one out of the sky, put the sparkle in your pocket.

Three slow and relaxed days paradoxically speed by. I forgot to take the hay bath. Shouldn't I have had a facial? All too soon, we board the cable car and begin our descent.

The Greek quote written on the spa door—now I know what it means: *Everything flows.*

Maialino da Latte, Purè di Pastinaca, Fave, e Mele

YOUNG PORK WITH PURÉE OF PARSNIPS, BEANS, AND APPLES, SERVES 10

A winter dish from Chef Filippo Zoncato, suitable for the great outdoor life at the serene Vigilius Mountain Resort. The chef's method given below is beyond the capabilities of most home cooks. You'll get great results from the regular oven roasting of a large leg of pork or a pork loin: a 350°F oven, 25 minutes per pound and roasted to an internal temperature of 145°F. Do take his method for the vegetable purée, such a good pairing with pork.

12-pound boneless leg of pork
Salt and pepper, *QB*
A handful of black peppercorns
10 to 15 bay leaves
12 parsnips, peeled and cut into disks
Milk and water, *QB*
6 apples, peeled, cored, and quartered
2 onions, sliced
Extra-virgin olive oil, *QB*
2 cups fresh fava beans, shelled

Season the meat with salt and peppercorns, and stud with bay leaves.

Lay the pork leg in a vacuum and cook in a steam oven for 20 hours at 150°F.

Remove from the oven and set the pork, still in its pouch, in a tray filled with ice water.

When the meat reaches room temperature, cut into slices, in portions of about 5 ounces each.

Cook the parsnips in water and milk in equal parts, until fork tender. Drain them (putting aside the cooking liquid) and blend with an immersion blender until a thick purée is obtained. Season.

Steam the apples over boiling water until barely tender. Mix them with an immersion blender until you obtain a purée. Leave to drain.

Sauté the onions in olive oil until translucent. Season with salt and pepper.

Blanch the beans in boiling water for 4 minutes. If they are fresh, no need to peel. If older, rub off the outer skin. Season and add a little olive oil.

If you like, brown the pieces of pork over a medium heat, to make the skin crisp.

Heat the parsnip purée and make egg-shaped little servings. Place a slice of pork on a plate and add the parsnip alongside. Spoon the fave over the pork slice. Finally, arrange the mashed apples on the side of the plate with a sprinkling of onions.

Ristorante 1500, Vigilius Mountain Resort,
Lana, Trentino-Alto Adige

Vipiteno

Vipiteno became Italian in 1919, quite recently by Italian standards. Formerly part of the Austro-Hungarian empire, the town used to be Sterzing, renamed from the original Roman Vipitenum. Although Italian for a century now, the Austrian heritage still thrives.

We park on the edge of the village and walk down a stage-set main street that's interrupted midway by Torre delle Dodici, a fifteenth-century clock tower dividing the old town from the "new," though it's hard to tell the difference. Tall houses in all the colors of macarons, with balconies of flowers, line the street. Arabesque iron shop signs, arcades, statue, fountain—a vivid scene. Lots of silly little dogs are paraded by their owners, and one couple pushes their collie in a perambulator. The dog barks like mad as they stroll. William buys a gray T-shirt and I buy a black bag to hold all the local jams and honeys we buy.

A trading center since time immemorial, Vipiteno is the northernmost town in Italy, hailing distance from the Brenner Pass, which was first mentioned around 13 B.C.

The pass is where our Stone Age ancestors with icy hair scrambled from the cold down toward the sun. During Roman times, the area thrived because of silver mines. And thrives still.

We order salads at an outdoor terrace. Here comes the collie, still barking. Two women near us drink the biggest glasses of beer I've ever seen. The waiter is Romanian and seems to speak neither German nor Italian. We point. It works out.

AT THE TOURIST office, I unfold a map. The vacation possibilities are fabulous. The Dolomiti are well organized for any walking, hiking, skiing, tobogganing, camping, or spa experience one could dream of. The map stars trails and places to stay, from rustic to five-star, and *rifugi,* mountain hut stops that serve food to hikers and sometimes offer rooms. William wants to stay in one of the Tyrolian classic houses— timber porches with ornamental balustrades and flamboyant flowers lining each floor. He's never seen *The Sound of Music* but a fantasy unfurls on its own: eiderdown, cheese, amber honey on bread, and goats outside. I look through brochures picturing dozens of these places. Oh, for the time to spend a month.

RIGHT IN THE *centro,* the frescoes in the Gothic Chiesa dello Spirito Santo show judgment day in no uncertain terms. Bodies emerge from graves and are shunted left for paradise, right for hell. Simple as that. The vaulted church feels intimate; I sit for a few moments of quiet and look at a happier fresco, Saint Christopher ferrying the Christ child across waters.

Thanks to Paul Blanchard's Trentino–Alto Adige chapter in the *Blue Guide: Northern Italy.* Otherwise, I wouldn't have known a revealing aspect of Vipiteno: the schools. Liceo Scientifico, the science high school, designed by Höller & Klotzner, and the Scuola Elementare, the elementary school designed by Cez Calderan Zanovello. The science high school's handsome and elegant juxtaposition of glass and slatted wood and its serene spatial relationships must inspire everyone who treads the halls. Zanovello's long colonnade supported by raw tree trunks surprises by evoking the nearby forests. Of what matters to the inhabitants of Vipiteno, the schools speak as frankly as the judgment day frescoes. What lucky students.

THE POINT OF the trip is shifting for all of us. We're still interested in towns, but the stupefying landscapes stun us constantly. On every walk, we remark on the *air*. Just breathing gives you vigor. Sloping, green upland meadows (*Heidi and Grandfather, where are you?*), with surging streams and those dreamy Tyrolian houses that look as though fifty could live there. In the fields where hay is being racked, men are wearing lederhosen. Forked hay falls from the pitchfork in a golden tumble. We drive across the Brenner Pass into Austria, just for William to set foot in another country. But we turn right around. Back into Italy, and on into the Dolomiti!

Campo Tures

Like Vipiteno, Campo Tures qualifies as a Bandiera
Arancione village, Orange Flag sites selected by the
Touring Club Italiano as particularly attractive or culturally
noteworthy. This place is blessed by the gods. The Aurino
(Ahr in German) River, narrow but swift, roars through.
A ring of mighty peaks surrounds the valley. At one end
of town looms Tures Castle. The little village—only five
thousand residents in the greater Campo Tures area—was
the field (*campo*) of the Tures family. Quiet today on our
late June visit but as a winter sports and market center,
it certainly sees many lively days. Surprisingly, only a few
houses are old. They look strangely Ottoman with their
stacked wooden mirador windows and plain façades.
Instead of marooned and seemingly abandoned in Campo
Tures, they'd look at home along the Bosporus. Mountain
gear shops cluster in the *centro,* then we find orderly
neighborhoods to wander in. A sign on the park invites you
in to "read and relax." Good idea.

A covered wooden pedestrian bridge crosses the Aurino.

Downstream, a red church spire, among lush willows and vines bordering the river, points up to zigzag peaks against gray sky roiling with clouds. *Alpenglow,* at sunrise and sunset—the play of rose and lavender light across the peaks. I'm mesmerized by the tumbling green and white water—how can it remain contained inside such tight banks?

"Now, why are we here?" William asks as we complete our walk around town in an hour.

"Look up! Those eighty peaks! We should come back in winter. You can sleep in igloos here."

"No way."

"Yes, and I read it's not even that cold. Sledding, cross-country. This is the place."

AT THE HOTEL Alpinum, our adjoining balconies look into a garden. Rooms are comfortable, albeit modest. There's an indoor pool but we don't take the time for a swim. William is catching up with friends on Snapchat. Ed falls into a major nap while I read my old favorite, *The Lawrence Durrell Travel Reader.* I copy in my notebook: *You enter Greece as one might enter a dark crystal; the form of things becomes irregular, refracted.* I recognize that strange feeling when the power of a landscape overtakes you. When in the Mani of Greece, I thought I would wear a white linen shift and grow very thin until my bones showed, so elemental did the place feel. Here in the voluptuous valleys and idyllic green hills sloping up to raw and haggard mountains, I close my eyes. The power and spirit of this landscape (Durrell would call it sense of place) must be that you enter it as an explorer. What lies over the next pass? The Dolomiti are in Italy but there's a bedrock German culture, too; these are mountains but not remotely like any seen before; the air is fresh but I want to gulp it like spring water; we're slowed by curvy roads but have a feeling of momentum; we hike one foot after another but harbor the desire to soar over the fields of hay, over the isolated wood and stone huts (*malghe*) of the summer pastures. I write: *You enter the Dolomiti as one might enter a dream of flying.*

ON OUR WALK, we found the Feldmilla Design Hotel. I should have booked there for its waterside location. It would have been thrilling to hear the torrent in the night. Like the Vigilius Mountain Resort, it is an eco, climate-neutral hotel. We looked at the menu for the hotel's Ristorante Toccorosso (red glass). All local products, with imaginative recipes and traditional fare as well.

We're back at eight. They've found us the last table. A wedding dinner is starting. "Oh, no," Ed says, "bad service coming up." We're put at the end table on the terrace, which is quiet and so out of the way that the waiter never will notice us. But, we hear the sweet sound of flowing water, not only from the river but from a sudden torrential rain as well. We're under cover but a fine mist wafts with every breeze. The waiter appears, prompt after all and smiling. We decide on plates of vegetable croquettes, potato dumplings, and grilled fish. There were lighter choices but we've gotten into these dumplings. I am pleased to see one of my favorite sauvignons on the wine list. It would be sobering to know how many bottles of Lafóa I have drunk over the years. A wine that sings, that inspires. Our friend Riccardo identifies one of the tastes as *pipi di gatto,* cat pee. (Others call that particular taste gooseberry.) To me it's a quality of some of the best whites, the velvet border on a silk dress.

The rain has rinsed the already pristine air. We walk back to our hotel along the river, chuting even faster through the night, a long skein in the moonlight, as though a woman has unfurled her silvery gray hair.

LAST DAY IN the Dolomiti coming up. We set out to look for a waterfall that William saw in a brochure. At the beginning of the ascending trail, there's the inevitable Italian touch: a bar. We stoke ourselves with coffee and head up, intending to see only the first of three waterfalls along the trail. The path leads through a forest where some glacial event once occurred: Enormous rocks covered with vivid moss fill the forest floor. Through tall skinny trees the light filters, a pellucid veil. There must be fairy houses everywhere in the ferny undergrowth. We follow a scent of coniferous green, pungent and sharp. A half hour of gentle climbing and we come to the first surging fall. Is there anything in nature more enchanting? The noise of it astounds—a crashing music.

William looks back at us. "Let's go on. This is fantastic." I say to myself a true line from Gerard Manley Hopkins: *There lives the dearest freshness deep down things . . .* The climb intensifies. In half an hour we hear a distant roar and scramble onward. Magnificent. We agree to continue. How could we not? This is one of the best walks ever. We're quiet, listening to silence, then silence broken by hurtling water.

Best for last. The long drop of the highest waterfall. The deafening sluice and slide, a violence sending heavenly mist everywhere. We're happily drenched. (Not happy that the camera is drenched.) *Remember this,* I think silently to William. *This is it.*

Going downhill is faster. We're back at the car, stunned as though we've been abducted by aliens. Not that drastic, but truly exhilarated. Such unexpected beauty keeps us smiling.

WE'RE THREADING THROUGH high passes. A geologist's paradise. "What does *dolomite* mean?" Ed throws out.

"The kind of rock," William guesses. He starts scrolling his phone. "Calcium magnesium carbonate."

"Yes, but why is it called *dolomite*?" He's got us. "Named for a French geologist."

"A geologist named Dolomite? You're kidding."

"Déodat de Dolomieu. Don't you love Déodat? He explored in the late seventeen hundreds. This range is unbelievably old, two hundred and thirty million years. This was a sea when Europe and Africa were still joined. Sea of Tethys."

"I've read that hikers still find marine fossils from the ancient lagoons," I add. "And there are dinosaur prints."

"Cool place," William says. "Good name for a dog, Déodat."

Indeed. I've seen mountains all over the world. These are unique. Inhospitable, formidable, and also sublimely mysterious, a never-never land to birth myth and legend.

BY LUNCHTIME, AFTER traversing many kilometers of oh-pull-over scenery, we arrive at Lago di Braies, another translucent emerald lake. The mountains hovering close to shore reflect in the water. On the Hotel Pragser Wildsee's terrace we have lunch before taking a walk across the golden beach and along a path by the water. The washed colors look like an old postcard. The rambling hotel seems like a venerable place where people come, year after year, for the hikes and good air. William suggests staying another night. Sunrise would be a prime time to set up his tripod for a time lapse. But we are headed back to Cortona today and all we have left to see is the rest of the Great Dolomite Road.

WE WONDERED HOW the mountain roads would be—precipitous and narrow, with infinite drop-offs? We should have remembered the strong tradition of the old Romans, whose roads endure to this day. The Italians have road engineering in their DNA. Traffic is light to non-existent; the roads are flawless. Easy to sit back, for William and me, and take in one jaw-dropping view after another. Conversation lapses into "majestic," "look at *that*," "spectacular," "those are over three thousand meters," and finally, "pull over, I feel sick."

I step out and breathe until my equilibrium steadies. I'm doomed to the backseat, since William is approaching six feet and can't fold enough to slip into the Alfa's afterthought of a backseat. Sips of water; on we go. Lawrence Durrell in Greece has fallen to the floor. I never found my precise image for what it's like to enter the Dolomiti. Anyway, even metaphorically, how does one enter a dark crystal?

Finally, we hit flat land. "What music do you want to hear?" William asks.

"k. d. lang, 'Hallelujah,' " I say.

"Never heard of it but okay."

Ed speeds toward the gentler terrain of Tuscany. Tonight, soul food—pasta al ragù. I write in my notebook: *Entering Tuscany is like climbing onto the lap of an immensely kind nonna.*

Veneto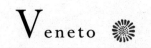

La Laguna di Venezia

Tamarisk trees are blooming along the canals of Torcello. Their dusty-white plumes, hazy in the still June air, blur even more in the water's reflections. At the Torcello stop, we're let off the vaporetto and there's nothing, just a path along a canal. Most people come to see the two ancient churches. They pause for a drink or lunch, then catch the boat again. By late afternoon, the island falls into somnolence. We'll stay for two nights in this old light and summer torpor, this odd spot where a Somerset Maugham or Graham Greene character might wash up.

I was here twenty years ago. Little has changed. The path was sandy, now it's bricked. Wild purple allium spikes the weedy fields. A few souvenir concessions and places to stop for a bite have arrived. Otherwise, the island remains trapped in time—a time before a place such as Venice could even be imagined.

On the voyage out, I took a photo. I caught a flat expanse of glittering water, a milky sky with high wispy clouds, and between water and sky, the low horizon line of a distant island, so thin it looks like a green brushstroke on a field of blue. This watery realm—so different from Venice, where winding canals are alive with working boats, and everywhere the waters shimmer with lights, colorful palace façades, striped mooring poles, and black silhouettes of gondolas. But way out in the lagoon: silence, a soft palette of tawny grasses, sand, and water turning from pewter to the old green of a celadon cup. Among islands barely emerging from the water, I'm back at the beginning. The city of Venice was once like these, just an idea of land. How bizarre to think of building on ground where the water table rises to about a tablespoon under the surface.

TORCELLO, YOU MIGHT say, is the mother of Venice.

The bishop of Altino, a town that had endured invasion after invasion not far away on the mainland, moved his followers to the then-desolate Roman island in A.D. 638. Some say the low and marshy settlement called to the bishop in a vision. There, his people would be less vulnerable. In the shallow waters around Torcello, channels had to be cut, and when attacked, the people of Altino pulled up *bricole,* deep-water markers, leaving enemies to founder in mud. After eight centuries of a thriving civilization, malaria and silt ruined life on the island. People migrated onto equally undependable strands that gradually became Venice. Thereafter, the island's five towns, and its many churches and palaces, were raided for building materials, reducing the place to the few remaining structures. Today, Torcello claims only ten residents.

I MUST HAVE been in a thousand churches during my years in Italy. Torcello's haunting basilica of Santa Maria Assunta, a crude relic with a powerful force, may be the most arresting one I've ever seen. Built in 639, rebuilt in 1008, altered again and again, it's barny and beamed, squared off and interrupted by rood screens. High windows, shafts of gray light, traces of fresco, shutters made of stone slabs. I was not prepared for the stunning mosaics. At the west end, a depiction of the Harrowing of Hell, the seven deadly sins, and the Last Judgment in gory detail. Serpents weave in and out of the skulls of the envious near dismembered parts belonging to the slothful; the gluttons eat their own hands. The messages are complex. Beware! A small child is actually the Antichrist in disguise. This is as alarming now as it was to worshipers in the eleventh and twelfth centuries.

The east wall mosaic is startlingly different. In a glittering, tessellated, and very tall apse rises the simple elongated Madonna holding her Baby. If you have binoculars, you see that she is weeping. Her right hand gestures toward the infant, as if to say *this way.* In her left hand she holds a small white cloth, which early viewers would have recognized as a foreshadowing of the shroud. Jan Morris, in her seminal book *Venice,* quotes a child of her acquaintance who described the mosaic as "a thin young lady, holding God."

The whole complex collapses time. What moves me most is the spolia, all the surviving stone and marble bits from across the centuries incorporated into the still-living building: exposed sections of mosaic from the original 639 floor, seventh-century altar, eleventh-century marble panels, fourth-century Roman sarcophagus, fragments of a thirteenth-century fresco, ninth-century font for holy water—this has been sacred ground as far back as memory goes.

Santa Fosca, the adjacent brick church, is a compact Greek-cross base topped by a round structure. Stripped inside, except for Byzantine marble columns, the space is still mesmerizing. Nearby, the two small archaeological museums with their cunningly cast bronze probes, tweezers, keys, spoons, and cups open to us intimate glimpses of life on Torcello. From many islands in the lagoon you can see the campanile, the exclamation point of Torcello. It was even taller before 1640, when lightning lopped off the top. Too bad it's closed today. I would like to have seen the brick-ramped interior, which must make it easier to climb up for the view.

ERNEST HEMINGWAY SECLUDED himself on Torcello to write *Across the River and into the Trees.* We, too, checked into Locanda Cipriani. You can sit under a pergola, sipping a Negroni and plotting the next year of your life. You can read by the window with the scent of roses and jasmine wafting through the curtains, or meander along paths lined with pomegranates and hydrangeas. The bare floors of our room are waxed and the simple curtain lifts in a slight breeze. Pristine, with austere twin beds, a marble fireplace, and reading chair: Emily Dickinson could feel at home here. In the bookcase, I find one of my favorites, *Timeless Cities: An Architect's Reflections on Renaissance Italy* by David Mayernik.

The inn is, by now, a large part of the recent history of the island. Here's Kim Novak on the wall, chomping down on a big bite of pasta. All the British royals come and go in faded black-and-white photographs. How young and slender Princess Diana was. There's Elton John! The waiters love to chat, the food is fresh from the sea, and the deep quiet makes my tense shoulders relax.

My favorite waiter says he has not been to Venice—only a half-hour trip—in five years. When I hear that, my perspective suddenly shifts. To those who live on the less-traveled islands, it's a world. Leaving Torcello, I'm ready to explore as much as possible of the 210-square-mile lagoon, only 8 percent of which is land. We'll hop on and off the vaporetti for a few days. They are working crafts—the metro and bus routes of the lagoon. Once off the busy Venice, Burano, and Murano routes, residents of the scattered islands are taking trips to the market, to the cemetery, to visit relatives, to school. Their days are lived on water, and their dreams must be of water.

AT SANT'ERASMO, WE step off for a bucolic walk along fields where the coveted *castraure* artichokes are grown. Castrated because the prized first buds are cut off, encouraging fuller growth for the plant. Those early two or three violet-tinged little prizes are tender enough to sliver, sprinkle with olive oil, and eat raw. The second wave is almost as delectable, and the third growth is the normal *carciofo* but still special for the large heart and particular taste that comes from saline dirt.

Others who disembarked jumped onto their waiting bicycles and sped off to the scattered farms that grow much of Venice's produce. There is a small hotel on the island with bikes for rent. Next time!

A STOP CLOSE to Venice, San Michele with its dark cypresses is the cemetery island. Extensive, well-tended mausoleums resembling immense marble chests of drawers give way at the wilder edge of the island to the Protestant plot, where many stones are broken, graves are in the ground, and the cypresses look especially moribund. This area seems cautionary for expats like me. Here are those who died far from home—the final stops of Great-Aunt Emily on the grand tour, seamen who caught fevers, and mysterious others like Archibald Campbell, died 1891, whose lonesome marker says: "The heart knoweth its own bitterness and the stranger intermeddleth not therewith." This, a story we never will know. Ezra Pound lies neglected and weedy, in contrast to the only tended grave in the section, that of Russian poet Joseph Brodsky, all covered in blooms. I can't help but feel the contrast of the exiles' abandoned stones with the elaborate private chapels of Italian families decorated with live flowers. Not lingering on such thoughts, I board the vaporetto again for the island of San Lazzaro degli Armeni, where another wandering expat found solace.

Lord Byron came here, possibly to escape his imbroglio of amours in the city. He rowed over from Venice to study Armenian with the monks, who were given political asylum and the island in 1717. By 1789, they'd started a printing enterprise known for producing works in many alphabets and languages, including Aramaic, Sanskrit, and Gaelic. They've been here ever since, in a monastery filled with curiosities and with art of varying quality. We arrive at a serene cloister and, with a few others, follow a copiously bearded monk around the complex. Since I have an aversion to tours, I break from the route and happily wander AWOL for a while, discovering mummies, marble busts, rose-water liqueur made by the monks, and a guest book where many visiting diasporic Armenians record their gratitude for this repository of their culture. What the monastery is most known for is its library of glass-fronted cases holding some of the monks' 150,000 volumes, ranged around a room beneath frescoes of church elders who are reading books. There, you easily imagine Byron taking out volumes and trying to decipher various languages. I then find the dining room, with tables set for the monks' silent supper, taken while overlooking, on the end wall, a huge painting of the Last Supper that must sober all their meals. San Lazzaro (Lazarus) previously was a refuge for sufferers of leprosy, as were other outposts in the lagoon. Paul Morand in his piercing memoir *Venices* credits the monks with importing Angora cats, but I do not see any sign of them.

• • •

WE SPEND A night at Venice Certosa Hotel, a simple inn on La Certosa. The island is under development as a park, but right now is only home to a sailing school, a kayaking center, and a boatyard for the repair of traditional small vessels. Kayaking in the lagoon looks fun and allows access to even smaller islands.

We're the only guests in the inn's restaurant, which serves excellent razor clams and pasta with shrimp.

The night should be as deeply quiet as Torcello. However, the loose rigging on a sailboat near the window dings all night. We depart early.

ACROSS OPEN WATER, the vaporetto speeds up en route to busy Burano, the island that explodes with color. What store offers house paint in magenta, ocher, grape purple, forest green? Why is no house painted the same color as the neighbor's house on either side? *Oh, you're doing yellow? Well, I'm going for Greek blue.* Burano—is there any place on earth with as playful a palette? We're getting off at the stop before—Mazzorbo. A small bridge connects them.

When I'm traveling, I often look at places with the question, *Could I live here?* Mazzorbo sets me dreaming of restoring a particular oxblood-red house with white trim right on the canal. Or is the yellow one more appealing? I don't understand why Mazzorbo is not a coveted residential area. Once it was, like Torcello, a prosperous ancient settlement. The Latin name was *Maiurbium,* large urban place. Also like Torcello, it succumbed to fevers and silt. It languishes now, but one family has staked a big claim to a positive future for Mazzorbo. The Bisols, known for their prosecco, have revived a plot of land where monks in earlier times made wines and farmed. By good fortune, the Bisols found the prized and rare *dorona* grape—only five vines—on nearby Torcello. A few dozen others were found elsewhere in the lagoon, and from cuttings they started a vineyard. The family converted quayside buildings into Venissa, a small inn with an *osteria* and an innovative restaurant.

The square pond of brackish water where the monks kept fish still ripples in the shadow of the old campanile, last vestige of the religious complex. About 90 percent of the restaurant's produce comes from the

garden. This is a "km 0" restaurant, kilometer zero, an Italian desig-
nation signifying sustainable and homegrown. Dining at summer dusk
on the edge of the vineyard in the quiet of the island is bliss. William
is intrigued by all the unfamiliar ingredients on the menu. Geranium
and rose dust are just the beginning. *Artemisia marina, ambretta, alga nori,*
latte d'angelica, basilico artico, calamansi, radice di acetosella, houttuynia, stellina
odorosa.

He surprises us and himself by ordering the tasting menu. Expensive, yes, but who cares? This is an adventure.

While we have a glass of spicy and cold prosecco, he looks up the
strange words. *Artemisia marina:* not what I have in the garden but a marine version. *Calamansi:* Filippino lime. *Alga nori:* a brackish seaweed.
Ambretta: a pink wildflower with fragrant seeds. *Latte d'angelica:* "milk"
of wild celery with a white flower; kin also to fennel. *Radice d'acetosella:*
wood sorrel root of an oxalis. *Houttuynia:* fish mint. (We have this weed
in our fields; I never knew the name. If you step on it, your shoes smell
like fish.) Also called chameleon plant and bishop's weed. *Basilico artico:*
a high-perfume basil resistant to cold. *Stellina odorosa:* a perennial little
star, a highly scented plant whose sweet fragrance becomes stronger
when dried.

I like a menu that makes you work a little.

WILLIAM ENTHUSIASTICALLY TRIES everything—*granseola* (spider
crab), *sgombro* (mackerel) in its silver skin, oysters with green apple,
the exotic local fish *gò* (goby), and roasted pigeon. The latter he enjoys
especially.

"So glad you like the pigeon," Ed says. We're about to end the dinner
with a lemon tart served with the exotic lime sorbet.

"Pigeon? I ate pigeon? Flying rat from Piazza San Marco?" In the
dim light, he'd thought "squab" was something mostly squash.

"No, wild pigeon. Nothing better."

"I ate pigeon," he laments. "It was good."

That golden wine! Maybe a bit of the setting sun melted into
the glass.

. . .

I AM HAPPY not to leave but to climb the stairs to our sloping beamed suite with a view of the canal. I hope this lively project lures others to the island and a little utopia flourishes again. Mazzorbo, otherwise, lies quiet in the lagoon time warp. Early walks around Burano before tourists arrive, around the perimeter of Mazzorbo, chats with women carrying home groceries from an expedition to market, a few people cultivating plots of tomatoes, onions, and zucchini: a slow honey in this hive.

JUST ACROSS THE bridge to Burano, two bright wooden boats moor near the vaporetto station. At the inn, I was given the number of the skipper, who will take me over to San Francesco del Deserto, the ultimate peaceful island. Wanting downtime, Ed and William stay behind, in our appealing mansard suite, wrapped in the hotel robes and watching movies on their iPads.

Only four Franciscans take care of the church, cloister, and gardens. One of them guides me. I'm the only guest. His voice is so soothing that I want to curl under a cypress and nap. He doesn't chatter, just lets me look at the silvery, glazed-water views all around, and watch a white egret that for a moment seems like Saint Francis returned. The monk relates that when his Francesco visited in 1220, he performed his miracle of the birds. In the dense cypress trees, throngs of them held forth with mighty song at the moment Francis wanted to pray. He told them to stop singing until he finished, which they did. It seems an easy miracle—I clap my hands and the cicadas always hush—but I hope it's true. True or not, the story survives, threading together all the days since on this small world amid other scattered small worlds.

AS WE WAIT on the Mazzorbo quay for a water taxi, I remember that many people consider "cellar door" the most pleasing sound in English. To my ear "lagoon," with its hint of the moon, sounds more melodious. Or maybe this thought comes to me because "lagoon" has now gathered to itself vibrant marshy salt scents, a vast reflected sky, lone seabirds, and the wavering and warp of time in secret places. The taxi speeds us to our hotel on the Grand Canal, back to the glorious, gaudy, fragile city

I have loved for many years. Now I may pass that love to my grandson, who will, I hope, adore it all his life.

NOTES:

Navigating the Lagoon—Pick up an Actv vaporetto map. On it, the routes of the many vaporetti, the people ferries that ply the lagoon, are numbered and color-coded. At the train station, the airport, or anywhere there's a vaporetto ticket kiosk, ask for this map called Linee di navigazione/Waterborne routes. Numbers on the boats correspond to the route numbers on the map. Note that the symbol N designates night routes.

Vaporetto stations are all along the Grand Canal and at Fondamente Nove. If you're unsure of your route, check with the attendant to make sure the ferry is going where you want to go. Rather than purchasing single tickets, you can buy an economical pass for a day or for several days. A three-day unlimited pass, at this writing, is forty euros. Vaporetti are efficient. They arrive on time and the schedule is no harder to master than a subway's.

Motoscafi, private water taxis, are plentiful. There's usually a stand near a vaporetto stop. If you're at a hotel or restaurant on the islands, the staff can call a taxi. Water taxis are expensive, but sometimes time is more valuable than money.

Sarde in Saor Sempre Croccanti

SARDINES IN *SAOR* ALWAYS CRISPY, SERVES 4

Chef Francesco Brutto, with the Venetian lagoon and the Adriatic all around him, impeccably sources the outstanding seafood served at Venissa. If I try to think of a more romantic setting for dinner than the garden of Venissa, I can't.

3 Tropea onions, thinly sliced
3 bay laurel leaves
1 tablespoon sugar
¼ cup raspberry vinegar with essence of rose petals
Salt, *QB*
¼ cup raisins
24 fresh sardines, bones removed, then frozen
All-purpose flour, *QB*
4 eggs, beaten
Fine bread crumbs, *QB*
Extra-virgin olive oil, *QB*

Mix the onions with the laurel leaves, sugar, vinegar, and salt. Boil briefly, 3 to 4 minutes. Stir in the raisins. Remove the bay leaves and set aside in a small serving bowl.

Bread the still-frozen sardines by rolling each in flour, then egg, and then bread crumbs. Fry in plenty of sizzling olive oil until golden brown.

On a platter, place the sardines around the bowl of sauce.

Ristorante Venissa, Isola di Mazzorbo, Veneto

Asolo

A winged lion, symbol of Venice, greets us in the center of
Asolo, the fountain still flowing with waters from a Roman
aqueduct. As we park, we survey cafés bordering the
irregular piazza. On the terraces, everyone seated faces the
piazza. Under an awning, a group of men at tables with red-
checked cloths enjoy plates of cheese and *salumi*. After the
Veneto traffic, the narrow street into Asolo—those one-way
traffic lights—and a couple of wrong turns, we could use a
Campari soda ourselves. A groomed sheepdog trots smartly
across the street like a politician on his way to cast the
deciding vote. A woman opens her car trunk and removes
an armful of white lilies. *Asolare,* a verb, means to "disport
in the open air, amuse oneself at random." Although coined
in the fifteenth century, *asolare* still looks like a good thing
to do in Asolo.

Even in Italy, packed with fascinating places, Asolo
stands out. Only sixty kilometers from Venice, this is an
appealing add-on to a visit to La Serenissima. Henry James,
Carlo Scarpa, Igor Stravinsky, the Italian poet Giosuè

Carducci, and many others agreed. Then there was Robert Browning. The English poet fell in love with Asolo and his last book, *Asolando,* published on December 12, 1889, the day he died, testifies to his feelings. Hemingway was here. Wasn't he, like George Washington, everywhere?

Driving across the industrialized Veneto plain, you suddenly begin a bucolic climb among cypresses and verdant fields, then arrive at this intact medieval town that looks like an illustration in a book of fairy tales. There's even a ruined thirteenth-century white castle, Il Rocco, perched above town, where a sleeping princess may lie in a glass coffin.

Maybe it was the exile here of fifteenth-century royal Caterina Cornaro, queen of Cyprus, Jerusalem, and Armenia, that put the stamp of exclusivity on Asolo. After she was forced to cede her reign to the rapacious Venetian republic, they granted her control of the town as compensation. Must have been quite a comedown but she took her position seriously and garnered an intellectual and artistic life to her provincial court. Even now that heritage endures. I have the sense that if all the cars were lifted away, we could be back with Caterina, arriving for a weekend of balls and courtly diversions.

WE CHECK INTO Albergo al Sole, small and exclusive, with a view over the town. I'm already looking forward to dining on the upstairs terrace with the moon shining down on Asolo. Our two tiny rooms are under the eaves, with two desks and an old-size double bed. I remember my freshman year in college when I had a similar room (not quite as nice) on the dorm's fifth floor. At least there's an elevator here. The bath is tiled in pretty, flowery green vines, a pattern someone surely would warn you against, saying that you will tire of it. Well, if you like it, you won't.

I'M ATTRACTED TO literary quests. Asolo holds a big one for me. The attraction isn't Browning (I barely can tolerate his poems), but one of my favorite writers, Freya Stark: travel writer, explorer, historian, archeologist, letter-writer, essayist, memoirist—yes, all of these—lived here. She died in 1993 at age one hundred, having participated to the nth in every day of the century she lived. She was first brought to Asolo as a small child in 1901, and her home, Villa Freya, was given to her by a family friend who died in 1941. The house became her touchstone during her travels in Iraq, Iran, Yemen, Kuwait, Syria, Egypt, India, Turkey.

We set out to find it, walking along via Roberto Browning, a narrow street edged by low arcades sheltering tiny high-quality shops. There is no tourist junk on offer. Instead, we find the intimate restaurant San Daniele, and Eleonora, an enticing clothing store in a beamed and frescoed building; Gelateria Browning strikes us both as funny. There is also the tempting Galleria Asolana, whose window glitters with antique jewelry; a wine bar; and a bakery selling homemade *pinza,* the local traditional sweet. It's a huge, loaf-like cake made with cornmeal, nuts, apples, raisins, and figs, without any added sugar. The owner says it's baked in a wood oven by his mother, Graziela. We buy a wedge. At a tiny fruit and vegetable shop, we pick up a bag of cherries and walk along eating one after another, down to the bottom of the bag. Of all the seasonal fruits, cherries are my favorites. Back at Bramasole, I've made cherries steeped in Chianti, cherry gelato, and cherry roulade every summer for a million years but perhaps they're best this way, bursting the plump fruit in your mouth, so sweet and juicy, tossing the pit into bushes.

"This is it," Ed says. At the end of via Roberto Browning, where the small Zen (a family name) fountain from 1572 stands at the intersection with another road, and timed one-way signals flash, a square three-story house, peachy-gold with green shutters, stands behind a fence. Did Freya plant the hydrangeas and jasmine? Virginia creeper crawls over the façade. In fall it will turn red, not a good color for the house.

All the shutters are closed. Does the revolving desk Freya designed still overlook the back garden, where the remains of a Roman theater were found? We have the number of someone to call who can show us the interior and garden, but I don't want to spoil this. Eudora Welty's modest home in Jackson, Mississippi, leaves no doubt that it is authentic; even Hemingway's house in Key West seems real. But Freya eventually sold this house, built another, and later sold that, so what can remain that is she? I am content to stand in front and imagine her joy as she welcomed friends from among her vast acquaintances, worked in her garden, set out on new quests. The surprise: Her house looks kin to my Bramasole. Three stories, like mine, square, peachy-gold, with green shutters. I'm pleased, as I feel affinity with her longing for travel, her weakness for pretty clothes, her enjoyment of picnics, her fabulous friendships, her passionate interests, and her austere let's-keep-moving philosophy of life. Quotes of hers serve as epigraphs to several of my notebooks:

—The beckoning counts, not the clicking of the latch behind you.

—To awaken quite alone in a strange town is one of the most pleasant sensations in the world. You are surrounded by adventure.

—Surely of all the wonders of the world, the horizon is the greatest.

And maybe the most useful:

—One has to resign oneself to being a nuisance if one wants to get anything done.

WE WALK ALONG the outside walls of her garden—too tall to peek over—where an old community wash station still stands: three descending stone troughs of clear water where you can scrub, soak, then rinse. Spring-fed, or from the aqueduct? Did her maid wash the sheets here? There must have been piles of them judging from the number of guests she entertained. Farther on, we're quickly outside town but on another narrow road where you could get your toes run over if you're not careful. Soon there are tall iron gates, proud and dreamy villas in the distance, a realization that town is only the nucleus for life lived large on grand terms.

CARS ARE THE bane. Everyone is on their way *through,* it seems. Many towns in Italy have banned them from the *centro.* But in Asolo, where else could they go? The ways in are steep and few and the way out very narrow. There's no level field for a parking lot. Somehow, cars are prohibited on Saturday, market day, and second Sundays, when there's a book and antique sale in the old commercial arcade. On walks, we must flatten ourselves against a wall when a delivery truck brushes our eyelashes. Yet around the piazza, there's little traffic.

I begin to notice that several storefronts are empty. Is Asolo losing its cachet? There are shops for shirts made to measure, but the *forno* is closed. Maybe it's temporary. "No, Signora," the waiter at the Enoteca alle Ore says, "*Asolo è pieno di turisti.*" Full of tourists. I don't see them. He pours glasses of DOCG Colli Asolani/Asolo prosecco, for which the area is famed. It's ethereal, full of pep. The chandeliers over the bar are completely romantic—drooping waterfalls of crystals shedding a golden light. Ed breaks off a hunk of *pinza*—moist, crumbly, tastes of figs. I think it could use a tad of sugar. (Maybe, like the Tuscan chestnut flour cake, *castagnaccio,* to love it, you should have been given your first slice at age two.) We buy a few bottles of prosecco to take home. We will remember, on a late summer evening, our visit to Asolo.

WHAT AN IMPOSING cathedral. "I'm churched out," Ed says. He sits down and consults his phone messages and I wander for a few minutes. Here's a painting of the Assumption by Lorenzo Lotto. Ed sees me standing still before it and comes to see. "The clouds around her look like clumps of popcorn." We laugh.

"This church is really old," I begin. "Built on the foundations of a much earlier church . . ."

"Let's go," he says.

TONIGHT AT LA Terrazza, the hotel restaurant, the moon cooperates, a waxing gibbous disappearing and appearing among high clouds. End of May and we're alone on the dinner terrace and the dining room remains empty. Where is everyone? We pretend it's all ours: this view, the sparkling prosecco, and the attentive service. We are overlooking the vast, sunset-colored Villa Scotti-Pasini, where Browning lived, and the Piazza Garibaldi. I'm happy with my little Parmigiano basket filled with mushrooms and fondue, Ed with his tempura scallops on a smoked pepper cream. By now Ed has looked up Browning, and quotes: "Italia's rare/O'errunning beauty crowds the eyes . . ."

"Is that from *Asolando*?" I ask.

"Yes. 'Crowds the eye' is kind of a bold choice, don't you think?"

"Sometimes you do feel that. Too much to take in. But bold is that

'O'errunning'—sounds like the word itself is overrunning." We're served our *secondi:* Ed's tuna in a pistachio crust, and my pork tenderloin with grilled polenta. We eat every delicious morsel. Our Browning talk fades and we turn to plans for tomorrow, lingering over coffee.

BACK IN OUR attic room, sleep won't come. How can the shape of a room throw me back to my first months of college? How at sea I felt, seven hundred miles from the home I wanted to escape. A churning time—and now, decades later, I churn again. Nothing is ever forgotten, is it?

Beside me, Ed wakes from a nightmare: He's in a closed car that has broken through the ice on the Mississippi and has been swept downstream under a thick layer. He wakes up. "Do you think we should have opted for the larger room?" He opens the shade that has blacked out any light and a faint glow enters.

Finally, I fall asleep.

ONLY TEN KILOMETERS away is Palladio's Villa Barbaro, designed in 1560. Of the Palladian villas I've seen, this one is my favorite. Instead of the monumental perfection of Villa La Rotunda and others, Villa Barbaro invites you to imagine the actual lives of the people who built such a house, and of those who still live there. There's a musical rhythm yet rigorous symmetry to the architecture. The residential central core, pure as a Greek temple, is flanked by long lower wings called *barchesse,* farming structures, which end in graceful dovecotes almost as tall as the central portion, their façades adorned with sundials. "Why such huge dovecotes?" I wonder. "Surely they didn't roast that many pigeons?"

"Must have been for getting messages to Venice. Homing pigeons. Can't you imagine Daniele Barbaro tying a paper to a pigeon's leg, *come for the grape harvest . . .*"

Inside is purely glorious. Where on earth are there more charming frescoes than these of Veronese that adorn Villa Barbaro? The surprise, after all the religious art that dominates one's Italian experience, comes from the scholarly Barbaro family, who preferred a splashy, whimsical celebration of love and harmony for their country home. Entering the villa in paper shoes to protect the floors, you're drawn into a fantasy of muses with musical instruments, trompe-l'oeil doors opened by renderings of Barbaro family members and servants, and idyllic landscapes behind painted balustrades. Gaze and gaze on the Sala dell'Olimpo, Hall of Olympus, for it is full of flights of fancy and a joyous design of figures emanating from the philosophy of the good life. In the center of the wide coved ceiling, there's—not the Annunciation of the Virgin Mary, as I first thought—but a female representing Divine Wisdom. So that's the center of this universe! Wisdom is surrounded by the Olympian gods and zodiacal signs. At the angles: figures representing Earth, Air, Fire, Water. Large medallions on the four sides show white, classical figures of Fortune, Fertility, Abundance, Love. (We could all do with some of these pagan values.) Below the ceiling are painted stone balconies, overlooking the room below. A parrot perches beside an elaborately dressed woman standing between a small boy and a dark-skinned wet nurse, who holds a little dog. Daniele Barbaro leans over his large hunting dog, and another Barbaro man is shown reading. There are dogs all over these frescoes, but I see only one cat. Other small details, such as a pair of slippers and a brush, add to the high-low program of these frescoes. Lesson learned: Harmony is found on both celestial and familiar levels.

There's more. In the courtyard behind the house, the Nymphaeum, a half-moon pool of spring-fed water, backed by a stucco wall with statues installed in niches. A short distance away rises Palladio's Tempietto, a severely classical temple that reminds me of a miniature of the Pantheon. Inside, as in his glorious church Il Redentore in Venice, the Tempietto is incandescent. The circular plan feels intimate and lofty; if you leapt, you might rise to the oculus at the center of the dome. Anyone laid to rest here will certainly ascend to heaven.

Villa Barbaro—Palladio's last work, an embarrassment of riches, a house out of a dream, and this Tempietto, where architecture gets to embody the word *holy*.

AFTER A LONG pause in our room, late in the day, we venture out. We turn onto via Santa Caterina, pass the Hotel Villa Cipriani, where

Freya and her friends used to dine, and continue down the hill and out of town, stopping to look at a magnificent villa and garden with a one-eyed, scraggly cat, quite out of place, and a view of another villa, so Platonically ideal it is like a cutout pasted against a hill of cypress trees. We're looking at Villa Contarini degli Armeni, which once belonged to Armenian monks, whose order still practices book arts nearby, on the Venetian lagoon island of San Lazzaro. We pause at Villa Longobardo, hard by the road; it's referred to in books as a palace, but it's really quite small—and strange. On the shutters we make out zodiac symbols. Inscriptions cross the façade above the windows. The structure has nothing to do with the Longobards. One inscription on the façade includes the word *longobardus,* referring to Lombardia, where the architect of the house was born. The curvaceous caryatids look as if they were sculpted out of sand. Mysterious, weird. Inside, a wizard might be mixing alchemical concoctions.

We are walking to the hillside Cimitero di Asolo at Sant'Anna, where Freya is buried. We see the grave of the Italian actress Eleonora Duse first. Just her name and dates. Someone has left primroses. A lizard suns on the stone. All quiet now, but what wild times she must have had with her lover, the flamboyant proto-fascist poet and World War One hero, Gabriele D'Annunzio, who changed the flowers around his bed three times a day.

We don't find Freya. We stumble upon some startling room-size mausoleums in the fascist rationalist style, but most of our discoveries are just plain graves decorated with photos of the occupant and many flowers. A woman has brought gardening gloves, clippers, and new plants. She's ripping out the winter dead. There!—Freya lies just a few feet from Eleonora. Her blindingly white stone says "1893–1993." And below her name, simply "Writer & Traveller." There's another name on the stone: Herbert Hammerton Young, died 1941. He was the great family friend who gave Freya her villa. I should have brought flowers; she has none.

WE COLLECT OUR luggage and load the car. In the market there are no flowers but I buy a healthy basil plant in a plastic pot. I'm sure Freya knew the Keats poem "Isabella; or, The Pot of Basil." Driving out of town, we stop again at the cemetery. I leave the basil on Freya's stone. I hope someone will water it.

NOTES:

Freya Stark's villa: Later, after coming upon an article by Kristian Buziol, who restored Freya's garden, I regret not seeing it. A visit can be arranged through BellAsolo Tours in Asolo. www.bellasolo.it.

Two excellent videos on Palladio's Villa Barbaro and the Tempietto:

https://www.youtube.com/watch?v=O5mZ_7qAEi4

https://www.youtube.com/watch?v=ETwMXnGpKsE

Visiting Villa Barbaro reminded me of Sally Gable's *Palladian Days: Finding a New Life in a Venetian Country House.* Said house is Palladio's Villa Cornaro. This is a moving text describing the joys and foibles of taking on a piece of the world patrimony.

Lucy Hughes-Hallett's biography *The Pike: Gabriele D'Annunzio—Poet, Seducer and Preacher of War* informs, amuses, and repels in equal parts. D'Annunzio was a prolific writer, a war hero, and a fascinating player in the history of fascism. Writing in *Atlas Obscura,* Romie Stott claims that D'Annunzio, being bored with bourgeois democracy and wanting more romanticism, "invented fascism as an art project." An egomaniac and an influential writer, he thought the business of the state should be music. D'Annunzio's novel *The Flame of Life* (*Il fuoco,* 1900) is a fictionalized story of his affair with Eleonora Duse.

Valdobbiadene

Prosecco land, just two hours northwest of Venice. *Cin cin!*
Ruggeri Vineyard won the award for best sparkling wine
of the year 2016 from the respected *Gambero Rosso,* whose
trusted guides rate wines and restaurants. To taste this
elixir, we've come by train, from Cortona to Mestre, seedy
gateway to Venice, and picked up a car. Would it really be so
much trouble to put up some signs in that chaos of a train
station? We find the rental car agency not in the station
at all but about a block down an iffy street where men are
loitering and drinking.

At least the exit from the city is easy. Soon we
are maneuvering the roundabouts, aiming toward
Valdobbiadene—Val-doh-BE-ah-den-a—what a fun word
to pronounce, and to Villa Sandi, a top vineyard and
restaurant with seven rooms upstairs. Since our room isn't
ready, we have an early lunch on the covered terrace. Barely
seated, we're handed a cold flute of Villa Sandi prosecco.
The tables are set with flowered crockery plates, each one
different, and vintage crocheted and lace tablecloths. Across

the lawn, hundreds of cyclists gather to register for a race tomorrow and to enjoy some wine and live music. American songs accompany scrumptious truffled gnocchi with a light guinea hen sauce: Jimi Hendrix, the Doors, Bob Dylan, Joni Mitchell—we could sing along.

THE SMALL BEDROOM has an alpine feel: cabinets of unfinished wood, plank floor, and a rustic bed with drifty mosquito netting. In the *Gambero Rosso,* we often look at recommended restaurants that have the little bed symbol. It's nice to have dinner and not have to drive. Climb the stairs and *buona notte.* The rooms are usually simple, as this one is, but satisfying for a night.

After a quick settling in, we leave to find that primo Giustino B. prosecco—only three minutes away.

ALREADY AT THE door when we arrive, Paolo Bisol steps out to greet us. In a pale floral shirt, he looks more like an artist than a man of the land. Slender and quick, he has warm brown eyes that instantly reveal a sense of humor. We hop in his Land Rover and bounce along narrow roads, looking straight up and down at steep vineyards, then turn onto the roughest, rockiest track I've ever been on. The car lurches and bumps. We pull up to a panoramic point of the vineyard where he brakes beside a gnarled four-hundred-year-old chestnut tree in a clearing.

He points to a large boulder with embedded fossils, then to a tall upside-down conical structure he calls a *cannone,* a cannon. We can see two others in the distance. "Stops the hail," he explains. To our quizzical looks he shrugs. "*Diccono,*" so they say. "There's some merit. The theory is that gas is siphoned into the cone and we make a sort of explosion that blows up and rearranges the air."

From our experience with olives, we know that hail is the most feared of the weather phenomena. Any desperate measure is worth trying.

La vendemmia, the harvest, started early this year because of intense summer heat and little rain. He's not trimmed back the foliage at all. The grapes needed the protection of the leaves. In the lush and green vineyards, golden bunches catch the sun and glow as though each little globe is luminescent. We sample as we go. A ladder made from a split log with rungs notched into the wood testifies to the long tradition of the hands-on life in the vineyard. Paolo shows us a section of twisted and gnarled vines seventy to a hundred years old; they produce a special vintage.

Returning to the office, we follow trucks piled with grapes. They line up at the back of the building. Paolo's vivacious daughter Isabella joins us but rushes off; she's setting up food on a long table for the harvesters. Growers drive up to a stainless-steel bin just the length of the side of the truck. With a marvelous whoosh, the grapes fall in, while a man with a long pitchfork helps ease them into the revolving crusher.

"Like looking at the fire," one worker observes as we stand watching the late-afternoon sun angling over the tumbling bunches. Paolo quotes Galileo, "*Il vino e la luce del sole tenuta insieme dall'acqua.*" "Wine is sunlight held together by water."

Upstairs in his sleek conference room, we taste, don't talk much, letting the Giustino B. speak. "One hundred percent *glera* grapes. Named for my father, who started the vineyard. Not the more floral style of other areas," he comments. I agree. There's a glass shelf of fossils on display and I imagine that a touch of minerality comes from the ancient shells deep in the soil. "Giustino B. is a reference point for all prosecco," *Gambero Rosso* asserts. High praise, justified. We select a mixed case of Ruggeri wines and prosecco to share with Tuscan friends.

VILLA SANDI IS overrun by the sleek and taut cyclists dining together. We expect a rowdy evening but they dine quietly and leave early. The beamed stone room looks inviting and the lacy tablecloths don't come off as dowdy, but charming instead. We order the *pollo alle brace,* a splayed grilled chicken (like our old favorite chicken-under-a-brick) with roasted vegetables and potatoes. Browned and juicy, the chicken is *perfetto,* with a bottle of Villa Sandi's big Còrpore.

A HARD START to the race. It's pouring; no blue breaking through the clouds. We wave; the cyclists have their heads down. Doubtlessly cursing. From the vantage of the car, the hills look dreamy in the rain.

Onward from Valdobbiadene, a blessed area. Besides our friends at Ruggeri and Villa Sandi, many wine magicians perform their sorcery in these *glera*-covered hills: Bisol, Adami, Bortolomiol, and dozens of others.

We keep two bottles on the backseat for tonight. Farther south, we'll be toasting with a friend.

Arquà Petrarca and Colli Euganei (The Euganean Hills)

Dropping deeper into the Veneto from Valdobbiadene, our destination is an *agriturismo* called La Tenuta La Pila, a kiwi, pear, and apple farm. Although a half hour away from the towns we want to explore, we couldn't resist reserving at such an intriguing place. We are meeting our friend Steven Rothfeld for the night. Based in Napa Valley, he frequently works in Italy on photography assignments—and we have worked together on several books. I feel lucky when we intersect somewhere.

Our first stop is brief—the late-eleventh-century Benedictine Abbazia di Praglia, just where the dramatic Colli Euganei, Euganean Hills, begin. A pity to visit on Sunday during mass, as the cloisters, chapter room, and refectory hall are closed. I'd especially wanted to see the library. The good work of the monks is mending books. In the shop, which is open, they sell extensive herbal homeopathic tisanes, acacia and chestnut honey, and various elixirs with substantial alcohol percentages. We do get to see the abbey church, a massive, rather squat building that makes me think of a puffed-up gray toad. It's packed inside. So lovely to step in and smell the spicy incense.

ARQUÀ PETRARCA SOUNDS as ancient as it is. Like Petra, it seems half as old as time. Arquà clings to a craggy hillside, a jewel box of stone houses that look carved from amber. The early humanist poet Francesco Petrarca died here. His ardent sonnets to a woman only identified as Laura strongly influenced the direction of Western poetry. What was supposedly his house remains. He was born in Arezzo, near Cortona, and that house also still stands. How likely is it that a poet born in 1304 has two extant houses? Only in Italy.

His shady, hidden house is closed and I can only stand outside and muse. Perhaps his idealized love never really existed, but there's a story that Laura de Noves, the woman likely to have inspired Petrarca's passions, was exhumed much later. A box holding a poem by Petrarca and an image of a woman tearing at her breast was found in the grave. Who knows? This Laura supposedly was married and the mother of eleven. She died at thirty-eight, still chaste in Petrarca's mind.

Whether she was or not, the poems are real. And the Petrarcan legacy is revered: His form and Shakespeare's give us our two principal sonnet types. He was the first to write so personally of his beloved's eyes and spun-gold hair. His work was immensely popular in his lifetime. He struck a chord, became influential, and traveled all over Europe. Arquà was his place of retirement. Still, I'd like to know, did Laura exist?

WE FOLLOW A sign to Ristorante La Montanella. The parking lot is full. The waiter finds us a table among dozens of well-dressed Italian families. Not a T-shirt or pair of tennis shoes in sight. The men wear sport coats or suits; the women, dresses and jewelry. Even little boys have on pressed shirts. Flowers on each table, white tablecloths, and big napkins. Wine is decanted, prosecco poured. The glass-walled room looks into a wet olive grove with the humped, volcanic Euganean Hills in the distance.

We love to fall into the fine ritual that begins and ends the week: Sunday *pranzo*. Both Ed and I grew up going to grandparents' houses on Sunday. Ed to a Minnesota farm table laden with homegrown produce, Polish sausages, and jars of his grandmother's pickles and beets. The table of my grandmother, Mother Mayes, with a perpetual bowl of wax grapes at the center, was graced with platters of fried chicken, mashed potatoes, biscuits light as butterfly wings, and my mother's watermelon rind or bread-and-butter pickles. My grandmother had a button under her foot to call in Fanny Brown, who had a heavy hand with pepper. I never eat a piece of fried chicken that I don't think of the dark-crusted breasts that made everyone sneeze.

At La Montanella, it's soul-food time on Sunday, too—but soul food means pasta with young nettles, celery, and asiago; saddle of rabbit with roasted peppers; grilled guinea hen with bay leaf aromas; and a seventeenth-century recipe for young duck with fruit. The prized prosciutto of the area comes sliced to transparency. Better than it sounds is the little hen of Padua marinated in Aperol spritz. At these lavish Sunday *pranzi,* no one is in a hurry. This tradition continues to thrive, and why not? It speaks of our best instincts: to gather with those we love and break bread.

FROM THE ROAD, the hills roll like tidal waves. The area is dotted with thermal pools and spas devoted to mineral waters. Another time, I'd like to check out Abano Terme and Montegrotto Terme, enjoy a soak. Instead, we check into La Tenuta La Pila with a big welcome from Carlotta, who lives at the farm with her family and her parents, Alberto and Raimonda. The guest rooms open onto a shaded loggia with dangling grapes and a garden with roses, pomegranate, jujube, and rows of kiwi. In mid-September, they've already covered the pool. The great barn with arches for carts to enter at either end serves as a lobby, a long, cool space with rush chairs and a table made from the ancient *pila,* unearthed when the owners converted the barn. The *pila* is a six-foot-long stone about four feet high, with three deep hollowed-out basins where rice was husked by gentle battering. We meet the whole vivacious, outgoing family. "Kiwi," Alberto tells us, "grows well here. Italy produces quantities of kiwi second only to New Zealand. And you don't have to pay for the airfare!"

"Tomorrow morning, you will have our jams," Carlotta says. She shows us the enormous game room and library above the lobby. We love the place—you could be nowhere else but Italy. *Agriturismi* are like that. You can forge relationships with local people. The farms can be spotty, but choose carefully and you will have an unforgettable experience.

Montagnana

Montagnana, a short drive from La Pila, is ringed by two
kilometers of high crenellated walls with twenty-four
hexagonal towers. The perimeter of this intact little city
looks constructed with those expensive block sets we used
to buy for William. Double gates and a greensward where
the moat once was. The interior is enchanting: arcaded
sidewalks; a piazza with its crown jewel, the soaring Gothic
duomo of pale stone; many cafés, gelato and pastry shops,
and a paternal Garibaldi, unifier of Italy, lording over the
piazza, as he so often does. A sign reminds: The porticos
of Montagnana are not a latrine for your dog. Indeed, the
streets are clean. We walk and walk. I love the clock tower
on Santa Maria Assunta. A star-studded face and intricate
gold hands tell us it's already five o'clock. We're lucky the
doors are still open because inside we get to see a pair of
Giorgione paintings. He's rare to stumble upon. Here, he's
painted an odd pairing. On the left, David holding the
head of Goliath. David looks robust, not the slight youth I
imagine. On the right, there's Judith, having just sliced

through the neck of Holofernes. She's looking down and what must be his head is a blur; the fresco is damaged. In the background, a white city and what could be read as the Euganean Hills.

OUR FRIEND STEVEN is going to be late. He happened upon a festival in a small town and stopped to photograph people in medieval dress. We meet at Antica Trattoria Bellinazzo, serving up *cucina tipica* since 1885 in tiny Carpi. Alberto recommended it to us as an authentic Veneto experience. Simple and welcoming, with square tables, typical farm chairs, and light that could be a bit less bright. As the prosecco is poured, Steven arrives in a rush. Hugs all around. "We do meet like this," Ed says.

"These old-style trattorias—I hope they last forever." Steven settles his lenses and camera in the empty chair. The *cin-cin*s begin. The talk. The laughs.

Among families with babies, lone diners, and couples, we are the only foreigners, as we were last night in Valdobbiadene. And this definitely is not a tourist menu. It features thinly sliced colt, a donkey stew, and another *secondo* of horse, along with many other meats. After such a staggering lunch, Ed manages to sample again the excellent prosciutto of Montagnana, and Steven and I order a platter of cheeses and grilled vegetables. We all choose the whole-grain *bigoli* pasta—a fat spaghetti—also with vegetables. There's no question that we will have the celebratory red wine of the area, *amarone*. My favorite. After every rich, sumptuous drop disappears, the waiter opens another bottle and offers three glasses. We linger until we're the last.

WE MEANT TO depart early, but we sleep late—dreams tinged, no doubt, with *amarone*—then feel so at home at breakfast that we don't leave until eleven. The cook has made scrambled eggs, the vivid gold of hens who eat—what else?—polenta. Alberto comes in and tells us about surrounding towns. We start calling him *professore*. Then the cook asks if we'll try her pear tiramisù. How can we refuse? Ah, creamy, with crunchy pears. I could eat the whole bowl.

• • •

FOR STEVEN, ON the way out we stop again at honey-colored Arquà Petrarca, seeing it with new eyes after Alberto explained to us that it was rebuilt after the death of Petrarca to honor his Tuscan hometown of Arezzo. Is that true? It does, now that he has said so, look like a stony Tuscan town. The skies open, slicking the streets, drenching us. No one, again, is out. Arquà, sleeping a hundred-year sleep.

USUALLY I WOULD be disappointed to visit a garden in the rain but the downpour that starts as we enter Valsanzibio casts a misty spell. Black swans with red beaks and wild eyes cruise the ascending pools. Through the veil of rain, all is dark green (boxwood hedges and cypresses) and glassy gray-blue water. The seventeenth-century Venetian owners stepped off a boat that brought them through a network of canals to their opulent landing, where a pavilion with statues of Diana and hunting dogs looms above the water. The Venetians of my imagining are elegant in silks and velvets. We wear wet tennis shoes and carry one broken umbrella among us. We wait out the rain under its shelter. The garden feels moody, as though the music of Erik Satie should be playing in the distance or someone on a white horse should gallop along the edge of the water. We're alone and feel like we might have just arrived in the afterlife.

When the rain pauses, we explore. The garden layout is the Roman *decumanus,* east-west, intersected by the *cardo,* north-south. There's a philosophy behind the design, as the walk symbolizes a person's journey toward perfectibility. The boxwood maze should conjure the kind of musings that lead to meditation in the hermit grotto. Soul-stopping are two historic weeping beech trees that seem alive with spirits of their own. We come upon dozens of statues of allegorical figures, some sacred, some pagan. The garden turns playful. A series of hidden fountains sprays on and off as you traverse the approach to the private villa. Under two flowing marble basins lie mythical canine creatures, water falling forever into their open mouths. The journey seems to end at the divine villa. I, too, might imagine I'd reached worldly perfectibility if it were mine. The seven steps leading up to the front garden are engraved with verses that extol the beauty of the place and tell you that you will laugh and not cry, that here Saturn does not eat his own children and Mercury loses all his fraud and Jupiter is smiling. The Christian goal seems to have been forgotten in favor of the pagans who might frolic in the garden.

Three stories, faded coral and cream, the house is bliss. The Venetians had a genius for domestic architecture. This one, not overly grandiose or forbidding, looks ready for someone to fling open the shutters and invite us to come in.

Gardens and houses. My obsessions. He was onto it, this Gregorio Barbarigo, the mastermind of this symbolic garden walk. Everything you bring or grow or create or care for in this realm moves you closer to the life more abundant.

TO CATCH A bite before Steven takes off for Vicenza, we drive into Este and find Trattoria Al Cavallino. All the pastas sound good. When we can't decide, the waiter suggests a *tris,* a third portion each of three types. A fine idea. We fall into reminiscing about other meals, other places. Steven will go to Vicenza for tonight, then on to Alto Adige. We will meet again, where? Este hadn't been on my list, but now after a walk around the piazza, I am smitten. We will drive on to watery Mira, the Palladian villa area, but will come back tomorrow. Here, in the rain, we part with Steven.

Este

We've spent time in Ferrara, a complex city of bicycles, memories of *The Garden of the Finzi-Continis,* and the historic crown jewel of the Este family. But the Estes were originally from this small town named for them in the Veneto.

Their castle grounds are now a public park, where the sweet scent of roses hits you from yards away as you enter. The Museo Nazionale Atestino, a spectacular archeological collection, too, is on these grounds. I know many people glaze over in the endless archeological museums in Italy (Ed often is ahead of me, checking his phone), but I fall into a trance when looking at the safety pins, tweezers, cooking pots, and jewelry of ancient people. *They were like us.* I like the skeleton from 900 B.C. She's wearing hoop earrings. She was just shy of five feet tall. Double hoop earrings. Yes, like us, and so long ago.

Este is the home of a graceful oval duomo, with a Tiepolo painting of Santa Thecla freeing Este from the 1630 plague. A run-down villa faces the duomo courtyard (awaiting an inspired restoration); and a path up leads to a dark wooden Alpine-style villa where poets Percy Bysshe Shelley and George Gordon, Lord Byron, visited. I'm smitten with the town's clock tower, its blue, star-spangled face. Ed favors the bar Al Canton, tiny, with black-trimmed forties wood paneling and nautilus-shaped lights they'll never be able to replace. There, we have a perfect espresso and tell the barista that Carlo Scarpa would have loved the place. He agrees. Italy: where the barista knows who Carlo Scarpa is.

SETTING PLACES FOR dinner gives me as much happiness as cooking—what's on the table being the complement to what's served. In the early years of our Italian travels, I began to buy a bowl or platter in towns with a history of ceramic design. I like taking down the lemon platter and thinking of Sicily. The rooster pitcher reminds me of Orvieto. And we have Cortona's eighteenth-century yellow pattern with a sunflower in the middle. How many broken pieces of that have I dug up in my garden? I abandoned the collecting because I ran out of space, but I'm still drawn to traditional patterns, curious about how they speak of the history of the town. In that spirit, we follow a sign beside the Duomo: Este Ceramiche. We find a SPACE (outlet) sign at the end of the street along a canal but the door is locked. From the other side of the street, a young woman, who seems to glow with energy, leans out of a doorway. She will open the shop for us.

Immediately we see that this is not typical majolica. Este Ceramiche Porcellane's designs are refined and exquisite. Since 1780, production has continued on this spot, with the canal once transporting the wares to Venice and Padua. Dior, Tiffany, Bergdorf Goodman—the marks on the bottoms of the seconds show the clientele. The items are totally reasonable in price. I buy several gifts and a—where will I put it?—platter for Bramasole. By now we've had a lovely conversation with Isabelle Fadigati, daughter of the store's owner. She invites us over to meet her father and to see the workshop, where the hand painting is in progress.

What a trove. A *trionfo* is a historic centerpiece for a grand table. They're still made here. Tall, extravagant, with vase shapes, piled porcelain fruit, little baskets and other removable parts dangling, they're often found on palace tables. I admire other objects, too, such as boxwood urns and grape-topped tureens. Anyone with a passion for china has to swoon over the dinnerware patterns—florals based on historic designs, charming hunt scenes, African animals, grape clusters and vines, and paste-white dishes with monograms or insignias. I like the playful plates with trompe-l'oeil ceramic fruits, olives, vegetables, or candies attached. These are said to have once signaled that a dinner had finished. Some of us need to be placed in restraints at this point. Time to go!

NOTE:

Nearby Nove, another historic ceramic center, has the Museo della Ceramica in Palazzo De Fabris, plus workshops around town.

Monselice

Named a hill of flint in the Roman era, Monselice served
as a quarry for the paving in Piazza San Marco in Venezia.
It's a walled town in a dramatic position, with a looming
background hill crowned by a castle. We are stopping,
at the recommendation of the Este Ceramiche's owner
Giovanni Fadigati, for a late, late lunch at Ristorante
La Torre, next to the town's thirteenth-century Torre
dell'Orologio, clock tower. We're late and in the restaurant,
only an ancient woman and her daughter are left dining.

Here's where I have the best pasta ever.

The waiter comes out with a box of white truffles. "The
first of the year," he says. "I recommend the ravioli filled
with *Taleggio,* served with truffles and a touch of butter."
We wait with a glass of prosecco. Then comes the pile of
thin *lardo* surrounded by quarters of figs and sliced smoked
goose breast with toasts and curls of butter.

The plain pasta bowls arrive and the woodsy scent of the
truffles rises. The ravioli is light, not chewy. *Taleggio* is one

of my favorite cheeses, and this has melted to a creamy richness that marries the generous shavings of truffle.

"This is good?" the waiter asks. No, it's heaven.

UP THE HILL after lunch. It's hot. This via al Santuario passes Villa Nani-Mocenigo, whose tall stone walls are decorated with eighteenth-century stone statues of dwarfs. They used to be the mascots at court, of course, and many have been immortalized by painters. What the story is for this villa, I don't know. *Nani* means "dwarfs." I recall a story of a rich family, all small, who didn't want their daughter to know she was different, and so hired only *nani*. The girl's companion, however, began to grow and I don't remember the no-doubt unsettling end.

The dwarf-topped wall is alive with the biggest caper plants I've ever seen. A vast stone stairway leads to some intriguing garden but, of course, the gate is locked. We climb to the top, rewarded with the Santuario delle Sette Chiese, six pretty chapels, each with a different painting above the altar. They're architecturally identical. The Villa Duodo (1593) and the octagonal Chiesa di San Giorgio, the seventh, larger chapel end the sanctuary walk.

On the way down, we veer into other streets. Now all we have to do is find where we parked the car.

Mira and Dolo

From Mira, drive twenty minutes to Felsina and you take the half-hour ferry right into Venice, stopping at the Zattere promenade. Easy day trip, then return to Mira before seven P.M. and find your great spot for dinner. This is a relaxing way to experience Venice and the watery world beyond it. We chose it because of proximity to the fabled villas of the area.

We're enticed by intersecting canals that hint at the vast network of work and transport that once existed among the major towns of Padua, Vicenza, Treviso, Venice. The advent of the railroads in the 1800s caused this way of life to languish, and, eventually, many canals clotted with silt and weeds. But once, the Venetians boarded lavish barges called *burchielli,* pulled by horses, for their country villas. Some were farms; others just dazzling holiday escapes. The number of villas around Mira is astonishing. Most are private but I'm happy to drive and drive along the canals imagining the rooms, the kitchens, the views onto the water. The road from Mira to Dolo passes many sublime places. In Dolo, we have the pleasure of eating at Ristorante e Pizzeria Al Cristo, right on a canal. Gnocchi with scallops and basil, little octopuses with polenta, and fluffy chocolate profiteroles. Rain again, lovely along the banks with their drifting willows and white geese. On the edge of Dolo we come upon a cluster of villas—Velluti, Badoer De Chantal, Tito. Intermittently, the twentieth century's uninspired contribution to the landscape crops up. The villas have lost some of their bucolic aspects.

WE'VE RENTED FOR three days an apartment on the Brenta canal. It's gorgeous. Amazing beams cross and criss like pick-up-sticks. When we look carefully, we home in on a few bizarre pieces of Indonesian furniture. An odd throne chair, and a wardrobe endowed with carvings of sexual positions. (How do they suspend like that?) Just opposite the bed—is this supposed to be inspirational? In the hall downstairs, there's an identical wardrobe. But overall, the pretty beds with lots of pillows, the comfortable modern sofa, and a well-equipped kitchen make this a fine choice for two writers—we need room to spread out our books and computers.

FOR HOW LONG have I wanted to see the villas along the Brenta? Palladio! Genius, who would be shocked to see his influence on everything from the finest Wren churches in England to American suburban megamansion stairway windows, from Inigo Jones to Tara, Thomas Jefferson, and my high school in Fitzgerald, Georgia. We don't say Wrightian, Corbusarian, Hadidian, but everyone says Palladian. His classical revival became part of our language. Near Mira, we get to see La Malcontenta.

In the ticket office, a distinguished older man in an oversize suit sits on a stool off to the side, obviously waiting for someone but gazing mildly at us as we buy books and talk to the ticket seller. "Yes, several of the books are by the owner of the villa." We look through them quickly. I see the man slightly smile.

Who was malcontent? A woman who didn't want to be here. A legend arose around her. Adultery. Exile from Venice. Or was it that the canal was *mal contempta,* badly contained?

How could this house not inspire stories? The name is actually Villa Foscari, designed in 1554 and built soon after. It is raised on a half-basement, giving loft to the *piano nobile*. Palladio loved entering directly a large central room with other rooms radiating around it. We only can see the main floor with tatty furniture and magnificent proportions. Frescoes and light from all the, yes, Palladian windows, make the rooms seem fresh and livable.

The farm buildings aren't connected to the house, as they sometimes are with Palladian villas. We walk around the grounds where a sculpture show is set up in a meadow. The lawns afford different views of the villa. Grand terra-cotta pots of oleander stand along the back of the house, and on the side a knot garden with brick paths is totally neglected. We run into the bookstore clerk and ask. Yes, he smiles, the man was the lucky owner of this monumental treasure.

A WALK ALONG the canal and around the sprawling village of Mira. Easy afternoon. Wandering. Last night, we only wanted a quick pizza and must have chosen the worst place in the Veneto. Slow, loud, and mediocre. Pony pizza, anyone? Well, that's a local tradition. For tonight, we're more careful. Ed locates Il Sogno, out in the country, and it is well named: the dream. These Italian waiters! Professional and helpful. Ours has a wide smile and a bald head shining like a rubbed chestnut. As he pours the prosecco, he recommends a Rosso del Milio from the nearby Treviso area, a combination of cabernet and *carmenére,* which reflects the maker's "velvet heart." We are the only foreigners in the long, glassed-in room packed with festive diners. The menu makes life hard. How, possibly, to choose? Ed orders *gallina Padovana in saor* and loves it. *Saor,* typically Venetian, is a sweet-sour marinade of vinegar, raisins, onions, pine nuts, olives. Sardines are most often in *saor* but here it's served with *gallina,* hen.

I choose little balls of fish in a crust of pistachios with a red pepper cream. The wine is a heart-breaker, and perfect with our *secondo,* the duck and white polenta. This is prime polenta country and in the Veneto it's more often white than the golden type we're used to.

. . .

VILLA PISANI IN the rain under steely skies looks like an etching of itself. This villa—not by Palladio but by Francesco Preti—has 114 rooms. We are alone here, rambling in the stark corridors while lightning strikes and thunder rolls. Adding to the atmosphere, some of the rooms have no lights. Others are furnished like some king's attic. The villa, built in the eighteenth century, has seen a maelstrom of history pass through: royalty, guests from the vile (Hitler) to the slightly less vile (Mussolini), from the rapacious (Napoleon) to the poetic (Lord Byron).

The villa originally was a holiday house for the Venetian Pisani family. What grand weekends they must have had. Room after room of miniature armchairs, silk basinettes, upright chairs, the draped bed where Napoleon slept. There is, unseen, an interior corridor that must have been used by scurrying servants. Otherwise, you go through one room to get to the next. In the Festive Salon, the ballroom, Tiepolo painted extensive frescoes of the Pisani family. This is considered one of his major works. The children all look pale and unhealthy, as though they exist on white polenta. Tiepolo is an artist I simply cannot appreciate. Everything he paints looks unfinished and wispy. But overall the ballroom is dazzling, the orchestra-level frescoes with monochromatic scenes, the glorious ceiling. Under the glow of the great chandeliers hanging from the four corners, we all could have danced away many a holiday night.

ON OUR LAST night, we return to Ristorante Margherita in Hotel Villa Franceschi, refined and sedate, with old-world atmosphere. We have come back because we stayed here the first time we came to Mira and remember it as romantic. We are immediately offered a Valdo prosecco from Valdobbiadene. We both order the risotto with tiny vegetables from the garden, then I launch into taking apart a plate of savory big scampi in broth. The waiter is pouring an Allegrini Palazzo della Torre from the Verona area. "A baby *amarone*." Ed swirls and inhales. "When they make this wine at harvest, they leave out some grapes to dry over the fall. They add them to the wine in January for a second fermentation." Hence, the deep raisiny taste of *amarone* but bright and fruity, too. Ed will order cod, that essential European fish, anytime he can. He especially likes this preparation, *mantecato de baccalà,* whipped and creamy baccalà on polenta.

Villa Franceschi is a perfect choice for a base in the Veneto. The intimate lobby nooks with sofas of crushed velvet, bookcases, and dark paneling are seductive and comfortable. I remember the returns from Venice, how welcoming it felt to step inside the hotel.

I TAKE MY clothes from the Kama Sutra cupboard and pack. From here, it's only twenty minutes to Mestre, where we board the fast Frecciarosa train for Florence and then home to Cortona. I google Petrarca's sonnets and as I read them, the lines are punctuated by my seatmate, who is sneezing and blowing her nose. The early autumn gold of poplars flashes by the window. Veneto!

Risotto agli Asparagi al Profumo di Prosecco

RISOTTO WITH ASPARAGUS AND PROSECCO, SERVES 4

The type of rice *does* make a difference. *Vialone nano* is a medium-grain and high-starch rice that renders the kind of creamy risotto Chef Gianmaria Cozza prefers in the Veneto. I also like *carnaroli* for similar results. *Arborio* isn't a favorite in my kitchen—too goopy. Optional: Top the risotto with grated Parmigiano.

1 large bunch (1 pound) asparagus, preferably white, stems peeled

4 tablespoons extra-virgin olive oil

1 onion, minced

1¼ cups Villa Sandi Valdobbiadene Prosecco Superiore DOCG

Salt and pepper, *QB*

1¼ cups *vialone nano* rice

4 cups vegetable stock

2 ounces *Casatella Trevigiana* cheese (or other soft cow cheese, such as *Taleggio*)

1¼ tablespoons butter

Cut the asparagus stems into small, round pieces, and thinly slice the tips.

In a small skillet over medium-high heat, warm 2 tablespoons of the olive oil, and brown half of the onion for 4 to 5 minutes, stirring often. Add the asparagus stems (not the tips) and cook until crispy and tender, about 3 minutes. Splash in ½ cup of the prosecco and stir, allowing it to evaporate. Add salt and pepper.

In a risotto pot over medium heat, warm the remaining 2 tablespoons of oil and brown the rest of the onion. Add the rice, and let it toast for 4 minutes, frequently stirring. Add ¼ cup of the prosecco and again allow it to evaporate as you stir. Add 1 cup of the stock, and stir the rice for 6 to 7 minutes. Add the stock in ¼-cup increments, letting each addition be absorbed before adding more. When the rice is close to al dente, after about 12 minutes, add the asparagus mixture and tips.

When the risotto is ready, add the cheese, butter, and the remaining ½ cup of wine. Stir to combine. Divide risotto among serving bowls and serve immediately.

Locanda Sandi, Valdobbiadene, Veneto

Gallina Padovana in Saor

PADUAN HEN IN SAOR, SERVES 6

The sauce called *saor*—meaning "flavor" in the Venetian dialect—originally may have been created to help preserve fish. The sweet-sour sauce for sardines and for sole is ubiquitous in the Veneto. At Il Sogno, Chef Silvano Libralesso serves it with a tender poached chicken. I find this outstanding for a summer dinner. Prepare a day in advance for the flavors to heighten and blend.

1 3¼-pound hen
1 carrot, halved
1 stalk celery, cut into 3 pieces
1 onion, peeled and quartered
1 teaspoon salt
Thyme sprigs

FOR THE *SAOR*
3 medium white onions, julienned
¾ cup plus 2 tablespoons white wine vinegar
1 cup extra-virgin olive oil
1 cup white wine
1 teaspoon salt
2 ounces pine nuts
2 ounces raisins
1 large red bell pepper, cut into strips
Extra-virgin olive oil, *QB*

In a large pot of boiling water, place the hen, the aromatic vegetables, salt, and thyme. Reduce the heat, partially cover, and simmer for about an hour. Test for doneness. Cool the chicken, then cut the meat off the bones, making sure the pieces are not too small. (You can save the light broth for a soup.)

Prepare the *saor:*

Toss the onions into a large skillet with ¾ cup of the vinegar, the oil, white wine, and salt. Bring to a boil and immediately reduce the heat to a simmer. Cover and simmer for 50 minutes, adding the pine nuts and raisins after about 20 minutes. Stir often, making sure nothing sticks to the pan.

Add the remaining 2 tablespoons of vinegar to a small pot of boiling water and blanch the red pepper for 3 minutes, then drain.

Mix the chicken, *saor,* and red pepper, tasting for correct seasoning. Leave to rest in the refrigerator for 24 hours. Taste for seasonings. Serve at room temperature with a drizzle of olive oil.

Trattoria Il Sogno, Mirano, Veneto

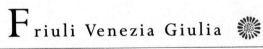 Friuli Venezia Giulia

Cormòns, Cividale del Friuli, and Palmanova

Now and then I'll get a text from our friend Robert in Washington. *Where are you on 26 May? Can we meet in Cormòns?* Or, *Flying in on 6 October. Cormòns?* I always answer, *Where shall we eat?* This time he's chosen Trattoria Al Piave, a place just outside town. We'll gather at eight. This will be a special event: We'll meet his fiancée.

These felicitous times together in Friuli began about ten years ago. Robert wrote to us in Cortona: *You need to know La Subida. Let's go.* We went. There's mystery at the heart of places that seem to belong to you. From the day he arrived, Robert experienced the same *colpo di fulmine,* lightning strike, that we felt our first summer in Tuscany. He began to come as often as possible.

Over the years, he's become local, at home in every restaurant and in the local *enoteca* where the great winemakers gather. He's accumulated that daunting kind of wine knowledge that includes the exact percentages in blends and which grapes are indigenous. With him, we got to know the Sirk family at La Subida, the epitome of regional cuisine and the meeting point of several cultures in one kitchen. We met Robert's friend Giampaolo Venica, whose family makes white wines you could weep over. Not your house sauvignon blanc, their whites are as complex as any red. Venica & Venica's sauvignon Ronco delle Mele is a big favorite of mine. We also visited vineyards, and collected cherished bottles of Edi Keber, Franco Toros, Schiopetto, and Gravner. What luck to have a friend who knows both terrain and terroir.

OF ALL THE undiscovered places in Italy, this little-visited corner bordering Slovenia remains an open secret. It has the Friulian Alps for skiing and hiking, pristine lakes such as Sauris, Adriatic beaches around Grado, the Duino coastal walk that inspired the poet Rilke, plus the capital, Trieste, with a strong Austro-Hungarian heritage. *Sopratutto,* above all, Friuli produces some of the tip-top wines of the world.

And it's close to Venice, where *everyone* goes. The Floating City suffers a plague of tourists, and rightfully so: Venice—where dreams rise out of the waters, where color spangles in your eyes everywhere you look, where the subconscious and conscious merge, where the mysterious east touches the west, and where any fledgling romance flourishes into full-blown passion. Being there saturates me quickly. Three or four days, bliss, then I'm ready to go. The Veneto and Friuli are perfect extensions to a Venice trip.

CORMÒNS, APPEALING AND livable, has a major attraction: Enoteca di Cormòns, owned by a consortium of vineyards for the promotion of local wines. And as a gathering spot for themselves. Many such tasting rooms around Italy are for tourists. This one is full of the local growers and winemakers every evening. How different they are from the slender Tuscan aristocrats in Ferragamo and Zegna. Their hands aren't soft, and some broad faces show Slavic heritage. Some are unshaven, all are full of zest. Because Robert knows many of them, they send over tastes and come to talk, mostly to joke with Robert. The women pouring all know him, too, and they serve us boards of cheeses, prosciutto, and smoked trout.

Cormòns straddles two major growing areas, Collio and Colli Orientali (Hills and Eastern Hills). Ah, Italy's finest wines are produced by these men laughing over their glasses. In other areas where I've tasted, the wines can seem similar. In these zones, even ubiquitous pinot grigio rises way above its station. With each glass, I'm sure these men with their eyes closed can identify a hillside slope, a slant of sun. Across five Friuli wine districts, the grapes play the music of their own plots. Easy to fall in love with the wines of the area when the vibrations of their very terroir rises from the ground you stand on.

WE'VE STAYED AT La Subida and at Castello di Spessa in Capriva, both of which we love. This time we check into La Casa di Alice, a jasmine-covered B & B with a pool and garden in a leafy residential neighborhood. Anna Brandolin converted her grandparents' barn and farmhouse and named her B & B for her daughter. For guests, she has four large rooms, each decorated in a bold color: yellow, blue, green, or red. We are put in the red, which is like being inside a big glass of wine. The atmosphere is light-hearted and Anna is *sympatica.*

We have the day and much to see, so we drop our bags and drive through the spring countryside over to Cividale del Friuli, only nineteen kilometers away. The thrill of the drive: With windows down for the freshest air, we pass fields of white asphodel in bloom.

WE ENTER THE storybook town over a high, double-arched bridge, Ponte del Diavolo, first built in the fifteenth century, destroyed in the infamous World War One Battle of Caporetto in 1917, then rebuilt by the Austrians after the war. The bridge spans the emerald-green waters of the Natisone. Why is it called the devil's bridge? He allowed it to be constructed in exchange for one soul but the canny builders delivered him instead the soul of a dog. Devilishly clever.

Parking is easy and soon we're under Gothic arches of the brick town hall that was started in 1286. We're looking out at a statue of Julius Caesar. He built a forum in 50 B.C. and started the town on its way. (The word *Friuli* derives from Forum Julii.) Pigeons poop on his head but still he surveys with dignity the ancient town.

Down the street, we try slices of *gubana,* the signature dessert of this area. The leavened dough is rolled around a filling of mixed nuts, candied fruits, raisins, and orange peel, then swirled into a cake pan. When it's sliced, you see a spiral of the filling. A lot like pastries I tasted in Hungary, even similar to strudel but cakier, *gubana* tastes of *mitteleuropa.* The name probably comes from Slovenian, *guba,* bent. I've read that it's sometimes served with a splash of grappa.

So pretty, Piazza Paolo Diacono, surrounded by three- and four-story palatial buildings in pastel colors. Paul the Deacon: his piazza. That's his chalky-white frescoed house. A monk and writer who lived in the eighth century, he chronicled the history of the Longobards. That he wrote a poem to San Giovanni Baptista fascinates Ed because the first syllables of the first six stanzas—*ut, re, me, fa, sol, la*—inspired Guido d'Arezzo to use them when he invented the musical scale.

The artistic remains of the Germanic Longobards, who arrived in 568, bring many to visit this town. After them, and after an incursion from the patriarch of nearby Aquileia, Charlemagne took over in 774 and the town came under the dominion of the Franks, who bestowed the name Civitas Austriae, eastern city, which evolved into Cividale. Longobards. Long beards. We find their Tempietto Longobardo, miraculously surviving from the eighth century in the oratorio of the Santa Maria in Valle monastery complex. Though small in size, this is the fullest expression of Longobard art and architecture remaining in Italy. The space is very pure, very pale, with exquisite stucco grape clusters and vines surrounding an arch, and a stunning row of six female statues above. "What do they remind you of?" I ask Ed.

He stares a while longer then nods. "The women in the mosaics in Ravenna. Same elongated archaic shapes." Just what I thought, too. The overwhelming impression is stillness, silence.

In the outer room, under restoration, we can only glimpse intricate choir stalls, and another arch with curly vines and grapes. We'll be back another day. The walkway out gives us a pretty view of the river, houses perched along it, and distant mountains.

Other Longobard relics are displayed at the Museo Archeologico Nazionale, along with finds from earlier and later times. Most arresting, an S-shaped fibula (garment fastener brooch) in gold set with garnet and amber; the jewelry found on a female skeleton—ring, belt buckle, hairpin, comb made of bone; sixth- and seventh-century necklaces of beads, filigree, glass, and amber. Take these home and wear tonight! Ed calls me over to look at a gold cross I could hold in the palm of my hand. It's embossed with vegetal designs, delicate and highly worked. Another, even more cunningly worked, has an antlered deer carved into the crux of the cross. Those Longobards—not just Frankish hordes from the north but skilled and aesthetic artisans.

Cividale is a town that takes outdoor life seriously. Bars and cafés with umbrellas and flower boxes are everywhere, and the townspeople are out strolling the appealing streets. Friuli is prosperous; local shops prove that. Along Corso Mazzini, a window shows exquisite embroidered linens. We pop into Scubla Antica Drogheria, now a gastronomy emporium, and buy polenta, *biologico* (organic) fruit jams, and *vialone* rice. *Profumerie* (perfumes and beauty products), hair salons, cool shoe and clothing stores are plentiful. My favorite shop, in the arcades on Piazza Paolo Diacono, is A Occhi Chiusi ("To Closed Eyes"). They sell exotic teas, spices, infusions, essential oils, and tea-making articles in a curated, attractive nook.

We stop for a light lunch (after all that *gubana*) at Enoteca de Feo, where we're surrounded by young businessmen in fitted suits and dress shoes with no socks. Very cool and likely to stay that way. Friuli is justly known for San Daniele prosciutto, which we're able to buy in Cortona. With our *Montasio* aged cheese, we're opting for D'Osvaldo prosciutto, arguably more delicate. Transparent slices seem to melt in the mouth, imparting the gentlest sweet-salt tastes. We're sitting at an outside table because the day is perfect, sipping a glass of Friulano, which used to be called *tocai*. The Hungarians won the right to *tokay* and *tocai,* and local makers renamed theirs Friulano. The elixir in our glasses is Schiopetto's Friulano Collio.

From the corner of two pedestrian streets, we see bicyclists' baskets blooming with fennel fronds, a toddler in red running away from his mother, and a tall teenage boy, insouciant of his beauty, who could have stepped out of a Bronzino painting. He will never lack someone to love him.

HARD TO PULL away from Cividale. In the afternoon, we push on for a look at Palmanova, only a half hour away. I was first curious about this

town because of reading W. G. Sebald's *Austerlitz.* He was fascinated by
the architecture of star forts such as Palmanova's. By the time they were
built, interim advances in armaments eclipsed the tactical advantages
offered by the star-shape design. They were obsolete before they were
finished, blending into his sense that enterprise is dispersing even as it is
conceived. Sebald saw in this a deeply melancholy philosophy that puts
life always in diaspora. Our reach never grasps.

On approaching, the lineaments of Palmanova's star are clear. Inside
the walls, we come immediately into a grand piazza, center of the town
plan. The center hexagon has eighteen concentric radiating streets and
four ring streets intersecting the radials, a mesmerizing spider web. Built
by the Venetians in 1593, Palmanova was meant to protect the area from
raucous invaders, especially Turks, but the plan wasn't just for defense. The
Venetians believed beauty promotes the general good, and designed ac-
cordingly. Their intention was utopian: Equal land was given to everyone.

The surprise—no one came to live there. Too perfect? Too regimented? (There is something deadening about planned communities.)

Finally, in 1622, the Venetians released enough prisoners to occupy
the ghost town.

What elaborate preparations, all for battles that never happened.
Without military parades or festivals, what to do with such an immense
piazza? A playground makes a tiny dent along one edge. Some old wooden

hoists used in the original construction occupy another small space. A café intrudes a few meters. Mostly, though, it is empty, a space still waiting for something to happen.

AS EVENING FALLS, we park in front of Trattoria Al Piave in Mariano del Friuli. Right on time—it's eight o'clock. Behind us, Robert and his fiancée, Kirsten.

Robert is one of those friends you pick up with as though you've seen each other last week, when it has been six months. And this beauty whom we already know to be brilliant, too—what a pleasure to meet her. The trattoria owner, Patrizia, throws her arms around Robert. Her family-operated place is welcoming, too—a fireplace, bucolic mural, white tablecloths. We're seated in an intimate garden drenched with the scent of jasmine. Patrizia brings out prosecco. There's catch-up, there's getting acquainted with Kirsten. Travel. Books. Politics. Food. News. Projects. Out come the house-made breads, a potato strudel with *bruscandoli* and ricotta with cubes of tomato. What luck, this is the season when it's possible to try *bruscandoli,* the mild green top shoots of hops. Pasta with raunchy wild greens and rabbit. Fall-off-the-bone veal shank. The wine honors go to Robert. He chooses first the Sturm Andritz Rosso Collio 2011, and when we have turned up our glasses for the last sip, he orders Raccaro Collio Malvasia 2016, both new to us. Best to trust Robert, who knows his way around Collio wines!

We love the old-fashioned trattoria, the owners' dedication to the gifts of the land. Love being with friends for a great feast to pull us back together again. Now we go in different directions. Next year? Same place?

IT'S LATE BACK at La Casa di Alice but we sit by the pool for a few minutes, letting the day settle into place, revisiting the menu at Al Piave, admiring the food of Friuli and the Slovenian, Austrian edge.

"What's better than *frico*? Like hashbrowns but not. I could eat *frico* every day," I muse. The shredded potatoes are mixed with the local aged cow's-milk *Montasio* cheese and sautéed until crisp. Some versions include apples or herbs.

"*Genuino,* that sacred Italian word." Genuine.

"Yes. Don't you love the frequency of woodcock, venison, and goose on the menus?"

"And fat white asparagus, best I've ever tasted; *canerino,* that canary-yellow radicchio. And all kinds of mushrooms . . ."

We trail up to bed in the red, red room.

ANNA'S BREAKFAST IN her big sunny kitchen: crostata with apricots, lemon, nuts. She's set out, too, local *caciotta* cheese with herbs, and a basket of breads. Anna is a sunny presence herself. We look with her at some of her cookbooks, then she takes us around the garden. This is like visiting a friend of a friend.

We stroll around Cormòns while it's still early. Ed beams as we pass a vending machine that dispenses bicycle inner tubes for seven euros. His kind of town. We greet Massimiliano I, his statue a vestige of the Hapsburg era of the town. The Maria Theresa yellow of several buildings also connects to the long Austrian heritage. The other color of Cormòns I like is a pale blue, ashen and calm. Particular to Friuli is the *centa* and we look into the entrance to one. *Centa,* from the word for "belt," I presume, is a single or double row of houses arranged in a U; they protect a church, nested inside.

Cormòns is an elegant, low-key town. Will Robert someday buy a house here? Maybe this one, with a celadon-green door and shutters, an arching bower of white roses tangled with wisteria, a calico cat on the step, and a red vintage Fiat Cinquecento parked outside.

NOTES:

Robert Draper's article on his Cormòns adventures in *Smithsonian* magazine: https://www.smithsonianmag.com/travel/venice-friuli-wine-region-vineyard -enoteca-italy-180956875/

UNESCO site on Palmanova: http://whc.unesco.org/en/tentativelists/1154/

Interesting connection: Plaza del Ejecutivo in Mexico City was based on Palmanova's design: http://worldurbanplanning.com/plaza-del -ejecutivo-mexico/

Gnocchi con La Lepre

GNOCCHI WITH WILD HARE, SERVES 4 TO 6

Hare is relished in Italy. Milder and readily available, rabbit is sold in most butcher shops, which every town has—we can shop at four in our immediate vicinity. Neither hare nor rabbit is easy to find in the United States, but there are online sources for ordering both. I hope this is not heresy, but this recipe from Chefs Patrizio and Stefano Fermanelli also works with chicken.

FOR THE GNOCCHI
2 pounds russet potatoes, peeled and freshly boiled
2 cups all-purpose flour
2 large eggs

FOR THE HARE SAUCE
3 tablespoons sunflower oil
1 whole hare (or rabbit), about 4 pounds, cut into pieces
3 onions, chopped
3 carrots, sliced
2 cloves garlic, minced
Rosemary, sage, marjoram, *QB*
4 juniper berries
3 tablespoons sweet paprika
1 bottle red wine
2 cups chicken stock, plus more if needed
Salt and pepper, *QB*
2 tablespoons all-purpose flour

Prepare the gnocchi: Crush the potatoes and let them cool in a medium mixing bowl. Add the flour and eggs and mix until the flour is completely integrated. Let stand for about 10 minutes. By hand, make cigar-shaped cylinders with the dough, about 1 inch thick. On a floured counter, slice the cylinders into ¾-inch pieces.

Prepare the hare sauce: Add 1¼ tablespoons of the oil to a large skillet and brown the pieces of hare over high heat. Remove and add the remaining oil to the skillet. Sauté the vegetables, the herbs, juniper berries, and paprika. Return the pieces of hare to the pan and add the wine and stock. Bring to a boil, cover, and simmer until cooked, 20 to 30 minutes, depending on the size of the pieces. Take the hare out, remove the bones, and cut the meat into small pieces.

Remove any excess oil from the skillet with a spoon. Pass the vegetables through a food mill or coarsely purée in a food processor, and return the mixture to the skillet. Season, then add the flour and mix quickly with a whisk to avoid lumps. The sauce should not be too liquid or too thick. At this point add the pieces of hare. Thin with stock if needed.

Cook the gnocchi in plenty of boiling salted water until they just come to the surface. Drain them and top with the sauce.

Trattoria Al Piave, Mariano del Friuli,
Friuli Venezia Giulia

Torta al Limone e Ricotta

LEMON RICOTTA TART, SERVES 8

Anna Brandolin serves this for breakfast, but I'd like a late-night slice and a glass of *malvasia* to take out to the pool.

12 tablespoons butter, plus a little more for the tart pan

6 tablespoons sugar

Zest and juice of 4 lemons

3 large eggs, separated

1 cup ricotta, drained of excess liquid in a colander

¾ cup self-rising flour

⅓ cup almonds, chopped

1 teaspoon vanilla extract

2 teaspoons baking powder

Confectioners' sugar

Preheat the oven to 350°F.

Line the bottom of a 9-inch tart pan with parchment and butter the sides.

Make the pastry. Cream the butter and sugar together in a large bowl. Add the lemon zest. Add one egg yolk at a time, and combine well. Add the ricotta and continue mixing. Beat in the lemon juice.

In a medium bowl, combine well the flour, almonds, vanilla, and baking powder, then add the ricotta mixture.

In another medium bowl, whip the egg whites until they form soft peaks and then fold into the ricotta mixture.

Pour into the pan and bake for 40 to 45 minutes. Test for doneness with a toothpick. The tart will be very *umida* (moist) because of the ricotta.

Unmold the tart, and let it cool for 5 minutes before sifting confectioners' sugar over the top. Serve at room temperature with fresh fruit, crème fraîche, or whipped cream.

La Casa di Alice, Cormòns,
Friuli Venezia Giulia

I Girini: Briciole di Pasta Buttata Condite dall'Orto e Funghi Porcini, Quasi Crudi

La Subida is a family enterprise. Fortuitous it was that daughter Tanja married a chef. Alessandro Gavagna stepped into the kitchen and the La Subida legend continues. I'm delighted to share his "tadpoles." Porcini are hard to find in the United States. Substitute portobello or any wild mushroom. When traveling in Italy, tuck a few bags of dried porcini in your luggage, along with small boxes of porcini *dadi*, bouillon cubes. The colander called for below should be one with good-size holes. I have an old aluminum one that works perfectly. When dropping the pasta into the water, it should be at a *dolce* boil, a soft boil rather than a hard boil. Remove the zucchini pistils with tweezers.

FOR THE PASTA

4 large eggs

1¼ cups all-purpose sifted flour

FOR THE SAUCE

1 tablespoon butter

3 ounces porcini mushrooms, chopped

1 small zucchini, finely chopped

8 pumpkin or zucchini flowers, opened, stem and pistil removed, coarsely chopped

Salt and pepper, *QB*

3 tablespoons aged *Montasio* cheese (or substitute aged Parmigiano-Reggiano)

4 grapevine leaves, washed and patted dry

Olive oil

2 to 3 tablespoons goat cheese, crumbled

Chopped oregano or basil, or the flowers of *ursino* garlic (wild garlic or ramps)

Dash of red wine vinegar

Prepare the pasta: Break the eggs in a bowl and beat until well combined. Let them rest for 10 minutes. Add the flour and mix vigorously. Let rest for another 15 minutes, then pour the mixture into a colander and push the dough through, dropping "tadpoles" into gently boiling salted water. Pour in small batches to prevent clumping. Break apart any clumps with a fork. As soon as they come to the surface, skim them from the pot and drain them in cold water.

Prepare the sauce: Melt the butter in a medium-size skillet and add the mushrooms, zucchini, and zucchini flowers. Sauté for 5 minutes and season with salt and pepper.

Stir in the cheese and add the "tadpoles" to the vegetables.

For each diner, take a flat plate. Lay down a vine leaf and arrange the tadpoles and vegetables. Sprinkle with a little oil and the crumbled goat cheese. To taste, add the oregano, basil, or flowers of *ursino* garlic. Finally, add a small dash of vinegar.

Trattoria Al Cacciatore della Subida,
Cormòns, Friuli Venezia Giulia

Aquileia

Only a half hour from Cormòns, Aquileia is another world.
A Roman world. Once you come here you cannot imagine
why you've never heard of it—one of the great sights of
Italy, of anywhere.

Founded in 181 B.C., Aquileia is a sleepy village of thirty-
five hundred. Once, its population was as many as one
hundred thousand, the fourth largest in Italy after Rome,
Milano, and Capua. First established as a military bastion
against barbarians, the settlement grew large as Rome
expanded toward the Danube. Rome recognized its position
on strategic roads, and saw that boats could ply the river to
the Adriatic outlet. Trade eventually extended as far north
as the Baltic amber routes and as far east as Arabia.

Entering town on via Giulia Augusta, you immediately
see on the left a spectacular row of fourteen tall intact
columns, plus a few stubs and bases, hints at what once
stood there. The whole site is like this: Everywhere you
wander, you come upon remnants of forum, circus, port,
town wall, houses with bits of mosaic floor, amphitheater,

all unguarded, open, just lying around among the cypresses, pines, and long grass, as though just unearthed. There must be much left to discover. As many ruins as I've seen, I've never, with the exceptions of tourist-central Pompeii and Herculaneum, felt the living reality of the town as I do here. The way it existed eerily rises in the mind's eye.

AFTER ROMAN RULE ended, Aquileia was subject to sieges, fratricides, martyrs, and plagues. The Christian patriarch Theodore built a basilica in 314. Attila destroyed the town in 452 and salted the earth. He left in his wake the legend that fleeing citizens forced slaves to construct a well that they filled with treasures; then they killed the slaves to erase memory. Fallen to ruin, the basilica was reworked from 1021 to 1031. After: a dizzying succession of power grabbers, patriarchs, earthquakes, and extraordinary artistic triumphs.

THE MUSEO ARCHEOLOGICO Nazionale di Aquileia, housed in a large villa, beggars description. Everything here was excavated locally. The cemeteries must have been like museums. The signage tells us that funeral monuments were arranged along roads leading into town: sepulchral roads organized according to social order. We get to see quantities of finely executed marble busts that marked the graves. Stone lions— protectors of tombs—from the first century B.C. A head of Venus. A headless, armless whole Venus, tall, realistic. A Janus face. Decoratively carved sarcophagi for those buried whole, cinerary urns for cremated bodies, with carved scenes like film strips encircling the urn. A dead man is shown nude lying on a bed. Ah, here's a surprise: Across from him, another man makes the sign of the *corna*. Index and pinkie pointed down, like bull's horns, the gesture that all over Italy means *let it not happen here*. The floors of black-and-white mosaics, exquisite, lifted from houses in the area. Fragments show scenes from the *Iliad*. One of the Trojan war, and a vast wave about to subsume all. Useless to catalog; you must see.

The marble portrait busts make me linger longest. Real faces. Full of lived life. One, very old. One, a boy with an ivy wreath. Delicate young woman with corn-row hair; most of the women show elaborate hair.

Some have smashed noses. We're alone here with these former citizens. Conversing.

In the garden, we find the *lapidarium,* an immense salvage yard of Roman stones—tombstones, stone carvings, bits of buildings, monument markers, stele, round pots for ashes of slaves. And more mosaics. Ed is photographing the carved, precise Roman lettering, no font ever as pleasing to the eye. Jumbled storerooms off the loggia are jammed with pots and glass objects—major craft of ancient Aquileia—surprisingly enduring all this time. Coins, of course. All speaking loudly of vibrant life.

NOT FAR AWAY, we're in a later era. The basilica, dedicated to the Virgin Mary, hid a secret for almost a thousand years. Imagine the surprise of Austrian archeologists in the early twentieth century when they lifted the eleventh-century floor and found under deeper layers of straw and mud the intact mosaic of the 314 church. What a moment.

This is the largest mosaic surviving from the ancient world. Traveler, this is why we find ourselves in places we never dreamed of! Scenes of the Old Testament surge across the huge floor. What is moving: You sense the presence of the maker. The person who picked up stone after stone and formed images of the allegories, stories, and symbols from early Christian times. Daily moments, too: a man sleeping under a pergola, a swimming octopus, many animals. Oh, Jonah and the whale, and the pagan Perseus, the winged horse. Fishermen—the Apostles?—wielding a somehow transparent net. I identify many types of fish, which speak of the citizens' riverside life.

THE WELL OF treasure was never found. For centuries, any property sales contract excluded buyers from the wealth inside the well if it were later discovered on the land. I'm dreaming. When I win the jackpot lottery, I'll fund a crack team of archeologists to uncover what must still lie under the earth. Magnificent sculptures, a preserved kitchen, a chariot. In an undiscovered dip of the ground, they'll come upon an octagonal stone, and when they lift it, they'll look down into the golden well.

Emilia-Romagna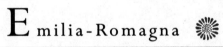

Parma

Called *Chrysopolis* ("Golden City") in Byzantine times,
Parma is a snow-globe town—shake and it dazzles—a
seventeenth-century steel engraving of a city on a river,
a place of street music and opera, a solid market town,
a stop on the antique via Emilia that ran from Rimini to
Piacenza. And a major food destination because of—what
else?—Parmigiano-Reggiano, plus the range of prosciuttos
and other *salume,* and the reputation for a bountiful and
varied table. But a major art exhibit of Correggio and
Parmigianino in Rome's Scuderie del Quirinale last summer
spurred us to visit. We were mesmerized by the portraits
from these two Parma artists, struck by how intimately and
precisely the subjects were observed.

Twenty years ago, we visited Parma briefly with a friend
who was writing her dissertation on the Correggio fresco
on the dome inside the city's Romanesque cathedral. From
that long-ago weekend, I remember buying a packet of
candied violets (violet—the signature fragrance of Parma),
the sweet-meaty aromas along a narrow street, a boar's head

leering down at me from a shop, a violinist playing something tremulous from Verdi in the Piazza Garibaldi. I remember a general sense of an elegant city on a small river and of staring up into the cathedral dome at an off-center figure whose legs seemed to be kicking. I thought, *how strange.*

We're settling in at Palazzo dalla Rosa Prati, right on the piazza of the duomo and baptistery. Wisteria, branching from a trunk thicker than any prosciutto, clambers all over the courtyard walls and up to the third floor. Gold-leafed in early December, it must have flowered for a hundred years. Our room is old world—a high wooden headboard, a dressing table, flowered fabrics, and a round table perfect for spreading out our books, maps, and snarls of cords. With bold confidence, someone selected a red rug and floral draperies in a riot of coral, pink, and rose geraniums. We're concealed from the courtyard but mellow light seeps in between wisteria leaves. Any old English duchess, especially one who smokes hashish, would feel right at home here.

After cross-checking the *Gambero Rosso, Touring Club Emilia-Romagna, Osteria d'Italia,* and *Mangiarozzo* restaurant guides and finding too many promising choices, we set out. First stop, Libreria Fiaccadori, the bookstore, open since 1829, just down the street. We find a regional cookbook and a couple of locally written city guidebooks, then head for Piazza Garibaldi on the spot of the Roman forum, where we settle in for coffee. We make lists of what to see, while taking in the grand yellow-and-cream building surrounding us and an arcaded building, the Portici del Grano, where wheat, fish, meat, salt, wood, and other goods once were sold. There's a predominant Parma yellow, like lemon butter cream; I'd like to paint every room in my house this delicious color. I admire the sundials on either side of the clock tower. I love all sundials, but especially those looming over piazzas. Time both slows and becomes more real as it falls across the face of your companion, across the cobbles, across the checked tablecloth and the empty cups. To know time by a shadow.

WE ENCOUNTER OUR man Correggio first in San Giovanni Evangelista, Saint John the Baptist, a substantial church with a soaring bell tower. Correggio is the nearby town where he was born and christened

Antonio Allegri. His dome here, frescoed prior to the duomo I remember from years ago, shows another dynamic mid-sky event with haphazard limbs flailing. Maybe it's Gabriel, maybe it's Christ; one or the other is descending from upper heaven to collect Saint John, who is old and surrounded by a crowd of Apostles in clouds, along with decorative *putti*. What is remarkable, other than the sulfurous sky, is how awkward the whole composition is—yet that awkwardness creates a frenetic energy totally lacking in most such scenes. (I've seen a few!) How bold and new his off-center placement, the odd sky, and the dynamic movement. Ideally, you'd lie flat on the floor with binoculars to see the details. The light shed by my euros in the machine hardly illuminates the particulars.

Off to the side over a doorway, and very visible, is Correggio's lunette of the young Saint John writing the Apocalypse, accompanied by an eagle. "That eagle, I know it symbolizes John, but signifying what quality?" I ask Ed, whose intense Catholic education gave him expertise in iconography that my Methodist background left lacking in me.

"Soaring upward. Ascension toward heaven. Here's a surreal quote. Let me look it up exactly; it's from Ezekiel." He scrolls around a minute then finds it. "Their faces looked like this: Each of the four had the face of a man, and on the right side, each had the face of a lion, and on the left the face of an ox; each also had the face of an eagle." He clicks off the phone and laughs. "That sets off a bit of an image storm."

"The eagle looks a little ratty. Not sure he'd ascend all the way."

Walking out, Ed says, "Check out this floor." A dizzy expanse of trompe-l'oeil colored marble cubes laid to trick the eye. During long sermons, you could hypnotize yourself by finding patterns in the connected squares.

A monk with a face the color of congealed oatmeal guards the entryway to the church's Benedictine monastery. We want to see the three cloisters and the library. His hooded, iguana eyes look at us as though we're barbarians at the gate, which I guess we are. My smile brings no response. Instead, he seems to puff up, the expansion that happens the moment before an explosion. Almost empty shelves around the room hold a few jars of fruit confitures that monks made somewhere back in time and space. I fear we would be poisoned if we spread a spoonful on our toast. Even out of good will, I don't buy. His head sinks lower into his cowl as he glowers and gestures toward a door.

The once-lovely cloisters stand empty. The library is closed. All dreary. I try to imagine life here when the monastery thrived. Wandering in and out of several thousand churches over the years, I often fantasize about how the world would look if all the money and talent and effort that went into church building had instead been lavished on libraries and schools.

We must exit through the stony monk's room. His rheumy, hard eyes look trapped. A chill runs over me. I think he might die today.

IN THE SAME complex, we stop into the old herbal pharmacy, Spezieria di San Giovanni. A round woman bundled in sweaters, her determined nose almost touching a crossword puzzle, smiles and waves us into dark rooms lined with cases holding ceramic jars labeled with plant names. In these old labs, nuns and monks were deeply into investigations of cures. They cultivated complicated gardens of simples (plants that heal). The workroom with its well and marble sinks remains totally intact. What if you depended on the monks to cure your TB or mushroom poisoning? We're out of there in ten minutes and off to lunch at number one of our eight meals in Parma.

ANGIOL D'OR, A greenhouse room with windows overlooking the great piazza, is a lucky choice. Risotto with crunchy pancetta, a touch of pumpkin cream, and sprinkled lightly on top, fine crumbs of amaretto cookies. Pumpkin isn't a favorite of mine but this tastes delicate and creamy. A glass of the wine I'm late to appreciating, *malvasia*, a dry one with a flowery upper note. Not of Parma violets. More carnation, if that undervalued, unappreciated flower were distilled to its most delicate note. And don't I recognize downfall when I see it? The owner brings over a basket of crisp, golden *torta fritta,* puffs of fried bread. I know it's lard. I don't care.

Wine at lunch. Dessert. What a way to start a trip. We cannot continue this or we will be leveled for each afternoon, missing half of what we want to see. But it's useless to resist the traditional sweet of this area, *sbrisolona.* The recipe comes out of *cucina povera.* Made with equal parts polenta and flour, with abundant toasted nuts, it's crumbly like shortcake but grittier in texture. In the tradition, grappa often dappled the top; but this one is raised a few powers by the little cup of rich zabaglione on the side. You break the crunchy pieces and dip. And dip. And I don't want more but I dip again.

WORTH THE TRIP to Parma: Cattedrale di Santa Maria Assunta, the duomo! It's good to stand on the opposite side of the cobbled piazza, near the bishop's palace, and rest your eyes on the buildings. The octagonal baptistery in pink Verona marble rises out of a dream. The duomo face is rhythmic with arches. Wider than you'd expect, it does not soar but sits solidly on the earth. Three large doors invite you to come closer, where gigantic lions flank the center, and the frieze above shows not the heavenly orders but people fishing, harvesting grapes and wheat— ordinary labors of the months, including a pig butchering. Yes, the *salume* tradition goes way back in Parma. High up, you glimpse a golden angel weathervane guarding the piazza. That's Archangel Raphael, a copy of the thirteenth-century one now protected in the nearby Museo Diocesano.

Inside, how lofty the dome. Layers of the happily dead in circles of cotton-candy clouds, along with wingless *putti* playing musical instruments, pile in layers toward the yellow vortex. I knew Correggio's subject matter was the Assumption of the Virgin Mary into heaven. She looks wonky, disjointed as she ascends. With the dome lit, I finally see what I missed on my previous visit. Not the Virgin Mary! The awkward figure just off center in the dome is Jesus coming down from heaven to snare Mary, who's jammed into the beatific crowd around the sides of the dome. Through my zoom lens, I see the soles of his big feet and his white garments billowing upward as he descends.

The risky choices Correggio made forever step out of line and jolt the history of painting. Why did he decide to paint Jesus coming for Mary instead of the usual Assumption into heaven? Possibly because it makes a more interesting *story*. And as we know, frescoes were narratives for those who had no books.

Ed is ready, again, for an espresso. He's sitting on a pew, reading a guidebook on his phone. "I like this." He looks up at the dome. "One observer from that time commented that all that commotion in the sky looked like a stew of frog legs."

FROG LEGS ACTUALLY appear on the menu at Trattoria dei Corrieri, the venerable spot we've chosen for dinner. It's brightly lit and packed with local people who've probably been eating here all their lives. The service is, for Italy, uncharacteristically chaotic. Also on the menu is *pesto di cavallo,* which someone might gloss over as *cavolo,* possibly some kind of cabbage. But there's the double l. *Cavallo*: horse. When I ask the waiter how it's prepared, he says, "*Caval pist. Tartara,*" as if to say any fool knows that. *Caval pist,* we figure out, is dialect for horse pesto. *Tartara,* we know.

Raw horse. I won't be placing an order but I'm interested when a bowl of fresh, bright red meat is served to the man at the next table. It looks good. He spreads it on bruschetta. "We eat cow. Pig. Why not horse?" Ed reasons. But he orders tortelli with *spalla cotta di San Secondo,* a hallowed recipe in Emilia-Romagna. Pork shoulder is soaked, then boiled in water with some wine, spices, and seasonings for around three hours. The meat is soft with a whiff of cinnamon and a hearty pork flavor. San Secondo is near Le Roncole di Busseto, the town where Giuseppe Verdi was born. An early foodie, he loved *spalla cotta.* He wanted a lot of things on his plate—especially *spongata,* a sugar-coated jam cake. Food crops up constantly in his letters. The tag on a *spalla cotta* in butcher shops features a photo of Verdi.

I'm happy when my plate of gnocchi with Gorgonzola and toasted walnuts arrives. This is an old-school trattoria where house wine rules. We order the red *fermo* and learn a new word. Not the same as unbottled house wine (*sfuso*) in Tuscany—*fermo* means "still." That's opposed to *frizzante* wines, a sparkling *malvasia* or *lambrusco,* so loved locally. At their price for a half-liter, they might as well give it away. A big, mouthy red with nice balance—it goes quickly. After we wave at the server a few times, he plops down another pitcher.

When the man next to us borrows our olive oil, I ask him, "How's the horse?"

"Excellent. My wife is pregnant and it's full of iron. Very good for her." No wife in sight. He goes on to order roasted duck.

SO OFTEN IN Italy, there's a way. Something is not possible, then it becomes possible. As Wallace Stevens wrote, "After the final no, there comes a yes."

Inaccessible, the sign says. And I so want to see the Bodoni museum. Any book lover would. Giambattista Bodoni, the pioneer typographer, revved up the art of composition and type design so forcefully that he's credited with being the first modern typographer. After he was tapped to become the official printer for the Duke of Parma in 1766, he jump-started the possibilities of printing. Many Bodoni texts remain on the top floor of the Palazzo della Pilotta. This is the ugliest pile of bricks I've seen in all of Europe, but the vast complex houses the Archeological Museum, the National Gallery, the Palatine Library, and the astonishing wooden Teatro Farnese that smells of resins and crosscuts. Stage, seats, walls, floors, ceiling—all strips of wood. What a feat, restoring this fantasy space after it was badly bombed in World War Two.

We visit everything. But we cannot see the Bodoni collection. No, we're told. Closed. Impossible. Then, as we're leaving the vast Palatine Library, the woman at the ticket booth follows us out into the hall and says conspiratorially, "Come tomorrow at nine." Perhaps she saw how long we lingered over the books.

ED EXITS OUR room at seven each morning for a three-mile walk. I wish I were not lazy. He gets to see the vegetable deliveries, the bread trucks unloading, early birds zipping to work on bicycles, students paus-ing for coffee. He returns bearing a cappuccino for me and observa-tions. The crowd of immigrant African men, all very tall, who gather on the sunny side of the baptistery, the Fellini woman in a white feather hat who walks three ancient white poodles, the pebbly river you easily could wade across, the quiet of the dignified city without cars or motorcycles in the historic center's streets, the coppery glint of sunlight on the angel atop the duomo.

It's getting late and we hurry to the Pilotta.

To our surprise, the ticket seller, a different woman, expects us. Top floor, she directs, and we climb. Immensely high ceilings double the usual stairs for each story. Early-morning-walker Ed sprints up but I'm pausing on the fourth (eighth!) floor as if I'm halfway up Everest. Signor Natalino ("Little Christmas") greets us formally and proceeds with a half-hour lecture on Parma history. His Italian is so clearly enunciated that we understand almost everything, even though he frequently uses the dreaded past remote tense.

This is Bodoni type:

FRIENDS, ROMANS, COUNTRYMEN, LEND ME YOUR EARS . . .

You can see the sculptural elements in the clipped curves and in the different widths of ink in each letter. You can also see a connection to the earlier, heavier Gutenberg type and to Gothic lettering, but it's hard to know the revolutionary aspect of this new type and the way forward it opened to subsequent printers, and the ease his type gave to readers' eyes.

As a young man, Bodoni left home in Piemonte, where his father and grandfather were also printers, to work in Rome. There, for his agile body, he was known as "the deer." After six years at the Vatican's print house for missionary publications, where he learned Coptic, Arabic, and other lettering, he returned to the north to work for Ferdinando, Duke of Parma, heading up his printing shop for official publications. Later, as his artistry brought him fame, he was allowed to open his own shop. He could publish whatever he wanted. His first book was the poems of Horace.

Loosed from Signor Natalino's lecture, we gaze at Bodoni's typographic tools and books. Wood, string, chisels. Creamy thick paper and elegant, simple type, all safely behind glass when I would so like to take out a book and see what's beyond the displayed page. And I wish for my California friend Robin Heyeck, who published my and Ed's early poetry on the letterpress printer in her garage. She taught us the aesthetics of type and paper, and also the tedious work that goes into handsetting tiny letters into a block. From her we learned to distinguish among Bembo, Arrighi, Centaur, and Garamond. She put in hours with sloshing buckets for dipping paper, pulling out marbled designs. Trial and error. Patience. How space is as crucial as print, and how, with pressure, the lead fonts bite into handmade paper. Back-straining work results in words given their full due. Her Heyeck Press books are in fine-edition libraries all over the country, and a row of them stands in my bookcase. We're all in Bodoni's debt.

As soon as he could branch away from printing the duke's posters, presentation volumes, and announcements, he turned to his own interests: Homer, Tasso, and Virgil. On to Aesop, Dante, Petrarca. Touching to see *Poems by Mr. Gray,* the English poet, Thomas Gray. I would like to peer inside the only existing replica of the calligraphy manual that Leonardo da Vinci consulted. It's a "xylographic syllabary," which I imagine for a moment to be letters with a glassy musical sound. A quick fact-check and I tell Ed authoritatively that the term means vowel and consonant syllables are printed by carved woodblocks, not type.

Thanks to Robin's hard work, we easily see how Bodoni's museum reveals fierce ambition. Eventually, he created twelve hundred volumes. What fascinates me most is the book he never saw. After his death in 1813, his widow, Margherita dall'Aglio (Margaret of the Garlic!), finished his magnum opus. The typefaces of *Manuale typografico* must have driven several typesetters completely mad: six hundred large pages of alphabets in all sizes, in script and italics, as well as in roman. He shows many examples of characters in other alphabets (Greek, Russian, Armenian), also with the capital letters. Preserved for us, too, are his musical notations, and all manner of numbers and ornaments. Though Bodoni had thoroughly planned the two volumes, bringing them to the light was a heroic effort by Margherita.

While staring at his statement, "The more a book is classical, the more the beauty of its typeface should be admired alone," I text a message: *Robin, did you ever visit Parma? The Bodoni Museum with all his books displayed?* As a respected printer, she might have dispensation to take them from the glass cases and turn the pages.

One book of his must have been radical at the time. He printed the Lord's Prayer in 155 languages. Lastly, Ed spots *Pitture di Antonio Allegri: Esistenti in Parma nel Monistero di San Paolo.* I'm hit by this—Correggio's pictures in the San Paolo monastery, which we haven't yet seen. The book where Bodoni pays tribute to an artist who died 206 years before he was born remains sealed in its cabinet. And 203 years after Bodoni's death, we're reveling in the immediacy of the works of both men.

THE FOOD STREET! It jogs off Piazza Garibaldi. Eat your way down the length of Strada Farini, jammed with bars, cafés, restaurants, fruit stands, and places to buy cheeses and *salume.* In the upper stories of the rose, saffron, and peach buildings I see residents at open windows, drying dishes, knitting, smoking—taking in the life of the street below. One man looks like the portrait of Bodoni except for the white ribbed tank top he's wearing. A cat sleeps on a sill four floors up. What if it turns over? I have to look away.

Charming metal and glass box structures like small train cars line the street. I've seen these along the Via Veneto in Rome. With their standing heaters, the cafés are open all year. It must be lovely in the snow to sit with a hot chocolate and watch the flakes falling. We choose the most crowded one and I order a *tris,* trio, of polentas—*funghi porcini,* fondue of *pecorino,* and truffle. Oh, my. Best polenta ever? Ed, across the table with his bowl of nutmeg-scented *anolini in brodo,* broth with pasta knots stuffed with beef, says he's pleased but I see him cast longing eyes at my polenta bowls and I take pity, passing them to him for a few tastes.

In the great Feltrinelli bookstore nearby—bottom floor is almost all café—I find three books by Wallis Wilde-Menozzi in the English section. *Mother Tongue: An American Life in Italy,* a memoir set here in the 1980s, naturally reaches out to me. I am a visitor here; living in a place is always different. From *Mother Tongue,* which I dip into as soon as I'm back at the hotel, I see how hard it was to be a free-spirited, intellectually curious woman in Parma then.

As late as 1990 when I became a part-time resident of Italy, few women went to college and even those few who did seemed to dead-end in jobs that demanded much and gave little. Most young women, even *liceo* (the highest-level high school) grads, stayed close to home. The admired word for a girl was "*semplice,*" simple. Someone not bothered by a vision of herself that rocked any boat. I couldn't fathom the lack of ambition until I finally understood the fierce family ties that keep young Italians close to the home fires.

After years of living here, yes, it's changed but not enough. Many still give themselves up to stay close to family. It's a hard aspect of the culture for me. I admire the commitment to family, even long for that, but rebel against the constraints. If I'd grown up in a close-knit Italian family, I might have been toast. Or a disgrace. But here's Wallis—a transplant with an extensive teaching career. A poet, essayist, with three books on the shelves at Feltrinelli.

I look at Wallis's website and impulsively send a message asking if she'd like to meet for coffee tomorrow morning. But how often does one check a website? I don't expect a reply.

WHEN SHOPS REOPEN after the afternoon pause, it's dark. While starting over at five seems fine in summer, I'm always thrown in winter. Many of the 32,000 students of the ancient University of Parma begin to gather along the streets in early evening. Even in December, the temperature lingers in the mid-fifties. Everyone drinks at tables and upturned barrels and in the glass cafés. Small streets off Strada Farini also are jumping, with chic or plain or vintage places to stop for a drink or dinner. The street buzzes with locals shopping for dinner and meeting friends for an *aperitivo*. I'm shocked at the well-dressed students and young couples with strollers. Great boots and fitted jackets and hair that looks five minutes out of a salon. Parma's rich but who would think that students would be looking so fine?

I buy some candied Parma violets and scented soaps (made for tourists, I know), and stop into a few shops just to look. We spend an hour in a wine bar smaller than a good-size closet, then cross back through Piazza Garibaldi to La Greppia, a sedate restaurant where the service is old-world formal—snowy linens, cordial and expert service, the menu for ladies showing no prices. Old-fashioned, yes, and friendly. I love *sformati,* crustless vegetable quiches, and their artichoke one with a fonduta of *pecorino* is feather-light. Roasted duck with pistachios follows. We eat slowly to prolong the pleasure. From the long wine list, the waiter recommends L'Ala del Drago, wing of the dragon. Better than hair of the dog. Again, how inexpensive these nice wines are compared to similar quality Tuscan wines.

· · ·

BACK AT THE hotel, I see that Wallis has replied. We arrange to meet tomorrow morning in the café at our hotel. I read further into her book about living in Parma, realizing at every page that her roots here show how a visitor like me only treads on the surface of a place. I want to ask her if the closed society she describes has opened. And what the immigrants (now 15 percent of the population of two hundred thousand) who pore through the cheap clothes at an outdoor market are bringing to the life of the town. And what winter is like, and if she will always stay.

AS A TALL, slender woman comes in the café, we know her immediately. Using a cane, tossing back a wave of silvery gray hair clearly Italian-styled, she's indisputably American—although I'm hard pressed to explain why. (What is that national stamp that makes one's country so clear?) The cane clatters to the floor as she sits down. "I'm recovering from a broken foot. I'm still not used to this thing. Thanks for contacting me." Ed leans the cane against the wall and it crashes again.

We order cappuccino and orange juice and I say how much I'm enjoying her book, how we're loving Parma—totally swept away by the art. She had the chance, during a restoration, to climb scaffolding up into the dome of the duomo. She could almost touch the Correggio.

We talk for hours. I know we'll be in touch again. I like thinking of Wallis in Parma, observing so closely and with wit all the machinations of Italian life.

AFTER WALLIS BOARDS her bus for home, we rush toward the San Paolo monastery. Across from the small park where you turn in, I see the local post office and glimpse a painted ceiling in the foyer. Immediately, I call Ed. "It's all Liberty design—glass-paned ceiling letting light pour in, and seductive paintings ringing the room." Crowded with people using the Internet and paying bills, and others who appear to be reading as though in a library, this post office should be a *jardin d'hiver* salon for the populace, with chaise longues and potted trees. I've never seen such a post office.

The morning is growing short. We find the doorway to Correggio's first (1518–19) major Parma venture—the decoration of a private chamber in the convent apartment of the *badessa* (abbess), Giovanna da Piacenza. Certain orders of nuns at that time were powerful. The abbess, elected to rule for life, had to be a skilled manager of properties and businesses owned by the rich order. This convent was known to house young women who were placed there, for whatever reasons, by their aristocratic families. I remember being told by an Italian that each large family had a "runt," the unmarriageable one shunted off to the nunnery or priesthood. A dim view of the holy orders. I remember a note in Sarah Dunant's novel *Sacred Hearts,* about a powerful, intricate order of nuns in Ferrara. She says that by 1600, dowry requirements were so outlandish that almost half of Italian women were nuns. But this wealthy *badessa* Giovanna da Piacenza must instead have been a handful—a badass. I'm suspecting trouble got her there, not lack of money or because she was a "runt." These nuns weren't cloistered. They enjoyed social events, festas, visits, involvement with intrigue and church politics.

The first surprise: not a Madonna and Child in sight. Nary a Jesus. Nor a saint. The fireplace wall is emblazoned with the mighty Diana, goddess of the moon and the hunt. The livable scale of the room and the fanciful antics of nude young boys—these erotically charged figures are *not* cherubs—make me wonder about this nun who wanted no Christian subject matter on her walls. She didn't even want images of women, except Diana, with whom she must have identified. Her family crest on the painting makes me sure of that. Emblazoned in Latin, the imperative: *You will not disturb the flame with the sword.*

Correggio created for her a leafy pergola effect under ribbed vaulting, with hunting motifs between each rib, and a running series of gray lunettes showing classical scenes, probably from ancient coins. The escape hatch of the *badessa* from the religious life? She liked the nude boys? And what on earth do the two dismembered feet in one scene signify? The meaning of the room's iconography resists complete analysis. Especially in that era of heavy Christian meaning attached to every painting, isn't it refreshing to enter this charged and sexy bower? After all the assumptions and Old Testament figures, and Madonnas, the room shows the artist early on as one who drew outside the lines. Even today, I easily imagine a round table set up for lunch here. Grouse, woodcock, and pheasant from the hunt. If the two large windows were not sealed, light would fill the room. I hope Giovanna had lute players, poets, and witty company. She was certainly a pistol herself. And I'm wondering: Did her design demands influence the future thinking of Correggio? Did her inspiration, as much as Raphael's and Michelangelo's, give him the impetus to break out of conventions?

After leaving Giovanna's marvelous room, we pop into a museum of an entirely different sort—puppets. Museo Giordano Ferrari. He was a puppeteer, as was his father, Italo. He collected more than five hundred of these creatures in the 1930s. I've never thought much about puppets. A birthday party, a matinee show for five-year-olds. "These spooky creatures," Ed says, "why are they so scary?"

"The faces. They're caricatures. Exaggerated. Like dreams." I remember how my daughter at two or three used to pull off the finger puppets, not liking my hidden hand beneath them. That's it—the manipulator is invisible; the puppets do the bidding of someone you can't see. There's a primitive fear in that godlike power. One lurid harridan with a big red mouth looks ready to pop out of the case and say something shocking.

Articulated dolls go way back to tombs in Egypt, Greece. Puppetry, a theater art with roots in primitive magic, sorcery, archetypal drama, biblical narratives, isn't at all a toss-away entertainment for children. The characters, scripts, staging of these shows reaches far into political satire, caper stories, mystery, fairy tale. The corsair, sailor, threadbare princess, soldier, devil with crooked horns—all highly artificial but somehow imbued with a strange life. "Let's get out of here." Ed heads for the door. The woman at the ticket window nods at us and she looks like a puppet herself. I think of Fellini. He must have been influenced.

OH, LUNCH. THIS at a passionate pizza place, Borgo 20, where the punched dough then rises to be punched again for five days, and after being baked in the hot wood oven is then topped with fresh ingredients. A new twist on pizza and a good one. There on the pizza menu—horse *tartara* again, with steamed onions and mustard. Also on today's menu, snail soup with polenta; rice with prunes and crisp pancetta. I like this use of *pancetta croccante* that I'm seeing a lot in Parma. Crumbled bacon this is not! Pancetta has a delicacy and, traitor that I am, more flavor than the southern bacons I love.

My pizza is piled with prosciutto, small artichokes, and mâche. Ed's has anchovies under oil, tomato, oregano, and capers. This is what happens when pizza gets in the hands of a starred chef obsessed with quality ingredients.

While we're savoring the strawberry semifreddo dessert, we start listing other delectables that we are eating, or want to eat, in Parma:

Culatello di Zibello: Only Zibello and seven other towns along the Po—all have foggy, damp weather said to be perfect for curing—can produce *culatello* legally. The lean hind leg is tied into a pear shape, aged, and treated with wine, pepper, garlic, and salt. Melting-on-your-tongue ham, layers of taste firing off in every direction.

Parmigiano-Reggiano: Of course, of course. This cow's-milk cheese has been produced here for nine centuries. After eighteen months of aging, it's ready. At twenty-four, the cheese becomes more crumbly, sweet but sharp. At thirty months or more, the Parmigiano becomes parallel to a "meditative" wine. Go sit in the corner and eat it by yourself. Dry, more complex, with a new fruity taste, flaky and granular. We bought a hunk and had it packaged *sotto voto,* shrink wrapped. You can even take a wedge back to the United States this way and parcel out servings over months.

Salame Feline: Named for a nearby town, which has a museum devoted to this home-favorite salami made from the chuck cut and other parts. By tradition, you slice this at a sixty-degree angle to show the grain.

Prosciutto di Parma: Loved all over Italy, prosciutto, sliced so thin that you can see through it the shiny tines of your fork, achieves transcendence on home court. Melon isn't in season, so we taste the transparent pinky slices with a plate of frittata and a bit of quince *mostarda* on the side. A very old taste, the fruit *mostarde* are popular all over Emilia-Romagna. Fig is favored, but all kinds of fruits are put up in sweet-sharp syrup. I like the quince, and also the Italian words for quince: *mela cotogne.*

Sacrao: Not sauerkraut, but a toothsome cabbage dish to accompany pork. It's cooked with white vinegar and juniper berries.

Tortelli: Though it may look like ravioli, cappelletti (little hats), or tortellini (knots shaped like the navel of Venus), tortelli is the name that you usually see on menus in Parma. Especially popular is *tortelli con zucca,* pasta filled with pumpkin and a smatter of crushed amoretti, and served with butter, sage, and Parmigiano. I don't care for this sweetish taste but I'm in the minority. My favorite is *tortelli d'erbetta,* the classic chard and ricotta filling scented with nutmeg, though I wouldn't turn down tortelli stuffed with potato or mushrooms.

We have yet to try *ragù di strolghino,* a pasta sauce made with bits of a particular small salami.

THESE ARE ALL standard fare in Parma. Local chefs are intoxicated with the plentiful *biologico* (organic) ingredients available and the exceptional quality of produce, grains, and meats. The result—a jazzed-up culinary scene. Chefs take these historic givens, plus the bountiful ingredients of the Po River plain, and perform their experimental riffs. If the *nonna* who stirred pots of polenta over the fire and the exalted chef of the Farnese rulers could show up tonight, they'd have plenty to talk about with those tossing pasta into boiling water. They might be mystified at every menu's lengthy claims and disclaimers about the impeccable sourcing of every damn herb or flour or grain of salt used by the chef, and the lack of preservatives or additives. May the residents all live to be a hundred!

AS WE WALK in neighborhoods during the afternoon pause, I fantasize about which house belongs to Wallis and where she buys prosciutto and what grows in the gardens behind the blank façades. I have an abiding interest in how *place* forms those who live there. I wonder how Parma shaped her, as I wonder the same about my writing. Would I have continued to write poetry if I still lived in San Francisco? Unanswerable: What would she have written if she had stayed at home? Isolation made her an independent thinker. Another day, I might find out more.

• • •

MANY EXCELLENT ARTISTS painted here in the Correggio years; unfairly neglected because they painted outside the major art cities, and on their home ground, they were eclipsed by the dazzling top boy. I get a chance to see how good are the other members of the Parma School: Rondani, Anselmi, Gandini, Bedoli, and Del Grano. Even Francesco Mazzola, known in the diminutive as Parmigianino, whose portraits are even more nuanced than those of Correggio, suffered in comparison.

Parmigianino's name—the suffix -ino being diminutive—came not from his size but from his amazing precocity. At fourteen he was an accomplished painter. His work is scattered around the world. Not a lot remains in his hometown, but at the renaissance church of Santa Maria della Steccata he left his six wise and foolish virgins, painted on the broad arch in front of the apse. Along the base you see small still-life paintings of books and instruments, revealing the love of details that makes his portraits so exact.

Santa Maria didn't work out well. When Parmigianino ran up debts, the priests drove him off the job. He died shortly afterward. The church is dim, and without binoculars, the frescoes are hard to see. A fabulous quest: to fly to all the cities with a Parmigianino—see them all. I would especially like to see the playful *Self-Portrait in a Convex Mirror* in Vienna. He was twenty-one, showing off a virtuoso talent by painting on a curved board the illusions created by a convex mirror.

SAVED FOR LAST: the baptistery. Best ten buildings I've ever seen? This is on the list. A pink marble tower, octagonal in shape and sweetly proportioned, four stories with arches rise to one blank story, then Gothic cupolas on top, columns slender as femurs, and four doors in the cardinal directions. "It was built for baptisms, I know," Ed says, "but doesn't it look more like something out of a fairy tale?"

"Yes! A wizard waving a wand could step out on that loggia and cast a spell."

At various times of the day, the soapy peaches-and-cream marble turns carmine, and as pink as the inside of a shell, and dusty white and rose. This can't be real, but is.

The building is a book. The carved panels on the outside tell all the stories of monsters, dragons, sirens, unicorns. Once inside, I have to sit down. I'll just say it—I want to cry. The baptistery is open all the way to the top. Rings of porticos, then under an umbrella of ribbed marble struts dividing the dome into sixteen sections, all walls are completely frescoed. I'm inside a kaleidoscope. The seasons, the zodiac, the Bible stories, the symbols, the mysterious alignments with the solstice so that the sun strikes the right place on the right date. There's the Madonna holding a playful baby who pulls on her scarf. There's John the Baptist baptizing Jesus.

And oh, a pleasure of winter travel—we have the place to ourselves for an hour. Antelami, architect back in 1196, thank you.

As we leave, Ed says, "You had a major attack of Stendhal Syndrome in there?" We realize we've not talked at all. We walk over to the Museo Diocesano, where amid the many artworks discovered during excavations in the piazza and duomo, they have an excellent interactive digital display of the baptistery, where you can see the art up close, all the way to the top.

YOU CAN GAUGE the wealth of a town by how many shops you see for fancy baby clothes. Parma's *centro storico,* historic center, has many. I stop to admire the tiny camel-hair coats, velvet dresses with lace collars, the little smocked slips, and rabbit-fur hats. I've never seen so many shoe and clothing shops anywhere—not ubiquitous brands, but individual stores with well-made classic clothing. Where's the fantasy and drama of Florence's stylish shops? I feel in a bit of a time warp. There's a hat store, its sign in nineteenth-century lettering. Borsolinos and tweed caps for the hunt, women's cloches in felt.

Many babies are ferried about in those high carriages instead of collapsible strollers. Their mothers are pretty, with small features and shiny hair. Another bookstore. I'm happy to find two stores specializing in handmade papers. Old print shops, endless high-end jewelry, and curious shops crowded with medical models, leather-bound books, ship models, and music boxes. Ed, a cyclist, finds out about Italia Veloce— where you can design your own handmade bike. Teatro Regio, the grand opera house, testifies to the active musical culture that thrives here. You see more images of Verdi than of the Madonna.

We stop for espresso. "We could stay. We haven't seen everything we wanted to," I say. We love the cafés, this one with ceiling paintings in blue and gold. Four old men, all dressed from the nearby tweedy shops, sit at a table discussing the world. On the other side of the bar, six women meet. Laughter. Clatter of cups. Someone stepping outside to smoke. The barista, "Are you Americans?" The men take out a pack of cards. It's not the first time or the last.

Ed throws back his espresso in a gulp. He's learned to like *ristretto*, the essence of coffee. "Want to split one of those puffy things with cream inside?"

Later, another wine bar, another dinner. We do the unthinkable and return to Angiol d'Or, forsaking the chance to try another new place. But this just seems like our place in Parma.

WE ARE TAKING the train to Cortona. We change in Bologna, again in Florence where we grab panini in time to board the slow mover that stops at every crossroads, towns I can tick off as easily as I anticipated all the do-wa-diddies between Fitzgerald and Macon when I was growing up in Georgia, my mother barreling down the two-lane highway in our blue Oldsmobile.

If I stepped off the train at any juncture, I'd find an alluring place to explore. Bare winter hills zoom by the window. Stiff wash on a line. Persimmons still hanging like gold lanterns in a bare tree. Isolated castle on a green hill—I know it's cold inside. What luck to have seen Parma. Now I always can go there in my mind. I flip open a guidebook. What's next?

NOTES:

Shops for handmade papers: Cartaria Parmense Ferramola, Via F. Maestri, 5; and Cartasogno, via N. Sauro, 22.

Old books and treasures: Credula Postero Antichità Libri e Curiosità: medical models, leather books, dolls, sleds, stuff! Ship models, globes, music boxes, old photos. Via N. Sauro, 16a.

Italia Veloce: Design your own bicycle. Stradello San Girolamo, 2.

I'm a long admirer of *The Splendid Table: Recipes from Emilia-Romagna, the Heartland of Northern Italian Food* by Lynne Rossetto Kasper.

Liguria ✹

Camogli

Camogli—possibly from Ca' Moglie, meaning houses of wives left at home when fishermen set off from this curve of coast. Gelato and pastry shops line the beach promenade. Behind the street, astonishingly tall buildings rise. Apricot, russet, gold, cream, ocher, these dense seven, even nine, story buildings face the sea, another layer stepping up the hill that ascends abruptly in back. Did they choose bright colors so home could be easily recognized by the men returning from sea? If you threw open the shutters, you could look far out over the water as a schooner cut the horizon, or a *leudo,* a compact boat with large sails, headed home from what was known as "the cruise of one hundred days," the length of an anchovy fishing voyage. I imagine a *leudo* pulled up on the beach, greeted by the wives and children rushing down from the steep hill, as men begin unloading barrels of salted fish.

If you've ever looked at a calendar of amazing photos of Italy, or watched romantic Italian movies, you've dreamed of Camogli. This is my third time here. I come back to soak in the blues of the sea, walk the sweet crescent of beach, sit in the sun with a lemonade, and admire the vividly painted houses from which generations of wives watched for signs of their husbands' return.

AFTER WE CHECK in at Cenobio dei Dogi, surely the most gracious hotel along the coast, Ed takes off on his walk. He has an exercise streak of three hundred and something days. Nothing deters him. I relish the time alone. How often in life can you sit on a balcony overlooking the Gulf of Paradise? The beach, empty in November, a castle and dome in the distance, a clock tower, the stacked buildings painted with trompe-l'oeil fantasies, then above, silky green hills, sky. How many layers of beauty? One fishing boat putting out across the water, a few gulls. Quiet. This much beauty: I feel a quick sting of tears.

AFTER GAZING BLANKLY at the view, I pick up *The Rain Came Last and Other Stories,* intending to find a calm spot with a view for a little reading. Just right—a bench under a well-tended umbrella pine. Which is better? Looking up into the sculptured branches, then at the smoothness of the sea's surface, or reading the prose of Niccolò Tucci? The writing is as nuanced and wild as Nabokov's. I choose all three. Gazing, reading, meditating. After an hour of taking deep breaths of salt-stung air, I shut the book. The stories are transporting, but right now, I want to be here.

BEYOND THE PICTURESQUE Castello della Dragonara, at the quay, I stop under a *Madonnina,* a shrine to the Madonna, the glass-covered image surrounded by a border of sea shells. I hardly can see Mary for the wavy reflection of Camogli houses, a doubling. I listen to the dings in the riggings of boats in the small harbor—red and blue boats, a man hunched over his nets, a few larger trawlers, lowly rowboats; we are eons away from the early Camogli's powerful fleets of tall sails. *Va bene.* Fish still rule. Menus list an excess of fresh squid, and other marvels. The grand celebration of the year takes place every second weekend in May when three tons of fish are cooked in a four-meter-diameter frying pan, blessed by a priest, then fed to all in a free feast.

. . .

EVEN NOW IN November, we have lunch outside under an awning. The waiter aims a water pistol at pigeons that encroach on our table. With the burden of a bird phobia, I am often driven to duck and cover. The waiter hates the pigeons. Nothing frightens me more than the chortling scavengers. The waiter has become my *deus ex machina*. He brings us bountiful salads and lobster and crisp white wine; then he takes aim at a pigeon's tail feathers.

WHEN YOU ENTER Museo Marinaro, you encounter big glass cases lining what feels like old schoolrooms with wan light. Large cabinets filled with objects display local seafaring history. Ships in bottles, sextants, barometers, log books, accounting portfolios in distinctive penmanship, telescopes, even needles used to mend sails—all the useful accouterments. But the 178 paintings commissioned by proud ship owners grab my attention the most. There are schooners, brigs, paddle steamers, pontoons, and fishing boats. I inspect the ship models made by seamen. (Imagine, in the tall houses, how many other relics remain as family treasures.) Who sailed away, who waited? I would like to have one of the ships in a bottle, crafted by men at sea, the precision giving shape to the days on that three-month anchovy run. A ship in a bottle cannot sink.

THE FORMAL HOTEL dining room, Ristorante Il Doge, must be dreamy in summer, all the windows overlooking the sea and the tables attended by such friendly staff. Off-season travelers, we're alone except for one other couple seated in a distant corner. I want to wave to them. Three waiters stand by to top off the water glasses and refill the wine. Ed and I have a leisurely dinner of tender gnocchi with pesto and mixed grilled fish as we talk about the Ligurian poet Eugenio Montale. He plucked words directly from the land and seascape: a sun-warmed garden wall, carob tree, flowering myrtle, iridescent scales of a dying fish, medlar fruit, the waters' somnolent blues. Place *will* have its way with you.

I love hotels and happily could stay in this one for a decompression week, strolling their gardens, eating on a terrace with panoramic views, and sunning at the pool. The proverbial *dolce far niente*. When do we ever achieve that?

THE GREAT ACTIVITY of Camogli is walking. First, around town to admire the faux architectural flourishes painted on the houses, to pause at Revello for a warm slice of tomato focaccia, to look up at windows where women shake out their dust cloths, to photograph the fruit stand's glowing clementines, tangerines, and oranges wrapped in tissue, to stop into Santa Maria Assunta with its patterned marble floor, its frescoed ceiling, and its many crystal chandeliers that sparkle in midair like ships floating on the sea.

The real walking is up. On an earlier trip, we took the hike to San Rocco for wide views. You can proceed farther to the twelfth-century San Nicolò di Capodimonte, built over a much earlier (345) chapel. You then reach Punta Chiappa for a swim, and onward (about five hours total) all the way to San Fruttuoso and Portofino, where you can hop on a boat to bring you back. In warmer weather, many boats ply this coast, making it easy to explore without driving.

OF THE MANY seafood restaurants along the water, we chose La Rotonda, a curved structure jutting almost into the surf. We are seated right next to the bank of windows. A pile of rocks is meant to stem the tide but still the water comes crashing against the glass. "What's it like in a storm?" Ed asks the owner. He shakes his head, rolls his eyes, tells us about the fresh catch of the day.

"Is the Mediterranean rising as quickly as other seas?"

"Now it is. Yes," the owner says, "it's getting *pericoloso*." Dangerous. Splat! We're startled at every other bite of the fritto misto and grilled vegetables. The place is packed with locals celebrating a birthday. The birthday girl, obviously surprised as she came in, didn't seem too pleased. She is dressed casually and everyone else isn't. Probably she would have done something with her hair. But soon she's in the mood, and we feel included.

We'll never dine closer to the sea.

. . .

OF ALL THE pleasures, my stand-out joy in Camogli is our visit to the
ex voto collection at Santuario di Nostra Signora del Boschetto. I've never
seen this church mentioned on a website or in a guidebook. A friend
who stayed here for a couple of weeks told me about it.

Ex voto means "from the gift." These small paintings—naïve, primitive—on tin or wood almost always have PGR written on them, *per
grazia ricevuta,* for grace received. If someone survived a terrible accident,
divine intervention was acknowledged. The Virgin or a saint saved you
from what surely was fatal. You commissioned a painting to record this
miracle. Each one is a gesture of thanks. You seek out the person in
town who can paint and you tell your story. You hang your *ex voto* in the
church where you can visit and remember. When you simply recovered
from an illness, you may have hung a tin liver or heart or foot but your
ex voto shows a more drastic event. Grace.

My daughter and I have collected *ex votos* for years. We've found
around sixty, each one precious. We have many that we like to point
to, and often to toast. Here's to the bride, shot as she left the church.
Here's to the man who burned in the fireplace. Here's to the family
slumped around the table, poisoned, as the priest knocks on the door.
We're attached to these scenes of a woman in bed with her jaw tied in
a kerchief, a child bloodied on the ground, a cart pinning down a man
flailing his arms. Some are crude, some finely executed. They're blunt.
The perspective is flat. They manage to be both literal and metaphysical.

This collection at Santuario di Nostra Signora del Boschetto brings
me much closer to Camogli. Here are the tall houses I've admired, but a
man is falling from the fifth story. Women are looking out from second-
and third-story windows as he hurtles downward headfirst. Laundry
hangs from other windows. The action takes place on only a fourth of
the painting. The rest shows trees in the garden, another house, and
Maria in the sky. I was reminded of Brueghel's Icarus painting. The boy
falls as his wax wings melt and the farmer plowing his field does not
notice. Life goes on while you are *in extremis.*

Others re-create ships tossed on high waves or listing in a storm,
a large ship bearing down on a small one, and a man overboard being

carried in the current. This is the flip side of the pristine paintings in the museum. I've been so obsessed with ship paintings, and models, and the sea itself. Now I witness the odd fact that these houses posed hazards enough for those not in peril on the sea. Many of the *ex votos* show a child falling off a wall. A boy with bloodied head sprawls on the floor while another child, who looks like a homunculus, rushes down the stairs toward him. Did he push the boy? I think so. Oh, Queen of Heaven, how can this happen? One man falls from scaffolding on a ship-building site. Falling. So many falling.

The main artists were Domenico Gavarrone in the mid-nineteenth century and Angelo Arp after 1889. I wonder where they lived in Camogli. They're known, but the norm for these little treasures is the anonymous local painter commissioned by someone with a powerful gratitude. Faced with the divine in every painting, the *ex voto* painters led enviable lives.

This is a homey church. The caretaker sweeps and dusts and wants to chat. At the end of the display, tiny finches chatter and flutter in a cage. Who does not hope for miracles?

Varese Ligure

We drive up into the hills above the Ligurian Riviera, surprised at how sharply they rise into real mountains. I think of deer as scarce in Italy, but one with two curling, pointed horns leaps across the road with a don't-hit-me look cast at Ed. Another, strolling along the verge, gazes at us, spooked. Tall spires rising out of the forest tell us there are towns but we pass few. "This looks like northern Europe," Ed says. "Even the bell towers look as though we're in Germany."

"Could be anywhere. We could be in the Smokies." But we're not. We're en route to Varese Ligure, chosen because it's one of the Arancione Bandiere, the Orange Flag, sites. And because of a pasta tradition I've read about.

For a country experience on a farm, we've chosen a simple *agriturismo* about sixteen kilometers from Varese. The road is hard to find; we're deep into the wilds. Finally, a woman with a big dog greets us warmly and I'm already thrilled to see sheep and horses. We get out in a muddy driveway. Sharp wind hits hard. She takes us into an outbuilding fitted with two guest rooms. Nice enough. Simple. But cold.

"We've just turned on the heat," she explains. She points out the window where a man is gathering wood from a pile. "The furnace is wood-fed," she says.

I put my hand on the radiator. Ice.

We still have a couple of hours before we drive out for dinner. Nothing to do but crawl into the refrigerated sheets under two layers of blankets.

Ed grabs a damp quilt out of the *armadio.* "It's colder inside than it is out. She said we are the first guests. This building has been unheated all fall. It's not going to warm up." We try to read. My nose is dripping.

"Let's drive into Varese and find a drink before dinner. It'll be warmer when we get back." He dives into his jeans.

THE NARROW ROAD dips and curves. Black dark. We are soon in Varese Ligure. Deserted. On a back street of the village, we find the Albergo Amici, whose restaurant is mentioned in our guidebook. We order an *aperitivo* in the high-ceilinged, empty dining room. A waiter sits by a stove reading a magazine. It's warm. "Why didn't we stay here?" Ed wonders.

"It looked dated on the website. I could take dated easily at this point."

Ah, dinner. The redeeming hour! Who cares if no else is here? When Ed asks the waiter what she recommends, she says, "*I croxetti.*" The little crosses. And yes, this is what we came for.

I've read about this Ligurian pasta formed into flat disks and stamped with a floral or geometric design. Formerly noble families had their *stemme,* family crests, carved into the small wooden rounds. The first molds probably were crosses of the Knights Templar and the monastic orders who pressed crosses into the dough, just as they were slashed into bread about to be baked. "Now the forms are rare," she tells us, "but you can visit one of the last makers in Liguria. Right near the church."

The pasta is tossed with a light pine nut sauce. In a mortar, the nuts are crushed to a paste with garlic, herbs, olive oil (or a little butter).

Some add a dash of milk to thin the consistency but here I don't detect that. The taste is rich, though surely the recipe comes from the *cucina povera,* the poor kitchen.

WE MAKE OUR way back in the Stygian night. We've left a light on in our room. Otherwise the farm is dark and we must use the flashlights on our phones. "Uh-oh. No one stoking that wood furnace," I surmise. And, yes, the room has not warmed a single degree. The bed feels damp and frosty. Ed speaks of winter in Minnesota, when he shared an un-heated room with his brother. Heat was supposed to seep up through a vent to the upstairs. It didn't. We burrow under all the blankets. "They know it's freezing, otherwise they wouldn't have left so many covers," I reason.

WE LEAVE WITHOUT showering the next morning. As we load the trunk, the owner comes out in a light sweater. It must be warm in her house. She blithely hopes we enjoyed our stay and ever-polite Ed thanks her, but I say, "We were very cold." The smell of manure is strong.

"Let's go." We speed out of there. I refrain from giving her the finger.

BACK IN SWEET Varese Ligure, it's market day. We admire the circu-lar plan of the streets lined with houses painted pistachio, coral, pink, ocher. The castle is also rounded; the humpback of the six-hundred-year-old bridge is a half-moon. And the form of the *croxetti* molds is round, too. We find Pietro Picetti at via Pieve, 15. He doesn't seem to mind being interrupted. He shows us historic molds and ones he makes. They're small, somewhere between a Ritz cracker and a hamburger bun. The carved stamp fits into a holder that you use to cut the disks. At the lathe, he demonstrates his carving skill. He allows us to buy a grape-cluster design carved into pear wood and finished in beeswax.

The appealing town is built along the gentle river Vara. The houses on either side must be snapped up the second one goes up for sale. The market spreads along the main street. Behind the stands, there's a nice linen store and a fabulous bread and pastry shop where we buy focaccia with pesto and pastries with ham and cheese. The bar at the end of the street is teeming with locals who've paused for a hot drink while shopping. One of my favorite things about cold weather in Italy is a busy bar on market day. Everyone bundled, the smell of wool just out of storage, the banter among men, and the efficiency of women accomplishing their shopping. I love to linger, feeling a part of this ritual but also separate. "*Americani*," we answer when asked if we are German or French. It's moving to me, how often the Italians say they love America.

We watch people buying honey, sweaters, jeans, and glowing autumn squashes and pumpkins at the market. I know that each person has a wooden form for making *croxetti* at home.

Genova

En route to Cinque Terre, Portofino, or other seductive Ligurian destinations, travelers usually bypass this ancient city by the sea. Why does no one go to Genova?

We have checked into Locanda di Palazzo Cicala, across a small piazza from the black-banded façade of Cattedrale San Lorenzo. Our room feels loft-like and airy, simple, too: tall windows, white sofa and chairs, and two huge beds, also dressed all in white. I hardly can stir myself to go out; this is a perfect place to read and plan. Ed, frowning at a map, says, "Prepare to be lost," and out we go.

We're near a zone of butchers, produce stands, and cramped shops selling olive oil, lentils, legumes, and slabs of dried cod. At one *frutta e verdure,* I see a scrawled sign: *Le signore che palpano la frutta saranno sottoposte allo stesso trattamento da parte del fruttivendolo.* The women who palpate the fruit will be subjected to the same treatment on the part of the fruit seller.

We're starving. A tiny trattoria lures us in for a feast of chickpea fritters, grilled vegetables, and *branzino,* sea bass, with lemon. Wine at lunch contributes to read-away-the-afternoons, but today we share a carafe of effervescent house white.

THE CENTRO STORICO, historic center, quickly overwhelms us—a warren of narrow lanes called *caruggi*. They twist, turn, dead-end, branch. A maze! Each is lined with shops of claustrophobic density and heavy aromas, bins of clothing, musical instruments, bolts of African cloth, and button and ribbon displays. Albanese, African, Romanian, and Arabic voices ring out, music spills into the streets, and shoppers push into fishmongers, stalls selling plastic housewares from China, shoe repair shops, tailors, and brightly lit stores gleaming with cheap watches and electronics. Not like Naples, not like Palermo: I'm in a souk! This is the largest medieval center in Europe. We're lost and might as well like it. At least there's no traffic, only the zing-zing of bicycle bells.

WE SURGE INTO a lather of old-world cafés with bentwood chairs and painted ceilings, hip new cafés serving green juices and French-looking pastries. Art galleries—I've never seen as many anywhere. The fast food tempts me at Antica Sciamadda and Antica Sà Pesta, specializing in tasty *torte,* a thick pastry filled with cheese and chard or other vegetables, and *farinata,* huge golden moons of chickpea batter poured onto a metal disk and run into a hot pizza oven. How can anything this simple be so good? Take it and go. How many focaccia, pastry, and snack shops? Hundreds!

We're drawn to Pietro Romanengo fu Stefano, where they've made chocolates since 1780. Glass and wood cabinets could as well be displaying emerald brooches and diamond necklaces. The two women meting out these treasures, though, are as serious as if they're serving subpoenas. Even Ed's enthusiasm cannot elicit a smile. He selects candied *nespoli* (loquats), sugared lemon and orange peels, marron glacé, and dark chocolates. We walk out, untying the box before we've closed the door.

Uphill, down to a glimpse of water, radiating streets, a scary lane with drunks leaning on walls and prostitutes hanging out of doors and windows. Dark alleys, slices of bright sunlight. Sun-baked, wiry men from Morocco, paler ones from eastern Europe, exceptionally tall

Africans, veiled women, and others wrapped in bright prints. Wash hanging on racks. This is a raucous port where you don't know what to expect where, or when. Even the Italian sounds foreign, a clattering dialect harsher than the more rhythmic Tuscan we're used to.

I RESERVE A table at La Forchetta Curiosa. Atmospheric, full of regulars who're greeting the owner with hugs, this is the true-blue cozy *osteria*. Wild salad greens with squid, linguine with broccoli and anchovies, rolled *branzino* with pistachios—and what's that: *totani ripieni di boraggine e crema di patate al limone?* Calamari stuffed with borage, lemon, and potatoes. That's for Ed, no doubt.

I'm surprised to see *cappon magro* on the menu. I translate this as lean capon but when the waiter sets one down on an adjacent table, I see that it's more interesting than a skinny chicken. *Magro* refers to Catholic days without meat. *Cappon* mocks the chickens the rich were enjoying, while fishermen's families made do with what the sea offered. Pieces of hardtack are soaked in salted water and vinegar, then layered into a pyramid with seafood, olives, vegetables, and eggs. Often topped with a lobster, it's served with caper and anchovy sauce. The genius of *la cucina povera.*

I decide on ravioli with pesto and creamed potato. Are babies of Liguria fed a tiny spoon of pesto for their first non-milk meal? Is it the most enduring memory of family feasts? I don't want pesto often, but in Liguria, it's unctuous and fresh. I'll have some of everything, please.

Perusing the desserts, Ed says, "What is *caglio*?"

"Let's ask." And so, we get to meet *caglio*, aka *prescinseua*, aka *quagliata.* The owner gives us the story: a soft, somewhat acidic local cheese, not easy to find, as it is perishable and production is small. It's made from milk of cows grazing for centuries in the hills above Camogli.

"Is it only for desserts?" Santa Madonna, no. It has been used by Genovese on focaccia, in fillings of vegetable *torte,* in nut sauces for pasta, in pesto, stuffed inside vegetable fritters, and baked with anchovies. The owner serves a white bowl of bright berry sauce over what looks like ricotta or buratta. Tart berries and the slightly sour cheese remind me that Italian desserts often shock with their faint sweetness. A happy end, memorable place, memorable dinner.

. . .

AS WE WALK around town, we check menus posted outside restaurants. Seeing ingredients not usually on Italian menus—ginger, saffron, mustard, and curry—reminds me of the far ports reached by Ligurian trading ships. A window display of patterned cotton draws me into Deca. I meet Gabriella, who tells me that her hand-printed cotton bedspreads and tablecloths are called *mezzari*. The word comes from the Arab *mizar,* meaning to hide or cover. Gabriella shows me the carved wooden stamps used to ink the designs. Imported into Genova from India in the 1600s, *mezarri* became fashionable among noblewomen, who wore the fanciful designs as mantillas and wraps. As silk later became available, the rich abandoned the *mezzari* and the cloth was taken up by lower classes, eventually becoming part of the folk clothing of Genova. Women wore the prints as shawls. The designs (especially the tree of life, with branches, exotic animals, and fruits) were believed to bring luck to brides. Workers and sailors, she tells us, wore cotton workpants dyed the *bleu de Gênes,* blue jeans. This "blue of Genova" came from indigo plantations in India. I buy three *mezarri* for summer parties under the pergola. When I set my table at Bramasole, I will remember the women of Genova.

ED AND I walk down to the sprawling Antico Porto, recently revived under the auspices of native son, architect Renzo Piano. He's designed Il Bigo, a giant white derrick that raises you up for a view of the harbor. It mimics working cranes of the port. His, too, is the famous aquarium that draws all the schoolchildren of Italy, and a hands-on science museum. In a revised cotton warehouse, we find a bookstore and Eataly, a good place to slow down and browse the plethora of Italian foods. The elaborately boxed *panettone* for Christmas are arriving, at least a hundred brands of this traditional brioche-type bread dotted with raisins and candied fruit.

This is the first sighting of other November tourists. A few Dutch and English people are eating focaccia and pizza, or stocking up on risotto, olive oil, and jars of pesto. At the far end of the warehouse, we find a table at Il Marin, with a panoramic view. Everything is perfection. I get to try the classic Ligurian tortelli with pesto, green beans, and potatoes. Ed prefers raw fish, and lobster with endive. The menu is adventurous: frog with Jerusalem artichokes, *finanziera dal mare,* a dish made with the *quinto quarto* of fish. *Quinto quarto,* the fifth quarter, usually refers to meat offal, specifically what's left after the prime cuts. I assume this fish dish contains the heads and other usually discarded bits. Ed is attracted to the scallops with little green beans and something called *taccole.* He tells me, "The word translates as 'jackdaw.'"

"Surely not. That's some kind of crow." But after *quinto quarto* of fish, I'm ready to believe anything.

GENOVA IS UNLIKE any other European city. Spokes from here wheel around the Mediterranean and beyond. They lived like kings and queens, those merchants of the seas, in opulent *palazzi* lining Strada Nuova. Who decided in the sixteenth century that they would all build along a new street? "Who's frescoing your house?" must have been the *aperitivo* banter of the time. The area around what is now via Garibaldi was Europe's first housing development. Fact: One hundred and fifty *palazzi* remain; forty-two are designated UNESCO World Heritage sites.

Pietro Paolo Rubens, as the Flemish painter signed himself while in Italy, painted the palazzo builders, the Genovese nobility, portraits that fascinate me more for the splendid clothing worn by the subjects than for the sometimes pinched and ordinary faces. Rubens became fascinated with palazzo architecture when he lived in Genova. I have the volume he published in 1622, *Palazzi di Genova,* drawings (not his) that record floor plans, room uses, gardens, and elevations of the most important homes—those owned by the *rolli,* first families listed on the city's "rolls." He intended his publication to be a source of inspiration to architects in the rest of Europe. He admired the style of a "perfect cube" and a central living room. By the time a second volume was printed, grand squares had been superseded by rectangles with courtyards.

I'm glad I read this book before coming to Genova; I had acquaintance with the floor plans, their niches, friezes, marble balconies, trompe-l'oeil loggias, balustrades, and sculptures—the architecture that reveals how a life is lived. The grand *palazzi* provide, too, a contrast with the crowded, serpentine clusters of housing for the hoi polloi in the medieval *centro*. (I wonder, *where would I have lived?* Oh, perhaps in a stone cottage on the shore.)

Is there a book on the frescoes of Genova? The houses were decorated, not usually with predominant religious subjects but with maps, battles, and mythological themes. The owners also collected art, and not just Italian art. An astonishing patrimony accumulated in the *palazzi*. Visiting dignitaries, popes, and princes would stay in someone's palace. Each had a grade, like Michelin stars; the more important the visitor, the fancier the accommodations assigned by the government. Imagine a courier dropping off a note: You'll be entertaining the king of Spain's third cousin for two months.

Some of the *palazzi* have become apartments; many are schools or part of the university, others are banks. Some are residences still belonging to the last of the nobility. Many are open to visitors. First, we visit Palazzo Rosso, then Palazzo Bianco, overwhelmed in both by the richness of the art, then Palazzo Tursi, one of Italy's most treasured.

Have I used the word *overwhelmed* several times? A recurring word for how I feel in Genova, especially after entering Palazzo Rosso: six floors of opulent living space and paintings. The sixth floor opens onto a walled roof where you can see the sweep of Genova to the sea. The art—Van Dyck, Veronese, Dürer, Ribera, Tiziano (Titian), Lotto, and many Genovese masters I've never known before. One is Andrea Sacchi, whose *Daedalus and Icarus* captures a fraught and tender moment as Daedalus is tying wax wings on Icarus's slender body. At this moment neither of them knows how it will end. A dreary underlying message: Don't reach for the sun. How regarded must have been Gregorio De Ferrari and Domenico Piola, who painted the four ceiling frescoes in the rooms named for each season. It would be nice, wouldn't it, to have a winter room, a spring room, others for summer and fall. Looking at De Ferrari's work, I'm not surprised to learn that when he worked in Parma he copied Correggio's frescoes. They share the style of dynamic, floating forms and bold color. Piola was top-tier in Genova for the last half of the 1600s. Such immense fame, now faded. Palazzo Rosso was bombed in World War Two, as were many historic places in Genova. The restoration is seamless.

• • •

THE ART IS even more compelling in Palazzo Bianco: Rubens, Zurbarán, Memling, Cranach the Elder, Van Cleve, Brueghel. Bounty from the noble bankers and canny sea-traders, all of whom seem to have been enchanted with art. Two of my favorite Italians are here, too: Pontormo and Filippino Lippi. Most magnetic, however, is Caravaggio's *Ecce Homo, Behold the Man.* Dark, like all Caravaggios, except for the vulnerable torso of Christ, whose naked chest is bathed in a luminous, buttery light. He looks not at all transcendent this moment after being crowned with thorns. Downcast eyes, thin frame, his suffering private. The torturer's expression haunts me with its ambiguous mix of pity and enjoyment. The face of Pilate is thought to be a Caravaggio self-portrait. I hope not. It's awful to think he might put his face onto that ironic, cruel character.

ART SATURATES ME quickly. Four hours, I'm done.

OUR ROOM IS a haven. High ceilings lift the spirit. Ed is reading about Renzo Piano. If only we could invite him to dinner! I'm reading the trusty *Blue Guide to Liguria,* then about Charles Dickens's sojourn here. "Beautiful confusion," he noted. When I fall into a nap, the iPad crashes to the floor. A hazard books don't share.

BY THE MORNING of the third day, it's clear that we are not going to see nearly all of Genova. This city needs you for a week, at least. We are not going to visit the aquarium, nor Piano's biosphere of tropical plants, nor the Galata Museo's history of seafaring exhibits. We are not going to climb to the top of La Lanterna, the second-oldest lighthouse in Europe, and we won't be able to see the residential neighborhoods on the sea. I am especially sorry we can't get to the cemetery of Sant'Ilario in the near-suburb of Nervi. Its nineteenth-century sculpture of mourning was on my list, as was an architectural attraction in another cemetery: Carlo Scarpa's tombs for the Galli family. (Ed doesn't share my interest in how the dead are buried. But what else is more revealing about a culture?) As the list of what remains to be seen lengthens, the desire to return takes root. When?

• • •

AT THE ERSATZ house of Christopher Columbus, a busload of German tourists crowds the entrance. Believe this was his home and you also can believe that Juliet's balcony survives in Verona. But this may well be the right area; Columbus's father is said to have been the gatekeeper at Porta Soprana, the entrance between two sculptural round towers in the fortified walls built in 1155. Turning away from the modest hovel, what we find nearby is the delicate cloister of Sant'Andrea, untended and unvisited, a haunting outline of delicate columns surrounding a weedy center. No trace of the original church remains but the cloister feels holy.

AS WE WALK, walk, and walk, we stop into various churches—and there are many. All the *rolli* families buried themselves grandly. Most are elaborate and dark: Ashen air hangs like cobwebs from high windows where light bursts in. By the time you've been in Genova a few days, you're familiar with the names of local gentry; Doria, Pallavicino, Grimaldi, Spinola, Adorno, Brignole Sale are carved on *palazzi,* tombs, monuments, and plaques. The harmonious Piazza San Matteo memorializes the powerful Doria dynasty with a black-and-white banded church surrounded by several *palazzi.* The black and white signifies importance in the city; not just anyone was allowed that distinctive design. In Genova's major church, dedicated to San Lorenzo, you come upon the Grimaldi and Fieschi tombs. San Lorenzo isn't Genova's patron saint (that's John the Baptist) but he gets top billing anyway. Above the receding striped columns of the major portal, there Lorenzo lies on a grill, enduring his martyrdom. (Yes, patron saint of chefs.) At either end, two small figures appear to be ramping up the heat with anvils.

San Lorenzo has been a cathedral since 1006 and fate since has brought a series of revisions. Major construction took place from 1118 until 1130: Romanesque, with interruptions of French Gothic. How impossible to absorb the church's wealth of symbols, didactic programs, ornaments, and iconography. But the religious bookstore, Libreria San Paolo, on the same piazza, gets me started with a brochure called "Cathedral of Saint Laurence." I spend a morning with this. I am thinking of something Margaret Visser wrote about another church in her brilliant book, *The Geometry of Love:* "Meaning is intentional: this building has been made in order to communicate with the people in it . . . The building is trying to speak; not listening to what it has to say is a form of barbarous inattention, like admiring a musical instrument while caring nothing for music."

Inside, I find paintings of San Lorenzo's life, including one by local artist Giovanni Andrea Ansaldo. San Lorenzo restores sight to Lucillus, an imprisoned blind pagan. Especially bountiful are the many paintings of the Virgin Mary, capturing tender moments as when she holds the Child and John the Baptist leans over and kisses the tiny foot. Endless repetitions of religious images can engender numbness in the brain, but now and again, such as now, one makes you feel washed clean. Wandering this cabinet of curiosities, I love getting to know artists I was unaware of: Luca Cambiaso, Giovanni Battista Castello (Il Bergamasco), Domenico Fiasella, Giovanni Battista Paggi. Genova! What astonishing flowering over a long period of time.

The word *overwhelming* comes to mind again. From Byzantine frescoes to a crystal plate from the Last Supper—such a heritage. Who would expect to see a blue dish that held the head of John the Baptist, and an unexploded bomb that hit the church in World War Two?

ON THE EDGE of the *centro storico,* we walk into the shock of Piazza de Ferrari—a grand fountain, vast open space (sky!), opera house, arcaded shops, cafés, and the enormous Palazzo Ducale. Developed in 1870, after the unification of Italy, this area is where Genova joins the modern world. Cars, taxis, buses! Busy via XX Settembre branches off from here, a long street of small shops and the Mercato Orientale, which would drive even the most reluctant cook to the kitchen. The "Eastern" market is one of the greatest markets in Italy, a two-story structure packed with everything that swims in the sea, cheeses, armfuls of basil, meats. Mounds of endive, Jerusalem artichokes, primitive red radicchio with twisting white ribs that look plucked from under water, escarole, dozens of lettuce—all prove the appeal of the autumn kitchen. Worth bringing home: bags of dried porcini mushrooms and pine nuts.

The grand bazaar—you can't help but photograph piles of *broccolo romano,* tangerines, radishes, and black cabbage. Squid, fish flashing iridescent under the lights, slick calamari, cockles, mussels, alive ho! Although there are artichokes up from the south, missing this time of year are the coveted thorny, sweet, and tender artichokes of Albenga in Liguria. (We must come back in March.) We buy a few *annurca,* not local but brought in from Campania in the south. These apples are harvested when green; they can't ripen if left unpicked. Because of short stems, they drop off. They're set out on straw or hemp to ripen, and must be turned every few days. Ripe, they're rosy and round, and smell like apple essence.

GENOVESE EAT WELL. Their food is fresh and true-to-source. I make a list of favorites from *pasticcherie* (pastry shops) and cafés so far:

Almond panna cotta

Tortina di patate e gorgonzola, a little potato and Gorgonzola tart

Chocolate and orange tart

Shellfish salad with puntarelle (a bitter, wild green)

Salad of shaved raw artichokes with bresaola and Parmigiano

Torta of rice and saffron

Torta of escarole

WE FIND LA Buca di San Matteo, near the Doria complex. "Ah, a date-night restaurant," I say, slipping off my jacket. Softly lit, high-backed upholstered chairs, a place for intimate conversation. For a few minutes, we pretend we are meeting secretly, he down from Milan, me in from Florence. A torrid evening ahead. But soon we fall to discussing what we will choose from the tempting menu. We share an order of very light *pansoti* (like ravioli) with rich walnut sauce, then Ed lights on the tuna with grilled polenta and I opt for chickpea purée with grilled shrimp.

We've missed as much as we've seen. At least we have eaten our way across the city. We can't possibly order dessert tonight but we do—who could turn away from creamy zabaglione semifreddo with a crunch of chocolate and hazelnut brittle? And we might as well taste the chestnut mousse flavored with orange as we polish off a liter of house wine.

AT ALL HOURS, as we come and go from our hotel, a violinist stands before the great portal of San Lorenzo. He's good. He sends his music as a gift into the air of the ancient piazza. I think of his parents. All those music lessons, all the hope. And this is where he plays by heart—with exuberance and joy. We leave euros in his instrument case and he nods. We nod back. *Grazie per la musica!*

T oscana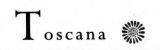

Scarperia

In the Mugello, north of Florence, the landscape rapidly changes. Geometric lines of vineyards defining natural slopes, and iconic terraced olive groves reshape into rugged woods and open fields. Villages often are not as appealing as those to the south. But the Mugello is Medici country— their villas remain—and they selected it for good reasons. Trading routes, yes, but also dramatic hills, bracing air, sweet rivers, hunting, and surely these blazing yellow poplars brushing their plumes against the sky.

On the way to Scarperia early this morning, we detour only fifteen kilometers to see the house we once rented for two weeks in Vicchio. Right down the road was the bridge where, so the story goes, Cimabue discovered Giotto, a shepherd boy drawing a sheep on the side of a stone. We find the bridge again. Nothing has changed in thirty years—the pretty little river Ensa still flows, as it must have when the artists met here. The house we rented only has a new coat of paint. The misty pastures are the same ones I walked in. Time warps, as it often does in Italy.

My daughter might still be drying her hair in the upstairs bedroom. The boy might still be here, trying to render the bulk of a ram onto a stone with a sharp rock. Does the refrigerator still ice over like an igloo, giving a big shock when you try to pry open the door?

WHAT REMAINS OF travels when decades pass? "Remember, that's where we picked string beans?" Ed slows in front of Villa Il Cedro.

"And we helped a farmer catch his pig." A ridiculous image of Ed, arms out, in hot pursuit of a grunting pig flashes in my mind. "What would you have done if you'd caught it?"

We're driving through the attractive and busy town of Borgo San Lorenzo, recalling with zest the *rosticceria* where rows of roasting chickens dripped fat onto potatoes below—forever after the paragon of crispy potatoes. We keep spotting shining *kaki,* persimmons, in bare black branches. Nothing says *autunno* more than these glowing orange lanterns in trees I never notice the rest of the year.

SCARPERIA. I'M COMING here to see Andrea Berti. He makes knives. Knives to covet. Handmade, balanced, honed to the nth. The town has been a center for knives, scissors, swords, and daggers since the 1500s. I met Andrea at a dinner in Cortona celebrating our local Chianina beef and our superb syrah. Famous chefs came from all over Italy. Andrea brought—what else?—knives. He said then, "Come to Scarperia."

We drop our bags at the thirteen-room Locanda San Barnaba across the street from a park where bright golden leaves pave the wet ground. Walking through the old town walls, we follow the straight road into town. In the Middle Ages, this was the main trunk road to Bologna from Firenze. Scarperia grew up on either side after the site was declared a fortification, along with Terranuova Bracciolini, Firenzuola, Dicomano, and others, protecting Firenze against invaders.

We've planned the trip around the curtailed fall opening hours of Palazzo dei Vicari (1306) because we want to see its knife museum, Museo dei Ferri Taglienti. The palazzo—more fortress and castle than palace—was the seat of vicars who administered the district. The structure looms over the piazza. *Stemmi,* stone coats of arms, with a few ceramic ones from the della Robbia workshop, decorate the façade, each one left by a vicar after his tenure. On the right rises a tower with a huge bell. Before we go in, we stop at a bar for coffee and look across at Chiesa dei Santi Jacopo e Filippo, balancing the opposite side of the piazza, and at the corner the small oratorio where the Florentine vicars swore allegiance.

The bar is full of joking men taking a mid-morning break. One, old, in an over-large black suit and sweater, polished black shoes, and a hat, takes his beer across the street into the piazza and sits alone at an out-door table. The sun hits the yellow-peach wall behind him with a burst of molten light, outlining him as if he were drawn on the wall. All the light stops at his black shape. He's squinting. His ears are long. His face, shadowed by his hat, is impenetrable. He belongs to no one.

WE ENTER THE Palazzo dei Vicari as did the horses and carriages, into a courtyard, also covered in coats of arms. I imagine the clip-clop of hooves, the neighing. Someone in the office must unlock the museum. We're pointed up the stairs where a large San Cristoforo fresco lords over the landing. Patron saint of travelers, Cristoforo is still my favorite, though he's been knocked off the church's saint list. He's knee-deep in transparent water, the Baby riding his shoulders and holding out a ball. The world, of course. A tentacled sea creature is faintly visible beneath the river surface.

Though there have been renovations and earthquake repairs over the centuries, nothing is over-restored. I can feel the palpable atmosphere of the time, even the chilly air. Designed by the Florentine architect Brunelleschi, the intricate mechanism that once drove the tower clock is on display in the first room, next to a Madonna and Child, which looks familiar. Ah, the tag says school of Ghirlandaio. Looking closely, I see that graffiti has been scratched into some of the borders.

The cavernous room of government chambers is covered with painted heraldic blazons, swags, wreaths, and faux red draperies, which would create a festive atmosphere if it weren't so dim. Ed sits down in the vicar's chair and I quickly snap his picture as he stamps a papal de-cree. I hope surveillance isn't always watched.

What I'd most like to do is open the glass cases and thumb through the handwritten parchment pages bound into thick books. Some on display are open to drawings of knives.

After seeing the knife collection at Palazzo dei Vicari, I doubt if I'll ever be content with one of those packets of six Japanese kitchen knives with colorful plastic handles that I've bought at Sur La Table. As with chocolate, coffee, shoes, and anything else, once you *know,* you can't go back. The artistry simply stuns us. The blades so accurate, the handles of bone, ivory, and horn exquisite. Agricultural tasks, sacrificial killing, murder, gelding, bread slicing—everything symbiotically fits its purpose.

We're fascinated to see knives in reproductions of paintings by Duccio, Donatello, Ghirlandaio, Giotto, Caravaggio, Pontormo, Fra Angelico. In Caravaggio's *Sacrifice of Isaac,* a strong hand grips a lethal knife used by shepherds to kill sheep. In Duccio's *Last Supper,* broad-bladed knives lie on either side of the meat on a platter. *Supper at Emmaus* by Pontormo shows three graceful knives in use at the supper Jesus attended after his release from the empty tomb. (One of history's oddest dinner parties.) All these appearances in art inspire local craftsmen. I see the Pontormo knife is reproduced by Andrea Berti.

AT THE HOTEL at lunch, Ed starts with three jumbo crostini—eggplant with garlic, *grana padana* cheese, and parsley; cannellini beans and *lardo di Colonnato* (herbed, thinly sliced dorsal fat of the pig); and the third with prosciutto, *pecorino,* and truffle-enhanced honey. I'm swooning over the vegetable *sformato* with Gorgonzola sauce. Then, I order hearty *robollita,* vegetable soup thickened with bread. Ed is happy with potato-filled *tortelli con ragù.* There's new olive oil to dribble on top of the soup. I can't finish it. We've found too many appealing choices on the menu.

Since we have a few minutes before meeting Andrea Berti, we walk across the park to Oratorio della Madonna dei Terremoti. The venerated Madonna is credited with protecting Scarperia from earthquakes. The sign outside says the painter is Filippo Lippi, a favorite of mine, but inside we find scaffolding and two white-jacketed men at work on restoration. "No, the sign's wrong and everyone knows it. The work is by just someone. It was in a roadside shrine before it was moved here," the burly one tells us. "Still worth saving." Yes, she's lovely and will be more so after her makeover.

WE GREET ANDREA at his retail store on the main street. Big-bearded, with black-rimmed glasses, he looks professorial but his smart cabled sweater with wooden buttons and the yellow knotted scarf show us that appearances matter. He drives us out to his laboratory where he introduces us to his wife and son at work in an office, then we tour the showroom. He picks up a serrated vegetable knife, just right to hold. A squared-off blade perfect for cutting gnocchi. The so aesthetically pleasing cheese set.

"I read there were five hundred knife makers in the Middle Ages. Why here?" Ed asks.

"No one knows. You need three things for making knives, a river for the grinding wheels, carbon, and iron. We have none of these."

A man is fastening together the two sides of the handle to those ivory-looking knives you see in very upscale restaurants. He's making holes and hammering. A woman is attaching handles onto cheese knives. Another is packaging. A calm workroom. They only produce twenty thousand knives a year. Obviously, they have to be expensive. This is craft raised to art.

Back at the shop, Andrea turns us over to his other son and we say good-bye. He has given me four sculptural steak knives. The young son is reading *On the Road* by Jack Kerouac. The photos of three generations of Berti knife makers look down from the wall above. "When are you getting your picture up there?" I tease.

"Probably never! You have to work hard in this family."

We send more steak knives home for Peter, my daughter's ever-grilling husband. Ed selects a cheese set for our friends Fulvio and Aurora, who are from Piemonte and know their cheeses. That perfect vegetable knife is for me, and me alone—don't touch it!

"DID YOU LOVE this day?" Ed asks. We're in the hotel restaurant for dinner.

"I did. And we're going to love this wine—mostly *sangiovese* with a swig of cab."

Ed picks up the bottle. "Dreolino Chianti Rufina Riserva. DOCG made over the hills in Rufina. That's right outside Florence."

"The Mugello area is so close to Florence. Wonder why it's relatively undiscovered."

The owner of the locanda is in the kitchen with his daughter, the wife out front running the show. We like staying in places that have a solid restaurant with simple rooms upstairs. It reminds us of Italy when we first traveled here.

"Are you ready to order?"

"Just bring us what's good," Ed says. That's my boy!

First, a plate of lightly battered and fried vegetables. So crisp. "Is there anything better than onion rings?" Then she brings out their special fried rabbit and chicken with roast potatoes and chicory. "Lots of southern-fried tonight," I observe.

"I'm not complaining."

We haul ourselves up to bed and sleep with the window open. I can't see in the dark but I know that a persimmon tree is right outside. When Ed is half-asleep, I say, "I should have bought the Pontormo knife. You know who should have that?"

"Yes. Alberto. I thought of that." He's our architect friend, who is also a painter and loves to cook. He would appreciate the knife and the connection to the painting.

"What's wonderful, I guess, is that when you find something special, it reminds you of people you love."

THE MUGELLO, EARLY. Hills shrouded in clouds, low slopes lapped in fog, and a distant opening of blue, promising a day of clarity. We pass a Medici villa under scaffolding, its noble stable decorated with painted flourishes, all soon to become a luxury hotel in this old landscape. A spiky-legged bird stalks the reeds along Lago di Bilancino. We wind down, skirting Florence, to the autostrada. Back to the velocity of the present. One day can seem like a week.

Buriano, Castiglione della Pescaia, Vetulonia, Montepescali, Campiglia Marittima, Populonia, and San Vincenzo

Is there a square inch of Tuscany that's unexplored? Yes. I constantly hear of towns I don't know. Hundreds of *borghi* remain out of sight. We've found that roaming the back roads yields pleasures equal to the delights of well-visited places because without preconception the sense of discovery intensifies. I'll venture this advice: Put down a water glass on a map of Tuscany and draw a ring anywhere. Pick a hotel in the middle of your circle, check in for three or four days, and venture out from there. You will make your own discoveries. This throws the emphasis on spontaneity.

WE DID JUST that. Wanting to explore the Tyrrhenian coast, Etruscan places, the Maremma—the low, formerly swampy stretch that now is primo wine country and lost-in-time hill towns, we looked on the *agriturismo.it* site and found a simple apartment in the country outside **Buriano**. I love driving thought flat agrarian land, fallow now, with distant blips of hills, castles, and towers. Plows turn up chunky brown clods that shine on the cut side. As we whizz by, the fields glitter and the earth smells of rain and dust and ground-down stalks of sunflowers and corn.

AN ALLÉE OF umbrella pines and old-growth cypress trees lines the long drive to a sprawling farmhouse with four apartments. A German couple lounges by the pool while their energetic toddler in water wings flays about with happy shrieks. It's only a few days until the *agriturismo* closes for winter, and these northerners are braver than we are. The water even looks cold. In our upstairs apartment, the kitchen occupies only an angle in the living room and there are two plain bedrooms, two baths. When we travel by car, Ed brings his espresso machine and the milk foamer for me. We don't plan to cook anything here, but it is nice to have excellent cappuccino and some bakery pastries in the mornings while we plan the days.

We unpack our oranges, grapes, cheese, and crackers. Put the yellow flowers I picked on the roadside in a glass, and we're off to explore **Castiglione della Pescaia** on the coast.

BEACH TOWNS LIKE Castiglione can be junky. In July and August, the Tuscan coast is *affollato,* crowded. Our friends flock to these wall-to-wall stretches of sand, every inch covered with umbrellas and relaxed people (no one wears a one-piece bathing suit) having a fine time visiting with each other. Bring three or four suits because after every foray into the water, the *costume* is changed, often under a skillfully manipulated towel. In the evenings, everyone swarms into restaurants and cafés, later promenading again through the piazza, stopping for gelato. The festive atmosphere means holiday. See and be seen. It's a cultural thing and you either like it or you don't.

I'm excited to see Castiglione della Pescaia in this season, returned to locals, along with a few tourists out for a fall weekend. The fabulist

Italian writer Italo Calvino kept a house outside town at Roccamare for thirteen years before his sudden death. That speaks well for the area, doesn't it? We park near a harbor of sailboats and small craft at the bottom of town, and walk along a broad pedestrian street lined with outdoor cafés under gay awnings. Flower boxes still rave forth, even in early October. Sand-colored or stone, the buildings climb the hill in tight cubes. Rather dreamy; was this fairy-tale setting in Calvino's mind when he wrote *Invisible Cities*? At the very least, it plays a prominent role in his last novel, *Palomar*.

This town isn't going to be junky even in touristy August. Chalkboard menus offer fish and fish, along with big salads and grilled vegetables. After the charming promenade, we climb up, up, skirting fortress walls, to the castle. Along the way we pause for broad views of coast and long, long beaches. The skies are overcast today and the opaque sea gleams like a hammered pewter tray. Many tiny streets are appealing, with picturesque doors and flowering balconies. Near the top—and it's steep—the barny and neglected church of San Giovanni Battista. And then we wind down again, going a different way. We're near the cemetery where Calvino is buried, but we don't stop. I prefer to imagine him looking out to sea and his character Palomar swimming out into a blade of light. Of the coastal Tuscan towns, Castiglione is a stand-out.

We drive along Pineta del Tombolo, a pine woods with paths to the beach. Curious about the all-inclusive vacations Italian friends often take, we stop at the beachside, four-star Riva del Sole Resort and Spa. The first thing we learn is that it fills quickly for the following summer; families return year after year. The rooms are contemporary and attractive, the sandy beach long and private. Your responsibilities fall away as you check in. Play activities, sports, and cooking classes keep the little ones busy. Three pools, biking, mini-golf, tennis, running tracks, restaurant, pizzeria, bars (one on the beach)—you don't have to leave the pine-shaded grounds. Relax. We had salads for lunch in a functional but pleasant café with super-friendly staff, sitting inside because of the cool day. But for most of the year, the terraces probably catch sea breezes and pine-scented air. Ed and I prefer small hotels. And I'm not one for endless sun exposure, but I can see the appeal of going with the flow here.

If I were a guest, I'd surely take a boat tour of nearby Diaccia Botrona reserve, a protected marshland of calm beauty and big skies, like the views in Dutch landscapes. Eighteenth-century efforts to promote agriculture in Maremma led the grand dukes to drain vast stretches of marshland, and Preglio, a large lake, is now the reserve for turtles, flamingos, and hundreds of other creatures and plants.

"You take delight," Calvino wrote in *Invisible Cities,* "not in a city's seven or seventy wonders, but in the answer it gives to a question of yours." I agree. His castle-topped fishing village answers my question about the quintessential Tuscan beach town. I also delight in at least seventy wonders. Lemon gelato, for one.

AS WE DRIVE up to **Vetulonia,** I begin to notice patches of pink haze on the roadside as we zip by. At a curve, I focus and am astounded to see that those blurs are beds of tiny cyclamen. Thousands! These woods must be enchanted, under a spell cast by the Etruscan past. A field of tombs lies just off the road. A round, slightly domed one looks like the ancient structures you see scattered in olive groves in Puglia, an archetypal primitive house. Below town, there are later ruins—a Romanesque abbey, some remnants of a Roman settlement—but never forget, this is Etruscan territory.

Vetulonia was one of the twelve major towns leagued together for reasons of trade, religion, mining, and common culture. Prime time for the Etruscans was long, 800 to 400 B.C., with more time on either end as they waxed and waned. Everything that remains shows them to have been advanced and resourceful. They drained the Maremma swampland! When Romans took over around 300 B.C., the area fell backward and gradually the boggy terrain returned. The Etruscans were highly artistic. I'll never forget the tomb paintings in Tarquinia, another of the twelve city-states. Frescoes show the dead and friends banqueting, dancing, enjoying life. Cortona, where I live, is another Etruscan center. A large metal chandelier with explicit erotic figures was found there, proof of a sensual culture. Tombs (called *melone* for their shapes), stairs bordered with stone scrolls, a thin, fragile bronze sheet covered with writing, and much else has come to light there in recent years; for always, farmers have been turning up bronze votives in their fields.

This little rook's nest has blissful views. Vetulonia's houses seem intact from medieval times. What a pity they have asphalted the street. Most Tuscan towns have retained stone and cobble streets; this looks incredibly wrong—ugly.

We have come to see the Museo Civico Archeologico Isidoro Falchi, which houses in seven rooms objects pulled from the local tombs. Falchi was a medical doctor with a passion for the Etruscans; his amateur, careful explorations continued for seventeen years. Grazie, Isidoro! This collection is haunting. Funerary urns for cremated bodies look like miniature homes fashioned in clay. Who could imagine that so many of these fragile vessels could survive? The black colander with a whimsical pattern of holes—someone rinsed the berries in that. Iron frying pan—cook the deer's liver. A finely shaped funnel for transferring the olive oil, a pair of bone dice with circles for numbers, a disk on a rod for a game of skills at drinking parties, which involved flinging wine lees at targets and uttering the name of your true love. What modern-looking hand scales. Many shapely jugs and storage jars. My hand reaches out, wanting to cup the curves. The warrior's helmet is pierced with holes around the face opening, perhaps for the lacing of the soft lining. One hundred and forty were found in a ditch; most were damaged but this one is perfect. What touches me most is fine gold jewelry worn to the grave. Any woman throughout history would covet the long gold necklace fitted with twenty-four coin-size embossed medallions. The gold, beaten thin, is almost like gold leaf. Earrings and rings loved by someone in the fourth century B.C., some so small they must have belonged to a young girl.

ON A WINDOWSILL of a modest stone townhouse, someone keeps a pot of succulents. I'm always photographing windows with curtains edged with handmade trim. Starchy white and prim—you know there's roast chicken for Sunday *pranzo* and the house is immaculately clean. A crafty woman has crocheted for each of the two sides of the window small squares in a pyramid shape at the bottom. They're connected by thin knotted strands of thread to meet the inverse pyramid of squares at the top. To work out this design, the woman who tends the succulents had an instinct for design that reaches back to those distant Etruscan ancestors.

As we turn into our *agriturismo*'s lane, a brindled cat leaps out of the bushes around a tumbledown barn. Barely older than a kitten, the little thing is a glorious patchwork of all the cat DNA in the neighborhood. Caramel, alley-cat spots, white, black, and tiger-gold, with a winning face: nose and mouth white, pale ginger speckled around celadon eyes, black ears splotched with touches of ginger. She slinks to us, tail in a question mark. Used to guests, she follows us up our outside stairway and waits by the door. We're smitten. Yes, milk. Yes, bits of bread and cheese.

The cat devours. Nudges at the stairway door, wanting in. We draw the line but are conflicted. Let her in? No. Yes. No.

After an hour, as we leave for dinner, she comes out of the brush to the edge of the bushes and stares.

LUCKILY, IN DEEP-COUNTRY Tuscany, you can depend on good restaurants. Tonight, we try Locanda Mossa dei Barbari, just below Buriano. We find a down-home, checked-tablecloth trattoria owned by the friendly Baldoni family. Why the name "Movement of the Barbarians"? Alessio explains that it's not barbarians but Berber horses that knights used to race on the road. We join a few local families and a jewel-laden woman with bouffant hair. Her husband is burly, blunt-jawed, and keeps going out to smoke.

Crisp fried vegetables, house-made tagliatelle with fresh mushrooms, and a platter of mixed meats grilled in the fireplace—pork, chicken, veal, and a slab of tasty bacon. Tuscan comfort food. He brings us a wine of the region, Elisabetta Geppetti Fattoria le Pupille Morellino di Scansano, 2014, ink-dark and serious.

The menu is in Italian and German. We ask Alessio if many Americans come in the summer. "Only a little drop, mostly tourists are from Germany and now some are Russian." He nods toward the bejeweled woman. "They are buying property here."

EARLY THIS MORNING, after feeding our feline friend, whom we've named Tabitha because it seems to suit her, we are returning to Buriano for a look in daylight. We break our own rule: Do not drive into the *centro* through a narrow gate designed for donkeys. We go because we followed another car in. Mistake. That car was a vintage Fiat the size of a grasshopper. How many times have we made a similar mistake? Okay, we're done for. We have to fold in the mirrors, as the car barely scrunches through. Then we're in a minute piazza with no exit sign that looks feasible. I jump out, and a woman points to what I thought was a sidewalk. Down we go. Unscathed. Released at last.

We park and walk back, up to what remains of a tower and the Rocca Aldobrandesca. Famous in Tuscany, the Aldobrandeschi family were feudal overlords here from the ninth century. They later lost the town, regaining it in the eleventh century. Siena and Pisa had their way with it, too. (I used to think Tuscan history was the most complicated until I learned more about Puglia and Sicily.)

In the piazza, a few women buy produce at a shoebox-size stand. Stony lanes crank up and around the hill, offering views over the Maremma. I look at the women's legs to see if they have well-developed calf muscles. The churches are closed, but we are offered a glimpse into the intimate history thanks to the photographs from the past posted on stone walls all around town. War, harvest, weddings, schoolchildren, festivals. Beneath them, names are listed. The faces are full of life. Young men carousing, a bent-over priest, girls with linked arms, chapped-cheek baby. *Ubi sunt . . .* where are those who came before us? Only 178 souls live in this tranquil hill town.

THIRTEEN KILOMETERS AWAY from Buriano, **Montepescali** is even smaller.

From our flat-land *agriturismo,* we can see it capping yet another small peak in the Maremma, its towers glowing at night.

These sights in Tuscany are common. Driving around the Cortona area, we can identify the profiles of Montepulciano, Foiano della Chiana, Sinalunga, and Monte San Savino. Since Italy is 40 percent mountain, you see a Monte this or a Monte that nearly everywhere you wander.

We asked Alessio last night about Montepescali. We knew its nickname, "the Balcony of the Maremma," and that Corsica could be seen from its ramparts.

"*Bella,*" he said, "and you'll have it all to yourselves."

"Meaning?"

"Meaning that the entire population is nine, down from ten a year ago." Someone had died. "Montepescali was different in the 1960s. People lived there. Now you have to say 'Buongiorno' every day to the same nine people."

TODAY, FULL OF sunshine, we take the excellent road up to see these nine people who live within the impressive medieval ramparts of Montepescali. Nothing about the town gate hints of life after the Middle Ages; time here is arrested. The eighteenth, nineteenth, twentieth centuries never arrived. The round brick fortification, high walls, and watch towers are straight out of fantasy. It's quiet as the day after doomsday. In Piazza del Cassero, three cats sleep on the steps of Chiesa di Santi Stefano e Lorenzo. Three women huddle outside a facility for the elderly. Most windows are shuttered but as we walk around the upper neighborhoods, I see over a wall a tended garden profuse with plumbago and jasmine. From a doorway where a woman is sweeping her stoop, the aroma of roasting meat drifts out. Is she dining alone? Would she like two guests?

"I've already counted twenty," Ed says, matter-of-factly. "And the 2010 census says two hundred seventy-five live here."

"Are you sure you're not counting the same people twice? That number is probably for the outlying areas as well." We're at the perfectly scaled Chiesa di San Niccolò, with its pretty campanile.

"Beautiful town, but a bit remaindered."

"Nine people isn't exactly a crowd!" I say. "Maybe the Russians will repopulate it."

FIFTY-EIGHT KILOMETERS TO **Campiglia Marittima.** Big town! Thirteen thousand people. The olive and the artichoke reign, along with the hazelnut and, of course, vineyards. Any script set in medieval times could start filming without rearrangement—like Buriano and Montepescali, this place is fabulously intact, but it isn't encased in amber. Campiglia's piazza is awake, the bar's terrace a hive of teenagers and locals stopping in after lunch. We're starving and happy with a prosciutto and cheese panino. I hoped to find *addormentasuocere*, oddly named "send-the-mother-in-law-to-sleep," but alas, I cannot find these clusters of caramelized local peanuts today.

Campiglia, like the other hill towns, has Etruscan roots. The remains reveal sulfur, iron, and silver mining, copper processing, and also marble quarries. They were, after Roman times, traded back and forth among feudal families, then became a Florentine military stronghold. Similar histories, these quiet places. The miracle is how they endure. Americans are accustomed to everything being leveled frequently. That the two white arches in the piazza, the stony lanes, covered steps up between streets, the clock-tower building covered with *stemmie,* coats of arms of local rulers, have endured untouched always seems so preposterous to New World people.

We look in the door of the public library and a woman comes downstairs to see who's there. The library isn't open, but would we like to see the paintings of Carlo Guarnieri, local artist who lived from 1892 to 1988? We say yes, though we do not expect to be enthralled. "He lived with his mother," she says, and that's all the detail we get as she leaves us among his paintings and engravings.

We *are* enthralled. He has painted six old men who might still be lingering near the stalls on the local market day, just as you still see all over Tuscany. One is seated, back to his companions, holding a cane. He's contemplative, a beret, a far-off expression on his face. Here's the artist's mother, sideways in a chair. The painting is as much about the folds in the drapery backdrop as it is about her. A portrait of a young woman in a blue armchair centers on a creepy fox stole around her shoulders, and the way her hand cradles the head. Marvelous, the woman in white against a red background. She's stern except for the white plume on her hat.

Ed is most intrigued by Guarnieri's many woodcuts, especially the one of Dante at the final moments of his journey. He calls me over to look at the clasped hands. The posted note says, "The vision just ended, the verses are over, the book is closed between the hands, and the eyes look down . . . divine prelude of a dream that dialogues with death and goes beyond life on earth . . ." His self-portrait shows him also with clasped hands and a strange coat of flowers, a forceful, chiseled face. The woodcuts—he began at age thirteen—are extensive, the technique masterful, and the intent stated on the notice seems accurate:

". . . woodcut is not only engraving an image on a wooden table that must be inked and printed on paper . . . it brings out that vitality restrained in the wood, mysterious in its nature of unconscious matter that suddenly offers a glimpse of the secret of life . . ."

We walk out rather dazed. "He had a big talent and who has heard of him outside his hometown? He should be known—he did significant exhibits in his time. Did you read? He was a war hero. World War One. He falls right into the Italian modernist traditions we've admired at Galleria Nazionale d'Arte Moderna in Rome and Museo Novecento in Florence."

"Many a flower is born to blush unseen . . . ," Ed quotes.

VIA CAVOUR, VIA Pietro Gori—under many street signs hang round frames with portraits of the person the street name honors. Marked with a marble plaque is the house of Isidoro Falchi, the archeologist who discovered Velutonia, carried out important excavations at Populonia, and practiced medicine in this town. His medallion shows a man with strong features and an unruly beard. Behind him a symbolic heap of stones.

On a second-story shuttered window I spot a for-sale sign, the property listed by Bella Tuscany Immobiliare. Since any Italian would say "Bella Toscana," I have to assume they have named their agency after my second Italian memoir, *Bella Tuscany.*

ED IS GOING through a Mina phase again. Mina being Mina Mazzini but everyone knows her as Mina—one of the great Italian voices. Speak of her in the same breath as Whitney Houston, more octaves than you can count on one hand. Driving back to our abode, Ed says, "I read that Gino Paoli had or still has a vacation house in Campiglia Marittima." He tells me that Paoli started Mina's career in the sixties.

He turns on his music. "What's this one?" I ask.

"'Il Cielo in una stanza.' You've heard it a hundred times. This is Gino Paoli. 'Heaven in a Room.' I read that he wrote it in a brothel."

"And I know you like Ornella Vanoni's 'L'appuntamento.'" Ed smiles. "It's coming up next."

Blissful to fly through the bucolic Maremma countryside with the music turned up.

TABITHA IS WAITING. She runs up to us and follows. I'm worried. The *agriturismo* is closing. I asked the housekeeper this morning if she belonged to anyone. "You take her," she exclaimed. "She is a good cat." We can't. We don't live here all year and though I might be foolish enough, Ed refuses to haul animals across the ocean. She's darling. I write my friend Sheryl in Cortona, who has two cats plus a couple who stop over daily for food. *Will you take her?*

WE ARE CURIOUS to eat at the Slow Food restaurant Oste Scuro Vin Osteria in a residential neighborhood in nearby Braccagni. We are the last guests of the season; the owners have packed their car this afternoon with prosciuttos and cheeses and wines for the drive to Sicily, where their relatives live. Unusual: He's out front, she's in the kitchen. The space has an industrial look, with bright yellow walls and contemporary angular green tables and yellow chairs.

After a long day, we savor a leisurely dinner. Red shrimp with farro, a plate of anchovies and parsley under curls of butter—we are off to a good start, especially with a bottle of Leonardo Salustri, Montecucco Sangiovese, 2013. We are big fans of Montecucco, and this one tastes as expansive as we feel tonight. The menu proves there is a chef who knows her traditions. Her gnocchi, made from the red potatoes of Cetica near Arezzo, are puffy and delicate. We go forward with tender lamb tornedos on a bed of spicy chicory. For dessert, a homey lemon meringue tart. It's dense and custardy, with the intense lemon flavor only Italy can achieve. Imagine, a restaurant of this quality in a town of fifteen hundred people. Miracle of Italy.

SHERYL SAID YES. (But her husband, Rob, is not thrilled.) Tomorrow I will find a box, food, litter, for the trip home. Ed remains dubious.

• • •

LATE START. I'M engrossed with Calvino's *Palomar.* Also, I look up Bella Tuscany Immobiliare. I am shocked at the comparatively low prices of houses, 30 or 40 percent less than in our part of Tuscany. Why? This is a stunning area, well located for exploring and for the beaches. Food, check. Wine, check. I send off links to two friends who've despaired of finding a Tuscan retreat.

Ed is writing a poem. Tabitha waits outside the door as we start to leave for **Populonia**. I give her milk and a can of food I bought yesterday. She weaves her skinny form ingratiatingly around my legs. Yes, I'm smitten. As we reach the car, all of a sudden another cat emerges from the bushes. Almost identical to Tabitha. Oh, no. Will Sheryl take two? I know she can't. The new one comes right up to Ed. "It was never meant to be, Franny. These are farm creatures. They'll be okay."

ON A BLUFF above the Tyrrhenian Sea, the village of present-day Populonia is the remnant of the only Etruscan town built directly on the water. Remnant, indeed—we find a stupendous view of sea and sky, a forested hill plunging to the strand, and a tiny village protected by massive fortifications. One atmospheric main street with a few shops and cafés, a side opening into a fortress-walled piazza with a small, plain church. Capers spill down the walls.

That's it. A brief turn around town and then down to the beach and fishing harbor. Glimmers of anthracite in the sand recall the Etruscan mines and the excavations of Isidoro Falchi, indefatigable archeologist. Ancient iron slag heaps once besmirched this beach. Now along the Bay of Baratti, there's this sweet curve of blond sand extending into a pine forest. A heavy-set woman braves the water, out to her waist. A short walk and we find ourselves seated on the terrace of a seaside restaurant. At the entrance, men play cards. Suddenly this seems like vacation. *Maltagliata*—"badly cut" pasta (usually made from leftover pasta dough)—with shrimp, zucchini, and tomatoes, with a mezzo-liter of house white. A view of boats and mimosa trees seems just right.

SAN VINCENZO, WHERE we came years ago to dine at the world-famous Gambero Rosso. The waiter wheeled over a cart of olive oils. Which did we prefer for our salads? We were dumbfounded, knowing little about olive oil at that point. I selected the greenest, and the waiter smiled and nodded. The dinner I still remember thirty years later. Gambero Rosso is gone now, and in early October, the beach town is getting ready to fall into a long doze. We stroll down the wide main street, made for the evening *passeggiata,* with ample bars and gelato shops.

What is glorious about October travel is that we walk San Vincenzo's eleven kilometers of sandy beach and have it to ourselves. San Vincenzo will be hopping in the summer, but now how peaceful. Costa degli Etruschi, the Etruscan coast, stretches from Livorno to Piombino, eighty kilometers of beach. Spring and fall, you'll have it to yourself. Resolution: Return to the Etruscans in spring and fall for my necessary beach fix.

TABITHA IS NOWHERE to be found, nor the companion cat. Ed leaves two open cans for them. Sheryl had to decline the gift of two. She does not want to become a cat lady. They must stay, and if I don't see them again it will be easier to go.

On our last night, we pop over to the village of Braccagni again. We noted Ristorante Bernasconi by the train station when we drove through last night. It's open, they have a table, though it's crowded with locals, and soon the waiter has brought us—his suggestion—the same wine we had in Buriano, the Elisabetta Geppetti Morellino di Scansano. We're right at home with the cozy red walls and white tablecloths, the old-style menus. We waste no time ordering the mixed antipasti and ravioli with classic ragù. What's better on a crisp fall night?

TABITHA, STORYBOOK CAT, we leave behind. She comes to the car as we pack to leave. Let me not anthropomorphize, though I could. Just to say, she knows. We drive away and she watches, tail straight up. "Turn on Mina," I say. "Loud."

NOTES:

"Many a flower . . ." from "Elegy Written in a Country Churchyard," Thomas Gray.

Other winning villages in the Buriano–Vetulonia area: Scarlino, Caldana, Ravi. Very well known and appealing are the wine centers Bolgheri and Castagneto Carducci, with a magnificent cypress-lined entrance. We love Marina di Bibbona for the pleasure of dining at La Pineta.

While in San Vincenzo, we were not able to go to Ristorante Il Bucaniere, owned by Fulvietto Pierangelini, son of the owners of the famous Gambero Rosso. A must on the next visit.

Massa Marittima

"Can we veer by **Massa Marittima**? It doesn't look far out of the way."

"We have time. Remember that church up on an angled stone platform, how the piazza goes wonky because of that?" Ed pulls over to recalculate our route. For three days, we've been wandering around the Tuscan coast and small inland towns and now are headed home to Cortona.

"Remember when I called it Massa Mari-TTI-ma?"

"Yes. You were corrected and admonished. Ma-RI-ttima. A trill with the r. She did it to me, too. I'll never forget the mocking 'Not *G-Ovanni*. Say *Joevanni,* all together.' Then there was *geometra*." A *geometra* is a quasi-architect who has to approve building projects. "I put the accent on -*met*. She let me know it was on the –*om*. I was humiliated."

She refers to our great friend the writer Ann Cornelisen, who preceded us in Italy by a couple of decades and spoke excellent, if a bit stiff, Italian. It was her mission to minimize what fools we made of ourselves those early years. She was always right. Would that she'd remained to correct other mistakes.

. . .

MASSA MARITTIMA—QUIRKY TOWN. Piazza Garibaldi, usually called
Piazza del Duomo, is ringed by medieval buildings—the town hall, the
wheat granary, Palazzo del Podestà (now the archeological museum)—
and by cafés well placed for viewing the imposing church. The placement is pleasing and disorienting, as though the piazza tilted to its side
and stuck.

Did I say quirky? On via Ximenes at the entrance to the *centro,*
we find the covered thirteenth-century public water fountain, Fonte
dell'Abbondanza, which has a tree-of-life fresco on one wall. On second
glance, I see that the branches are decorated not only with leaves but
with testicles and erect penises! How bizarre, this Albero della Fecon-
dità. And next door, a reminder of fascist Italy, Casa del Fascio, built
in 1935 in the prevailing rationalist architectural style, with the requi-
site balcony for speeches, and the carved, flat eagle over the door. This
architecture, which used to scream Mussolini, now takes on a period
patina. The rigid, some say brutal, architecture of the era always had,
in Italy, a foot in classicism. Travertine of the area links this building
with a longer past. Here, the primitive phallic tree and the stylized eagle
coexist.

WE SIT DOWN on the church steps overlooking the lively piazza full of
older residents. "The cocktail party," Ed calls our intensely social mornings in the piazza in Cortona. Of course, instead of cocktails, people
are sipping cappuccino. Parties going on all over Italy every morning of
the world. Growing old in Italy seems a kinder thing than in America.
The old aren't isolated and don't get the not-so-subtle message that they
should be. Four women, two with canes, hold court at a table under the
arcade. They're having fun on this chilly October morning.

"Here's the brief," I say to Ed, as I check the *Blue Guide.* "Under
dominion of Pisa. Then a free city in 1225, the period when all these
buildings were accomplished. 1335, conquered by Siena. Downward
spiral, plus malaria and bubonic plague. 1555, town goes under the control of the Grand Duchy of Tuscany and old mining (active in Etruscan times) of silver, lead, iron, copper recommenced and prosperity

returned. Nutshell. 'Massa' is from Latin, meaning a group of properties. And 'Marittima' doesn't mean it was once near the sea; it refers to the area, Maremma."

"Okay. And 'Maremma' means sea-swamp, doesn't it? *Mar,* sea, and *—emma,* marshland."

How nice to sit in the mild autumn sun, the Duomo looming magnificently. Blind arches run along one side and on either side of the entrance. The campanile is a joy; the zigzag of steps so unusual, a rose window with stained glass (not very Tuscan), the octagonal cupola instead of a dome, and the bas-relief over the big door, portraying the life of San Cerbonius, whose works seem kind of goofy. They involved a gaggle of geese he met en route to see the pope, bears who were supposed to devour him but licked his feet instead, deer who allowed themselves to be milked to slake the thirst of guards accompanying Cerbonius to Rome. And he heard angels sing. How childlike, these narratives for the populace, and strange how tonally different these stories are from the tree-of-fecundity phalluses.

EVEN IF YOU'VE seen a hundred archeological museums, you haven't seen the belt buckle, storage jars, safety pins, and weapons from *this* particular area. And I always appreciate the shock of obvious aesthetic pleasure taken in fashioning a pitcher or necklace. After photographing the dignified façade covered with coats of arms, we go inside to see the small collection, which ranges from the Etruscans (sites still being excavated in this area) to the Romans. And, yes, there is a cunningly wrought belt buckle. And to contemplate: a prehistoric sandstone figure, about sixty centimeters high, in the shape of a triangle. Mysterious: Barely etched in are crossed arms and slits for eyes that looked at we know not what.

WE WALK ALONG via Moncini, the main street spiking off the piazza. Knife shop, bookstore, wine bar, house concept shop, and toward the end, La Padellaccia del Viggia, a small café where we sit outside for a quick lunch of mushroom bruschette and salad. Up from here, Piazza Matteotti and Sant'Agostino, also from the boom-time thirteenth century.

There's a 1228 clock tower to climb for a view over the countryside, but we don't. Instead, we take a few side streets, quiet and mostly residential, where Ed stops to pick up bread and I buy some pretty paper. What for? Lining drawers, wrapping gifts? I just have a weakness for paper.

LAST STOP, THE interior of the Duomo. What a beauty. Seen from inside, that odd octagonal cupola on top stuns me with eight wedges of alternating black and white bricks. A deep, receding illusion. I wonder if it was meant to have been stuccoed and frescoed. But the effect could not be more dramatic. Dazzling, too, the magnificent *Madonna delle Grazie* almost certainly by the great Sienese painter Duccio. Raffaello Vanni's *Annunciation* shows Mary, with a what-am-I-to-do expression on her face. Uncharacteristically, she's wearing a bright red dress. Behind the altar, generations of crass visitors have scratched their names and initials on the marble. A relic preserved here—a finger of San Cerbonius.

NOTE:

Thirty-two kilometers away: the evocative ruins of Abbazia di San Galgano. Not to be missed.

Sansepolcro

On the way to Sansepolcro, we stop at Busatti, maker
of traditional Tuscan fabrics. Anghiari, the striking hill
town, is Busatti headquarters, where you might be taken
downstairs to the industrial-age-looking looms, or see
Giuseppe Busatti himself, stirring a large pot of onion skins
on the back porch—for dyeing wools and cottons.

While I'm looking at tablecloths, Ed strikes up a
conversation. He often finds someone to talk to while he
waits for me to finish shopping. He claims he's practicing
his conversation skills. But really, he just likes talking to
Italians. After some exchange about Anghiari restaurants,
he says to the woman, "How did Sansepolcro get its
name?" She isn't entirely sure but another local chimes
in—some pilgrims brought relics from the Holy Land,
pieces of the sepulcher where Jesus was buried and
arose; built themselves a monastery; and called it Holy
Sepulcher—Sansepolcro.

Not by coincidence, then, that Piero della Francesca's
most famous painting, *The Resurrection,* was created in the

city of his birth, Sansepolcro. I select a muted orange cloth woven with a renaissance design.

WE'VE TAKEN THE famous Piero della Francesca trail many times—the Basilica di San Francesco in Arezzo, with frescoes of the *Legend of the True Cross;* the Duomo for his small portrait of Mary Magdalene with her hair wet after drying the feet of Jesus; nearby Monterchi, birthplace of Piero's mother, for his stately *Madonna del Parto,* the pregnant Virgin Mary, and, of course, the Museo Civico in Sansepolcro, featuring *The Resurrection.* Aldous Huxley proclaimed this to be "the greatest painting in the world." Christ rises from the tomb; four guards sleep beneath. The one in brown on the left is said to be a self-portrait of Piero.

I like the story, and I hope it's true, of an American pilot in World War Two who had orders to bomb Sansepolcro. As he flew, he had a memory of an art professor lecturing about the great painting hanging in a museum in Sansepolcro. He dropped his bombs elsewhere. Be thankful for a good liberal arts education.

Also at the civic museum, we find Piero's *San Ludovico* (Saint Louis) and *San Giuliano* (Saint Julian), the blond youth with an other-worldly look in his eyes. I love the riveting *Polyptych of the Misericordia.* A larger-than-life Virgin Mary shelters eight people under her cloak. The panels of saints are equally brilliant and moving. Although Piero magnetizes us always, there is more to see. I'm especially fond of the work by local artist Santi di Tito, most of all the lovely *Rest on the Flight into Egypt,* the Raffaellino del Colle paintings, and the Mannerist Pontormo's *San Quintino.*

I CAN IMAGINE living here. Though the setting lacks the drama of hill towns, the flat streets and spacious Piazza Torre di Berta invite lingering, bicycling, window-shopping. Droves of well-dressed young people throng streets lined with fashionable shops and bars. Cortona friends come here to find distinctive clothes at Ballerini. Busatti has a branch. La Nuova Libreria is an excellent bookstore. Look up! Several medieval towers spike the façades of handsome *palazzi.* One sidewalk menu offers pasta with goose sauce, roast duck, osso bucco, rabbit. Just your ordinary old fare.

We've brought guests here many times, as the town is a bit out of the way and many do not know of it. We always take them to Ristorante Locanda da Ventura. We have to have completed our sight-seeing prior because you stand up from the table in a food coma. We order from the antipasti cart, as was the custom for many decades in Tuscany. Grilled eggplant and breaded peppers, slices of frittata and *salumi.* For *primo,* the ribollita or the ravioli with truffles, then the roasted pork with crackly skin, or the savory *brasata,* braised beef.

Today we visit the gorgeous and appealing displays of medicinal plants and herbs in Museo Aboca, a few meters down from the Museo Civico. Antique ceramic pitchers and jugs, blown glass distillers, bottles and storage jars painted with names of what they held: opium, roses, arsenic. All the tools for making cures. Old monasteries had their garden of simples; and much of the lore, of course, is now known to have scientific basis.

While I'm looking at books in the gift shop, Ed talks to the women at the desk. He is told that Osteria Il Giardino di Piero, the restaurant across the street, is associated with the museum—which he finds out is associated with the farm Aboca, 2,000 acres of vegetables and organic medicinal herbs. We have to try it. This means no lunch at Da Ventura. Will this be a rival for our affections?

The garden room of the *osteria* faces the Piero park, which Aboca has planted with healing plants in beds all around the statue of Piero della Francesca. Since we're at the end of October, we sit inside. As we walk in, we see glass flasks (*fiaschi*) filled to the top with beans in the fireplace coals. We have to taste that ancient Tuscan specialty. First, we split the *bringoli* pasta (similar to the *pici* of our area) with a pesto of kale, saffron, walnuts, and almonds. Then the smoky white beans with a plate of fried artichokes. A slender slice of almond and ricotta tart with a hint of lemon. We love this—everything top quality, organic, curated, and served on Richard Ginori china painted with a scene of the park across the street. We'll have to come back to Sansepolcro twice as often now.

Walking out, we find the Cattedrale di San Giovanni Evangelista open—not always the case in the afternoon. The first church was revised to Romanesque in the thirteenth and fourteenth centuries. Because it faces via Matteotti, a side street, not the piazza, it's easy to miss and that would be a pity, because inside is a resurrection painting, earlier than Piero's and almost certainly an influence on his. Niccolò di Segna's composition is similar, with Jesus resting one foot on the edge of the sepulcher with toes curled over, same powdery-pink garment. I feel a little shiver, thinking of Piero standing in front of this painting while contemplating starting his own.

I always visit the *Ascensione di Gesù* by Perugino, with Christ ascending in an oval of cherub heads surrounded by musicians, angels, and dangling ribbons. Mary and the crowd below look up in wonder. The colors and shading are harmonious, and always with Perugino there will be a glimpse of sublime landscape in the background. Quite magnificent but after spending time with Piero, Perugino looks static.

In an inconspicuous spot, I see a Piero look-alike. *Baptism of Christ* by Christiana Jane Herringham (1852–1929). How curious. This copy, painted in 1909, of one of Piero's famous works is excellent. Herringham would have seen the original in London's National Gallery. When I look up the copyist, she is one of those formidable, fascinating Edwardian women who carved their way in a society that expected little of them. Lady Herringham translated a fifteenth-century book on tempera and fresco, reviving interest in those methods. She started funding organizations, still active today, to protect British works of art. She traveled to India to copy Buddhist paintings in the Ajanta Caves, leaving an important record of their condition at that time. Her last years were, sadly, spent in mental institutions. I wonder how her painting found a home on a side wall of the cathedral in Sansepolcro.

"Piero's town," Ed says. We're walking along the substantial town walls toward the car.

"Why do we always call him by his first name?"

"We want to feel on intimate terms with the local boy."

NOTE:

There is a biography of Christiana Jane Herringham: *Christiana Herringham and the Edwardian Art Scene* by Mary Lago.

U mbria ❋

Montefalco

Isn't this the way an Umbrian hill town should look? Yes. A circular piazza, just the right size, with seven radiating streets, some leading down cobbled lanes into charming neighborhoods of stone cottages with arbors covered with grapevines, tumbling potted plants, and a multihued cat asleep in the street.

The piazza is anchored by a handsome thirteenth-century Palazzo Comunale, town hall, with a bell tower to climb for wide views. Directly across, Teatro San Filippo Neri formerly was a church. What a good fate for unused religious buildings, staging pageants of a different kind. At an arched doorway surrounded by datura plants, I step into the intimate oratory, Santa Maria di Piazza. The apse fresco of the Madonna and Child was painted in 1517 by local boy Francesco Melanzio, whose name you see around town, but the oratory dates back to the beginning of the thirteenth century. Melanzio's blues are vivid, his Madonna pensive, and off to the left Pope Gregory I holds up a huge communion wafer. I almost didn't notice the aedicule (small shrine) to the right of the fresco. This niche is a remnant of the older oratory. Along the sides, the tourist office has mounted copies of many important paintings in Montefalco. If churches are closed, you can still see what you're missing.

Via Goffredo Mameli drops down to the frescoed Porta Sant'Agostino, the main entrance into Montefalco. Along the way, *enotece* for the tasting of the local *sagrantino* wine, textile shops selling pastel linens in traditional patterns, and *trattorie,* including our favorite, Olevm. On this street, it's easy to pass right by Chiesa di Sant'Agostino. I love the haphazard arches and windows inside and the faded and fragmentary frescoes, almost all "attributed to" someone or by unknown Umbrian painters of the fourteenth to sixteenth centuries. Via Ringhiera Umbra, off the piazza, takes you to the museum and church of San Francesco. Others lead you to panoramic views. No wonder this town is known as "the balcony of Umbria." We identify the compelling towns of Trevi, Spello, Spoleto, and Assisi, scaling distant forested hills, shining white against green like fine two-color drawings of themselves. When I look at them, I always feel a surge of hope. Maybe this comes from the biblical "A city set on a hill cannot be hidden."

MONTEFALCO IS ONE of my favorite towns. We discovered it early in our years in Italy, arriving with two friends at dark in winter. Ed wanted to taste *sagrantino*—the grape is indigenous to Montefalco— then mostly unknown outside its sphere. The town was not the lively place it now is. One light across the deserted piazza, an open door with barrels of wine inside. No one home. We sat down at a rustic table and waited. Finally, a scruffy man in old wool ambled in and gave us a glass of the "little sacred wine." He'd been playing cards in the bar. I thought the tannins had tied my tongue in a knot. The man laughed and gave us another taste, an aged *sagrantino,* mellow and deep, with just enough tannin to make me sit up straight.

"Smart wine," Ed remarked. "The complexity makes you think. Makes you want to analyze, talk about it."

We bought a bottle. Arnaldo Caprai, it said. We have been drinking those wines ever since. We've had lunches at the vineyard, tasting their *passito,* dessert wine made from first drying the mature grapes in the sun, and their vintages. A first sip always brings back the image of the lighted doorway across the piazza, a bare bulb casting shadows on our faces, the dark crimson wine pouring into our glasses.

WE CAN NOW buy *sagrantino* in Cortona, even in North Carolina. Still we come to Montefalco for its beauty and major art holdings, especially for the captivating frescoes of Benozzo Gozzoli. When our French friend, Veronique, worked on the restoration years ago, we were able to climb the scaffolding and see faces and details up close. How cold she was in winter, all bundled up, painting on fingernails and earlobes, and cleaning faces with vile-smelling potions. Now the frescoes are in their glory again. The museum attached to the church displays rooms of paintings by unknown artists. Powerful paintings, crucified Christ in wood and tempera, another devastating Crucifixion painted on a board mounted with a carved sculpture of bleeding Christ on the cross. Disturbing and weighty. Who gets remembered, whose works? Many of these pieces rival or surpass others by artists whose names are well known, hung in city galleries. Being from a remote place, not producing a body of work, not known by those who could promote you, that was the fate of Painter from Spoleto, 1280; Umbrian Painter, fourteenth century; Circle of Niccolò di Liberatore; and others.

Before the museum rooms lead into the church, we visit the lapidary rooms down in the crypt. Local archeological finds include several Roman funerary *stele* from the first century. (Some were discovered just outside town at San Fortunato, where we are going later.) The prize in this room: a white marble Hercules, 117 centimeters tall from the first century B.C. or early first century A.D. Although found here, its provenance is unknown. He is holding the skin of the Nemean lion, his first challenge in obtaining forgiveness for murdering his own children in a fit of pique. Since the skin couldn't be pierced, he strangled the raging lion and created a coat and a helmet from the head. He holds a club in one hand and an apple in the other, a symbol of one of his other labors. A mysterious hello from ancient history.

• • •

ONLY THREE OTHER people are in the church. What luck. Soon they leave and we have Signor Gozzoli to ourselves. On the back wall, we find Perugino's sweet nativity against a bucolic landscape background. It's painted in a coved space perhaps six meters high. Above the nativity, God looks down benevolently and at the top, the start of everything—an Annunciation, with the angel in soft corals and blues.

There is much to see along the walls. Gozzoli's chapel of San Girolamo with many weird clouds that look like splats of whipped cream. Other chapels depict the Annunciation, Assumption, and lives of Saints Bernardine and Antonio. In the choir chapel, we arrive at the frescoes of the life of San Francesco. The space is crowded with scenes on three levels and on the vaulted ceiling. From left to right, follow the narrative of Francesco's life from birth in a manger setting like that of Jesus, to youth when he renounced his family's wealth, meetings with saints, a dream, expulsion of devils from Arezzo, and then the familiar stories of preaching to the birds—thirteen different kinds mill around his feet in attentive postures. In the same panel, Francesco blesses Montefalco. The scenes reinforce the parallels between Jesus and Francesco. The fait accompli occurs when Francesco receives the stigmata, the only saint to be so honored. Then, death.

The work is dense. Though each panel looks packed with detail, the story is clear and explicit. Art! A holy ferment of creativity in this small town centuries ago. The museum and church are immense treasure troves, worth any detour.

AND NOW, PRANZO. Umbrian food is hearty everywhere, but especially over in Norcia, where every part of the pig is celebrated. The local lentils taste like the earth smells. Big unsalted breads, full-bodied olive oil, the old-world bean *cicerchia,* farro, chestnuts, and fava. Truffles! This is the season. We're at Olevm, where three tables are squeezed in downstairs and upstairs, slightly more spacious, another few. Everything homemade. On the way in, I spot the pie-sized chocolate *budino* on the counter, trays of fresh pasta, and my favorite cheese bread with walnuts.

The young couple next to us drinks two bottles of wine with a plethora of courses, all scarfed up quickly. We admire their fortitude. She giggles. He has a nose ring that in profile looks like something dripping from his nostrils. Don't look.

What could be finer than just-pressed olive oil on bruschetta spread with black truffles? Especially when paired with a glass of *sagrantino,* followed by *zuppa di cicerchia,* dense puréed soup made with a bean that looks like an irregular little pebble and tastes like time itself (similar to chickpeas). And, ah, a basket of breads. The house *sagrantino* is Monte-falco Sagrantino 2013 Montioni. Quite a house wine! I love semifreddo desserts but can't manage theirs, which is made with *sagrantino*. I guess the owner saw my admiring look at the chocolate *budino* on the way in. She cuts us each a sliver of this delicate pudding cake as we pay. A mighty espresso sends us on our way.

Some shops, including Tessitura Pardi and Tessuto Artistico Umbro—the linen ones—have stayed open during the *pausa*. Textiles are a major weakness of mine and the holidays will be upon us soon, so I have a good reason to go in. I am drawn to the dusky fresco colors of the Umbrian designs. I select placemats and napkins in old gold and a stack of kitchen towels to give to dinner party hosts. There's a yellow tablecloth like a skirt in a renaissance painting. I don't buy it but I can always come back.

BENOZZO GOZZOLI PAINTED his first four frescoes in the Chiesa di San Fortunato, just outside town. Some of the funeral *stele* we saw in the museum were found on this ancient holy site founded in the fifth century, and paintings in the museum were moved from here. We walk into a small cloister. The church is closed. A smiling priest gets out of his car and walks up to us with his hand out. He's new here, trans-ferred from Israel. Not only is the church closed, it's not going to open anytime in the foreseeable future. Seismic, he explains. Recent earth-quakes will have Umbria sorting out possible damage for a long time. We do get to see a chapel in the cloister, charmingly painted by Tiberio d'Assisi in faded green, lavender, saffron, and buff. A resurrection with Christ emerging from a pink sepulcher. Two lithe and delicate angels, as lovely as Botticelli's, accompanying San Francesco on a bucolic walk. He already has the stigmatas but is carrying a bouquet of flowers. In medallions above, two martyrs are shown with knives plunged into their shoulder and head.

Sebastiano must be the most popular subject among all saints. Here, he's pale, tall and blond, pure frontal nudity except for a wisp of lavender scarf tied around the strategic spot. He survived the arrow attack. Infections from arrows were thought to cause plague. Since he lived, he became the saint people beseeched when plague settled on their towns. The priest doesn't know the painter, he says. He's new, he repeats. "Tiberio d'Assisi," I tell him. We leave an offering but not enough to restore San Fortunato.

DRIVING AWAY, WE stop several times to photograph undulating hills planted with grapevines, delicate plumes of gold poplars, lindens turned flamboyant yellow, even evergreen oaks and ilex leaves gone to sepia from the summer drought. The grapevines blaze dark, russet red, embers with sparks of fire, the color of *sagrantino*.

NOTE:

"A city set on a hill . . ." Matthew 5:14, English Standard Version of the Bible.

Bevagna

What amazes me most about Italy is that I travel a few kilometers and everything changes. A different pasta, a dialect incomprehensible from the last town's. Different artists. There you have the Romanesque, here the Baroque, there the Venetian Gothic. Pastries, wine, the color of the stone, even the most popular tint of women's hair, the preferred dog. We do it *our* way, each town maintains.

Bevagna lies only seven kilometers from Montefalco. Both are walled, both have Roman roots, and both are unspoiled and intact. And yet: They are light-years apart.

PIAZZA FILIPPO SILVESTRI, Bevagna's main piazza, has an off-center fountain and the buildings zigzag, cutting each other off at odd angles, giving Bevagna's *centro* a disorienting sense of surprise. I'm not lulled by beauty but fascinated by the dynamics. The intimate nineteenth-century Torti opera house, the severe church of San Domenico, a lone column standing next to an outdoor café where people are enjoying the first day of November sun, a surreal flight of steep stairs, an arcade—a harmony of disharmonies.

Two facing Romanesque churches, San Silvestro (1195) and San Michele Arcangelo (built shortly after and by Binello, the same architect), have raised altars that must be approached by many steps. From this exalted height, the priest looks way down onto his congregation. In San Silvestro, the square plan seems overtaken by two rows of robust columns out of proportion to the space. "This looks like an Egyptian tomb," Ed says. Rough gray brick walls are stripped of ornament.

"Gloomy," I agree. "But monumental." Unless I miss something in the dimness, there's only one painting—a damaged fresco of a saint, who must be Silvestro, holding a book and a long iron object that might be a key, as Ed guesses, or what it resembles more, handcuffs.

SAN MICHELE, NOT perfect with an odd oversize round window (was a rose window added later and not finished?) and cut-off top (was a matching campanile lost?), has a marvelous entrance. The wooden doors are topped with carved bull heads, foliage dangling from their horns— such a primitive welcome. In the tympanum above, Michael slays the dragon. Best of all, on either side of the door, carved into stone, are crude, long-legged birds. Not artistic, but here's the hand of the maker. The symbolism is lost on me—it's not the pelican often associated with the Virgin, but they meant something.

Inside, it's light and airy, the rhythmic arches supported by a double row of stone columns of a pale buttercream color. There's Catherine, with the wheel on which she will be tortured standing beside her for the portrait, and a fresco fragment of the heads of Mary and Jesus. The six pots of flowers on the altar stairs are arranged haphazardly— everything is wonderfully off-kilter!

WE'RE BROWSING ALONG the main street, Corso Matteotti, reading menus of restaurants, popping into the cashmere outlet, when Pasticceria Panetteria Polticchia's window entices us. Mid-morning, time for a little something. We buy a few each of *sagrantino*-flavored cookies, fig pastries, *pastarelle di San Nicolò* (clove, cinnamon, nutmeg spice biscotti), and *roccette alle noci* (hazelnut biscotti). Then there's *pancaciato* and some marron glacé for our neighbor who loves them. Ed may eat the whole loaf of *pancaciato* before we get to the car. The walnut and *pecorino* bread has slightly crunchy crust and a texture like cake. (It makes perfect toast.) I've heard of *rocciata,* decorated with streaks of red sugar and piled on a plate. Typically baked around All Saints' and All Souls' days, *rocciata* is one of the most historic Umbrian pastries. Often you see it formed into the shape of a snake. The dessert is a simple olive oil pastry rolled around a filling of dried figs, apples, raisins, walnuts, cinnamon, lemon peel, and a moistening of wine. The recipe jumps straight out of a medieval cookbook. We are having people over for coffee tomorrow morning; all these treats will be fun to serve.

QUITE A BIT of the Roman endures. A curve of houses follows the ancient theater. There's a bit of a temple. But nothing sings out from that pass like the mosaics that line the *frigidarium* in the Terme di Mevania, the public thermal baths. Black-and-white sea creatures—giant lobsters, octopuses, dolphins—must have appeared to swim as the waters of the second century moved over them.

BEVAGNA INVITES STROLLING. We climb up to the medieval neighborhood and come upon the *cartiera,* the place where rags become paper. The workshop is only twenty years old but it expertly employs the oldest methods, re-creating the once-upon-a-time of torn linen and cotton, mauling, slurry and vats, dank air, and emerging pristine pieces of thick white paper. We meet Francesco Proietti, the paper-maker who works with these medieval techniques. He runs through the process for us. Open all year, the *cartiera* is also a main part of Mercato delle Gaite, the June festival where old crafts such as candle-making and silk weaving are demonstrated, jousts are fought among the four *gaite* (sections of town), medieval music and food are in abundance, and, judging from the photographs, the entire town parades about in period dress.

• •~•

BEFORE WE LEAVE we stop into the Baroque Chiesa di San Francesco, which posseses the very rock the saint stood on when he preached to the birds outside Bevagna. We sit down and read the sermon. They should be grateful that they could fly, he told them. After his gentle words, the birds rose into a murmuration in the sky and formed a cross, before breaking into north, south, east, and west flocks and flying away.

L e Marche

Sant'Angelo in Vado

At the end of October, we're in northern Le Marche for truffles. The Roman poet Juvenal thought these pungent *funghi* were born from the strike of thunderbolts. That seems as good an explanation as any for the gnarly little jewels. Sant'Angelo in Vado is truffle central. On the final weekends of October and the first ones of November, they celebrate with music, food stands, and colorful markets lining the streets. Restaurants feature menus rich in truffle dishes and the town fluffs up for visitors by opening any closed churches and monuments.

ONLY AN HOUR out of Cortona, we've already crossed mountains, curving through unsettled land, climbs, sheer drops, and jagged horizons. Ever since I've lived in Italy, I've heard that Le Marche will be "the next Tuscany." Le Marche ("the Borders") certainly are as physically alluring: the varied landscape dotted with hilltop villages, noble historic towns, the 180-kilometer-long Adriatic coastline.

Does any region of Italy have mediocre food? No. Everywhere, *si mangia bene,* one eats well. But the cooks of Le Marche excel. The food is robust, bountiful. As we drive, I'm dreaming of a salami made with figs, a duck stew, and *vincisgrassi,* a much-loved pasta layered with mushrooms, béchamel, and rich ragù. And a walnut cake dense with nuts, citrus flavors, and raisins. But, no, Le Marche have not become a fevered destination and these spiny mountains see to it that they won't. Excepting the coast, it's hard to get around in Le Marche.

Once over the rugged Apennines, we dip into the sweetest countryside imaginable—hummocky green hills with isolated farms. Tractors on the verge of tumbling sideways as they plow steep fields, overturn hard clods, and break them down into rich brown earth. What are they planting now? Cover crops? Winter wheat? Substitute oxen for the tractor and this scene has been playing for centuries.

Ed loves to drive, especially in Italy where you can speed and other drivers know what they're doing. You rarely meet a duffer cruising the left lane at fifty miles per hour. He would be blown off the road. Here, we're meandering; hardly anyone is out. It's delightful to find yourself alone on winding back roads, some that run out of pavement. Even the GPS can give up and improvise, sending us through someone's cow path marked PRIVATO to land on a gutted dirt road that finally leads to a pristine village.

DRIVING ALONG THE lush valley of the Metauro River, I see a road sign near the village of Làmoli: ABBAZIA SAN MICHELE ARCANGELO. One of Ed's major talents is his ability to swerve into small roads when an intriguing glimpse of a tower or a sweet slice of landscape appears. We hop out in front of a seventh-century Benedictine abbey. Middle of nowhere, although in Italy you learn quickly that what you'd have thought "middle of nowhere" is a considerable somewhere. Often a small *borgo* existed since long before the Romans, and has stacked up a dizzying history along the lines of who begat whom, who begat and begat.

In Làmoli, since pilgrimage years fourteen centuries back, Archangel Michele's inevitable lines have graced the lives of those who lived within the sound of its bells. For now, it's all ours: wooden ceiling like the skeleton of a sailing ship. High oculus of white light, carved-out side windows, the silence of the arched interior, on whose columns muted remnants of frescoes remain.

The Romanesque, my favorite style for any church, keeps to a purity and human scale. The elemental lines seem closest to the spirit. This *abbazia* is plain as a pancake outside, and obviously restored, but the dark and quiet inside—we are all alone—calms and claims me. Dio, it's cold. Must be frigid here in winter.

BLACK OR WHITE? We'll go for either or both, but this is the season for the more prized tuber *magnatum pico,* the truffle currently selling for two thousand euros a kilo. That sounds, and is, outrageous but a kilo is more than two pounds of truffle. Fortunately, the taste is so prominent that a few quick and thin shavings over a mound of tagliatelle is enough to send that dish into the category of sublime.

Sant'Angelo in Vado since Roman times sits on the banks of the Metauro, a bucolic little river that, I read, in stormy times suddenly can turn vicious. "In Vado" means a place to ford the river. I can't wait to see the recent excavation of a Roman villa but first I'd like to gaze on those toffee-colored little fists, the white truffles.

Sant'Angelo's Piazza Umberto I is surrounded by a bell tower, proud civic buildings, and two churches. Chiesa di Santa Caterina delle Bastarde, Saint Catherine of the Bastards—odd name for this miniature church. Once an orphanage for females, the narrow interior is overwhelmed by looming oversize statues of the cardinal virtues and the church doctors, whereas the altar painting shows the martyrdom of Saint Catherine on the wheel. Must have scared the little girl "bastards."

Nearby, San Filippo, a tiny, octagonal treasure box. I always admire the country Baroque, where the ambition for grandeur exceeded the budget. The creative builders constructed of wood what richer churches would make out of stone and marble. Skilled painters used their talent for faux, painting the swirl of marble's white and cream and greens on wood. San Filippo is one of those, although plenty of gold was lavished on the square ceiling frescoed in gilded panels. Almost hidden on a side wall I find a tender *Annunciation* by Raffaellino del Colle. Of all the set religious subjects, the Annunciations appeal to me the most. She wears a pomegranate-colored dress, reading a book. Maybe that's why I'm drawn to these paintings—Mary is often holding a book, or there are books nearby. Mary before she became who she became.

WE DIDN'T RESERVE but are late enough to secure a table at Trattoria Taddeo e Federico, where we succumb to the white truffle. Our server authoritatively tells us what to order. "You will be happy," she assures us, and we believe her. Only two diners remain in the room; they surreptitiously feed their dog when the server exits. They look over at us, hoping we don't mind. We don't.

"What's your dog's name?" I ask. They are dressed in scruffy walking clothes, hoodies, and boots, a late-middle-aged couple both with straw-colored hair and ruddy cheeks.

"Pietro," the woman says. As his name is called, the dog stands and looks hopeful. He's carefully groomed, with thick, curly toffee-colored fur that invites petting.

"Oh, a truffle dog!" The Lagotto Romagnolo is my favorite kind of dog. Smart, adorable, so alert. Brown with white underbelly, Pietro looks at me with "I-speak-Italian" eyes. The breed goes way back: Lake dogs of Romagna, working dogs used for hunting and for water retrieval, now famous as keen searchers of truffles. "Is he finding truffles here?"

"No," the man says, slipping Pietro a sliver of prosciutto. "We're from Piacenza. He's trained for black truffles and shows no interest in the white, only in digging up the ground."

"Just the same trouble at home," the woman adds. "They like to dig everywhere. Especially daffodil and tulip bulbs." She looks at him fondly. "He's terrible." *Tremendo* is what she says, a word often applied to a rambunctious toddler.

I wish she were not saying this in front of Ed, as I've been lobbying to get this kind of dog.

As the server brings my tagliatelle and Ed's *passatelli,* a super-size policeman comes in the door. Someone is parked illegally in the piazza. "My husband," our boisterous server announces. "Isn't he lucky to have a wife like me?" We agree and turn to admire bowls of steaming *passatelli* redolent of sliced truffles. Not truly a pasta, *passatelli* is a local favorite. The tender little cylinders are formed from bread crumbs, lemon, eggs, Parmigiano, and nutmeg. The batter is passed through a special press with holes, or a ricer or sieve. The little dumplings are poached, like gnocchi. I've tried making them twice, only to have them fall apart. These don't. They're in a bit of fragrant broth, with, yes, truffle slices crowning them.

We vow to come back for the truffle with red potato gnocchi, and *paccheri alla carbonara. Paccheri,* the big tubular pasta, is one of my favorites for ragù. The rolled and stuffed rabbit, *rollè di coniglio farcito al tartufo bianco pregiato,* sounds fine, too. Anything with the precious white truffle.

Pietro's ears lift and he's wagging his tail. Maybe if they fed him a few tastes, he'd get the idea. For us, with one bite, the action in the room fades and the pure experience of this simple and ancient flavor takes over. Musty, earthy, mysterious. If there's ever an occasion for that overused word *umami,* this broth with *passatelli* is it.

We sometimes get summer black truffles in Tuscany and relish those days, though sometimes the texture resembles wood chips. These are both firm and tender. Order another portion? But the tasting platter arrives and all I want to do is stay in this room and eat—a fluffy omelet with truffles, polenta with truffles, crostini with *fonduta* of *pecorino* and truffles, a potato *sformato.* A blur of truffles. It's over too soon. I'm almost expecting truffle dessert. Since we're headlong into indulgence, we order another true taste of fall, the *tortino di castagne con scaglie al cioccolato caldo,* chestnut torte with melted chocolate.

Now that we've simmered down, and coffee is ordered, I wonder about the painted restaurant sign we saw outside the door of two gentlemen, Taddeo and Federico, namesakes of this restaurant. A note on the menu explains that the two Zuccari brothers, born in Sant'Angelo, were artists in the mid and late 1500s.

Over coffee, Ed reads to me. Taddeo had left for Rome by age fourteen, quickly establishing himself. He painted frescoes in the Villa Farnese. He died in his mid-thirties and was buried in the Pantheon, where his neighbor is Raphael. Federico was already working at the Vatican by age eighteen. He became famous, too, later painting in Spain, the Netherlands, Belgium, Florence's duomo, Galleria Borghese, all over. He was a pupil of Correggio from Parma. His twenty drawings of brother Taddeo are at the Getty.

"Both brothers from this tiny and remote town. How did they make their way to Rome as boys? What was in the water?" I never stop marveling at the level of culture that has thrived in Italy for centuries, even in back-of-beyond corners.

"The father was an artist," Ed says. "He must have wanted more for them and pushed them out the door."

Three-thirty seems like a good time to finish lunch. We go in search of our car, which we parked somewhere. Then we recall, the magic phones will tell us where. Soon we won't have to think at all. Just eat.

WE CHECK INTO a B & B just on the edge of Mercatello sul Metauro, only six kilometers from Sant'Angelo. Third floor of a simple house, small room, simply furnished with a wrought-iron bed. Cold. We've been on the move since dawn. We'd like to relax, prop up on pillows to read our *Blue Guide* to Le Marche, go over today's photos, check messages. I mean cold. The shower is minuscule. One of those folding panel doors that slide open at the corner. You have to squeeze in sideways. We take turns freezing. Fortunately, the bed feels good and the fluffy white duvet soon warms. The radiator makes encouraging sounds.

HAVING DRIVEN SEVERAL hours, we want a nearby restaurant for tonight. At the recommendation of the B & B owner, we try Ristorante Pizzeria Barbara, just down the road toward Sant'Angelo. He calls for a table for us. Lucky he did. When we arrive, the very large, well-lit restaurant is totally packed with local families and groups. We are the only lone couple. Clearly, this is where to go on Friday night. Everyone visits from table to table, stopping to greet a dozen people as they enter and exit. The waitstaff knows everyone. We order a liter of house wine and survey the ample menu, finally deciding to try the pizza, since everyone else seems to have done just that. Here's a sense of community. Here's where you came after your first communion, for your first date, with your kids, with your grandchildren. One of those important neighborhood classics we all long for. Our place. Where we have our special corner. Where the young girl waiting tables is your dentist's daughter. As flies on the wall, we participate in this weekend routine that everyone here knows so well. And the pizza is terrific. Margherita with sausage for me, *capricciosa,* chef's fantasy, for Ed. Only a small slice of chocolate *torte* for dessert. No truffles tonight!

AT BREAKFAST IN a glass sunroom, the owners' King Charles Spaniel keeps trying to leap to the buffet table. Two other guests, Francesco and Maria Grazia from Venice, sit with us. Over the dog's antics we strike up a conversation and linger talking to them for a couple of hours. Maria Grazia owns a family palazzo in Mercatello. They're here because it's the Day of the Dead. She comes back every year, as Italians do all over Italy, to her hometown to decorate the family graves with flowers. They don't stay in their palazzo in winter because it's too cold. They must have a warmer room here than we do, though ours has heated to a bearable temperature. They're working on repairs, enjoying visiting with family and friends. We swap photos on our phones, talk Venice, talk Tuscany, talk interesting places in Le Marche. I take notes of towns they know. But finally, Francesco says, "My life in Venice is a joke. I am from Naples and I must go to Naples every month. I fly. It's close. I have to go because it is my reality."

I'm always drawn to people who are indelibly bonded with a place. Maurizio, a Cortona friend from Naples, says that those who were born and lived there never can be satisfied with anywhere else. Francesco, case in point. Maria Grazia (Mary Grace, such a nice southern name) smiles indulgently. She's heard it before. Instead, she is wed to Venice and to this small village in Le Marche.

WE RUSH BACK to Sant'Angleo to the Saturday morning market stalls, where not only truffle vendors are set up, but hundreds of stands selling clothing, vegetables, and every household item imaginable. I buy some shiny *marroni,* the most prized of the chestnuts. Score! Six euros a kilo. Bins are mounded with walnuts, the preferred Italian nut, and with *nespole,* which are a popular fruit. When I lived in Palo Alto, we had loquat (also called medlar) bushes that seemed always laden with fruit. Seeing them rot spurred me to make preserves, but as the fruit simmered, the color turned from translucent orange to gooey gray. I should give them another try. Sacks of red potatoes labeled La Patata di Sompiano are obviously a special local potato. Duly noted.

The weekend market weaves down a long street, branching into narrow side passageways, spilling out the gate and onward. It's vast. As we walk by the cluster of truffle stands, we catch the unmistakable scent. Ed looks askance at the truffle-flavored olive oils on sale. Usually adding something to olive oil means the oil isn't top quality. A few hunting dogs hang out around the truffle sellers but they aren't the famous truffle sniffers. "What kind of dog is that? Does he have a good nose for truffles?" I ask one seller about his shaggy friend.

"Bravissimo," he answers. *"Un bastardo, il migliore."* A bastard, the best.

Signs on restaurants shout out today's specials: pastas with white truffle, *vitello al tartufo scorzone,* beef with black truffles, and *fagioli con cotiche,* the robust dish of stuffed pig's foot and white beans. *Trippa* and *cinghiale,* equally full of force: tripe and boar. Those guys manning the tractors out in the wheat fields will feast.

AFTER SOME TIME happily lost, we find the Romanesque complex Santa Maria dei Servi Extra Muros, outside the walls. There are thirteen altars from the seventeenth century (much younger than the walls themselves), each one donated by a local family. Imagine the competition! Many gifted painters never become household names, and here I see some of them, although I should have known Raffaellino del Colle, whose *Annunciation* I saw yesterday. I read about him last night. He's prolific and marvelous, as in *Madonna e Bambino con Santi,* his work at one altar. A fluid style and colors that wash over you. We're the only ones in the airy church, so the bored guard accompanies us to the museum wing, assuming the role of guide. From room to room, he points out what we shouldn't miss, watching to see if we are as impressed as we should be.

We get to see one of Federico Zuccari's paintings. I photograph close-up the exquisite hands on several of his saintly figures, and a young boy's sweet face. He's thoughtful and staring right at you. Could that be his brother Taddeo?

IN A PERFECTLY flat field on the edge of town, we find the Domus del Mito, House of Myth. This is mysterious. Archeologists in 1999 uncovered an intact mosaic floor of an A.D. first-century Roman house of one thousand square meters. How could it not have been found before? It lies barely under the ground level. Hasn't anyone ever plowed this land? What else lies under the grass? The perfectly clear floor plan could be a good one for a house today. The mosaic designs in each room functioned like rugs. Stunning images of Bacchus, Acteon, Medusa, Neptune, some of them colored and others black and white. Then the subjects pivot from mythology. Here's a hunting and fishing scene with an eel biting an octopus who catches a lobster, all surrounded by geometric patterns. Optical illusion patterns of diamonds and squares surround the central depictions. Of all the many mosaics I've seen in Italy, Greece, Spain, this is the most intimate and domestic; the most touching, because it's easy to imagine the furnished house, the splashing of a fountain, the lives in the rooms.

BACK IN THE *centro* and waiting for lunch, when Ed stops for yet another espresso—how does he not fly into the sky?—I wander on along a narrow street. In a doorway, a blur of candlelight catches my eye and I look into a room just below street level. Stepping down, I find myself in a small cave-like space completely covered with photographs. Faces of people, or standing front and center, posed in their finery. All over the walls, framed or thumb-tacked or lying loose on the table. A memory room for the town. There's a place to kneel, a metal stand where you can light a candle for someone dead. The bride whose eyes brim with life. The boy who fell down a well, the ones who went to war, grandmothers, all gone. Everyone. All the past equally over. And for those who remain, a space on the wall waits for them.

Over a flower-covered altar hangs crucified Christ, He who died for all these smiling faces. The scent of roses, carnations, waxy yellow begonias, blazing pink cyclamen, dried hydrangeas. Hot wax, dank air. Like burying your face in the hair of the young woman who has lifted off her hat.

Mercatello sul Metauro

Orange Flags, Bandiere Arancioni, are awarded to villages deemed especially attractive, historic, and interesting. I've listed these small places, most of which I've never heard of, in my travel notebook. Tuscany has thirty-eight, Piemonte twenty-six, and Le Marche twenty-one. What a quest—to see them all.

THAT'S HOW I found Mercatello sul Metauro, right down the road from Sant'Angelo. What a good place to stay for two months, working on a novel, paintings, or an opera. Peace and quiet, a still point on the spinning world. On this late October day, hardly anyone is out, though they must have been earlier, since this is market day. The large piazza, grand enough for a city, is a gift for the fourteen hundred inhabitants. Church, arcaded loggia with shops and cafés, grand and imposing town hall. Branching off, streets are lined with upright *palazzi*. How such a rural market town became so prosperous, I don't know. Sheep? Herds clump on many hillsides. Wheat? Probably.

THE USUAL COMPLEX history from Etruscan settlement to a small coin in the Papal States coffers, and lots of action in between. Across the ages, the town somehow remained intact: clean and proud streets, houses with interesting doors, an arched and pleasing Roman bridge over the river. I keep saying the word *idyllic.*

It's quiet. The two museums are closed. No cars to disturb. We walk every street, making up stories about the lucky residents of the *palazzi.* Which one belongs to Francesco and Maria Grazia, the couple from Venice we met at our B & B? I wish they'd lean out a window and call us, "Come up for a drink." Would the rooms hold old chests of drawers stuffed with parchment printed with music, photographs of dead babies with cotton stuffed in their noses, wills with names angrily scratched out? I've been in many old places where nothing has been disturbed in certain rooms for generations. Hunting clothes in the *armadio,* stiff nightgowns folded in a chest, a mangy toy elephant on a windowsill.

WE WIND OUT of town on country lanes through bucolic country-side, wondering if we're on the wrong road. How can a restaurant be so far from anywhere? But Osteria del Boscaiolo, recommended by Maria Grazia and Francesco, is everyone's destination for a traditional Sunday *pranzo.* Boscaiolo is packed. If it were warm, we'd be sitting along the river under a pergola. Instead, we are stuck at a table by the kitchen door. We're fine. Lucky to be here! A party takes up half a room. Children run outdoors, play on the lawn for a few minutes, then dash in again. A family-run place; the staff seems calm as they race around a capacity crowd.

Much to choose from. A liter of house wine appears as we try to decide what comes after the pasta with truffles. But wait, here's *gnocchi di patata rossa di Sompiano,* the red potatoes I saw in the market yesterday. The server says they're unique to this area, grown in the nearby village of Sompiano without any chemicals. He recommends the town's festival celebrating this local favorite the last weekend in August, with all the traditional foods of this area and a big emphasis on potato tarts and pastas.

We must try this gnocchi, and, yes, we can have truffles on top. We both think the stuffed pasta with ricotta, ginger, and bacon sounds interesting, so we order that to share, too. Boar, guinea hen, pigeon, duck, hare, veal—I opt for the guinea hen and Ed for the pigeon, one of his favorites. I partially kill my appetite because the bread is too good. Should we have chosen the ravioli with pumpkin and chickpea filling? We continue to go over the menu, speculating about the sweet-and-sour boar, and anticipating the desserts.

Guinea hen, *faraona,* is fantastic to roast. You hear "tastes like chicken" about everything from frog to rattlesnake. No, *faraona* doesn't taste like chicken. It's richer, more savory, with a hint of the wild, though the birds usually are farm raised. My neighbor keeps a flock and always has one turning (along with pork liver and sausages) in his fireplace when we go over for Sunday lunch. He knows I love the crispy skin and herb-infused taste. Guinea hen was never popular in the South when I was growing up, but it wasn't unheard of, either. My mother insisted on serving these birds at my older sister's wedding dinner. Enormously popular and *normal* in Italy, guinea hens appear in every butcher shop. Compared to plump chickens from good markets in the United States, the guinea hen looks skinny. What they lack in quantity, they compensate in flavor.

This one is tasty. So are the special roasted potatoes that come with it. I liked the gnocchi, too, but couldn't detect anything particular about the special potato in either. To appreciate the nuance, I'd probably need to taste one simply boiled, served side by side with a common potato.

Not a bite left of the cinnamon gelato with pear and wine sauce.

AFTERWARD, WE DRIVE a few kilometers to almost-deserted Castello della Pieve. Up, up, an aerie with sweeping views of the river valley. We planned to hike in these verdant hills, but the *pranzo* knocked out that idea. We stroll the tiny stone village instead. It actually has an inn and restaurant but no one is in sight. A plaque says that here in 1301 Dante Alighieri was sent into exile by Charles of Valois. Who knows why the king of France's brother was in residence and what this hidden place had to do with the poet. The up-and-down buildings look like a setting for a tale with goblins and fairies and a magic child somehow raised by an ancient woman who casts spells. I twist my ankle. We sit on a wall drinking fizzy water and taking pictures. Then we see a couple, quite normal looking, shaking out a tablecloth and setting out glasses and wine. Maybe everyone is just asleep.

WE WALK INTO town just after dark but still too early for dinner. Seeing a glow at the end of a street, we find the cemetery on this night of All Souls' Day. Every grave is lit with a votive candle, both the graves on the ground and the stacked ones like square drawers in walls. Flowers, everywhere. Mostly yellow chrysanthemums. (I learned long ago never to give that flower to the living.) White cyclamen lit from below glow cold and perfect. On each grave—here and everywhere in Italy—a framed photo of the person below stares back at you.

I've never, even on a Halloween dare, been in a graveyard at night—but this one, warm with candle glow and vibrant with flowers, seems friendly. A large moon, gold as a Roman coin, shines down on all. I try a few lines from "Blue Moon." Ed isn't sure the dead need my serenade and we walk quickly back into town.

Another meal. We are heroically capable, but even we falter after such a *pranzo.* "Let's order sensibly," Ed says, glancing at all the tantalizing choices. Most Italians enjoy a feast with family or friends on Sunday at lunch, then order pizza, or make an omelet or something easy at home. But here we are. We decide on ravioli with—what else?—truffles, and salad.

Ristorante da Uto, part of an inn, is two small rooms. The owner's young daughter, about ten, periodically glides through on roller skates, providing us with a Fellini moment. She looks neither right nor left as she sails past like a spirit. The weirdness doubles as the owner shuffles through in slippers. Scuff, scuff, glide, glide.

OUR ROOM NOW is toasty warm. We set the alarm. Up early and onward to other towns in Le Marche.

. . .

WE SKIP THE large breakfast, wave good-bye to the friendly owners and their dog.

We're heading to Ancona on the coast. En route, we make several stops:

Fermignano, also along the Metauro. We enter this pale brick town over a three-arched Roman bridge with a medieval tower perched nearby. We stop for a cappuccino and a little wander, then move on.

Fossombrone. A sprawling market is in progress. I find two sweaters for my daughter, and a scarf. The long town with arcaded sidewalks along cobbled Corso Garibaldi also spurs the shopping instincts. This town is incredibly rich in archeology, Baroque churches, handsome *palazzi,* and lively cafès. I'd hoped to see the *Nativity* by Federico Zuccari, our discovery in Sant'Angelo in Vado. But Sant'Agostino is closed, as are other churches and galleries. Everyone must be at the market. Fossombrone deserves at least a day or two.

Mondavio. This is a spur-of-the-moment stop, and a lucky one. Hugely fortified with brick walls and towers, the town also owns several wooden catapults, huge launchers of whatever they once flung at approaching enemies. I'm surprised to see that they, and the imposing castle, La Rocca, were designed by Francesco di Giorgio Martini, who was the architect for one of my favorite churches in Cortona, Santa Maria del Calcinaio. The earthquakes terrorizing Le Marche recently have shut down the museum and the Teatro Apollo, whose floor rises to meet the stage and form a dance floor. The bakery, however, is open and we get to sample polenta biscotti and other cookies made with fava bean flour.

WE'VE BEEN TO Ancona before. It has treasures but it's not an easy place. A port town. Confusing to drive in, confusion heading toward frustration and perhaps some sharp words about turns that should have been made. This is an improvement in travel: With all the navigation prompts, the curses get directed at the disembodied voice that steers us astray. Not at each other.

Finally, we are checked into the super-serene SeePort Hotel overlooking the Adriatic. A few hours to unwind, take notes, read. The in-house Ristorante Ginevra shocks us out of our country ways with its glamour and finesse. Ah, the pea and garlic risotto, the succulent langoustines.

News is that earthquakes are shaking the area where we are going. Onward early tomorrow.

Sirolo

Si— and —rolo. The break, hiss, roll of waves. Sirolo, what an
evocative word for this jewel perched above the Adriatic, a
pastel, leafy town where the main order of business seems
to be gelato. Everyone else is strolling around on this warm
October day, gelato in hand, so we follow. Coffee and
hazelnut for Ed, plain vanilla and melon for me. We find
a bench and gaze through the trees at the sea. The town
may be medieval in origin, but the new and old blend so
seamlessly that the place seems timeless. For Ed, gelato calls
for espresso afterward. We light at Caffè Centrale, surely
the heart of this town, for a chance to watch fellow travelers
and dogs and babies in strollers already displaying their *bella
figura* clothing.

SIROLO IS ONLY a half hour and a world away from **Ancona,**
the ancient Greek port, now a convoluted town where we
were lost more often than found. Ancona has important
monuments and museums, as well as the stunning Trajan

arch, built in A.D. 115, a veteran of millennia of war and earthquakes. Since we'd been here before, we surveyed port activities from our windows overlooking the docks at the cool SeePort Hotel and spent the afternoon reading, then taking a long walk. Sometimes, while traveling, the greatest luxuries are the quiet hours spent with a notebook and a companion.

Last night, we were thrilled by Ginevra, the hotel's ambitious restaurant. Arched windows overlook tankers, ships, cranes, and fishing boats, but I was glued to the interior. I took pictures of the distressed walls and layered paint, thinking of our bedroom at Bramasole that I want to revise—something more interesting than white walls and white linen.

WE EXITED EARLY this morning, ready to see Monte Conero and the Conero peninsula. We're only passing through Sirolo, en route from Ancona to Loro Piceno in Le Marche, but I'm checking out Sirolo's hotels for when we can come back. At the end of a street of artisan shops, I see Locanda e Ristorante Rocco. It looks secluded and I imagine a room overlooking the sea.

We're off, driving to the coast before heading inland to Fermo and Recanati.

A FEW KILOMETERS from Sirolo and we're in another seaside town, **Numana,** whose charms must not be apparent—we didn't see them as we made our way down to the beach at **Portonovo.** The Adriatic can be green-gray like the Atlantic, but today shades of blue and aqua layer out to the pencil-drawn line of the horizon. Although they're hell to walk on, I love white stony beaches. It's as if millions of little moons have fallen. Who can resist taking home one of these smooth white rocks, perfect paperweights? I pocket one that looks like a round of pizza dough. We have the beach to ourselves: another checkmark on my pleasures-of-off-season travel list. Flocks will swarm in warm weather but today no one is out. We can walk the edge of the strand and look back at the Napoleonic fortress (now a hotel) and marvel at the limpid water.

· · ·

I DID NOT expect this morning to see one of the most magical objects I've ever encountered. I did not expect it to be inside one of the most soulful buildings I've ever entered. Leaving the beach, we look for the church I've just read about. We follow an arrow to La Chiesa di Santa Maria di Portonovo, but we almost turn back because we're walking a path through fenced residences with private property signs. I'm glad we pressed on because soon we face a white stone Romanesque church of such pleasing proportions and grace that we fall silent as we walk around it. It seems that only ascetics in long robes should be here. Pine, scrubby bushes, and olives surround the area, cutting the church off from views of the sea just below. We walk twice around the exterior. Such sweet curves and shadows cast by deep-cut windows and blind colonnades.

This is holiness living in a form. Three naves, three apses, three domes, a low bell tower. (I would like to hear them ring.) The interior is all curves. Compact as the space is, there are two side aisles, both arched. Here is the argument for less is more: I'm spinning from the beauty. The church is unadorned, silent, and luminescent. Easy to imagine the eleventh-century Benedictines chanting in the nave, the dove of the holy ghost flapping against the dome, even if you don't believe.

I'm indebted to Ellen Grady, who wrote *Blue Guide: The Marche and San Marino.* If I hadn't opened the book to the page on Monte Conero, I would not have known about the unusual object in the narthex of the church. It's hidden behind a standing bulletin board announcing church activities. With no one to stop me, I squeeze around the notice board. Embedded in the wall, I see a smooth marble disk with a carved Maltese cross and mysterious letters arranged around it. You can find disks of Saint Benedict in religious shops and on the Internet, protective medals with letters and symbols. But this one is ivory-colored marble rubbed to the sheen of wax by centuries of hands touching it as they entered Santa Maria.

Ellen Grady says this is "a talisman used by exorcists." The letters on the disk are the first initials of the words *Crux Sancti Patris Benedicti. Crux Sacra Sit Mihi Lux. Non Draco Sit Mihi Dux. Vade Retro Satana! Nunquam Suade Mihi Vana. Sunt Mala Quae Libas. Ipse Venena Bibas. IHS.* (The Cross of our Holy Father Benedict. May the Holy Cross be my light. May the dragon never be my guide. Get behind me, Satan! Never tempt me with your vanities. What you offer me is evil. Drink the poison yourself! In the name of Jesus Christ our Saviour.) Rubbing the plaque is part of reciting the prayer.

Of all my thousands of church visits, I've never seen anything like this. I rub it. Exorcism! Drink the poison yourself!

Recanati and Fermo

As we drive south from Portonovo, we hear more about last night's earthquakes in Le Marche. Macerata, where we've been in summers for the opera season, is shaking. The exquisite Ascoli Piceno has escaped major damage but is also trembling. After some jolts last week, Recanati and Fermo now seem calm.

Recanati, birthplace of the poet Giacomo Leopardi. And there he stands in the middle of his piazza, high on a pedestal, arms crossed, looking down on us voyagers. The piazza is empty. In the one open bar, we hear the word again. *Terramoto.* Earthquake. No restaurant is open. We eat ham and cheese on focaccia at the bar and that's that. The barista tells us that public buildings, including the Leopardi library, the historic Teatro Persiani, and the museum, are closed until possible damage is assessed. She looks a bit shaky herself. "Yes. My nerves are torn up. You know what happened to Norcia and Amatrice." We do.

. . .

WE'RE LEFT TO admire the handsome town hall, arcade, and Torre del Borgo with its clock running since 1562, and to walk the streets of this pretty town. How much the citizens revere the poet! Many wooden pallets are hung on walls. Studded with succulents and flowering plants, each displays a poem. Leopardi, however, did not admire Recanati. How could he? His over-protective family practically imprisoned him: He was not allowed outside alone until he was twenty. He considered the Papal States village an ignorant backwater that he could not escape. At that time, you had to have a passport to leave town; his father made sure he couldn't get one.

The tall, neoclassical palazzo where the poet spent his miserable youth looks like a fine place to grow up. Leopardi practically lived in his father's library, where he began writing seriously as a boy. By fourteen, he'd written *Pompeo in Egitto* (*Pompey in Egypt*), a book about Caesar. Sources and his own writing agree that his parents were tyrannical, fanatical, and loveless. His mother thought it best for children to die before they could be spotted with sin. The general wretchedness he endured was alleviated by his closeness with his sister and brother. At least his aristocratic father (gambler, failed writer) accomplished the remarkable library, where the boy learned Hebrew, Greek, and Latin. He wrote across subjects from philosophy to philological treatises but is loved for his lyric poetry. Unlike his English contemporaries, his was not a poetry of elegiac romanticism; his message is unrelentingly dark. Leopardi seems to have landed in Recanati from the future, bringing atheism, alienation, and confirmed hopelessness. As an adult, he finally escaped to other cities.

He possessed the rare gift to re-create sensory experience with a palpability that predicts modern poetry. His *I touch the world* talent gives joy, even though he found his subjects in the "unhappy and terrible strangeness of life in the universe." He is still read. Most Italians I know can quote the Leopardi they learned at school.

Besides his poems, perhaps the most astonishing work he left is the commonplace book, *Zibaldone di pensieri* (Hodge-podge of Thoughts), 4,526 pages of ideas, fragments, quotations, speculations, and responses to readings.

Frail, with failing sight, and suffering from scoliosis (and possibly cholera), he died at thirty-eight in Naples.

Leopardi's descendants still live on the upper floors. Outside, they've constructed a little glass-fronted take-a-book-leave-a-book box. Saul Bellow and Marguerite Duras are side by side.

WE'RE LOOKING FOR Casa Azzurra, our inn outside Loro Piceno. We're lost for a while—there's another inn of a similar name—and have the chance to see big swells of agricultural land and sweeping skies. Fallow fields have been plowed, and I roll down the window for the sweet scent of turned earth. Finally, we arrive at a blue house in the country with a lauded organic restaurant, Seta Cruda. Nothing special architecturally, the two-story farmhouse looks homey and casual. We know it's all green, with environmentally friendly heating and cooling, and even feng-shui attention to arrangements. I'm delighted to be greeted by two *Lagotto Romagnolo* dogs, the truffle hunters. They're matted and rowdy, jumping on me with dirty paws. Barking. We meet the friendly, bearded owner of inn and dogs, Elia Quagliola, and his assistant Giusi. They show us the glass-box dining room, a library of art books, and the pool and spa. Giusi asks if we want ground floor or upstairs. "You might feel better down because of the . . ." Her voice drops. "Earthquakes."

Having lived so many years in San Francisco, we're wary. We check in downstairs and quietly discuss leaving altogether. We don't. When I take a shower before dinner, a torrent of water runs onto the floor. Flood and earthquake. Not good.

WHAT IS GOOD: Seta Cruda. It's warm enough to have a spritz under the mulberry tree. Ah, I get it: The restaurant name—raw silk—is because of the mulberries on the grounds. The dogs join us. Although we are the only guests at the inn—they're closing for a winter break—the dining room soon fills with locals. I love this kind of restaurant, where the food is like what you'd have at the home of a friend who happens to be a super cook. We choose salads and pizza margherita, the most ordinary of orders. But the salad is a toss of several lettuces, all primo, with green and piquant olive oil. The pizza is classic and superb. Crunchy crust not too thin or too doughy. A lot of cheese and a few accents of truffle. "Best pizza you've ever had?" I ask Ed.

"That would take an hour of calculating but it's definitely up there."

Ed chooses an extraordinary Le Marche wine, Tenuta di Tavignano Verdicchio dei Castelli di Jesi Classico Superiore Misco. That's a long name for something that doesn't linger long in the glass. A hint of pear, a slight flash of minerals, a wine that calls for a second bottle.

AT THREE IN the morning I wake up because a hard flash of rain hits the window. All those dusty fields soaking. They were filled with sunflowers all summer; now what will be planted in the friable soil? Winter wheat? I am about to drift off again when a low, unmistakable rumble starts shaking the bed.

"Ed! Wake up. Earthquake." Glass rattles like teeth chattering.

"What? Oh, Christ!" We fly out of bed. As I stand up the room seems to tilt. We rush outside in the rain. I'm in a thin nightgown, Ed in underwear. Dark. We're on the back side of the house. My feet feel the current in the ground. Then it stops. How long do we stand out here getting wet? After a few minutes, we cautiously enter our room. Nothing seems amiss. Maybe the feng shui kept the lamps and chairs in place. Was it the rain that woke me? Or primal instinct? I think we'd better go home until these seizures stop.

ALTHOUGH THE MORNING is innocent again, we cancel our next three days. For me, the 1989 Loma Prieta earthquake in the Bay Area never faded away. We leave right after the warm pastries and commiserating conversation with Giusi and Elia. I regret not having another night at Seta Cruda. The dogs quietly follow us to the car and stare as we leave. We snatch a quick look at tiny Loro Piceno, which has an unbelievable number of churches and a castle. We must skip for now the lakes and trails of Monti Sibillini National Park, and San Ginesio, selected by Touring Club Italiano as one of the most beautiful villages in Italy. Suddenly having to make hard choices, we opt for Fermo.

DIGNIFIED AND NOBLE like Recanati, Fermo surprises us by looking lively this edgy morning. Surely they shook, too. We quickly find out in the tourist office that, yes, public buildings are closed until inspected for damage. We won't get to see inside the asymmetrical Gothic Duomo, but we do get to admire its façade with many grapevine carvings. The inspiration came from a quote: Jesus said, *I am the vine.* An angel holds out her gown to collect in her lap the grapes she is picking. A woman hands grapes to a child who puts them in a basket. A bird pecks grapes. A hooded creature eats them. All grape imagery. The early viewer would have known the symbolism: Eating the grape means tasting the mystery of the Eucharist while on earth. There are also puzzling shellfish images. Then I read that they symbolize the resurrection because they shed their shells in spring. Dragons, lions, scorpions—a rich panoply of meaningful images. And what a pretty rose window! Twisted stone spokes radiate around circles and circles of curvy carving.

I ESPECIALLY WANTED to see the town library. Established in 1688. Imagine! In photographs, it looks magnificent: An enormous old celestial and terrestrial globe, double tiers of mellow wooden shelves lettered with Roman numerals and stacked with pale volumes bound in vellum. Can't we see it? Impossible. But the helpful young woman at the tourist office offers to unlock the Teatro Comunale dell'Aquila, the 1780–1790 "eagle" opera house. Ah, the people of Fermo at that time were enjoying opera! A thousand seats. I make a mental note to check future schedules and bring friends for a weekend in Fermo. I would wear my best velvets and jeweled shoes! The gilded wedding-cake tiers rise to five levels. The ceiling frescoes by Luigi Cochetti depict the gods of Olympus singing to Apollo. I hope to hear a pure Monteverdi opera where they play the sackbut and cornetti and the voices rejoice.

OUR YOUNG, SERIOUS woman from the tourist office offers to let us see Piscina Epuratoria, the *cisterna romane,* the Roman cistern behind Piazza del Popolo, built between A.D. 140 and 160. We follow a back street and she unlocks a door that leads us down into thirty lofty, cavernous, dank, domed underground brick rooms for holding and cleaning water. Astounding. Underground vaulting in chamber after chamber where aqueducts poured fresh water for the inhabitants of Fermo. Oh, how smart they were. Levels were controlled, channels ran off the extraneous, other systems made sure the water was potable. Some of the cisterns were used up until 1982. Interesting in earthquake times—they're secure in letting us see something this old.

THIS TOWN OF five thousand is a place you can see in a morning, and yet you could live in for a lifetime and not see everything. Its history, convoluted as for all Italian towns, goes back forever. Bits of clay vases from the fourteenth and fifteenth centuries B.C. have been found here. And the beat has gone on ever since.

Gamberi alla Griglia con Finocchio e Olive

GRILLED PRAWNS WITH FENNEL AND OLIVES, SERVES 4

What a fresh and surprising preparation from Chef Carlo Candria. In his kitchen, prime ingredients are allowed to shine.

1 fennel bulb, cut in large dice

20 prawns or large shrimp, shelled and deveined

2 tablespoons extra-virgin olive oil

Salt, *QB*

2 oranges, peeled, sliced, and seeded

20 small black pitted olives, sliced thinly (*taggiasche* if you can find them)

Boil the fennel for 3 to 4 minutes, drain, and let it cool. Grill (or quickly sauté) the prawns and season with oil and salt. Add a bit of oil and salt to the chopped fennel, and then put the prawns on the top. Scatter the slices of orange and the olives on top.

Seta Cruda di Casa Azzurra, Loro Piceno, Le Marche

Lazio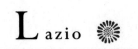

Sabaudia

Mussolini did many worthwhile things, other than make Italian trains run on time. For one, he finished what others before him—back to 162 B.C.—had tried to do. He drained the vast Pontine Marshes, ridding the area of malaria and creating vast agricultural lands that pulled the economy out of a quagmire. And he built Sabaudia. Of all the charms we expect of Italian towns—ancient piazzas, flowering balconies, villas of ocher, saffron, and rose, cart-narrow streets, Romanesque churches—Sabaudia has none. The architecture is post–World War One *razionalismo,* rationalist, the Italian offshoot of the modernist international style: functional, unornamented, pared-down materials, and composed mostly of squared-off volumes. *Razionalismo* was the preferred style of the fascist government.

We are visiting Sabaudia, just a two-hour drive south from Rome, for its twenty-three kilometers of beach and the four beguiling lakes just behind the strand. May has arrived, balmy and soft. We check into Hotel Il San Francesco, built of white cubes with curvy details. Our all-white room looks out at lawns sloping to a lake. Early check-ins are a bonus to off-season travel. Ed has time for his walk and I have time to sit near the lake and read before lunch.

The dining room personifies the word *airy*. Doors are open in the glass-walled room where breezes send all the sheer curtains drifting. We share a large fennel, orange, black olive salad, then grilled octopus on a bed of chicory and fried shrimp. "Push through," Ed says over coffee, when I am leaning toward a long siesta with the doors to our balcony open.

We do. We drive the five minutes to the beach, which is blessedly undeveloped, with wooden access paths every few kilometers. No one! Not a soul. How rare. No concessions and umbrellas and beach lounges. A few houses at the far end toward a picturesque watchtower, a couple of hotels, a few bars and fish shacks. Waves, gentle, clouds, busy, sand, soft and gold, air salt-tanged, sweet.

I DO GET my short rest. I tuck my watch with its news alerts and dings reminding me to stand up into a pocket of my suitcase. I'm switching to beach time.

Late in the afternoon, we walk around Sabaudia. I expect to be disinterested in the town, but we find a lively place with palms, plumbago, and oleander in bloom. Almost a hundred years on, rationalist architecture has acquired its own historicity. What was never lost in the Italian version of modernism is the human scale of the buildings. With such a long distance from the fascist era, the eye begins to see less demagogic purpose and more of the adherence these severe buildings have to classical architecture. The Italians never let go of their love for the Romans and Greeks. Or of travertine and marble over concrete. The Piazza del Comune must have double-functioned as an outsize military parade ground. A small market of local honey and organic products stands where the Blackshirts held forth, and farther out tiny boys are playing soccer. Electronic music blares from one of the cafés lining the perimeter. Stores sell beach toys and flip-flops along the sidewalks, and gelato shops send genial troops of teenagers out with towering cones of melon and coffee and hazelnut gelato. Well-dressed, prosperous, the *sabaudiesi* are all out for a stroll. Wouldn't the five architects who won the design competition for planning this place be shocked? Their rigorous, utopian town, designed for workers and transplants from poor sections of the north, now thrums with a relaxed seaside vibe. Flip-flops and beach hats replacing military boots and helmets.

Over Campari sodas, with a view of the official buildings and a clock tower, we check our books. Started in 1933, Sabaudia was built in a miraculous 253 days! Six thousand workers labored, accomplishing a Roman grid design down to a *decumanus* cutting through the center. The old post office stands out. The oval form and bold staircase are not at all like the severe volumes of the vertical clock tower, the horizontal town hall. Now a library and documents center, it's the only major structure not designed by the selected team of five but was conceived instead by a man named Angiolo Mazzoni. Maverick lurking in the wings: shiny blue tile, red marble, and primary yellow trim instead of the somber grays of the overall plan. "I bet Mazzoni wasn't a real die-hard fascist," Ed says. But I look him up and he was. He designed many, many post offices, train stations, and other public buildings across the realm for Mussolini. Yet something says *liberty* in his designs; he must have been torn. He fled to South America after the war.

We walk over to the municipal buildings. I always feel a creepy shiver when I see the fascist symbol, the ax and bundled rods, carved into a building. But inside the regime's tower, now the Museo della Torre Civica, we find a surprise: two hundred artworks inspired by Dante.

WE DRIVE THE tree-lined Appian Way over to Pontinia for dinner at Ristorante Essenza. Finding it isn't easy but we have a little tour of the town, which was also a fascist endeavor. Teatro Fellini. A blur of other rationalist buildings. Stuck out in a nondescript residential neighborhood, the restaurant's premises look a bit shaky. We're drawn inside by its Michelin star. Very chic and inviting and the staff super friendly. What a treat. Everything outstanding: a soup of Parmigiano, hazelnut, saffron, and potatoes with a Parmigiano foam. The mellow background music just serves to relax us for the next course. Which is, for me, shrimp on a red pepper *sformato* (a puffy quiche-like tart), and for Ed the catch of the day—didn't catch the name of the fish—with panzanella and smoked burrata. Just for taste, we shared the baby pig with peanuts, chard, and mustard.

Throughout this feast, we're impressed with splendid, surprising wine parings from very particular sources: Terra delle Ginestre Lentisco, 2014, a local bianco made from the scarce *bellone* grape and fermented in chestnut casks, which gives a hint of smokiness to the airy wine; Stefano Antonucci, 2011 Tardivo Ma Non Tardo (late, not too late), a spun-gold *verdicchio* from Jesi in Le Marche; Alma Mater Consoli from Damiano Ciolli in Lazio, dark and fruity, made from indigenous *cesanese* grapes; and Noelia Ricci, La Vespa 2015, a *sangiovese* from Emilia-Romagna. Their labels show drawings of vineyard animals and insects. The *sangiovese* label design is a *vespa,* wasp. And this wine, full-bodied, with enough tannins to deliver a little sting.

Generous pours, a dessert of white chocolate meringue with raspberries; espresso, we're off. Down the arrow-straight Appian Way, this ancient road from 312 B.C. Maybe it's the wine: I start singing "Do You Know the Way to San Jose," until Ed says, "Mio dio, Frances."

Back to Hotel Il San Francesco, where a boozy wedding dinner is wrapping up in the garden. The last music floats up to our room, over the lake, over the dunes, out to sea.

ED IS OUT early. When we meet at breakfast, he shows me photographs he took of jasmine. Hedges, tall, trained up over trellis gates, jasmine tumbling from balconies and climbing onto roofs. Our jasmine arbor at Bramasole blew down in a storm. We're inspired to replant.

What else to see? The fabulous Garden of Ninfa. But we cannot get a reservation. Another time. Instead, we set off for Sermoneta.

ON BACK ROADS, we pass through sweet countryside of olive groves and yellow wildflowers, then a castle on a tall mound with chopped-off edges, leaving the castle perched precariously. How does anyone enter? The walled town of Sermoneta spreads across a spur of a green mountain, situated much like Cortona, our adopted Tuscan hill town.

High above any marsh problem, the medieval town, also topped by a castle, takes us back into the Italy we know. Twisty up-and-down cobble streets, some scarcely wider than a person; sudden long views between stone houses; pastry, cheese, and wine shops. There are tourists, mostly Italians out for a Sunday *gita*. Not thronged but enough to fill the few restaurants. We end up at a tiny place named Street Food. The owner squeezes us into a nook adjacent to his friends who are playing cards. Street food it's not; we love the huge and hearty roasted vegetable sand-wiches on crunchy bread. And love joining for a little while the boister-ous group next to us. I'm always heartened by the genuine friendliness of Italians. Boundless! "Americans? I have a brother in Pittsburgh!"

"How did he happen to go there?" A story ensues. We're bonded. He offers the coffee, now that we're friends.

What a romantic town: branching and twining streets full of mys-tery and surprise. A friend used to have a house here. When I mention her name to the owner of the ceramics shop, she remembers her well. "Ah, la Susanna!" We take a photo together to send to her. When I buy a platter, she gives me a big discount. Everywhere, the human touch. The natural intimacy that sets apart life in Italy from life anywhere else.

I photograph the *lavatoio comunale,* the three-part stone basins with circulating water for washing your clothes. I think I would like to rinse out my blouses here. Sheets, probably not. We wander up to Santa Maria Assunta, the thirteenth-century church built on top of a Roman temple. The façade is somber but graced by a lovely rose window carved from stone. Outside are posted the rules for entering: silence, turn off cell phone, no smoking, dress decorously, no American chewing gum.

TONIGHT, BACK IN Sabaudia, we're at a simple trattoria near the hotel. A platter of grilled razor clams with crispy French fries, half a carafe of local red. We are the only customers so the waitress lingers, telling us about her cousin's fishing boats and her son who wants to be a deejay.

WHEN I WAS growing up in Georgia, my family went at least once a month to Fernandina, just barely into Florida. We all loved the beach. There, most of the time, we resembled a normal family. My daddy and I got up to see the sunrise over the ocean. I rode, arms out for balance, on the backs of turtles as they made their way back to the water after laying eggs in the warm sand. Daddy would, or so he told me, give the bottles I stuffed with notes to the shrimp boat fisherman to throw in the water far at sea. *Write to me. I am from Fitzgerald, Georgia.*

Therefore and forever after, I'm seeking the right place where water meets sand. So many Italian beaches are narrow or rocky or full of people. Sabaudia is unique. The long beach is separated only by a narrow road and then dunes from a series of lakes. The largest, Lago di Sabaudia, reaches fingers farther into the interior, creating vast amounts of lake frontage.

I can't get enough of the beach. Are any of the well-hidden houses for rent? I'd like to come back for a week. Meanwhile, early and late, I walk.

A WATCHTOWER, TORRE di Paola, anchors the Monte Circeo promontory jutting into the sea. Driving south from the beach road, we turn uphill near the tower; we're en route to the small town of San Felice Circeo; Circeo, yes, that's Circe, who zapped Ulysses's crew, turning them into pigs.

Both Sabaudia and San Felice Circeo are located within the 21,004-acre Parco Nazionale del Circeo, established in 1934, when the marsh was drained. The park has recently been expanded. Trekking trails, twenty kilometers of dunes, ruins of cyclopean walls and an acropolis, extensive forests, Mediterranean maquis and holm oaks, lakes, and coast—a rich ecosystem and resource. Amazing that long ago the fascists saved this bountiful resource. From the other side of the tower, you can go by boat to explore forty-odd caves where Neanderthal remains have been found; people have appreciated the beauty of this area for eons.

San Felice Circeo, starting point for many leisurely-to-strenuous walks. And what a delectable village: a main street lined with butter-yellow-to-golden buildings, a fountain, casual clothing shops, gelato, gelato, gelato, and cafés where pensioned men sit talking under umbrellas. The town hall was originally the house of the Knights Templar. At the entrance gate, the inviting cinema is dedicated to Anna Magnani. On display in the tourist office—we always stop at the tourist office—there's a head of Circe, found by a shepherd, quite stunning and more so for being exhibited alone. From the port, you're close to the island of Ponza and can jump on a boat and be there in an hour. The activities seem endless, but we are on the road again tomorrow.

AFTER A LONG fish, fish, fish lunch, we repair to the hotel to replenish. I have research to do on my laptop. (Exactly how many lakes are there?) Ed is on the balcony with his notebook. On the lawn below, a first communion party moves into its fourth hour. A long lunch under umbrellas, table laid for maybe sixty, is over. Half have gone but the rest linger in the mellow afternoon. A few men still sit at the table, smoking and talking. Cards come out for a game of *scopa*. Women lounge in the lawn chairs with children playing games all around them. Two fairy princesses, the honored ones, in their white dresses spin and cartwheel. Another child is on crutches. Badly dressed among the swans. The one who hurts. The others cavort in their lacy dresses. Someone plays a sweet guitar. How many such celebrations I have attended—sometimes bored with the endlessness of it but usually lulled and carried by the timelessness of what Italians do best, celebrating life.

I'm sinking into the pillows, dreamy, thinking strangely that if I were to die now, this would not be a bad ending, listening to an Italian party on a spring afternoon.

NOTES:

The architects of Sabaudia: Gino Cancellotti, Eugenio Montuori, Luigi Piccinato, Alfredo Scalpelli. The post office architect: Angiolo Mazzoni.

The lakes behind the beach are Lago di Sabaudia, Lago dei Monaci, Lago di Fogliano, and Lago di Caprolace.

Article of interest on Sabaudia by Michael Z. Wise: https://www.guernicamag .com/michael-z-wise-mussolinis-new-town/

Sperlonga

The extravagant beauty of Sperlonga will never leave
me. I first saw the twisted whitewashed village above
the sea twenty years ago and at many moments those
blue views through arches, white laundry flapping in
the wind, waterfalls of magenta bougainvillea have risen
unbidden in my mind. Such a place gets at the heart of
the Mediterranean fantasy: *Here is my place in the sun.* Stone
stairs curving up to a simple room, a table on a balcony, a
breeze—breath of gods—a pot of rosemary and basil. A
few books, and solitude all the way to the horizon.

Maybe the same people are still visiting under the trees
in the small piazza. That scent of focaccia always has been
wafting out the *forno* door, and the same (American?) girl is
still playing the bohemian exile in her gauzy dress, sandals,
and a hundred bangles. Maybe we haven't changed, either.
No longer the innocents abroad but still bedazzled by the
charge and fierce life of the old world.

We've been traveling a long time this year. Today I want
to stop and sit here without thinking of anything other

than this air that smells of mimosa. I'm not even curious; I just want to observe the hugely pregnant woman going about her shopping and bent men huddled around a table of sports newspapers and cigarettes.

"Brimful," I say.

"What? Oh, the cappuccino?"

"No."

"I see what you mean." A gift to travel with someone you don't have to explain everything to.

THOUGH THE VILLAGE remains as it was, the development along the beach below has certainly expanded. I don't recall many hotels and restaurants, but now they follow the strand for quite a distance. Sperlonga—from Latin *spelunca,* cave—always receives awards for its clean beaches. Friends tell me it's a perfect family vacation spot, low-key and easy. We don't go down to the beach. This is a brief stop, just to check up on *paradiso.* In the *centro storico,* there is nothing in particular to accomplish, other than enjoy grilled octopus on a high terrace, wander, sit in the sun, and read a guidebook. It's a place to climb up streets narrow as veins and to look at how people have planted their stoops with cacti or geraniums, to notice how someone has glued seashells up the drainpipe, and how many people choose to paint their doors blue. The stone streets, polished by centuries of use, shine as though they are wet when they're not. I buy a pair of yellow espadrilles and a sun hat.

THOSE ANCIENTS, OF course, knew just where to build lavish marble villas for their escapes from Rome. Just out of town, we find the Museo Archeologico Nazionale on the spot where Emperor Tiberius vacationed. His twenty-three-year reign was from A.D. 14 to 37. Villa di Tiberio, built along three hundred meters of coast, included a secret sea cave, magnificently decorated with sculptures and mosaics arranged around fish pools. Miraculously in 1957, ruins and many of the artworks were found during road construction.

The little museum is not to be missed. The male nudes are startlingly monumental, the marble relief of a woman and a winged creature is delicate and regal. We see Ulysses blinding the giant cyclops

Polyphemus, and Zeus in the form of an eagle kidnapping Ganymede, both well-known scenes from *The Odyssey*. A major discovery shows the tentacled Scylla monster attacking Ulysses's crew. Dating the statues is still problematic. Are they Greek originals of the Hellenistic middle period, or are they first-century Roman copies? Were they the actual figures from Tiberius's grotto dining room? Whatever they prove to be, they are daunting and powerful.

HOW SMART THE citizens were to block the road when the government tried to move the newly found trove to Rome. They kept their patrimony; they got their museum. The memory of Ulysses, who roamed this coast, belongs to Sperlonga.

Gaeta

From Sperlonga to Gaeta, the coast is punctuated with Genovese watchtowers on rocky outcrops. Along the twenty-minute drive stretch the heavenly beaches of Lazio. One requires descending three hundred steps. One is a hidden cove you only can reach by swimming. The rest are splendid walking beaches at this season, early May, but in summer, I've seen in photographs, they become the typical Italian lidos with closely placed umbrellas, concessions, and changing rooms. I'm not enamored of the beach life Italians love, but what feels claustrophobic to me is convivial and fun to everyone else. Ed says you have to get into it. He likes being able to stroll a few meters and order a lemon granita. Italians visit with friends lounging around them in the sand, often renting their station for an entire vacation.

LEGEND SAYS AENEAS landed along this strand after leaving Troy. Here he buried his wet nurse, Gaeta, naming a town for her. (Legend doesn't say why a grown man was traveling with his wet nurse on this voyage.) Alternately, the name comes from *Kaietai,* Greek for concave, cavity, for the mouth-shaped harbor. Gaeta was a resort for the ancient Romans. Hadrian built a villa. Not that it went well for all the Romans. Cicero was decapitated while trying to escape on a litter. When Marc Antony displayed Cicero's head in the Roman Forum, his wife, Fulvia, pulled open his mouth and jabbed his tongue with a needle, posthumous punishment for his inflammatory speeches.

Later, the Byzantines, the Angevins, the Spanish took their turns with the seductive harbor. Who wouldn't want to hold this strategic and gorgeous land?

WE CHECK INTO the Villa Irlanda Grand Hotel. Parklike gardens and a pool with an island surround a peaches-and-cream neoclassical, nineteenth-century villa and several handsome outbuildings. Right on the sea, although separated by a road, the hotel is close to town and a great choice for a quiet and pretty stay.

GAETA, FABULOUSLY BUILT along the water, is a quiet town of around 22,000. In the relatively newer part, eighteenth century onward, fishermen set up their market at evening, when everyone is suddenly flooding the streets, out shopping for dinner. I have not seen this before; usually markets are held in the morning. The *lungomare* is lined with stalls for every wiggling octopus and breathing fish hauled in today: anchovies gleaming like just-polished sterling silver, boxes of mussels, plus mounds of the famous red shrimp of the area.

Just inland, narrow via Independenza is also thick with shoppers at produce stands and tiny grocery stores. Some strollers are ready for an *aperitivo.* Teenagers roll along in clumps. The street ends in a group of crammed cafés. All this under a benison of late-afternoon light off the water, a soft luminosity that can rise at evening.

A WALKWAY ALONG the sea leads out to the jutting peninsula where the *centro storico* sits under its tower, flat-topped castle, and cathedral.

A small church falling into ruin, quiet residential streets, boatyard. We decide on Antico Vico for dinner and happily fall under the spell of Chef Walter De Carolis, another of those young, intrepid cooks who go off to train, then happily bring home their talents and new skills. The restaurant is in the lower part of a palazzo that goes back to early Gaeta history. A piece of medieval wall and two Roman cisterns were found under the floors during restoration. The restaurant's rustic elegance is enhanced by a charming modern mural showing a marriage feast in progress. Costanza, in the fourteenth century, is marrying Ladislaus, later to become the king of Naples. The artist used local people as models, dozens of them dressed in colorful clothing that wouldn't be out of place in a Renoir painting, and though the mural creates a marriage scene from long ago, the artist has left a portrait gallery of striking faces from our own time. If you're from here, you can dine with Uncle Giacomo or Zia Maria looking on. Imagine how many of the models have come in over the years and pointed out their own faces to friends.

"Do you think Cy Twombly liked or loathed this?" I wonder.

"I think he'd have to like it. How long did Twombly live here?"

"He came to Gaeta in seventy-nine and kept a place here until he died in 2011. Long time. Of course, he lived in Rome, and he had another place north of Rome. When he was old, he took a place back home in Lexington, Virginia, again. His partner still lives here in a palazzo that goes back to the year 1000."

"These Italian remains. There's no fathoming them."

We sample across the menu: ravioli with burrata; octopus with capers, tomato sauce, and olives; sea bass in *acqua pazza* (crazy water poaching broth) and vegetables; crispy baby pig with truffle fondue. Walter presents each course with a knowing little smile: *They are going to like this.* He brings us a Lazio wine, the chaste white Antium Bellone, 2015, golden as the light that bounces off the harbor at sunset.

BACK AT VILLA Irlanda, we sit by the pool with our feet in the cold water, talking about how we came to spend so much of our lives in Italy. Early on, both of us heard all the usual siren calls. (Others do, too, but they don't run off and buy abandoned houses.) Separately, on first trips to Europe, both of us experienced unexpected and irrational flashes of *this is for me.* Ed hopped off the airport bus into Rome, looked around, and surprised himself by thinking *I'm home.* On my first trip to Italy, I remember walking along the Adige River in Verona on a golden fall afternoon and realizing that I wanted to stay. Italy snared me. We have by now stayed half of forever.

I'm beguiled by Cy Twombly's half-century and more in Italy. He was a southern eccentric, going his own way when his compatriots Jasper Johns, Robert Rauschenberg, Andy Warhol went theirs. He lit out for Italy in 1957. Myth, literature, classical art, gods—these were his idiosyncratic muses. Often poetry went right on the canvas, as well as graffiti, collage, drips, and huge blank spaces. On the Riviera di Ulisse, Ulysses's coast, he breathed the myths that pushed him to paint his cryptic impressions of Hero and Leander, Leda, Venus, a ten-piece work on the Trojan war.

I often wonder *what if I had stayed at home?* Did he ever look back and wonder, too?

AT THE LAVISH breakfast in the garden room of the hotel, I ask the young woman who brings our cappuccino where the best *tiella* can be found. "There are many best," she says, "but why not go to Calegna."

The *pasticceria-forno* is unassuming but bustling. *Tiella,* a local specialty, is a two-crust pie filled with anything you fancy. Perhaps most loved is the octopus with tomato, capers, olives. There's a range on view in the glass cases: chard, spinach, potatoes, leeks, cod, broccoli. "Is it possible to see them being made?" Certainly. We're shown to the kitchen in back where a Romanian woman glowing with sweat rolls out rounds of pastry and flops them into the round pan, actually the *tiella.* (The word varies all over the south: *tegella,* Latin, *tegame, teglia.*) She fills them from large pots, then fits the top pastry over, sealing the edges with big pinches. A man is making *taralli,* those appetizing crunchy, variously flavored (hot peppers, herbs, cheese) little twists that are so perfect with an *aperitivo.* They're first boiled to cook then baked for texture. He's stirring a vat, scooping them onto baking sheets and into the oven. He's making a sweet version flavored with limoncello, grated lemon rind, and sugar.

We buy four quarter pieces of *tiella,* the octopus, spinach and ricotta, broccoli, and escarole and onion. Ed picks up several sacks of *taralli* to take home.

WE LEAN ON a sea wall, eating. We're at a park, Monte Orlando, with a spectacular cliff overlooking the sea, and a stony path to a place where two enormous rock hills almost meet, revealing a V of impossibly blue sea between them. What's that George Herbert poem?

> *Having a glass of blessings standing by,*
> *"Let us," said he, "pour on him all we can . . ."*

That must have been the creation idea for Gaeta, too. A fortunate landscape everywhere you look. Below, a perfectly empty beach. The *tielle* are browned, flaky, and savory. Not perfect picnic food. I spill spinach on my shirt. There are soft almond biscotti at the bottom of the bag, a gift we didn't know about.

AT THE END of the afternoon, we've walked eleven kilometers. We've breathed the air of Aeneas.

THE BLISSFUL DAY ends at a terrible restaurant. We didn't mean to eat here but a wild storm came up, we got lost in nearby Formia, and eventually had to pull over until the rain let up because I was sure we were going to have a wreck in the claustrophobic traffic and savage wind. Our first choices were booked by then. It's hard to find a bad meal in Italy but we manage tonight. A tired old trattoria with greasy plastic menus. Even the bruschetta is bad. How can that be in this glorious tomato land? Really sad olive oil. The waiter is watching a game on TV. We are the only customers. Chalk it up!

Late, it clears and we walk again in the freshest air along the water, the spit of land that is old Gaeta sparkling ahead of us.

. . .

WE'RE GOING HOME to Tuscany today but decide on a detour this morning. The olives of Gaeta are famous all over the world. I'm shocked to find that they actually come from **Itri,** about twenty minutes inland, and are called Gaeta only because they're shipped out of here. Itrana is the particular cultivar of the prized olives. Lazio grows many kinds of olives, including *canino, Tuscia, Ciera, Marina, Sirole, Sabina, Colline Pontine.* All new to my Tuscan ears.

With the best weather in Italy, fertile plains, and sea breezes, everything grows in Lazio. Surprisingly, a major crop is kiwi. This region is a main European exporter and Italy is the largest worldwide producer. More familiar, the famous Roman artichokes are grown in vast quantities, along with every other vegetable, grape, and bean imaginable.

We stop in lower Itri—bustling newer part of town, much of it rebuilt after suffering fifty-six aerial bombings in World War Two—where we pop into a *frutta e verdure* and buy a cone of maroon-colored brined olives, one of dark, salt-cured olives, a bag of wild greens, and also a bunch of *sedano bianco di Sperlonga,* the elongated celery of Sperlonga. Can a vegetable be elegant? Yes, this is. Crisp, with the palest bulb, and ribs like flutes in Doric columns.

Itri is on the lava-paved Appian Way, construction of which began in A.D. 312, the world's first autostrada, stretching 563 kilometers into Puglia. The old town is dominated by a picturesque castle, which Charles Dickens once said is "like a device in pasty, built up, almost perpendicular, on a hill."

We could but don't linger, driving on through the Parco Naturale dei Monti Aurunci, a vista of blue hills and dips of valleys, and isolated farms, on to the village of **Campodimele**. Field of Apples. Who could resist a town with such a name? You could hold this secret place in the palm of your hand. The ancients knew how to site their villages. Circular Campodimele sits on top of a hill, its panoramic views sweeping around hills of holm oaks and beeches, and valleys of olive groves. No apples? Ah, the Latin name was *Campus Mellis,* having to do with honey production, not apples.

Where are the six hundred people who are said to live here? We walk all around the village walls with its half-cylinder towers. No one. A water main has broken (or is draining?) and the streets are running. No one out looking alarmed. The town is clean as can be anyway; now it's getting a wash. Actually, there's no town, just vertiginous, densely packed stone houses in pristine condition. A church up top.

We find a small grocery store, the Municipio building and its spreading elm planted in 1799. And, ah! A bar. Here they are. A dozen people, all older, having their morning visit in the sun. *Paese della longevità,* the village is called. Town of long life. Also of robust food. Locals feast on their fine cheeses, pasta with goat sauce, and snails picked from the stone walls and cooked in green sauce. Is it the air, the food, the lack of stress, or a genetic fluke? People here are studied for their low cholesterol and low blood pressure. Often they live to one hundred; more over-eighty citizens live here than in any town in Italy and general life expectancy is stunning: ninety-five.

Lack of stress, I said. But at the end of a walk past the school and community center, we come to a war memorial and the somber reminder that the idyllic was not always so.

In World War Two, Campodimele was directly on the Gustav line, a main German supply route. Alberto Moravia, deported by the fascists to Campodimele, wrote a novel, *La Ciociara,* which became the famous Vittorio De Sica film *Two Women.* After the victory at Montecassino, the French Allied commander Alphonse Juin allowed his Moroccan troops fifty hours to do what they wanted among the Italian population. His horrifying proclamation: If they win this battle, for fifty hours they will be the absolute masters of everything they find beyond the ranks of the enemy. Nobody will punish them for what they do, nobody will ask them for explanations . . .

Widespread rape—even of children, of the elderly—and terrible pillage. Moravia gathered his novel around the event. A new word entered the vocabulary. The raped were said to have been *marocchinate,* moroccaned.

I don't want to imagine this whole area wracked by violence and loss. The recovery looks sublime but with many residents over the age of one hundred, brutal are the memories that must still haunt them.

The flowing has stopped. The stone streets of the newly washed town glisten. A woman, unbent but surely one of the lucky, century-old residents, hangs her wash in a small back garden. Three dish towels, an apron, and two pairs of big, white underpants. Her black cat glances at us with disdain and goes back to sleep on the warm wall.

. . .

ED HAS FOUND Caseificio Paolella, a *mozzarella di bufala* maker in nearby **Fondi,** an attractive market town surrounding a fairy-tale, round-towered castle with merloned walls. We stop at a produce market for directions and find such gorgeous vegetables that we stock up on things to take home. *Torpedini,* torpedo-shaped tomatoes, are strictly local and prized, the owner says. They look like bigger San Marzanos. We take some other Sicilian tomatoes called Marinda, ridged like small pumpkins, and luscious strawberries.

What a thrill to see the artisan mozzarella production. As we arrive at the *caseificio* in the industrial zone, the workers are just finishing the morning's work. We only can stand at the entrance, for hygiene reasons. Four women in white with shower caps lean over tubs with egg-shaped mozzarella balls floating in greenish-milky liquid. They pack the pure white balls into plastic bags. Other cheeses—shaped like cherries, eggs, knots, and braids—still float in vats. The floor is wet, with the white water sloshing around.

We're lucky to meet Signor Paolella, the owner, whose grandfather began the work in 1933. Where did the water buffalo come from? I wonder. He says no one remembers. I've read that perhaps originally Hannibal brought them. That would have been around 200 B.C. Or maybe they came ten or twelve centuries later with the Normans via Sicily, where they might have been brought by the Moors or Saracens. Water buffalo have been raised in Italy as far back as memory. His herd is kept down the road, milked twice a day, the milk rich with twice the fat of cow's milk.

I love scamorza grilled on the fireplace, and scooped onto bread. The name means "beheaded," for its lopped-off and tied shape. We often buy the smoked, cow's-milk scamorza. These are buffalo-milk *scamorzine,* small versions with a fresh fragrance, not smoked. We select a few of the ribbon-tied little sacs for ourselves and to take home to friends. We want ricotta, of course, nestled in pierced plastic containers that imprint a pattern recalling the straw baskets that once were the forms used for ricotta. Signor Paolella gives us tastes of *casatica di bufala,* a soft Camembert-type texture, and his buratta, which is melt-in-your-mouth soft and creamy. He piles all our cheeses in a Styrofoam box for the drive home.

THE MORNING HAS turned warm and, as we skirt Roma, from the backseat rise the humid scents of tomatoes, celery, strawberries. Lazio! When you travel, you're trying on a life to see how it fits. We're always asking, "If we were moving to Italy today, where would you live?" Lazio would be an easy life to choose. Close to Roma, close to Napoli, Gaeta especially seems ideally balanced between the place of myth it occupies in history and the vibrant, everyday market and fishing village of today. We have the stash of mozzarella, a box of mixed Lazio wines, bags of *taralli,* the olives of Itri. Our own heart's needle, chosen long ago, lies north of here. We can't wait to get home.

NOTES:

Article from *Vogue* archives on Cy Twombly in Gaeta: https://www.vogue .com/article/from-the-archives-cy-twombly-a-painted-word

Ciociaria is an unofficially named area around Frosinone—the lands of those who wore *le ciocie,* thick leather soles tied over the feet with straps.

Orata all'Acqua Pazza

SEA BREAM IN "CRAZY WATER," SERVES 2

Si mangia bene, one eats well, in Gaeta and nowhere better than at Chef Walter De Carolis's table. *Acqua pazza*—seasoned water—is a common cooking medium in Italy.

2¼ cups fish broth
16 cherry tomatoes, halved
2 cloves garlic
A handful of parsley, snipped
Extra-virgin olive oil, *QB*
Salt and pepper, *QB*
2 large sea bream fillets
4 slices bread, toasted

Boil the fish stock and add the tomatoes, garlic, parsley, a little oil, and salt and pepper. Reduce to simmer, and add the fillets. Poach for 4 to 5 minutes.

To serve, place two slices of bread on soup plates, lay a fillet over them, and ladle the broth over. Drizzle some oil.

Ristorante Antico Vico, Gaeta, Lazio

Puglia ❀

Trani

Early spring, far south. "Of the great experiences of our travel lives, does *anything* rival seeing these olive groves?" Turning onto a back road, soon we are passing far-as-the-eye-can-see stretches of olive groves, casting dappled shadows on mosaics of yellow and white wildflowers in the lush grasses. The fabled *oliveti* of Puglia! Twisted old dancers, gnarly dwarves, sinister giants, personifications of *endurance*. Silvery green seas of trees abut blooming fields of plum, peach, and cherry trees, then almond orchards fluffed out in white. I let down the window to sniff but only catch a faint dusty smell.

Driving from Cortona, we skirted Rome, then Benevento, heading for the Adriatic coast. Italy is *long.* I'm reading aloud to Ed about Puglia's convoluted history. We've never heard of the early settlers, the Messapians or the Peucetians. And we barely can keep track of the successive invasions: Greek, Ostrogoth, Lombard, Byzantine, Norman, Saracen raiders, Swabian, Angevin, Aragon, Austrian, Spanish, French, on and on. Everyone had their turn. I'm liking the most prominent ruler, Holy Roman Emperor Frederick II, *Stupor Mundi,* astonishment of the world, born in Le Marche to an older mother who, it's said, gave birth at age forty in the piazza to prove him legitimate. Of the invaders, he seems to be the only one who loved the land and was loved by the people. One legacy: He scattered his red-headed genes among the Puglia population.

Puglia seems to have been an open invitation for every warmonger-ing brute who took a fancy to its ports and peasants. After Frederick, his son Manfred was loved as well. He quickly came to a bad end. Puglia: wars. (And sheep. In the seventeenth century, four and a half million of them roamed the land, gnawing it down to the dirt.) The Risorgimento, unification of Italy, made more chaos. Mussolini began to pull Puglia up, but then it was bombed and occupied by Germany. Dio! I'm not sure why I had to study so hard in college. American history is a snap. Italian students must truly suffer—it's as if the American Civil War lasted two thousand years!

THE DREARY OUTSKIRTS of Trani quickly become narrow lanes lined with pollarded trees not yet in leaf. Palm trees, my favorites, announce that we have left behind any remnant of a cold climate. The cafés look inviting but in early afternoon no one is out. These towns in the south shut down firmly in deference to the after-*pranzo pausa.*

Was the old town carved out of a huge, single clump of stone? This color—ivory as piano keys. The stones trap the light and send it back out, transparent. Trani glows. Sunlight strikes the campanile and skit-ters along the water. As long as I'm here, I will be watching the play of cloud shadows on the surface of the harbor and the façades of buildings reflect shades of cream to cool gray to pearly blue. "Reason enough to live here," I say to Ed. "Imagine the privilege of this light."

"The Tuscan light is special, too," he maintains.

"Yes. Different. This is white light. Tuscany is mellow."

WE MEET AND are warmly greeted by Michele Matera at Corteinfiore, the restaurant we've chosen for tonight. Anticipating dinner, we look into the glassed-in dining room, which is crisply laid with white linen.

Down the street we'll be staying in his six-room *residenza,* or residence hotel. Michele's friendly colleague walks us there, along the harbor to a quiet piazza where boys must dodge benches as they kick around a soccer ball. Nothing keeps Italian boys from soccer.

A few years ago, the B & B concept didn't exist in Italy. There were signs for CAMERE, rooms, but they were spare rooms in someone's house, very cheap and incredibly plain. Recently, what has cropped up are suites of rooms—a *residenza* in a renovated building where someone operates a mini-hotel with minimum staff—or a *diffuso* plan, rooms let around town by an agency. You're met at an appointed time and given the key. We enter Dimora Corteinfiore through its welcoming common room, where breakfast will be served and we can make coffee or tea anytime. Our bedroom and living room overlook the piazza. Wood floors, dark gray walls, monochromatic beiges, sand, and white for the sofa and bed—a trendy minimalist design. Two rooms help because of all our electronics. What did I used to do without these devices to charge constantly? I carry two zipped bags of cords. I can push open shutters and see palm trees full of chattering birds.

THE FIRST PLACE we look for is a *forno.* The bread of Puglia is known to be the best in Italy. We find one but morning customers have decimated the daily supply. We're able to buy only a quarter of a ten-pound loaf—sixty cents. The baker looks amused as we immediately reach into the sack. "I've never had bread before," Ed claims. "It's cakey and the crackly crust doesn't rip out your teeth the way Tuscan bread does."

"Semolina softens the texture of the hard wheat flour," the baker tells us. We must look hungry; he wraps four pistachio biscotti in tissue and hands them to me.

"I could live on bread when it's this good," I tell him.

THE HARBOR INSCRIBES a large C, like a crab's reach. The startling white buildings follow the curve, with a street between for the capricious drivers to indulge their wrongful turns and random parking. Fortunately, there's not much traffic.

What inspires instant happiness more than blue fishing boats, weathered row boats, nets drying in the sun, people walking peppy little dogs, a boy selling a pile of lemons, and an afternoon to wander? Trani's harbor gives way to a walk along the sea and to the open piazza where rises the astounding cathedral San Nicola Pellegrino. Because of the great space left open around the building, you're allowed to admire the four differing sides. The magnificent siting is also odd. The church does not face the sea but is angled so that the back, with its three graceful apses, and the long side of high arches are on the water side. People have been repeating this walk for almost a thousand years.

My mind spins. This little town's magisterial cathedral took a visionary to build. How? The structure is vast and high and complex. Ancient. And someone once stood on the beach and said *let's do this thing*. A pity the word "awesome" is worn out by things that aren't because this truly is.

A BEGGAR WELCOMES us into the lower church crypts. Inside, many marble columns support the arches of the grand edifice. I have a flash of center poles holding up a vast tent camp of desert fathers. The upper church, cool and bare, lets the architecture have its way, unlike churches covered in gilt and frescoes and paintings. Any Baroque additions have been banished and without all that, the raw energy of the building asserts itself. I slip off my shoes, since the nave is empty, to feel the white stone floor still holding on to winter chill. As we leave, we give coins to the gray-skinned beggar, who is so wizened that he might very well have been standing here when ginger-haired Frederick II's son Manfred swept across the esplanade with his Greek bride, Helena of Epirus, in 1259. Bells are clanging. How far out at sea can you hear them?

ACROSS THE EXPANSIVE piazza, we skirt Castello Svevo, one of Frederick II's stalwart fortifications. Formerly, a seawater moat surrounded the walls. The massive, blocky building became a prison in 1832, and held that ugly role until 1974. It's now a small museum and exhibition space.

Ed spots a café with red velvet chairs outside and we pause for his—what?—fourth espresso of the day, then wander the old town. In medieval Trani, there were four synagogues, all refashioned as Christian churches after the Kingdom of Naples demanded that Jews become Christians or go into exile. One, Scolanova Synagogue, recently returned to its heritage. Even though there are few or no Jews living in Trani, services are sometimes held there. Puglian history is littered with conversion motifs—become a Muslim, or die; become a Christian, or die—according to which group was invading.

OFF THE PIAZZA della Repubblica—which contains two immense piazzas with rows of shapely trees—we happen on Anice Verde, a café with walls papered with pages from old books and retro lightbulbs hanging on single cords. A perfect place for an intimate talk over tea and biscotti. A perfect place for an *aperitivo,* too. We talk to the pretty Romanian waitress, who is surprised to see Americans. She wants to know what New York is like. And how did she get here? We want to know. Came on vacation and never left. Ah, I can see that. The appeal seems obvious: arched entrances to narrow streets, many leafy piazzas, and most of all to be bathed every day in this swimming light.

GOOD THING WE reserved, even off-season. We take Corteinfiore's last table. As we come in, we pass the fish on ice. Ed has his sights on a bright-eyed San Pietro but we check the menu first. Many fish! Only fish! If we were in a group of friends, we'd order the chef's choice antipasti—five tempting preparations from a list that includes cod, octopus, mullet, swordfish, anchovy, and *canocchia,* the large Mediterranean shrimp that look like a cicada. When Ed asks the waiter what he recommends, he comes over with the glistening San Pietro. This fish (John Dory) has a darker round mark on its side that's supposed to be the thumbprint of Saint Peter, fisherman. We begin with spaghetti and sea urchin sauce for Ed, and spaghetti *alla chitarra* with red prawns for me. *Chitarra* (guitar) refers to the frame with bronze wires that cuts the pasta into spaghetti. Bronze cut assures better adherence of sauce, and over the years I've opted for that method when using dried pasta.

Our San Pietro arrives at the table, where it's deftly filleted, the delicate pieces tumbling onto our plates and served with olives, capers, and sautéed *datterini* tomatoes, the oblong ones shaped like dates. Oh, chef of the New York temple of seafood, take a trip to Puglia! All around us, platters of the freshest catches arrive to the big smiles of diners. Lemon slices I've learned to ignore ever since our friend Edo said, "Do you want to taste lemon or do you want to taste the fish?" I don't think I've ever seen an Italian squeeze lemon juice on seafood.

Now to begin tasting Puglian wines. Michele helps us select Vigna Pedale Castel del Monte by Torrevento, a 2012 reserva, which comes full-mouthed and winningly right out of the bottle. The *nero di Troia* grape ensures a deep garnet color and a touch of fruit. Big red with fish? At tables all around us that's what's in the glasses. Why not?

First night in Puglia. Tomorrow we turn even farther south.

Spaghetti alla Chitarra, Gamberi Rossi, Olive Leccino, and Calamaretti Spillo

SPAGHETTI ALLA CHITARRA, RED SHRIMP, OLIVES, AND SQUID, SERVES 4

The wooden form with bronze strands that cut the pasta resembles a guitar. *Chitarra* is known for the way sauce clings so nicely. Chef Alessio Di Micco's quick and easy shrimp recipe is redolent of the South. I add a few shakes of hot red pepper flakes.

2 tablespoons extra-virgin olive oil

16 cherry tomatoes

12 *leccino* or *taggiasca* olives (or niçoise), pitted

16 red shrimp, shelled and deveined

½ pound young squid, cleaned and cut in small pieces

Salt and pepper, *QB*

1 cup fish stock

1 pound spaghetti *alla chitarra*

In a large skillet, in the oil, sauté the tomatoes and olives. Add the shrimp, squid, and seasonings. Add the fish stock, bring to a boil, then immediately lower the heat and simmer for about 12 minutes.

Cook the pasta al dente in copious salted water. Drain. Serve on a hot plate with the seafood and sauce.

Ristorante Corteinfiore, Trani, Puglia

Ruvo di Puglia

Leaving Trani, we pause in Ruvo, just south and slightly inland. The tree-lined main street is of normal width but the sidewalks are wider than the street; this town favors strolling. People sit on their white iron balconies that front the creamy-stone residences, looking down as their friends and neighbors take a *passeggiata*.

Weirdly, as we walk, we see effigies of an old woman in black hanging from electrical wires above our heads. Is that a fish hanging from the wire? She's holding a spindle. Near the Museo Archeologico Nazionale Jatta, we spot two of them. What's with that? I'm from the American South; a hanging black figure counts as nightmare.

THE MUSEUM, ON the bottom floor of the Jatta family's nineteenth-century palazzo, is closed. We weren't expecting much anyway, just brothers Giovanni and Giulio's collection of locally discovered artifacts and vases. Two women sit by a stove in a side entrance room and when we ask about opening hours, one of them takes a key and lets us in. Four rooms, just as the paterfamilias collectors left them. I love the tall wooden cabinets, with wavery glass doors and sequential Roman numerals, filled with objects and hand-inked tags. House museums fascinate me; they manifest individual passion. The brothers gathered their trove in the early nineteenth century, long before anyone regulated digging in a field or your backyard and unearthing a pre-Christian frying pan, Roman pins for a cloak, or stunning red clay vases painted with scenes from mythology. There must have been late-night furtive knocks at the door; some stealthy man unrolling a blanket wrapped around a small statue with an archaic smile. The brothers must have been awed by the terra-cotta drinking vessels shaped like animal faces, whimsical and graphic. I imagine Giovanni wandering down here at night with a glass of wine, moving among his cases, taking out a red-orange plate from 340 B.C. and admiring the two painted *orate* (sea bream) and the flowing tentacles of *seppia* (cuttlefish) filling the surface, exactly what he had for dinner. He picks up the even more ancient beads—his wife has worn them to celebrations—turning the pre-Roman glass and stones over in his fingers.

Just as he did, I can run my hands over the amphorae and precious vases displayed outside the cases. Oh, they're vulnerable, up on pedestals in the open. Watch that backpack! Several *kraters* (wide-mouthed urns used for mixing water into wine) found here were imported from Greece from the eighth until third centuries B.C. and were used not for all-male *symposia* parties, as they had been in Greece, but as accompaniments to the departed in their graves. What a pleasure to see these vases up close, the delicate leaves and spiraling tendrils of a grapevine, a half-reclining nude and winged woman—long before Christian angels—holding aloft what appears to be a casserole topped with a mountain of whipped cream.

Outstanding, among a lot of outstanding objects, is the vase depicting the death of Talos, who was invulnerable except for a vein in the malleolus—the bony knob on the side of the ankle. Sent by Jupiter to guard Crete, Talos was bewitched by Medea and somehow banged his malleolus on a stone and died—a rather ignominious death for such a hero. His pale body is supported on either side by Castor and Pollux. What dark night yielded this treasure?

The woman with the key returns after leaving us alone for an hour. She knows everything about the collection, the family, and the gardens behind the villa. On one vase she points out, a serpent twines around a tree, slithering upward to a young woman who holds out a plate to feed him. "The snake and the beauty," she says, "and we read about this pairing centuries later in the Bible." Among the iron objects, I see a crusty grill much like my Tuscan neighbors use for veal chops in their fireplaces. The quotidian items bring close the ancient people of Puglia.

LIKE MOST ITALIAN towns, Ruvo has a well-stocked tourist office with a helpful staff. We ask a raven-haired young woman, whose ancestors must have been settlers of Magna Grecia, about the black-robed effigies hanging around town. "*Quarantane! Vedove* [widows]. They hang for forty days. Inside their robes they hold an orange stuck with six black feathers and one white, one for each week of Lent and then the white for Easter. For the end of Lent, they explode on Easter morning."

This sounds so deeply pagan that it makes me dizzy. "Why old women?" I ask.

"Widows—they are mourners, yes? As widows of carnival, they symbolize Lent."

"Why the orange and the fish and the spindle—what do those mean?"

"The orange signifies the end of winter. The herring is about the lack of meat during the deprivation of Lent. The spindle is the woman's work." She tells us about numerous celebrations around Easter. When we go out into the streets again, I notice signs on churches announcing schedules of processions. One church, San Francesco, has a portal surrounded with skeletons. Photos show all the old wooden figures that will be carried through the streets. I start imagining the Easter *pranzo* that will take place in every house. These narrow streets of stone houses will throw the windows open, all the scents of roasting lamb and potatoes, steaming chicory and fennel drifting through the air. Which leads us to lunch.

WE STOP IN at the very casual Sesto Senso, the first place that looks good. We meet Giacomo, the owner, who brings over wine even though we say we want only water. Then two platters of grilled vegetables arrive.

His wife and two boys, nine and fifteen, come in with their Jack Russell, who immediately tries to jump in my lap. The younger boy chases him about while the older boy stares hypnotically at his phone. Giacomo is bringing out various courses for them and seems disconsolate when we tell him the vegetables and great bread are all we can manage. We're the only guests. Americans, they marvel. As Ed savors an espresso, I look up the *Quarantane* tradition. Towns that honor this ritual hang up seven widows. Some disapprove because, as I guessed, the deep tradition is pagan, going back to agricultural and Dionysian fertility rites. In Ruvo, one *quarantana* was stolen this year. The writer speculated that the thief might have been a priest.

PUGLIAN ROMANESQUE! ALL through this region we'll be visiting these great cathedrals of the eleventh and twelfth centuries. I want to see each rose window of carved stone, not stained glass, as in French cathedrals. Romanesque, my favorite church architecture, with a Puglian twist—the local mix of Arab, Byzantine, French, Spanish, Venetian, Norman architectural influences. Ruvo di Puglia's church may have less grandeur than Trani's but its proportions are pitch perfect for the intimate square where it's situated, with radiating streets of low stone homes. The *cattedrale,* spare in ornament, focuses on its rose window with the roofline angled sharply down on either side. The carved-stone ornamentation looks like cut-out pastry designs pressed into a piecrust. Mythical animals always astound me on medieval churches. Some of Ruvo's are eroded, like sand castles when a wave washes over. Beneath the church, as is so often the case, lie remains of an earlier religious site and below that, another. Puglia: layers on layers. Mosaics, tombs, paths—it always has been thus. One religion gives way to another, the truer one, until the next truer one comes along.

Ruvo we like. Idyllic village. Eat from the clean street! Natives nod at strangers. The Jattas still haunt. Probably there's more to be discovered in groves and byways. The grilled vegetables, perfect lunch. The hanging widows, I don't know. Exploding on Easter. A bit creepy. "Fetishistic," Ed says.

"Are you sure that's a word?"

"Haunted. That orange with seven feathers piercing the rind."

Ostuni

A white, shimmering mirage. As we drive from Ruvo, approaching Ostuni, I see sugar cubes, stacked willy-nilly up and down hillsides. "This looks like Greece. Santorini. Or those pared-down towns in the Mani."

"Not even remotely the Italy we know. It's not called 'the white city' for nothing." Ed navigates through an industrial area and starts up into town.

We've reserved at La Sommità Relais, and as we come closer we understand why the hotel asked us to call when we arrive. We meet their driver below the ramparts and pull into a parking lot that looks rather dicey. Ed says what I'm thinking: "Is our car going to be stripped to the wheels if we leave it?" The driver's spotless Mercedes turns into the gate and the hip (shaved-head, all black clothes) driver assures us that our darling Alfa will be fine. We wind up, up, yes, to the summit. A Relais & Châteaux, always a good sign. The staff is cool, too, like the driver, and we're given a tour of this multilevel hotel seemingly carved out of rock. Small spa, Michelin-starred restaurant, two living rooms with uber-chic furniture, and finally to our huge minimalist room over-looking, at some distance, the sea.

Ed installs himself on the white sofa, his devices and cords arrayed about him. I prop up on pillows to read *Old Puglia.* It's late in the day; we lingered long in Ruvo. Too late to venture out. Too early to contemplate dinner. Perfect time for a long shower with luxurious bath products. A shift into a dream state, then the chance to dress in whichever silk blouse is not too wrinkled at the bottom of my suitcase, and gold slippers with straps instead of sturdy walking shoes. Gold slippers are one of my packing secrets. Signaling glamour, they magically transform casual into dressy.

Ed shakes out the folds from his gray sport coat and off we go to the anteroom of the restaurant, where we sink into a cushy sofa by the fire. We would put our feet on the coffee table if we weren't in a superbly curated and sophisticated hotel. The waiter brings out a still life on a board: tiny mozzarella balls, crunchy *taralli,* olives, and an array of local *salume.* Though we've ordered only a glass of Pastini, he leaves the whole bottle. (We do make a dent in it.) The golden prosecco is light and peppery.

On the way into the dining room, we pass Cielo's kitchen. Spotlessly clean, the open plan whets the appetite, though I have eaten too many *taralli,* those boiled then baked little twists of dough seasoned with fennel or peppers. All seems serene in Chef Andrea Cannalire's work space. He comes out and greets us warmly. He's intense and friendly, a young chef who has made a special place in his home territory. Many talented young Italians go off and study in the kitchens of those we kneel before, then come back to their roots because they want to be home.

The rest of the prosecco has followed us to the table. We are looking forward to a long evening.

In Cielo's poetic dining room, all pale stone and glass overlooking a grove of orange trees, we peruse the menu and, after a dazzling array of amuses-bouches, I select lobster with slivers of radishes and Ed chooses a crusted fish. The waiter helps us find a Puglian wine—Masseria Li Veli, 2010—made of *negroamaro* (black bitter) and cabernet sauvignon grapes. Doesn't take much to make us happy. The wine is gorgeous. The night is gorgeous. Andrea is having fun in the kitchen and we are, too.

. . .

WE FLOAT BACK up to our room, where the bed rests on a raised plat-form and I hope I don't stumble off in the middle of the night and break an ankle. It's too far away to hear the sea, but Ed opens the window to feel the bracing air. We fall into profound sleeps. I, to dream of my daughter riding her horse across the Andalusian countryside. Ed dreams of trying to revive his dead brother.

ALL DAY WE wander the up-and-down streets—so windy in March. Ostuni, a fortified town, still rests on the steep ramparts that must have been tough to scale. Narrow lanes are lined with whitewashed houses. White was used to prevent plague. Many doors are painted bright aqua or blue. I photograph distinctive knockers, imagining proprietors of these look-alike houses giving directions: *Mine is the one with the oak leaf knocker.* The maze of tiny streets that end abruptly or zigzag up lure us to turn and turn, glimpsing balconies hung with wash, and inviting angles with brief glimpses of the sea. Over some streets, buttresses arch from one house to the neighbor's across the way because some facing façades have collapsed in a heap, leaving rooms as exposed as open dollhouses. Like dice stacked every which way, the homes present a surreal aspect: Many of these plain structures have elaborate Baroque door surrounds. You think you're seeing a palazzo but then you recognize a plain little house behind the flourishes.

At lunchtime, we discover the place we'd frequent every week if we lived here: Osteria Piazzetta Cattedrale. This is the prototype for my favorite kind of restaurant. Intimate, elegant but also homey, mirrors, tureens, hanging plates, and round tables full of local people. Oh, the *tortelli di agnello con carciofi* (pasta with lamb and artichokes), divine focaccia baked in a muffin tin with sun-dried tomatoes, little baskets formed of Parmigiano with crispy bacon and pesto tucked inside. So good, the fried balls of cod, potato, and lemon, then orec-chiette with broccoli rabe, anchovies, and toasted bread crumbs. Madonna! All celebrated with a house *primitivo.* You might say we go overboard. We usually don't but today we fall into it. Walking all af-ternoon helps.

Cars scurry around the lower Piazza della Libertà but do not venture up into the older town. The town hub, this lopsided piazza stays busy with local shoppers and lingerers out for visiting. We're all presided over by a looming statue of Sant'Oranzo. Just a few yards up, we're in secretive alleyways, finding an architecture that valued privacy. It's hard to imagine that ordinary life—homework, laundry, TV—takes place behind the closed, blank-faced houses. Inside, it seems, the woman of the house lounges like an odalisque on a daybed covered in Matisse-colored cloth, the man strums a guitar and smokes a bitter cigarette. All the furnishings are pillows and low tables, and in the kitchen only bowls of lemons and pomegranates.

No tray of cat litter, no stopped drains. But reality intrudes. There's a brown dog staring us down from a balcony, there's a hand on the lace curtain, an ancient man turning an ancient key into his home.

ON THE SECOND day in a place, more details come into focus. I begin to notice all the lettering carved over windows and around doors. Ed's high school Latin isn't up to translating but in a souvenir shop I find a city guidebook that helps. Incised on Palazzo Petrarolo: *The just will prosper like a lily—unmoving stones among waves.* Bit of metaphor mixing there. On Palazzo Siccoda: *The spending has not to exceed the owned wealth.* And: *It is necessary to get wealth with work.* What a sanctimonious little directive. On the house I would like to live in, at number 26 near the cathedral, the message is also a bit dreary. *Everything in due time* is carved over one window, and over the other: *The moderate things continue.* On via Bixio Continelli, one of my favorite streets, a portal remains at number 2, all that's left of what once was a house where the arts were celebrated. Here we read: *Amuse ne Ingreditor,* which my guidebook translates as *He must not come in, the one who does not know music.* Down the street across from number 10, *Who says bad words will listen to bad words.* On vico Pasquale Villari, this inscription was carved over the window of number 11: *Who has fear of God never will meet the devil.*

"These homilies make me wonder," Ed says, "what kind of people they were. A kind of uptight motif runs through these, even the artist's. Not a welcome to those who love the arts but a warning to keep out if you don't."

"I've never mentioned it but I would like a Latin phrase at our house. I've had it picked out for a long time."

"I hope it's not like these. And not like the fortune cookie that said 'Work hard'."

"Not at all. It's from Virgil, *The Aeneid*." I look at my notes to get it right. "*Flectere si nequeo superos, acheronta movebo.* If I cannot move heaven, I will raise hell."

"It's not what I associate with you—Miss *carpe diem*. Pretty macho for a southern belle."

TONIGHT WE CHOOSE the less formal bistro room at our hotel. The menu is casual. Is Ostuni all about eating? Small focaccia squares, rough grainy slices, and warm puffy rolls—we try them all. "What was the best thing you saw today?" I ask Ed.

"That would have to be the twenty-five-hundred-year-old woman." This local find, a major display in the museum, is a reclining skeleton with the barely discernable little ribs of an unborn child tucked inside her. "But," he continues, "there was that shop where the guy and his son—I have his card, Giancarlo and Piero Maglionico—make *taralli*—all good. Those from various grains are stupendous." We bought several packets to take home, along with some local honey.

"Imagine. Twenty-five hundred years she's lain there with her unborn child."

"Sometimes even the dim past is overwhelming. *Taralli,* never." Ed selects a Kebir Torrevento, 2007, which causes us to put aside the *aperitivi.* Then come *freselle,* round crunchy rusks with a hole in the middle. These are a popular snack or antipasto all over Puglia and they couldn't be simpler—just rub the *fresella* with a cut side of tomato, top with a few chopped tomatoes, add salt. After this rush of breads, we're content with grilled fish and *buona notte.*

WE ARE GOING south today, all the way down to Lecce. But before we leave, we take a last look at the cathedral. Its beauty is compromised by a building that juts out into the piazza, partially blocking a full view. Nevertheless, this one is right up there with the other beauties along this coast. A large central rose window is flanked by two smaller ones, each centered over a portal. Christ is at the center, holding up the world. A comfort to imagine. Slender columns and circles radiate out from Him.

We make a last *taralli* stop. The father-and-son duo gives us tastes of several flavors and we choose bags of potato, rosemary, tomato, mixed grains, and *grano arso*. The latter, the father tells us, "comes straight out of *cucina povera*. After wheat harvest, when the remaining stubble was burned by the landowners, the farmers gathered the charred grains. That's back-breaking labor, picking up tiny grains from a scorched field." And probably carcinogenic, I think. Now selected grains are toasted and prized. In Puglia, the flour from these grains is often mixed with regular hard wheat flour in the making of the region's breads and the favorite pasta: *orecchiette,* the little ears.

WE WIND SLOWLY down from the hills of Ostuni, turning south toward Otranto and Lecce. I turn on the radio and rip open a bag of *taralli.* Adele is belting out "Set Fire to the Rain." On we go.

NOTE:

Old Puglia: A Cultural Companion to South-Eastern Italy by Desmond Seward and Susan Mountgarret.

Spaghettino Freddo con Ostriche Crude

COLD THIN SPAGHETTI WITH RAW OYSTERS, SERVES 4

Similar to medieval *garum, colatura di alici,* an Italian fermented anchovy sauce, salty and full of umami flavor, adds an ancient-as-the-sea flavor. *Colatura* means "leakage," referring to the method of allowing the juice of fermented anchovies to leak through holes in the bottom of the barrel. It's easily available online. A couple of anchovy fillets can be substituted but the flavor will not be as pronounced. Chef Andrea Cannalire serves this as an elegant and unusual *primo,* first course. For the pasta, he recommends the Puglian maker Benedetto Cavalieri.

¼ cup extra-virgin olive oil

⅓ cup hazelnut oil or roasted walnut oil

1 tablespoon lemon juice

4 teaspoons *colatura*

2 tablespoons chopped chives

1 shallot, minced

1 pound thin spaghetti

Salt and pepper, *QB*

12 oysters, freshly shucked

In a food processor, emulsify the olive oil, hazelnut oil, lemon juice, *colatura,* 1 tablespoon of the chives, and all of the shallots.

In a pasta pot of boiling, salted water, cook the spaghetti for about 10 minutes, until al dente; drain. Cool the spaghetti in ice water and again drain well. Mix the pasta in a large bowl with the emulsified blend. Divide among four plates. Top with the oysters and the remaining chives.

Ristorante Cielo at La Sommità Relais,
Ostuni, Puglia

Lecce, Corigliano d'Otranto, Specchia, and Otranto

Spur and heel of the boot, Puglia forms a long peninsula into the Adriatic and Ionian Seas. Therefore, there are beaches. Dreamy Adriatic beaches with cliffs and coves and caves, and then those along the southern Salento area on the Ionian Sea with grainy golden sand like polenta. Italians, sun-worshippers, flock to them, and now with cheap flights into Brindisi, English and Europeans also have discovered this captivating region. Since it's March, we're not here for fun in the sun, though the mild, full spring of the south is perfect for walking on empty beaches.

Leaving Ostuni, we're moving down into the heel. Today we will reach **Lecce**! Wildly Baroque fantasy land. Treasure of the south.

WE DETOUR ONLY once. In Puglia, we want to take every turnoff! Near the Brindisi airport we stop at a special church, Santa Maria del Casale, which I read about in an

Italian travel magazine years ago. I'm translating slips from the article I tore out: Built around 1300 by Philip of Anjou. Knights Templar held court here. Frescoes from Byzantine era. Little prepares me for the beauty of this church, stuck incongruously near military grounds and airport parking. Pale apricot marble in geometric patterns cover the small Romanesque-into-Gothic façade. Inside the single-nave church, frescoes, faded sepia, blood, ocher, and blues, are also framed by bold geometric designs. Above the altar, the paintings stack into four rows, with separations between scenes, like panels in a comic book. Such quiet. Not even the roar of a plane taking off for London. There's Santa Caterina holding the torture wheel of her martyrdom. Christ crucified against a tree of life. Faces, all with haunting Byzantine eyes. In the cloister, a single fruit tree has burst into blossom, along each black branch an explosion of white flowers. This was a lucky stop we almost didn't bother to take. My *Blue Guide to Southern Italy* doesn't mention it. What else are we missing?

BY THE TIME we check into Vico della Cavallerizza, our centrally located B & B, Lecce is just reopening after the *pausa*. We have been here before, but only for a morning, when the cruise ship where I was guest speaker docked south of here at Gallipoli. We came in by bus for a whirl of a tour. The majesty of the city imprinted and I've always wanted to come back. *Cartapesta,* papier-mâché, is Lecce's unusual craft, especially figures for crèches, but also life-size religious figures for carrying in processions (so much lighter than wood), peasant figures, and accessories for the crèche such as trees, animals, fireplaces, and blacksmiths, candle makers, and butchers working at their crafts. And angels! I bought an ethereal one with billowing skirts for our Christmas tree. Every year since, I think of Lecce when I affix her to the top.

Perfect for walking, with its low buildings and flat terrain, Lecce feels open to the sky. Once a four-gated city, its remaining magnificent arch, Porta Napoli (1548), could be at home on a significant Roman triumphal route.

Lecce is a town for those hundred thousand people who live here, not a tourist town. The ornate *palazzi* look private; I long to go inside one pale confection made, it seems, by a wedding-cake baker. Most buildings are ornamented to the hilt with Baroque carved supports for balconies, surrounds of doors and windows. The local sandstone, *pietra leccese,* was easy to carve into beasts, beauties, acanthus, flower medallions. Then it hardens. By now, much is worn. Lions have lost their fierceness; the dresses of caryatids are pocked; *putti* are missing their wings. We look into one extravagant church after another. Right in the center, the ruin of a Roman amphitheater reminds me of a long history behind the flamboyant Baroque era. Only excavated in 1938, it's still not fully explored. A few intact seats remain where people watched barbarous animal torture games. At the center of the piazza stands Sant'Oronzo, the saint we met in Ostuni. His statue is surrounded by shops and Caffè Alvino, a righteous coffee stop.

LEADING OUT OF the Piazza Sant'Oronzo on via Trinchese, we find Natale, a glamorous pastry shop already full of fanciful giant chocolate Easter eggs and lavishly wrapped *panettone.* We select some chocolates, which are then packaged like gifts for royalty to nibble. The tarts and cakes are flounced and dolloped and edged with lime-green or pink ribbons of icing, feasts for the eyes. On this street are modern shops, including Zara, which at the end of the day resembles a place that tornadoes blew through. The sales staff looks defeated over the heaps of clothing strewn on the floor and a million lopsided hangers. Dusk, everyone out. Lecce is a university town, which guarantees liveliness. Also guarantees bookstores. I spend time in Cartoleria Pantheon, the booklover's companion store, full of journals and agendas in leather and paper, real ink pens, wrapping paper that is so pretty for lining drawers, and nice notepads and leather satchels.

BROS'! THEY MIGHT not, with their hard-edged décor and idiosyncratic presentations, think they're in line with the Baroque but I do. Playful, way over the top, dramatized, but still taste-forward, this restaurant belongs to Floriano Pellegrino, a bright light born in 1990. The super-talented pastry chef, Isabella Potì, was born in 1995. They represent a youthful version of Lecce. We are the only ones dining except for a lone woman with her laptop open on the table. Ed thinks she must be a Michelin reviewer. Olives are served in a hand of ice made by freezing water in a rubber glove. Mushrooms appear on a mossy log. Jellied kumquats on a bed of charcoal. And what are these, salted plums lined up on a piece of driftwood? The bread is beautiful on a simple board.

For antipasto, there's a roasted red onion with *ribes,* currants, and tiny pearls of tapioca; a soft cheese with lavender and cress; a little terrain of *sedano rapa,* celeriac. Everything is gently treated and delicate. We're rolling with this. Onward to the *primi.* Lentils with coconut and dill. Big fusilli with scampi and black sesame. The waiter suggested Taersìa, a white of the area. The chef comes out to chat. Our *secondo* seems almost ordinary, crunchy-skin duck breast with green apples and juniper. Ed doesn't mind that the duck is so very rare, while I'm slicing around for the more done edges. We're given a glass of a local big blood-red, though we never find out what it is beyond *negroamaro.* In advance, we ordered one of Isabella's gossamer cheese soufflès, what the angels eat. Before we go, the waiter brings a citrus soup with floating jellies in the shapes of B R O S. What fun.

EARLY, WE'RE OUT. Piazza del Duomo, the grand heart of town, is one of Italy's finest. Its drama is increased by the entrance. Curved walls topped by statues narrow then open into the vast space occupied by the Duomo (1114), its sixty-eight-meter-tall bell tower, the elegant bishop's palace, and other buildings that look important enough to host world-changing councils. The scale and harmony stop me with awe. A tiny bodega, squeezed in among the grandeur, belongs to an artisan *cartapesta* maker. A group of Dutch tourists jams into his shop, where he has almost nothing for sale but is gamely explaining the process. The large figures are first made of wire and stuffed with paper, then the wet strips of papier-mâché are wrapped around and shaped and dried and sanded and . . . We slip away. The tour guide is outside smoking and looking at her phone. She's seen this before.

ERENE, WHO WORKS at our B & B, sends us around the corner to La Vecchia Osteria. It's crowded. We meet true-blue regional food.

Wonder if the Bros' cooks eat here on their day off. We order the vegetable antipasto, six small bowls of chicory greens, peppers, mozzarella,
cabbage, mushrooms, and potato croquettes. Puglia is a great choice
for vegetarians; the repertoire weighs heavily that way. Then *ciceri e tria,*
chickpeas and *tria,* a local broad, flat pasta topped with crisp fried strips
of chickpea batter. Big seafood fritto misto. Orecchiette, the favored
pasta throughout Puglia, appears on the menu with *cime di rape,* turnip
tops. What makes it great, the waiter says, is a few pounded anchovies.
Everyone around us seems to be ordering the same things we are, and
also the bright red raw beef or horse meat. Horse figures prominently,
with tomatoes and chili peppers, as *escalope,* and as a filet. I'm studying
the menu because this represents fully the Leccese traditions. Lamb
rolls with heart, liver, and lung. Snails. And a whole page of grilled fish
and other seafood.

Tonight, further forays into the heart of the Puglian kitchen at Alex,
a glassed-in restaurant in a park. *'Ncapriata,* a fava bean purée, wild chicory, olive oil, garlic, and red pepper. This has to be straight from the
cucina povera tradition. Then there's braised beef glossy with kumquats,
a gratin of eggplant with smoked mozzarella, almonds, and sweet-sour
cherry tomatoes. Just a glass each of Masseria Maime, Negroamaro,
2011 Tormaresca, and lots of sparkling water. All bright flavors in the
florid atmosphere of a garden room.

AFTER BREAKFAST WITH other guests—a group of young Chinese
travelers who innocently arrive at breakfast in their pajamas—we leave
for the day. We finally find the lot where we've parked the car and
drive into the Salento, the far south of Puglia. First stop, **Corigliano
d'Otranto,** intriguing because it is one of nine villages where Griko, a
dialect surviving from when this area was Magna Grecia, still can be
heard. A Bandiera Arancione, Corigliano is immediately appealing.

We walk to the striking, symmetrical Castello di Monti with four
round towers, then to La Chiesa Matrice di San Nicola. As we're admiring the rose window and statues on the façade, a slender middle-aged
man wearing a suit introduces himself as the town historian. Would we
like to see the church? Originally a much older church, the current one

was built in the sixteenth century, then renovated in 1622. On the bell tower, there are letters carved in Greek that were found in the medieval era. As he opens the door, light falls down the center aisle in a burst. "The mosaic on the floor," he tells us, "is the tree of life." Highly stylized figures. The trunk of the tree runs all the way from the door to the altar, with biblical scenes along the branches. I can't place the era. "No, not old," he says in answer to my question. "Only 1878. The brothers Maselli accomplished the work and design."

I don't know who these brothers were, but they were bold. He tells us more about the town history and its current ambiance. "We are only six thousand. With many philosophers." I forget to ask if he speaks Griko.

We walk out through a park with a row of weird ceramic sculptures, each one emblazoned with the name of a different philosopher. Later, I read that the mayor has employed a philosopher to be available to discuss problems and issues with citizens one afternoon a week. Special town!

NEXT STOP: SPECCHIA. On a nice inland rise that protected citizens from Saracen coastal raids, Specchia began in the ninth century. Driving through olive groves and wildflowers, we pass a *pajare,* one of the ancient stone agricultural buildings that look like an upside-down flower pot. Some of these have spiral stairs. Lookouts? One source suggests a climb for star-gazing.

The square Piazza del Popolo, flat-top buildings, palm trees, balconies all give a fleeting impression of North Africa, or southern Spain. Castello Risolo, also looking quite Moorish in design, lines one side. This is a distinctive small town; it's easy to see why it has been named one of the listings in *I Borghi più belli d'Italia.*

Where is everyone? Any minute a hand might part curtains and peer down at us for a better look.

At least the *Pasticceria* Bar Martinucci is open. One of the delights of Italy is that every bar has freshly squeezed orange juice, *spremuta d'arancia.* Here I try *spremuta di melagrana,* juice of pomegranate. This is going to become my afternoon drink in Puglia—what Persephone must have drunk to increase her powers on the way down to Hades. We're the only customers and the barista wants to chat. He recommends their *pasticciotto,* which is a favorite and famous pastry of the Lecce area. "You need to try the chocolate," he advises, but we split the one filled with pastry cream and wild cherries.

"Wouldn't this be good for breakfast?"

"Anytime," Ed says. He's had more than his share. *Pasticciotto* is made in a small oval mold. The old ones were copper. *Pasta frolla,* a soft pastry dough, is formed into a cylinder, then cut in little slices that are pressed down by hand and put into the form. Next comes the filling (chocolate does sound good), and then another flattened oval of dough over the top. We buy a few *mustaccioli* to go. This chocolate-covered cookie, popular in Naples as well as this part of Puglia, has a soft, cake-like interior flavored with spices, honey, and candied fruit.

I CAN'T OVERSTATE the beauty of the Salento coast. We spend the afternoon driving to different beaches—walking, stopping for a sandwich and coffee, sitting on bluffs watching the mesmerizing colors of blue shift to turquoise and back to blue. Oh, for a boat to wend our way along the shore. The clear water reminds me of Lawrence Durrell writing about Corfu. He's tossing cherries and watching his wife dive down to the white sand bottom and bring them up in her teeth.

About transparent water, there is something life-affirming. Even if summer is crowded, there are so many beaches that it must be easy to find a plot of sand and immerse yourself in the delicious water. I am ready to come back to **Torre dell'Orso** with its gentle swath of beach and the two monumental off-shore rocks, Due Sorelle, two sisters. Also Torre Saracena, with dramatic rock formations, and the sandy inlets around Melendugno. If I could forecast an ideal time for the Salento, I'd say early June; although, for me, the spring offers solitude and a chance to be alone with Ed and the beauties of this coast.

FOR DINNER, OUR last night in Lecce, we choose Osteria degli Spiriti, a family-run restaurant with the cozy atmosphere of a home. We order fried mixed vegetables, beef filets braised in *negroamaro* wine, and salads. The Polvenera Primitivo 17 is from seventy-year-old bush vines. It's deep red in the glass, with purple fringes. Lecce at night looks glamorous and, in places, almost unreal. Few are roaming about at this hour. "Do you think we've somehow ascended into heaven?"

"No. They don't have espresso in heaven." Last coffee of the day. Ed always has a nip before bed, as he thinks it gives him the strength to sleep.

WE DEPART LECCE early on our way north to a cluster of small villages around Troia and Lucera. Today's detour, a half hour south: **Otranto** on the coast, the ancient port for trade to Greece, Turkey, Asia. Albania is only a sail away, less than a hundred kilometers. Otranto was strategic and often raided. A Turkish attack in 1480 was unusually brutal. After a wholesale slaughter of the citizens, the remaining eight hundred were offered their lives if they renounced Christianity. They did not. Their bones remain in Santa Maria Annunziata. More uplifting to see in that church is the mosaic tree-of-life floor and the portrayed seasonal activities as in old books of hours. Ah, the brothers who accomplished the tree of life in Corigliano must have been inspired by this.

Long ago and far away, I first heard of this place in high school when I read *The Castle of Otranto* (1764) by Horace Walpole. This book birthed the gothic novel. The real fifteenth-century Castello Aragonese dominates the town, but looks less forbidding than the one I imagined when reading Walpole's book.

Strife now seems remote in this *centro*. On summer evenings, it must hum with contented beachgoers, through for the day, and ready for strolls and dining in a charming town.

The wind is pushing us through the streets where most of the tiny shops catering to tourists are shut. We find an open bar for cappuccino and a *cornetto*.

"End of April," the barista tells us. "That's when the town wakes up."

"YOUR ROOM IS ready. Documents, please." As we check into the hotel in Lucera, I open my handbag and realize that I left my passport, camera, and wallet in the drawer of the bedside table in Lecce.

NOTES:

Mamma li Turchi is a phrase known all over Italy, a cry of alarm when danger of intruders arises. Or, used ironically for other invasions such as a swarm of tourists descending. Mama, the Turks are coming!

A must to read in this part of Puglia: *Honey from a Weed* by Patience Gray, eccentric Englishwoman who lived, foraged, and cooked in a primitive house nearby for many years.

When I get back to Lecce, I'll book at La Fiermontina. I saw photos from friends who stayed there and raved. www.lafiermontina.com

Fusillone, Scampo, Sesamo Nero

LARGE FUSILLI, PRAWNS, BLACK SESAME, SERVES 4

A wildly inventive and surprising restaurant, Bros' is in the hands of Chef Floriano Pellegrino, still in his twenties, and also the young and gifted pastry chef Isabella Potì. Their playful recipes usually feature at least one rogue ingredient. Here we get to play with toasted black sesame seeds (I order them online). He recommends Gentile fusillone, made in Naples, but large fusilli is widely available. The philosophy of the plate, Floriano wrote to me: "In this dish, we wanted to use in a different way the usual toasted broth soup, combining vinegared shallot with bitter black sesame." For the broth, I recommend first sautéing the shells in olive oil, then adding 1 cup of water.

16 raw prawns, scampi, or large shrimp, shelled
    and cut in half lengthwise (reserve shells)
Salt, *QB*
¼ cup white wine vinegar
4 shallots, thinly sliced
¼ pound toasted black sesame seeds
5 tablespoons sunflower oil
1 cup broth
¾ pound fusillone
4 tablespoons extra-virgin olive oil
Fine salt, *QB*

Make a broth with the shells by simmering them with salt in a small pan of water for 30 minutes.

Pour the white wine vinegar into a small bowl. Add the shallots to the vinegar.

Toast the black sesame seeds in a 300°F oven on a parchment-lined sheet pan for 4 minutes. When cool, emulsify with sunflower oil in a food processor.

Cook the fusillone *al chiodo,* nail hard, in enough boiling salted water and 1 cup of the broth.

Sauté the scampi for about 3 minutes in the olive oil.

Serve with sesame sauce on the bottom, then the fusillone and prawns, and finish with the shallots in vinegar.

Bros', Lecce, Puglia

Lucera, Troia, and Pietramontecorvino

What luck to land at Le Nicchie Guest House, outside **Lucera**. It looks like a typical large brick modern house in a rural neighborhood, nothing venerable at all. But inside the welcome is genuine and the response to my missing passport is *"no problema."* Ed calls Erene, the lovely student who helped us at the Lecce B & B. She goes up to our room and locates my forgotten things. I am so embarrassed. Credit cards, insurance cards. Library card from Hillsborough, North Carolina. Even the card they punch when I buy beauty products in Cortona. "Tomorrow," she says, "or the day after." She is calling DHL. Dee-occa-elle-eh. "Do not worry." But we do. We are here for two nights; will the package arrive?

Our two-room suite is a tranquil haven. All shades of white-to-taupe. The immaculate duvet, the bed draped in gauzy fabric. Perfect bath, and a living room with natural sofa and two light taupe chairs. Good Wi-Fi, not always a given in Puglia. What a gentle base for seeing a few of the many villages in the area.

We're in the province of Foggia, inland from the spectacular Gargano peninsula, the spur of the boot, where we last year spent a blissful week exploring Vieste, Peschici, the national park, and numerous beaches. Ed kept saying "Why go to the Amalfi coast? This is stupendous." That trip prompted our interest in coming back to explore more of Puglia. We're lucky to be here in spring, when each turn off the main road leads us into *oliveti* and almond orchards. These massive olive trees make our Tuscan ones look like twigs.

Only one other guest is dining, a business traveler glued to his phone and wine bottle. Francesco, owner of the hotel, likes to talk and we spend the evening with him, though he is serving and going back and forth to the kitchen, where a local woman is in charge.

We learn about his family, about the relatives who control the other half of the house and have their own hotel and restaurant. One of those Italian stories I've heard a million times. A falling-out. A truce but no going back. Family businesses often come to this and, side by side, they all somehow go forward. Since Francesco is passionate about wine, much of our talk is about local production. The cook feeds us well. Stuffed rings of calamari. Oh, bread! The bread is everywhere the quintessence of what bread should be. Where does she get hers? In Troia. We are going there. Dinner is leisurely; Francesco pours liberally. "We are drinking a lot of wine, Francesco!"

"Local, can't harm you," Francesco maintains. "2011 Ferraù Cacc'e Mmitte di Lucera, Paolo Petrilli." That's a mouthful! Francesco now speaks quickly and I'm not sure I follow. The wine is the local grape, *uva di Troia*. But. There's a baffling list of other grapes that balance it out: *montepulciano, sangiovese, malvasia nera*, or doses of white local *bombino* and *trebbiano*. Sounds unholy but the taste is full and spicy, dark as a Puglian night in the country.

Ed asks, "What does Cacc'e Mmitte mean?"

"Um. You drink one and then another? But actually it is what's pressed and the holding tank."

Out come *friselle,* rounds of bread usually topped with tomatoes and basil, but here served with sautéed wild mushrooms on a bed of mâche. *Friselle* is to Puglia what bruschetta is to Tuscany—soul food. A vegetable *sformato* with cannellini, a squash soup with crisp guanciale and Gorgonzola. Pause. Roasted baby pig with prunes and pine nuts. *Molto buono!*

•⁻•⁻•

YOU CAN'T BE long in this part of Puglia without becoming enthralled with Frederick II. He ruled as Holy Roman Emperor from 1220 until 1250. He's responsible for most of the castles and fortifications scattered throughout the countryside. In Lucera, the ruins of his castle fortress stand on a hill just outside town, overlooking the Tavoliere, the immense plain where golden wheat ripples in the wind. He built castle, mint, treasury, and, some say, a harem, when he brought twenty thousand Arab Muslims from Sicily—a bold troop buildup. Loyal to Frederick, they became his royal bodyguards.

Later expanded by his successor, Charles of Anjou, the brick walls reached nine hundred meters. Towers, bastions, remains of Frederick's palace and, inside, stones of a Roman acropolis, proclaiming *we were first*. Actually, the Daunians, an Iapygian tribe, were first, but who *were* they?

Citizens' DNA swabs must have fascinating results. Lucera spins out the spectrum of conquerers: Lombards, Swabians, Byzantium, Angevins. Rome left its mark. Only in 1932, also just outside town, an amphitheater was uncovered. From a distance, it looks like a football stadium. Built in the first century B.C., it seated eighteen thousand for its gladiator games.

ELEGANT JEWEL-BOX LUCERA. Everyday busy wine town, market town of thirty-four thousand. The gate into the *centro storico,* Porta di Troia, bears Arabic inscriptions testifying to their problems with Christians. Walking toward the heart of town, we pass many noble *palazzi;* people have lived in elevated circumstances here for hundreds of years. So much time present in the sand-colored buildings, the stone streets. The Angevin church, built in 1300, looks like a strange northern import with its flat brick face and angled roofline. Something else is odd, too. On the left, the slender tower is obviously a Muslim minaret! In 1269, the Angevins invaded and murdered the Arabs, except for those who escaped to Albania or converted to Christianity. They destroyed the mosques. Santa Maria Assunta was built on the ruins of the town's last remaining mosque. Was the minaret left for its grace?

I look in an interior design shop. Fur pillows and extravagant glass vases. Expensive cookware. Someone's not looking toward the past. In a hardware store, we buy packets of *cicoria,* and fava seeds. The best wild greens in the area are said to grow on the grounds of Frederick's castle.

Not wanting to take the time for a restaurant, we pause in a bar for *friselle* with tomatoes.

I WILL NEVER forget Troia. A pleasant, tiny village with views—there's one reason you must come here. Simply unforgettable and sublime, the 1039 church of Our Lady of the Assumption. Small, in just proportion to the piazza it dominates, with three blind arches flanking either side of a *portone,* big door, fashioned by Oderisio da Benevento in 1119. The bronze door shows scenes from the lives of saints and bishops. The glory, the jaw-dropping, fall-to-your-knees glory is the façade's stupendous stone rose window, more delicate than any lace doily my great-grandmother ever crocheted. "Let's just don't say anything," I whisper. Who made this? Who designed a wheel on a piece of parchment, an intricate design that recalls fine lace and Arab tiles? Eleven radiating spokes with the pie-wedge pierced-stone designs in between. The wedges recall screens dividing nuns from view, the patterns on miradors that Muslim women hid behind, or mandalas. How intricate this stone lace: crosses, clover shapes, interlocking curvaceous framing borders. Eleven ribs. Often there are twelve, for the Apostles. Was Judas's section removed or did the design just achieve equilibrium with eleven? Surrounding all, a simple stone edging under an arc of carved stone phantasmagorical figures—simian animals, a man on a lion, rams, others I can't identify. I'm glued to the ground by this enchanting, out-of-the-way church. Lions peer from behind columns at the upper windows. Bulls, ubiquitous symbol all over the Mediterranean world, poke out under the roofline.

Isn't this why we travel? To be lifted thus? To be seduced and refreshed? I look around at people going about their morning, wondering if living in constant contact with such beauty transforms their faces. Even if nothing shows, the structure of their thoughts and dreams must be influenced by the filigreed fineness of the stone carving in the rose window; the eleven dividing bars must structure their days;

the circular center with its six-pointed star must give them strength to hold all else in balance, and the small center hole: What is most loved resides there.

What finally lures me away is wafting scents of baking. In Pasticceria Casoli, we sample a soft tiny cake with pistachio frosting and a rosette on top that looks like a design in the rose window. In such a small town, we pass three pastry shops. Couldn't one of them please move to Hillsborough, North Carolina?

UNTIL LATE AFTERNOON, we drive in the countryside, around the plain dotted with windmills and up to the village of **Alberona** with its Knights Templar tower and panoramic views. We start out on a walking trail but the wind picks up and we turn back to a café where we have lemonade and I read bits of *Old Puglia* to Ed. I would like to spend more time in **Pietramontecorvino**. We discover Santa Maria Assunta with a charming campanile of green and yellow tiles, buildings buttressing each other with arches, stepped streets, and some houses built into rocks.

Near where we park, a man is selling produce from his panel truck and a group of women in dark dresses and neat pumps crowds around him. Ed walks over to buy some fruit. The object of all the attention is a crate of what looks like gnarly onions. Soon we are in deep discussion about this delicacy. *Lampascioni.* Something to do with raspberry, *lampone*? No. They're amused that we've never heard of *lampascioni.*

"They're wild," the man says. "Just peel and cook like anything else," one woman says as she holds out her sack to be filled.

"*Un tipo di cipolla?*" I ask. A type of onion? Another laugh.

"*Muscari,*" another says. "*Com'e un giacinto.*"

What? Hyacinth? Yes, a type of hyacinth. I didn't know they were edible and the ones I plant are too expensive to eat. These are small and covered with papery layers. We buy a bagful.

The man approves. Yes, you will like this. He cradles several in his palm. "This is something we wait for. Especially good with sausage."

By now, Ed has looked up the word. "That's right. Hyacinths. *Muscari comosum.* After you eat them, the next day blossoms come out of your ears."

•⁻•⁻•

AWAITING US AT the hotel, the package. DHL was fleet of foot, and Erene a princess to dispatch my things so quickly. Dinner at Nicchie again rewards us for a crammed day of travel. There are other guests tonight but we get to tell Francesco about our exploits and to confer with him about wine. He brings over what will surely become a favorite: Polvanera Gioia Colle Primitivo, 2017, a beautiful pour of ruby red from the Murgian area near Bari. Before we leave tomorrow, he will put together for us a case of this area's best. Dinner begins with stuffed calamari and rolls of cod filled with green olives and a sauce of red carrots. Then classic Puglian orecchiette with wild greens, anchovies, and bread crumbs. Home cooking. Ed has a local fish in a crust of crushed *taralli,* and I quit at this point. In Puglia, I could survive on the divine bread alone.

AFTER WE RETIRE to our room, in my notebook, I try to draw the rose window of Troia from memory.

NOTES:

Frederick II is for me the most interesting of all early rulers. He was born in what is now Le Marche, and although he ruled over a giant swath of Europe, his affections were always for Italy. This is a brief summary of his life: https://www.britannica.com/biography/Frederick-II-Holy-Roman-emperor

Angevin and Anjou: Angevin means "from Anjou," western France. When a building is Angevin, it was built in the twelfth to early thirteenth centuries, when kings of the House of Anjou ruled England. Henry II, Richard I, and John were Angevin kings.

Sformatini di Pancotto su Paté dell'Orto con Cascata di Cannellini

SFORMATINI OF COOKED BREAD WITH A VEGETABLE PÂTÉ AND WATERFALL OF CANNELLINI, SERVES 6

A *sformato,* kind of a crustless quiche turned out of its mold, is usually served as part of an antipasto platter, or as a side dish. Chef Anna Maria Piccolo's *sformatini* (small *sformati*) are different. Bread and broccolini line the ramekins, which are then filled with savory vegetables and cannellini beans. *Pancotto*—cooked bread—also is used all over Italy for a base for a much-loved soup that makes good use of leftover bread.

FOR THE *SFORMATINI*

2 bunches broccoli rabe, any tough stalks removed, chopped

4 slices of day-old bread, diced

1 tablespoon olive oil

1 clove garlic, minced

FOR THE PÂTÉ

2 stalks celery, chopped

1 onion, chopped

1 carrot, sliced

1 potato, chopped

FOR THE TOPPING

2 cups cooked cannellini beans, with a little reserved cooking water

20 pitted black olives, sliced

15 cherry tomatoes, halved

Salt and pepper, *QB*

FOR THE GARNISH

¾ cup bread crumbs sautéed in olive oil

1 handful parsley, snipped

Prepare the *sformatini:*

Immerse the broccoli rabe in boiling water for 5 minutes, add the bread, then drain. In a medium skillet, sauté the garlic in the oil, then add the bread and broccoli rabe. Season and allow to cool.

Oil 6 four-inch ramekins and fill with the bread–broccoli rabe mixture. Cool the ramekins in the fridge to set.

Prepare the pâté:

Steam the celery, onion, carrot, and potato over boiling water. When barely done, season and blend with an immersion blender until a homogeneous mixture is obtained.

Prepare the topping:

In a saucepan, heat the beans with a little of their own water, along with the olives and tomatoes. Drain away the liquid. Keep warm.

With a spoon, spread the vegetable pâté in six circles on a flat baking sheet lined with parchment. Unmold a ramekin on top of each circle, then bake in the center of a 350°F oven for 10 minutes. Serve the *sformatini* using a wide spatula. Spoon the beans on top, then garnish with the bread crumbs, parsley, and a drizzle of oil.

Le Nicchie, Lucera, Puglia

Orsara

Last day of the trip. After a leisurely breakfast and a long wine talk with Francesco, we load the car, not forgetting passports! Orsara, only thirty-two kilometers away, is another of the many highly individual villages in the Foggia province. This one has a particular lure: bread. Pane e Salute, Bread and Health, is the object of our quest. Francesco told us that this *forno* has been baking bread since 1526. We find it in a lane that looks unchanged since then. Crude small buildings, stony street. No one home but the door is open, so we step into a dingy room with a black oven in back. Ladders are hung sideways on the wall and enormous loaves of dark brown bread rest on the rungs. Into the top of each has been slashed a cross.

Crude sink, iron-burnered stove, large basket of eggs on the floor, and an antique *madia* with cutting boards inside. This is a classic Italian open-topped chest that no household in the past was without. Usually chestnut, the *madia* lid opens into a trough for letting the dough rise, and for storing bread. A cupboard is below.

(Now you often see these used as drinks cabinets in restaurants.) A table is set for three. Two blue chairs, one red, checked napkins, and a white tablecloth. Could be 1717, or 1817.

While Ed tries to call the phone number on the sign, a glistening woman comes in, carrying a bag of groceries. The owner, Angelo Trilussa, is away today. She calls him. "Americans are here." She asks if she can cook for us even though we've just turned up unexpectedly. In the adjoining room, another table is set. "He says yes," she calls out in Polish-accented Italian. This is an unexpected pleasure; we'd thought to buy bread to take home to Tuscany.

She starts to cook in the primitive kitchen. She plops a pitcher of red wine and two tumblers on the table, and a selection of flat breads filled with ricotta, tomatoes, and herbs, another with wild greens, and, our favorite studded with olives, almost-blackened tomatoes, and onions. A log of *salume* and a bowl of olives. From a back room she hauls in ingredients and soon she brings in two round loaves of bread, each with the top sliced off. Inside, the bread has been hollowed out and is filled with steaming fava, chicory, and potato soup. A basket of the house special bread. It's cooked in a straw-fired oven; the quick flash of flame gives the crust its darkness.

The cross makes it seem even more special. When baking for the community, initials were cut into the dough for identification. These loaves are tremendous! They weigh around six pounds, an armful! Beneath the brown crust, the golden cake-like interior. Bread like this they eat every day around here; for us it's a phenomenal treat. I see big flour bags by the door: Molino Campanaro, *semola rimacinata di grano duro.* Hard wheat semolina twice milled (fine grind) in nearby Castelluccio dei Sauri. They probably have their secret mix of flours; their "mother" yeast is seventy years old. I'm terrible at bread baking and have no wood oven but I'm inspired to try again, although my bread is, historically, best for doorstops.

Old photos on the wall: two soldiers young and smoking, a couple on a motorcycle from the 1930s, a *contadino* group of eleven farm workers, four of whom are holding ducks. Several *pale* hang on the wall, the flat peels for poking into a deep oven to retrieve the pizza or bread. A line of sausages dangling from a pole, bunches of tomatoes drying on strings—I love this place. And she is shockingly good. She brings an omelet with bitter greens. A beef stew appears, too, but we have to say no. She's shocked that we don't want our *secondo*. "Truly, we are too happy," Ed tells her.

When we want to pay, she calls the boss again. "They didn't eat," we overhear. He tells her what to charge. So little. We are happy that we get to buy three of the enormous loaves. My preferred breakfast is a piece of buttered bread toasted under the broiler. I can freeze hunks of this bread and have perfect breakfasts all spring.

WE ARE SIX hours from home. We decide to drive a couple of hours into Le Marche and spend the night in Ascoli Piceno, one of our favorite towns. We munch on bread as we drive through the countryside.

Monopoli, Bitonto, Lecce, Altamura, Matera, and Alberobello

One winter night over dinner with close friends in Hillsborough, I said, "What if we all went to Puglia?" That afternoon, I'd come across a listing for a palatial and evocative villa outside Monopoli. Ed looked at me: *What?* We hardly ever travel with friends.

"Monopoli. Where's that?" one said.

"Mid-Puglia below the spur but above the stiletto heel," I explained. "We were near there in March. In May, the weather should be *perfetto*." Ed pulled up the villa photo on his phone. Curly iron gates, an allée leading to the grand villa of long windows, a glass loggia, and a façade of dark oxblood stucco, peeling just enough to give an aura of decadent romanticism.

Ed and I have been to Puglia four times; still not enough. We talked Puglia. The crystalline water, massive olive trees, the vegetable-centered cuisine, Romanesque churches, stone walls crisscrossing the landscape, perched white villages that let you know the Greeks once lived there. What fun to share it with good friends. We drank a lot of red wine. We decided YES.

FIVE MONTHS LATER we all meet in Rome, where Ed has found a house that I could move right into. Three stories, refined taste, comfortable. I know I'd like the owners though I'll never meet them. The dining room says who they are: a long walnut table with candlesticks and epergnes piled with fresh fruit, walls like buttercream frosting, old portraits, window seat with apricot velvet pillows, sideboard full of good linens.

We're near Piazza Navona but on a quiet street near one of my favorite small churches, Santa Maria della Pace. By day, everyone goes in different directions since some of us never have been before, some have, and one was born here. Ed and I are on a quest to see the many-splendored Biblioteca Angelica and other great historic libraries of Rome. We all buy flowers, wine, cheeses. At seven, we meet for drinks in the living room—three roomy sofas—then proceed to dinner. In warm mid-May, we can eat outside at Santa Lucia, at Pier Luigi, on the terrace of Hotel Raphaël, and at sidewalk trattorias.

For the third day, we've arranged a seven A.M. tour of the Vatican libraries and galleries, and the Sistine Chapel. We get to enter before opening hours. This works well with the art galleries—we're almost alone—but we're bustled right along, as other private groups are bringing up the rear. We get a few moments alone with Caravaggio's *Deposition*. I have always loved that long Vatican corridor with the early maps on the walls. It's a pure delight to see them again after many years. We pause at a coffee bar while our excellent guide lectures us on what we're going to see. By the time we enter the Sistine Chapel, many other private groups have arrived and soon the floodgates open. We're treated to guards constantly shouting about no photos. I think of Michelangelo lying on his back on scaffolding, paint dripping down on his face, the cramped position he held for hours. Crushed by now, I think maybe it was better up there than down here. I want out.

Is any meaningful experience with art possible when you are trapped like a chicken in a transport crate? Ed, who suffers at times from claustrophobia, already waits at the exit. "Tell me we never have to come back to the Vatican again."

A drastic idea. "I promise."

In the gift shop, we buy a thousand-piece puzzle of the Grand Canal.

WHO DOESN'T FALL in love with Rome? A walk along the Tevere, a raucous lunch at Roscioli, the Spanish Steps, the Pantheon, Antico Caffè Greco's pastries and coffee, little cakes at MADE Creative Bakery, shopping in Monti and fantastic lunch at Trattoria Monti, wandering Trastevere, a grand finale dinner at creative Il Convivio Troiani.

The four days are gone.

OUR FRIENDS BOARD the train for Brindisi, where a car will be waiting to take them to the villa. We retrieve our car from long-term parking. They arrive before we do.

Here's our group of merry pranksters:

Susan—cookbook writer, extraordinary cook, nutritionist, and former food editor at *Food & Wine,* later owner of a book editing and production service. Fascinated by India; lover of Bollywood.

Ann—agent for avant-garde photographers, curates shows, lives in her family home, the oldest house in Chapel Hill, is up on every culinary event, first to appear at the weekly Carrboro Farmers' Market.

Randall—trial lawyer with a houseful of books testifying to his English-major past. Married to Ann. Articulate with a wry humor.

Robin—former chef and owner of several restaurants, serious interior design talent, and always cooking for twenty or more.

Andrea—head of design at a major telecommunications company, walked the Camino de Santiago de Compostela, reader of books about consciousness and creativity. Married to Robin.

Michael—literary novelist, bon vivant, former head writer for a major soap opera. Just retired from teaching in theater arts.

Francesca—theater designer, recently quit professorship to freelance. Born in Rome to a complex family she's producing a film about.

•⁓•⁓•

ED, SUSAN, FRANCESCA, and Randall, our intrepid drivers, go off to pick up a rental car and groceries. The rest of us unpack and check out the villa. I knew there would be *some* quirkiness—but now we have a lesson in what photos of a rental don't show. The huge pool with umbrellas in the photo actually is surrounded by rough tarp-like material. If it gets hot, will it bubble like tar? The formal garden is enchanting with statues and a stone boat in a fishpond, a pergola, and an orangery—but the photo must have been taken twenty years back. In a futile gesture, a few clumps of lurid petunias and geraniums have been installed, probably for our arrival.

The bedrooms are fine, large and square, with antiques, soaring frescoed ceilings, and marble floors. The blankets are ancient mites. Only one bath was shown in the pictures. With good reason. Even the photographed one was only adequate. At least every bedroom has a bath, however primitive and minute. The two grand salons run the width of the house. In the main living room, the owners' son, who lives on the lower floor, tells us not to sit on the horsehair sofas as the fabric will split. There is nowhere else to sit. The other salon is airy and charming with family portraits, buff marble floor with inlaid concentric squares of ocher marble, and a Venetian chandelier. The Empire furniture, stiff and upright, marching around the perimeter, won't be comfortable. At least we can sit down. We pull everything in around an oval table where Michael dumps out the jigsaw puzzle we bought after our Sistine Chapel visit. A tall door opens onto another formerly formal garden with a view in the distance of the sea.

The dining room table seats eighteen. (We later find that it's extended with plywood panels. If you lean on your elbow, the other side flies up.) A playful fresco of a trellis, vines, and birds covers the ceiling. The walls, unfortunately, have been painted in an awful attempt to resemble wood. Angels and dog portraits that commemorate pets must have been painted by an untalented family member.

The kitchen. Let's not go there yet.

What is lovely: The front door opens into a two-story glass atrium with a marble plaque on the wall testifying in Latin that the villa was built in 1792 for the concept of *otium:* leisure, friendship, and relaxation.

Stone steps ascend through the greenhouse into a foyer. This must have been divine when full of flourishing plants. Now it seems a false kindness to keep the stalky and dusty specimens alive, but barely.

ANN, ANDREA, AND I set the table outside. Limpid late-afternoon light casts its spell on the skeletal garden. I'm worried that everyone is just being polite and they're seething that I've spent their money on this ruin when there are lovingly restored *masserie* (the old fortified farms) we could have rented for less. But everyone seems excited to be in Puglia. We're laughing as we cobble together three folding tables. Thrown over them, a white tablecloth I found in a cupboard in the dining room. We set votive candles all along, and a vine of greenery. Mismatched plates and ugly cutlery. It almost looks like one of those clever settings on social media I've seen, where someone who wouldn't consider ironing napkins lays out dish towels, cuts a few twigs and plops them in a jar, spontaneous anti-décor. Oh, contrived and fun.

SUSAN AND ROBIN are throwing something together; the rest of us sit drinking prosecco on a sun-warmed stone wall. Michael and Francesca think we should write a play to perform in the bereft garden. Randall makes his way into the kitchen to find another cold bottle. A chair must be wedged against the refrigerator door because it won't close. "Do you smell gas?" Susan asks him. "The guy said the stove is brand new."

"Yes, I do." Twisting the cork, Randall looks on with alarm. Robin is shaking a pan of sausages over the flame. The kitchen provides a study in inefficiency. I do love the wall of dozens of mid-century aluminum colanders, frying pans, and saucepans. Do not love the cluttered low table that serves as a work space, or the oilcloth-covered table near the sink, which must harbor generations of germs. We layer paper towels over it. Shopping list: sponges, disinfectant, scrubbing powder.

Robin arranges olives, *salume,* tiny mozzarella balls. Susan improvises with fresh orecchiette, tomatoes, and zucchini. Sausages, salad. Ordinary, but elevated. "How is it that everything *tastes* amazing?" Ann asks. Toasts into the night. Some quotes from *A Midsummer Night's Dream.* Andrea describes the brilliant twentysomething digital designers she mentors. Randall says what he can about a headline case he's defending. We talk about tomorrow. Monopoli! Far out at the edge of the view, a knife-edge of silver where the moon reflects on the sea.

We drift off to our rooms. A life-size marble woman by the rear entrance, although headless, bids us good night.

We are kept awake by a maniacal kennel of barking dogs across the road.

IN THE MORNING before departing, I go outside and knock on the young heir's door. He's sleeping in. Opens an inch and grimaces. "There's a problem. The dogs. What can you do?"

He squints into the sun. "Oh, sorry. Yes. The dogs. There's nothing to do. The owners are away. They've been barking since October. You get used to it." He wants to shut the door.

"Isn't there a caretaker? Can't you call the police? There must be noise rules in such an exclusive area."

"No. I'm sorry. There's nothing I can do."

And I do know about neighborhood vendettas in Italy. Calling the police on a neighbor might incite a generational war. "Well, I'm sorry, too, must be awful for you, but we need a solution. Otherwise, obviously, we will have to leave. Obviously."

He suddenly seems awake. "I'll try." He frowns. Pesky Americans. Wanting to sleep at night.

MONOPOLI CORNERS THE market on charm. A line of whitewashed houses with blue doors opening onto the equally blue sea. A tanned and hairy man up to his waist in water pulls up a squirming octopus. Harbor of bright boats, green water. Cafés and *osterie* line the piazza. We come upon a Byzantine rupestrian cave church, dark and mysterious, down a flight of stairs. Under an arch, a shrine painting memorializes the story of roof beams strapped onto a raft. The raft washed in and landed in the harbor in 1117. A miracle: the very wood needed to complete the construction of the cathedral begun ten years earlier. Found on the beams like a gift card, an icon of the Virgin Mary and Child, now displayed in the cathedral, venerated and celebrated with festivals.

We overwhelm the tiny Olio e Vino shop and stock up on good wines and artisan olive oil. Fish lunch outside at Dal Ghiottone. After we eat, and the table is cleared, there comes that moment when, ah, *vacation* kicks in. Shoulders go down and at the same time a different energy surges forth. We linger over coffee. We have nowhere we have to be other than this ancient village where the air is room temp and the waiter has a megawatt smile you've been waiting all your life to see.

Afternoon stretches out. We're lazy cats, reading, napping, lounging by the pool. Recovering from last night's dog yapping. Michael types on his lap in an upright chair, legs up on a stool. Under his white straw hat with a black band, he looks like Truman Capote. The edges of the puzzle are finished. The heir comes up with a repairman to see about the gas. Someone has been called about the refrigerator. He has talked to the caretaker and, *miracolo,* the dogs have been moved. "Imagine," Ed says, "he's lived with that racket for months and all it took was a trip across the road."

AT SIX, WE'RE picked up by Giacomo in his Mercedes van for a trip up to Polignano a Mare. Robin made this dinner reservation months ago. She'd seen a photo of a spectacularly positioned restaurant, so spectacular that we won't even care if we're served mediocre food. Like Monopoli, Polignano a Mare is a dreamy white village on the sea. Near the entrance into the old town, we see a statue of Domenico Modugno, who wrote "Volare," which must be belted out all too frequently at many outdoor bars.

We reach Ristorante Grotta Palazzese by going down, down, down many stairs until we emerge into a cave above the sea. In front, the sunset splendidly splashes the sky with lavish orange and purple, and the water reflects the colors in ripples and swirls. In back of us, a blue grotto. Impossibly gorgeous! Robin orders the best Champagne because why not? When will we ever be in such a setting again?

Raw board: everything pulled out of the water today. Grilled red shrimp, whole fish, glistening oysters that surely must have pearls. The light behind Ed, sitting across from me, appears to emanate from his hair, showing him to be the beatific creature that he is. We are swimming creatures. We are finny and fine. The sky, now fading to nacreous pink. We do not sing "Volare," although the notes strum through my head as we take photos to remember such a memorable night.

UP AND OUT early. Giacomo will drive us to our far point of the week: **Lecce**. We've reserved at Bros', the edgy restaurant Ed and I discovered when we were there in March. Once let out in the *centro storico,* we keep losing each other. "Where's Ed?" "He's gone to a bar he liked before near the amphitheater." "Where's Ann?" "She's looking for sunglasses." Herding cats. We decide to meet at lunch.

Ed and I neglected the *cartapesta,* papier-mâché, tradition when we were here in March. Today, we visit the small Museo della Cartapesta in the Castello di Carlo V, where the city has collected some of the best examples of the craft. We're enchanted with the detail of those original artists' work, with how the figures reveal life at that time through what they wore, work they did. Known as "poor man's marble," *cartapesta* was early *arte povera,* art made from humble stuff, as their seventeenth- and eighteenth-century materials were rags, glue, plaster, straw, wire.

Now there's more to it than religious figures and crèche furnishings. At Tonda Design, artisans display statement necklaces and rings. I buy colorful dangling earrings made of squares and circles of *cartapesta.* Tonda is primarily a furniture and lighting gallery, with very particular objects made from olive and other local woods. Then we meet the exquisite Francesca Carallo in her eponymous art gallery on vico dei Pensini, 1. She's one of those women with short, stylish hair who make a white blouse and black skirt look chic. She welcomes us like friends and shows her abstract sculptures, two of which are pierced honeycomb wall lamps that cast radiating shadows. She's apologizing that most of her work is away at a show. I think she must be the new Lecce.

I find La Casa dell'Artigianato Leccese and immediately call Ann. When I described the *cartapesta* angel I bought here years ago, she wanted to find one. And here they are. I pick three small ones. She's here in a flash, sporting new sunglasses. There are many angels to choose from. They are artistic, not simpering. Ann finds one in a blue dress she likes—and now must get it home without breaking off a wing.

Bros'! Once again, but more so—more fun to be here with friends to enjoy the zany and creative presentations. Out come the first tastes served on blocks of wood, charcoal, driftwood, even atop a potted olive plant. Behind the pomp, the food is fantastic. Pasta with sea urchins; lentils with coconut and dill; calamari with leeks and miso; duck with apricot sauce; quail with plums and green beans. Several of us order the quail, delightfully presented in nests of straw. They're plump, glistening gold, legs tied, heads still attached. We have different wines with each course and I never know exactly what we are drinking, except for a Taersìa Negroamaro in Bianco, Duca Carlo Guarini, a Salento wine as ethereal as an angel's wing. Dessert is called, inexplicably, Fucking Cold Egg. Served in a whacky box covered with graffiti slogans, it looks like a real egg, but tap the top and a sweet crust breaks open. Inside, creamy vanilla custard.

Lunch ends at four. Far south in Italy, where the sun hammers hard, how strongly somnolence can hit after a midday feast. Good thing Giacomo is waiting at the gate.

WE HAD INTENDED to sample country *trattorie* in the area but when we return from our explorations, we want to stay home. The gas smell is cured in the kitchen, but now has migrated to outside the salon door. No more candles lit at the folding tables, I suppose. The heir is disgruntled that we've noticed that a leak has sprung outside. I raid the chests in the dining room and set the tables with vintage linens. Tonight, Michael makes a grand caprese. We don't want another course. Just the usual flowing prosecco and vino.

SOME OF US want to go to Rudolph Valentino's birthplace and museum. Others want Bitonto. Can't we do Castellaneta later, en route somewhere else? It's in the Taranto province, not on the way anywhere. We pick **Bitonto** and pile into the cars, Randall following Ed, whose GPS leads us through idyllic groves of ancient olives and past concrete factories and block apartments, finally into Bitonto, big town of 57,000, where parking is a headache.

Finally, we're standing in front of the Cattedrale di Bitonto, mesmerized by the intricate carved portal and weathered stone griffins standing guard. Over the portal stands that peculiar Christian symbol that always seems to me to belong on an Egyptian obelisk: the pelican. Far-fetched, but the derivation of the symbol comes from the gruesome idea that the bird pecks its own body to feed blood to its young, equaling Christ giving of himself for mankind.

This church repays walking around it: The geometry of the design of the side's arches and the strange little balcony that connects the church to another building can only be appreciated by circling the sturdy structure. Here's the classic Puglian Romanesque with a dash of the Moors, partly from the arcades and perhaps because of the palm trees in front.

It's open courtyard day, a city *festa*. We can peer into usually gated private living space. Some have left their wash to hang, others use their *cortile* for cars. A few tend small gardens. By chance, we come upon the Chiesa del Purgatorio. Skeletons flank the door, so anatomically precise that they look articulated. One holds a scythe, the other an hourglass. The hourglass skeleton wears a halo carved with the twelve hours and the phrase *NIL IN CERTIUS*, nothing is certain. Their unfurling scrolls say *QVA HORA NON PVTATIS*, you do not know the hour, and *VENIAM ET METAM*, I come and I finish. Meaning finish you. Above the door, a line of crowned skulls, topped by a frieze of ten people licked by flames. Over the burning ones fly two succoring angels who can lift them to heaven. Nothing subtle about these messages.

Purgatory churches appeared after the Protestants in northern Europe began pooh-poohing the concept of purgatory, and especially the scandal of indulgences, the practice of paying the church for some points toward a quicker ascension into heaven.

Meanwhile, small churches were constructed by confraternities, lay organizations dedicated to prayer, for those trapped in purgatory. Twenty purgatory churches exist in Puglia, concentrated between Manfredonia and Brindisi. *Memento mori.*

We squeeze into tables at a *panini* bar at the back of the cathedral. Big sandwiches, a wind with a hint of balm, and a view of this grand memory palace. *Carpe diem!*

WE SUGGEST A deviation because we loved **Ruvo di Puglia** in March. My friends must see the graceful Romanesque church built on top of Paleo-Christian ruins, and its Byzantine campanile converted from a watchtower. Everyone agrees and we happily meander around the livable, clean, clean village. As we're determining the route home, a man backing out of his driveway bumps into Randall's car. He doesn't want to give us his insurance information. We note his tag number and dread dealing with the rental agency over this. Luckily, most of the damage wipes away. Then we're on the highway. When we turn off, we are soon lost on bumpy one-track farm roads. Hard to imagine a better place to be lost: ancient twisted olive trees, grasses that make you want to graze, bountiful yellow and white wildflowers.

OVER A STRAIGHT-FROM-THE-SEA dinner in the piazza in Monopoli, we're settled in with cold prosecco. The two drivers are proposing that we hire Giacomo for the rest of the day trips. Those who rode in the backseats immediately agree. Divided nine ways, the van seems quite reasonable. Ed calls. Yes, Giacomo is ready for our big food day tomorrow.

GIACOMO ARRIVES, CHEERFUL in his beret, with a crate of cherries from his garden. Once on back roads, we hardly make any progress because we constantly want to stop for a photo. We are in trulli country. "Stop the bus!" we call out, imitating Diane Lane in the *Under the Tuscan Sun* movie. The beehive-shaped houses are cunningly made of flat stones without mortar. They rise from the land like rounded pyramids. Seeing one, the mind turns on its ratchet, for the shape is out of archetypes, out of prehistory, out of space, out of fairy tales and desert tents. We can't get enough of them, especially ones in olive groves, or ones that link to two or three others in a wheat field. Elves might march out the door.

There's a continuum of stone structures in Puglia. Square and low dolmens are the simplest: standing stone slabs, and slab top. Some are thought to be funerary in purpose but no one really knows; they could be shelters. Menhirs, like ancestors of the trulli, are stacked stone structures, often narrowing at the top. The oldest are Neolithic and seem kin to the Nuraghi ruins in Sardinia. Trulli must be durable—we are seeing many.

Obviously, they were made from the building material at hand. Stony fields must be cleared for planting. Make use of the stones. The form, indigenous and inevitable, goes far back into dim history, but the story goes that more recent sixteenth- and seventeenth-century trulli were built for the ease of destroying them. Tax man arriving from the feudal lord or the Kingdom of Naples or whoever lorded over the peasants. Pull the keystone from the top and the trullo collapses. Tax man gone: Rebuild.

Ed has made an appointment for us at La Florida, producer of *mozzarella di bufala* outside Putignano. As we pull in, we see pens of brown, sweet-faced water buffalo. In an adjacent barn, brand-new piglets. Are they cute? Not to me. They're basic and determined, snorting and rooting and pushing. The newest water buffalo are kept in individual stalls, each with the birth date on the door. They are cute! The open but roofed pen shelters the milk givers, clean and mildly curious. They come to be petted and look at us with goony brown eyes, their horns swept back as though by wind.

Yes, we see the mozzarella process. Rich *bufala* milk swirled with rennet until it thickens. This is hands-on. The workers stir with a pole but when the cheese starts to form, their fingers are their tools. As the cheese comes together in the vats, handfuls are scooped out and put in a machine that forms snowballs. They plop back into the water they came from and two women scoop each one, along with some of the milky water, into plastic bags they tie off. I love how long strands are braided underwater to make *treccie*, plaited mozzarella.

In the retail shop, we fill a cooler with *bocconcini*, little mouthfuls, burrata, and the softball-size creamy mozzarella we've just seen lifted from the vats. Giacomo looks amused that the *Americani* are enamored of the animals. "Let's go," he calls. "There's too much to see today." Back in the van, we compare too many photos, later to be deleted, of the faces of the water buffalo.

Ed and I are fans of the *Gambero Rosso* wine listings and rankings. Each year they do the impossible and select the one best white, red, and sparkling wine. Puglian wines are late to world-class status; this year's red choice, Chiaromonte's Gioia del Colle Primitivo Muro Sant'Angelo Contrada Barbatto, 2013, is quite the coup for the region, and precisely for the vineyards of Acquaviva delle Fonti. Tenute Chiaromonte dates back to 1826 but when Nicola Chiaromonte took over the family business in 1998, the winery began to climb the difficult ladder of national reputation. Today, he tells us, they produce about 120,000 bottles a year.

His vines are bush-trained and range from sixty to more than one hundred years old, at an elevation of more than three hundred meters, on very mineral-rich limestone subsoils with thin topsoils of *terra rossa,* red earth, and clay. *Gambero Rosso* says: "The Tre Bicchieri and Red Wine of the Year, remains a benchmark for anyone wishing to produce a *primitivo* that is not just close-woven and fruity, but also elegant and drinkable. Here the nose notes of black berry fruit with spicy nuances usher in a palate whose sturdy alcohol is balanced by fresh acidity and rich flavor." We get to try their wine with our feet on the exact terroir.

As is typical in Italy, there is no tasting room, per se, but we're welcomed to a storage building by Nicola, who starts opening bottles. "Deep nose," he says. We load cases to take to the villa and to Bramasole into the van. As we drive away, I mull over Nicola's statement on his website: "My parents taught me that the earth is different one inch from another, each one producing a different product. I like thinking that diversity is a sort of richness and a resource which increases the value of human work." Hmm. Wisdom beyond the subject.

GIACOMO SPEEDS TOWARD **Altamura**. This is a town worthy of investigation, especially the cathedral. Never mind, today we're on another quest. Bread. Of all the Puglian bread, none is more revered than Altamura's, especially Forno Antico Santa Chiara, in operation since 1423, even older than the great Pane e Salute in Orsara, which we visited in March. We dash there, as we've lingered long with the water buffalo and the lucky tasting of Chiaromonte. In an arched, cave-like room with a rustic table loaded with flat breads and pizza, two women are shoving the last loaves of the morning into the deep black oven. May we order a few? Yes, come back in an hour. What luck. We take a turn around town, stopping in at Panificio del Duomo, Giacomo's favorite *forno.* It's plain and without romance, but the loaves are righteous and we buy a couple, breaking off chunks of cake-like golden bread with dark brown crust and eating them as we walk.

We have a moment to pause in Piazza Duomo to see Santa Maria Assunta (1423), with its fifteen-rib rose window, a lamb nestled in the center circle. Built by Frederick II, the church's stunning portal shows a last supper with Jesus seated on the far left rather than in the center of the table laden with beakers, fish, and, of course, bread. Who is that kissing Jesus? A woman? John, his favorite disciple, or is this the kiss of Judas transferred from where it is supposed to have happened, in a garden? How many have paused in this intricate doorway before entering the church to admire the flanking lions, the carved vines growing from urns on the heads of two women?

Ed finds a bright and contemporary restaurant, Tre Archi, where we meet Mina and Peppino, the owners. Most everything served comes from their farm and from local producers and farmers. Sacks of grains, lentils, and beans are available for takeaway and a gleaming case of cheeses tempts us as well. Clusters of tomatoes hang from a rack with dried herbs, and fresh herbs grow in jars on the tables. At a wooden board, a young woman shapes small orecchiette from a mound of pasta. She smiles but doesn't speak, as she concentrates on the rhythmic beat that turns out the little ears so quickly.

We're served boards of grilled vegetables and *grissini,* bread sticks, that raise the bar with their toasty taste of wheat. Some carafes of red and white wine make their way around the table. Of course we order orecchiette, some of us choosing a sauce of fava, some chicory. Ed opts for the pebble-shaped legume *cicerchie* served with tagliolini. Little known outside the region, *cicerchia* is a Puglian classic that comes with a caution. Too much of it can cause paralysis, muscle atrophy, or aneurysm. But by discarding the soaking water and eating these delicious peas in moderation, not twice a day for months, *cicerchie* have nourished the Pugliese for many generations. Since we're into full lunch mode, we end with silky panna cotta with berries.

We buy *cicerchie* to take home, along with chickpeas, my favorite, and hustle back to the *forno* for our giant loaves of bread. Giacomo meets us nearby with the van, which is good because each loaf weighs five or six pounds.

We're not on the way back to Monopoli. Giacomo takes us on an excursion because it is truly a pity that we are here for only a week when there is so much to see. He insists that we must go to **Matera,** not far away and unforgettable, even if we just pop in briefly. Once in Puglia, Matera is now located over the border into **Basilicata**.

He's right. He stops at a view point outside town. In the distance, we see a strange hive: stacks of cave openings that served as homes, shops, and churches for centuries, then were largely abandoned, and now are being restored as residences, boutique hotels, restaurants, and shops. The strangeness reminds me of Mesa Verde, the ancient Native American ruin. Above, we see the modern town. Giacomo drives into the *centro,* a leafy and pleasant piazza from which you can clamber down into the cave paths.

Ed and I were here more than twenty years ago, when Matera was dismal and depressing. How it has awakened! The population looks young and vibrant. Girls stroll arm-in-arm and clumps of young men saunter around laughing and carousing. My memory is of old women in black, empty caves that gave me the creeps. Actually, they still kind of give me the creeps. Of all the structures to live in, a cave is bottom of my list.

BACK AT THE villa: downtime. The puzzle is two-thirds done. Francesca tells us about her fascist relatives and their lost estate. I'm reading about purgatory! Michael takes over the kitchen. He presents a gigantic platter of our fresh mozzarella, rolls of bresaola and rucola, and beauteous bursting-with-taste cherry tomatoes. Robin makes bruschette from thick slices of Altamura bread drizzled with the olive oil Bitonto is famous for. With this, naturally, the Chiaromonte wine of the year. Bowls of Giacomo's cherries. Feast for the gods.

GIACOMO WANTS AN early start. We think he has plans we don't know about. We're ready, and soon we are outside **Alberobello**. As in Matera, Giacomo knows a viewing spot outside town that gives us an orientation to this surreal town of trulli.

He lets us off with a meeting time and point. On one side the district called Aja Piccola, the other, Monti, both with dense concentrations of trulli. Does anyone really live here? When we came to Puglia with writer Ann Cornelisen years ago, she warned, "We are *not* going to Alberobello. Too touristy. It gives me a headache." But this trulli town remains above what tourism can discount. The curlicue, cheery lanes lined with the secretive white cones have to enchant anyone with an ounce of imagination.

First fact: the skill of the masons. The dry stone so artfully constructed connects with the world's first architecture. *Trullo* comes from Greek *tholos,* dome, and/or from Latin *turris* or *trullum,* which means tower. Oh yes, it's touristy—but this is a unique place in the world. We see a two-story trullo, and joined pairs called *trulli siamesi,* Siamese, which have no windows. Ed gets claustrophobia just looking at them. The shops are geared toward kitschy fridge-magnet replicas of the trulli—though we do find quality linen shops and a place with well-made olive wood kitchen spoons. I always marvel at how shop workers manage to stay friendly in heavily tourist areas. At the linen shop, the man who sold attractive dish towels, place mats, and shawls to Ann, Susan, and me was so genuine and personable that we almost were invited home to meet his mother, who makes many of the items for sale. He gave us gifts—ceramic replicas of the tops of trulli. "Put it on your table," he said. "It's a symbol of hospitality." The trulli are topped with finials, usually simple balls, or a crowning shape that looks like Monopoly pieces. I read that status is reflected in the quality of the spire. A cross or star or pyramid showed that the mason had skills. Some cones have white-painted symbols that look like mysterious and portentous fertility symbols and religious signs, but the book I buy in town says symbols were never seen in Alberobello before 1934. They were painted in anticipation of a visit from Mussolini. *Old Puglia* doesn't mention Mussolini's visit but about the symbols in general, says they were crosses, swastika suns (the ancient design had nothing to do with Nazis), hearts, and magic charms for averting evil. In summer, this place must be totally overrun, but in May few people are here.

Between the two trulli areas lies a swath of modern shops and cafés, including one bar with two glass-front fridges lined with fabulous cakes whose whorls of frosting would self-destruct before we could get one back to the villa. I let my eyes eat. So many vivid window boxes of purple and red petunias against the whitewashed walls. How many suggestive doorways can I photograph? There are no ancient women making lace. Doors are shut.

We all gather at Giacomo's van. We are heading to **Ostuni** for lunch at La Sommità, where Ed and I stayed in March.

This time, we're seated at a long table in the walled garden of orange trees and a small pool. What a fantasy! When I travel, I often think, oh, I wish X could be here, X would love this. Now here we are with friends all ready to celebrate.

The food is just as spectacular as it was in March. The great breads and tall, twisted *grissini* served in a glass vase. You feel healthy just looking at the tender salads of crisp vegetables and tendrils of pea shoots. Someone isn't happy with her sea urchin pasta but the rest of us are swooning. Guanciale with crackly skin. One dessert looks like an egg. When Andrea cracks it, the sugar crust opens to panna cotta and exclamations of "Oh, how clever." Another, called "caprese," resembles that salad but is a ball of panna cotta, and one of chocolate disguised as a tomato. Another chocolate dessert is served on a garden trowel. Like the chef at Bros' in Lecce, the chef plays amusing tricks. (I do wonder if chefs will tire of this. Isn't cooking challenging enough without having to dream up fantastic presentations?) After all, it's a renaissance tradition—spun sugar cages, swans roasted then redressed with their feathers, and birds flying out of cakes.

After lunch, everyone walks around Ostuni before Giacomo urges us on. He has other places he insists we must see. Such a good ambassador for Puglia! But it is already after four. We stop to photograph swaths of wild *ginestra,* yellow broom, in bloom. Ed and I don't mention that it's an invasive intruder at Bramasole. We only get to see the gleaming white hill town of Locorotondo from a distance, and take a brief drive-through at Martina Franca. Yet another reason to come back.

POWERING DOWN! AFTER yesterday's exploits, we're ready for beach time. Too bad Robin and Andrea left by train for Roma this morning. Work called . . . Calling us, cherries and cappuccino for breakfast.

The beach, only fifteen minutes away, is deserted this early, though by eleven a few souls are combing the rocks. Ed meets a man looking for octopus. He wades in and scoops up one from the rocky water then rolls it against rocks to tenderize the flesh. Then he grabs up another, almost as long as his leg. Michael, Francesca, and I walk as far as we can. Others are sitting on towels, listening to the slight tide scrooch in and out.

We wanted only a light lunch but find ourselves at a light-infused waterfront restaurant in nearby **Savelletri**. Thin pale curtains lift in the slight breeze and the white room takes on the tint of the sea. Mounds of freshest fried fish, whole lobsters that look formidable to deal with, big grilled shrimp, and carafes of cold white wine. The wavering reflections from the turquoise waters make us all appear to be subaqueous.

We drive home through the most ancient olive groves. Ann and I cause a halt so we can run into the field and say hello to a few of the thousand-year-old giant crones that emanate *survive, survive.* They're ancient souls writhing out of the earth, their crowns of leaves as green as in their early years. Leaning against one, imagining what this place was the day it was planted . . . "Let's go!" we hear them call from the cars.

IN THE LATE afternoon, the owners' son shows us his family art collection in a romantic building at the back of the garden. We've been drawn to the elegance of the ripe-peach stucco façade with faded green shutters, niches for statues no longer there, and a parade of busts along the roof. The place looks as if it could dissolve into a reflection in a Venetian canal. When he opens the door, light floods into a room lined with marble busts on pedestals mounted around the walls. Statesmen, poets, gods. "Roman copies of Greek statues," he tells us. He has seen them all his life and looks at them affectionately. "There was also an archeological collection, but much of it was stolen and the rest has been moved to a safer location."

Some of the pedestals are empty. Faded ocher walls with arched marble molding, and fascinating trompe-l'oeil tile floors, blue and yellow squares within squares—dazzling. There are maybe fifty of the astonishing busts and one palest white marble full-size naked goddess with a cherub at her feet.

• • •

PEDESTRIAN OF ME for sure, but I whisper to Ann, "If they sold some of these to a museum where someone could see them, they could restore the villa." As I say this, I am remembering what I know: Italians don't think that way. That's American practicality that doesn't comprehend what comes to you from eleven or twelve generations back. Perhaps he does not at all see the villa as we do.

NO ONE WANTS to drive any more today. When Ed and Randall turn in the rental car, the clerk waves away the info about the accident. "Not worth bothering about" is his surprising reaction. (That's not going to happen in the United States.) After the long lunch, dinner seems redundant. Ed takes off at nine to pick up pizza. He gets lost in the dark, dark countryside, and we've gone through a few bottles of wine while waiting. Our last dinner in the grand old dining room with the planks of the table flying up! *Otium* was the house philosophy and we certainly have embraced the concept.

A discovery for me: A new context deepens friendship. At home, we have our dinner parties, walks, fund-raisers, birthday parties, etc. Traveling together moves us out of preconception. Though some travel only to confirm their held convictions, this group is ready to be amazed. Seeing what is new gives our friendships new grounds. We'll be reliving Puglia for years.

"GOOD-BYE, GOOD-BYE," AS the Lucio Dalla song goes. *Andare via e non tornare mai.* Go away and never come back. That we won't; not to this dreaming-in-time villa. But somewhere else? We're talking about Venice next May. Or what about the Aeolian Islands? The future begins rushing toward us but I'm still saying good-bye to Puglia.

Our car is loaded with wine, bread, bags, all the flours, dried beans, *taralli* we're lugging home. *Con un foglio d'erbe in tasca te ne vai . . .* "With a blade of grass in your pocket, you leave."

NOTES:

We missed the Santa Maria del Suffragio, another purgatory church, in Monopoli. It has not only carved skulls on the façade but also full skeletons on the door. Inside hang preserved bodies of eighteenth-century Monopoli officials, plus one desiccated little girl. The figures must look like gruesome piñatas.

Fondazione Rodolfo Valentino in his hometown, Castellaneta: www.fonda zionevalentino.it

Ann Cornelisen wrote *Torregreca* and *Women of the Shadows,* both of which came out of her experiences living in the south of Italy in the 1950s and 1960s. She spent her last years in Italy in Cortona, where we became friends.

Sardegna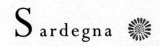

Pula and Teulada

As we approach departures at Fiumicino, the Rome airport, Ed calls Park and Dream. We often use this private long-term parking service. We wait in the passenger drop-off area called Kiss and Go. "Park, dream, kiss, go," I say. "Even flying in Italy is romantic." Kiss and Go means you can kiss for fifteen minutes and then depart. Within six, Dario arrives to take the car. "Where are you going for only one week?" he asks. He's used to us leaving the car for months when we go back to the United States.

"Sardegna! Last week of summer on the beaches." Ed unloads our two carry-ons and Dario speeds off.

THE PLANE QUICKLY ascends and as quickly descends. We've landed in Sardegna. Passing Cagliari in our rented car, we see a steep hillside town of pale stones stretching out to a plain and the sea. We're coming back here at the end of the trip. For now, we take only a few wrong turns while leaving the tempting town in the rear-view mirror.

In less than an hour, we've checked into Is Morus Relais, a hotel in pine woods on the sea. The gardens are rampant with trumpet vine, oleander, hibiscus, lantana grown into bushes, and entwined pink and white bougainvillea spilling over the wall and into trees. Two beaches lie just beyond—crescents of golden sand—and a wade-in pool designed to look natural in the landscape. Our room looks through pines at the glorious sea and a ruler-drawn line of purple horizon. The bedspread, headboard, and rugs are traditional Sardinian woven natural wool, the floor smooth tile. A balcony with two chairs—perfect—where I will reread D. H. Lawrence's *Sea and Sardinia*.

Ed notices many eucalyptus trees. Why would those be here, so out of place? They're out of place everywhere, according to me, except Australia, where they belong. In California, we had several that shredded constantly and stained everything. They were never mentioned without the word *damned* attached to their name. Other than the damned, the rest of the garden is all Mediterranean; beyond the hotel, the hills are covered with the low, scrubby, fragrant plants known as *macchia*. I was surprised to read that Sardegna once was a forested island, until those northern Savoy rulers in Torino clear-cut vast swaths of trees to use for their projects. By now the low *macchia,* home to birds, seems the true natural habitat. The desk clerk tells us that eucalyptus was planted extensively in some ill-advised government program. Ah! Like kudzu overrunning the American South. Good intentions turned to disaster.

WE ARE IN Santa Margherita, close to Pula. Sand beaches line this southern section of coast. Unlike the northern Sardinian coast, famous for its "villages" of tourist accommodations and seaside resorts such as Porto Cervo and Costa Smeralda, the landscape here remains unspoiled.

We chose Is Morus for the first two nights because it's near Teulada, where we will meet friends of a friend for a visit, and because the archeological site Nora is nearby. And the beaches! At the end of September, the sea is still warm but most summer visitors have returned to Milano and Rome.

• • •

DARK AS TAR. I would not want a flat tire on this road. We're driving up to Pula for dinner. We're late. What stars! Crystal clusters, the evening star, the diamond my mother wore. For braving the blackness, we arrive at our reward: Cucina Machrì, an inconspicuous restaurant half on the sidewalk, half inside—a dozen small tables.

When bread is this good, I indulge. I've had *carta di musica* before, dry flat bread thin as a sheet of music, crackly but pretty tasteless. Hard wheat flour, water, yeast rolled very thin then baked. It puffs and is then split in two and rebaked. In Sardegna, it's called *pane carasau,* meaning "bread crust," from the *sardo* word *carasare.* This savory version has been enlivened with rosemary, sea salt, and a bit of olive oil. The whole basket disappears—irresistible with a glass of *bollicine,* crisp, sparkling wine.

Sophisticated restaurant! We're served an amuse-bouche, a miniature zucchini timbale that tastes like the essence of summer. Ed passes me a bite of his Verrigni spaghetti with two bottargas, one of the great pasta dishes of Sardegna. I love my rich eggplant parmigiana but Ed is absolutely raving over the bottargas. After he almost hugs the waiter, the chef comes out. He looks cool in his whites, even though it's hot and must be steaming in the kitchen. "*Complimenti,*" Ed says. "Please tell us the secret of this!"

"Verrigni is a dried pasta from up in Abruzzo but the *bottarghe* is one hundred percent *sardo.*" Ed knows about the dried fish eggs that are grated over certain dishes, but that's not, the chef tells us, how he prepares this. "I mix the spaghetti in a cream of fresh fish eggs, either *dentice* [snapper], *muggine* [mullet], or *ricciola* [yellowtail amberjack], then add more *muggine* eggs. The entire egg pouch of a red mullet is salted and dried, *then* it grates onto pasta, like Parmigiano." His pasta, we quickly learn, is special. Organic, whole-grain durum wheat, cut through bronze or gold, then slowly dried at a very low temperature. All this care causes the pasta to remain porous, absorbing the tastes of the sauce. (We'll be ordering some of these Verrigni products when we get home.) Gold-cut! I thought bronze was the best—never heard of gold—but can see how it would keep the dough smooth. Always something to learn at the Italian table.

Now, the wine. We initiate this first night with a bottle of Iselis Argiolas, 2014, made from *monica,* a grape we don't know. Nice to meet you. You're plummy, spicy, and your tannins are tamed and behaving.

• • •

ON OUR RETURN, the dark and looming hills block the moon, if there is one. Back in our room, the terrace doors open to a sea so calm that reflections of stars wink on the surface. We hear the soft sluicing of retreating waves. I dip back into *Sea and Sardinia.* "Comes over one an absolute necessity to move. And what is more, to move in some particular direction. A double necessity, then, to get on the move, and to know whither."

So he begins. Lawrence, difficult and fierce, his wife Frieda, irritatingly called the Queen Bee, spoiled and capricious, on a brief trip shortly after World War One. Memory has tricked me; I recall from reading it years ago that the book was about the place, the sea. No. It's about the voyage by ship from Sicilia and then about travails of travel, with passionate bursts of description. Mostly, it's a novelist's book. What interests him is how to write vigorously about people and character. "A jaw of massive teeth," "an ancient crone in a crochet bed cover," "drooping-lily sisters, all in white, with big feet." He records long conversations with rough men slurping soup, glimpses of "wild peasants" dressed in black sheepskin tunics, and a man with two black pigs wrapped in sacks, each face appearing "like a flower from a wrapped bouquet."

The horrifying inns and meals Lawrence and Frieda suffered would have put anyone off visiting this island. Just as I'm getting tired of the banter from along the road, he launches into a gorgeous description:

"Another naked tree I could paint is the gleaming mauve-silver fig, which burns its cold incandescence, tangled, like some sensitive creature emerged from the rock. A fig tree come forth in its nudity gleaming over the dark winter-earth is a sight to behold. Like some white, tangled sea anemone. Ah, if it could but answer! Or if we had tree-speech!"

Buona notte, D. H. and Queen Bee. I'm lucky not to have to tie up my hair in a white kerchief to avoid contact with an unsavory pillow.

OUR FRIEND CRISTIANA, who lives near Siena, restored a house in nearby Teulada. She put us in touch with her builder, Antonio, and his partner, Elisabetta, because she wants us to see her favorite view in the world. They've agreed to take us to a point above Domus de Maria for her mystic site. We arrive in front of the Municipio, town hall, as they pull up in a truck. We climb in the backseat. They're young, bright-faced, and welcoming. Elisabetta's hair is pulled back tight, showing off her smooth tawny skin and big smile. How generous of them to give up their morning. Antonio heads right out into rugged hills where no one lives. What I thought was an especially heavy rock outcropping is the five-part ruin of a Nuraghi settlement. Those prehistoric people built conical rock fortifications with domed roofs. Now flat or collapsed, they're hard to distinguish from the natural landscape.

He turns off the two-lane highway onto a rutted road going up. We bounce along as they tell us about plants along the way: the brush that the lean, horned cows eat; the *lentisco* bush with bright berries that yield a prized oil (used like olive oil but less copiously); the *canna* (reeds) used in buildings; *fichi d'india,* prickly pear, which is everywhere, erupting its spiky, rosy fruit.

At a sharp upward turn, Antonio jumps out and opens a gate. After a couple of hundred yards of jouncing along, he stops at the low house of a friend who is not there. Yes, here's Cristiana's hallowed view. We look between branches of pomegranate and wild olive at the distant blue crescent of a Roman port, and the coastal points—Antonio names each—of Perdalonga, Tuerredda, and Torre di Malfatano. Home to them, these ineffably gorgeous places. "One of the great views in all of Sardegna, no doubt," Elisabetta says. Another great view is her big genuine smile.

WE THOUGHT THEY'D drop us back at the piazza, but instead, we take a looping tour along the stupendous coast, stopping at the Marina di Teulada for lunch. Their friend Enzo brings out a platter of shrimp and octopus, then another of sharp local *pecorino, salume,* and prosciutto, along with tumblers of cold white wine. He's from Piemonte. Married a local girl and has been here for twenty years. He pulls up a chair and we talk wine and Piemonte and food. The fishermen sell their catch right here on the dock every morning. Fresher than this doesn't exist. Then Enzo suggests a *mirto,* the Sardinian *digestivo* made from the maceration of myrtle berries in alcohol. Just a sip! It's pretty—dark, as though garnets melted into the glass—and the taste of the ripe berry leaves a slight rasp of bitterness on the tongue.

We've mellowed into the afternoon by now and when Antonio suggests a visit to his cousin, we climb back in the truck. Up into the rocky hills to a house with another staggering view. His cousin, a coiffed woman dressed as if about to lunch in a fancy restaurant, shows us her airy indoor-outdoor home where she expertly fashions fishing lures. The living room is strewn with her tackle and trim. She's a serious fisherman and lives in this remote area with her husband, dog, blown-up movie posters, an eggplant garden, and a shelf of dictionaries. Surprises everywhere.

Antonio drives another dusty road to show us Cristiana's house, which he restored from a broken-down farm. The ceilings are *canna* reeds, hand-tied. Juniper beams have been rubbed to a waxy patina. What is on the land becomes the house. Simplicity itself—minimal furniture and views of the hills. Her neighbors are cavorting goats.

We feel uneasy, taking their day, but we are having fun. Antonio makes a quick stop and runs into a store. He's bought us a bottle of *lentisco* oil. I can't wait to try it.

We must leave them; we're close to sunset. I hope they will come to visit us in Tuscany.

EN ROUTE BACK to our hotel, we stop for dinner at Mirage, an enormous restaurant with a crowded parking lot. We're stuck by the kitchen door, lucky to get a table. We don't expect much but the seafood fritto misto comes to us hot and crisp, and the grilled fish under a heap of chopped celery and tomatoes is fresh and simple. So is Ed's selection of wine: Mesa's Carignano del Sulcis Buio. How inexpensive good wine is here! We often order red wine with fish. Ed thinks if you're going to have wine, it might as well be red, and so often in Italy, fish will be served in a robust presentation.

The *carignano* grape, grown all over the world, is most at home in Sulcis, southwest Sardegna. *Buio,* dark. "What's the first word you think of?" Ed asks me.

"Blackberry."

We split a lemon tart and the last of the wine and the last of the tart make a happy ending.

I'M SLEEPY BUT manage a few pages of *Sea and Sardinia:*

The great globe of the sky was unblemished and royal in its blueness and its ringing cerulean light . . . It was a savage, dark-bushed, sky-exposed land, forsaken to the sea and the sun.

The right book in the right place.

WE'RE OUT EARLY to see Nora, near Pula. First finds indicate Nuraghi settlers from 1500 to 700 B.C. Later came (possibly) the Iberians, then (certainly) the Phoenicians, the Carthaginians, and finally the Romans. What great town planning. The siting is brilliant. The ancient town spreads across a splayed and irregular spit of land jutting into the water. A stretch of beach, and a sudden hill where there once was an acropolis. The peninsula used to be bigger; parts of the town lie underwater.

You can't wander here; you must join a guide. Ours is succinct and very good. Most intact is the amphitheater, constructed not for games but for performances. Somehow they know that cloth sails were rigged overhead to protect the viewers. Events are still held here; folding chairs are set up in front of the tiers of stone seating. Much of the structure of three thermal baths is still discernable. We can identify areas where the *frigidarium, tepidarium, calidarium* once were, and also changing rooms, benches, steam rooms. The mosaics on the floor of the *frigidarium* show a pattern of waves.

The guide points out which structures were residences and which were stores. Water came by aqueduct from over a kilometer away. A ridge in a threshold shows where the shop owner slid shut the door. Homes are ranged around courtyards. He points out sewers visible in houses and streets. So much remains that it's easy to imagine life here— the forum, cisterns to catch water, niches for storage, street drains, stone manhole covers. Miraculously, four columns of a house survive, as does a public latrine with marble seats and channels for running water that join the sewer. Sitting on the toilet was evidently a chance to socialize; the seats are close together. (I remember a similar setup at Ephesus.) Looking at the House of the Tetrastyle Atrium, I flash on Palladio. This ancient house was built around a covered atrium with a hole in the middle of the ceiling, like the Pantheon. Rain collected into a cistern and the rooms were arranged around this large central entrance. Extrapolated, Palladian villas follow exactly this plan. At La Malcontenta, you enter directly into a large circular room with six rooms around it. No opening in the ceiling but the concept is the same.

We'll get to see the vessels, masks, stele, busts, sculptural stones, and votives found here—some date to the second century—when we go to the Museo Archeologico Nazionale in Cagliari.

OVER A QUICK bite in a bar, I read this to Ed, who was amused by the public bathroom at Nora. From *Sea and Sardinia*:

> We went up a little side-turning past a bunch of poor houses towards a steep little lane between banks. And before we knew where we were, we were in the thick of the public lavatory. In these villages, as I knew, there are no sanitary arrangements of any sort whatever. Every villager and villageress just betook himself at need to one of the side-roads. It is the immemorial Italian custom. Why bother about privacy? The most socially-constituted people on earth, they even like to relieve themselves in company.

Ed laughs. "That was, what, a hundred years ago."

"It hasn't stopped—you still see men on the side of the road."

"Not like when we first came to Italy."

"Right. End of era."

We stop to pick up grapes and apples, then turn back, following the gorgeous meandering coastal drive with changing colors of water—lucid blue, turquoise, emerald, pale aqua—and tempting slivers of beaches and small coves. We then set off into the hills, inland.

NOTE:

Guttiau is another version of *pane carasau*.

Santadi

On our friend Cristiana's advice, we visit Santadi for a particular reason: to eat at the *agriturismo* La Grotta del Tesoro. *Tesoro* means treasure. Not sure what the treasure is but we're hoping it's the dinner because this is a detour.

On the drive inland, the landscape changes dramatically from jagged hills covered with rock outcroppings to bucolic rolling farmland. We pass through small towns of low buildings along a straight one-road-in-one-road-out. I admire the houses' paint combinations of russet, turquoise, and squash yellow. In the countryside, the wheat has been cut, leaving pale stubble. The harvest over, the grape leaves already shrivel and brown.

LA GROTTA DEL Tesoro is a few kilometers outside the hilly town of Santadi. We turn into the driveway at a big not-old, not-new farmhouse. Paola, the owner, is watering plants. She's tiny and wiry but obviously strong. An ancient relative in the old-school black dress and kerchief tends her birdcage, which seems to have way too many birds in it. Then she starts to sweep with one of those witches' brooms made of dried *ginestra* (yellow broom) twigs. I love those and haven't seen one in Tuscany in probably five years.

"Cristiana sent us. She says you're one of the world's great cooks!"

"*Ah, la giornalista Cristiana.* How is she? What would you like tonight, the pork or the kid?"

We choose the pork. She's amazed that we are American. "Not German?" she asks twice, as though we might be mistaken.

She shows us to our room, which is plain as can be, and says "Eight o'clock."

WE TAKE A walk around the farm. Pork, we ordered. Huge pens of the donors to the meal are arranged by age. They are clean. Some gargantuan pigs with those prehistoric darting eyes, some medium Three-Little-Pigs ones, who might want to build a brick house, and lots of small ones, like Toot and Puddle. "Dio, Ed, I remember that Paola said *maiolino*." That's one of these little ones. I walk on before he can tell me that if you eat meat, you have to . . . And before I tell him once again that I could be a vegetarian, and he tells me that I've always said that, but I have not become a vegetarian. We let it go and drive in to look at Santadi.

EVERYTHING'S CLOSED. NOT sure why, as it's only six. Supposed to be open, the archeological museum is shut tight. We're on its steep street and the sun is low, sending a benison of sweet light over three women talking in a doorway. They don't know they are illuminated. They are beatific, as though they might be angels announcing to someone beyond the door a new coming. We quietly stare.

To their right, a house the color of butterscotch, no—lighter—marigolds. Old rosy roof tiles scallop along the top. Beside the closed, recessed door, a trumpet vine has been trained into a Y. I take a photo and when I look at it, I think: *This is why I came to Santadi.* The delicate leaves of the vine cast a filigree shadow. The golden color of the plaster looks as if light surges out from inside. Benign luck! Or, the gods who made the three women into momentary angels tapped my camera with a wand and gave me a gift.

OTHER PEOPLE, NINE, I count, have checked in. Germans! Everyone fresh and ready at eight, when the dining room opens. Overlit. The table is set with blue paper tablecloth and napkins. Again, plain as can be! Already, the antipasti are waiting. Prosciutto, fried bread, roasted peppers and eggplant, cheeses, *salume*. Ordinary but extraordinary because the prosciutto, thin as tissue paper, has the salty-sweet balance just right, the vegetables were picked this afternoon and roasted in good oil, the *salume* made at home, and the two goat cheeses fresh today, while the *pecorino* is crumbly and well aged. Fried bread, which is so much better than it sounds, needs a light touch with the batter. Paola has the magic.

Santadi is where some of Italy's best wines come from. We order Rocca Rubia Carignano del Sulcis, 2014, made eight minutes away from where we sit. The simple tumblers on the table are replaced with proper glasses. Paola's son congratulates us on a good choice. Ed takes a long sip and pronounces it sound and fantastic. "Tastes like dry stalks after rain, and violets crushed under a boot." Poet! It's a lusty, full, juicy wine with lots of stamina.

Out comes the pork. Crusty, crunchy skin all bronzed and shiny. The succulent meat needs no knife. Chicory, zucchini, roasted potatoes, salad. Just what you'd cook but squared and cubed because of the quality of the ingredients. Talk about terroir!

BACK TO THE room. Why does it feel spooky? It's clean. Bathroom light makes me look like fresh goat cheese. Bed is okay. Roosters crow all night. Are they crazy?

We leave early. Grazie, Paola!

We're catching a ferry to Isola di San Pietro.

Isola di San Pietro and Carloforte

A last-minute deviation, a confusion about where to buy the ticket, and we almost miss the car ferry from Portoscuso to Isola di San Pietro. The ramp rattles up just as we pull in. We park down in the hold, squeeze out, and abandon the car, ascending to a low-ceilinged room with benches along the windows.

Something about a ferry suspends time. In a way that planes and trains are not, a ferry is Limbo. The coast recedes. I try to read. The high churning sound is not unpleasant. We walk up on deck. People on benches face the sun like rows of seabirds on telephone wires. There's espresso, also pastries for this ten-kilometer journey.

We were late because I spotted an intriguing line of block-shaped buildings along the road, with a white wall in the foreground. Shades of buff, pearl, honey, and stone, rooflines of varying heights, and windows that looked cut out by a knife. Jagged hills formed a background. "What is that? Looks like a painting by Morandi—all volumes and subtle colors. Let's go see."

We'd found the abandoned village of **Tratalias**. Eerie empty piazza with a well, houses with balconies not festooned with flowers, a thirteenth-century church built of stone and volcanic limestone. Inside (door open—okay, eerie again), simple, with three naves and odd, scary cantilevered steps leading up to the belfry. No railing. (You could not pay me any amount to climb those stairs.) The village moved away, a water issue. "The town looks like the rapture has just occurred," Ed says.

"Is there no one? I haven't seen even one face peering out a window and yet it looks like each house is cared for. What a pity." One abandoned lot is strewn with magic: wild and overgrown with white datura. Ghost faces, poisonous but lovely.

"It would make a great artists' colony. You know what? We are going to miss that ferry to San Pietro."

LEANING ON THE rail, sipping a macchiato and looking down into the wake, I feel a sweep of exhilaration. The island looms into sight, a strange place coming toward us. An island off an island, the bottom of Sardegna. We get in our car and roll into the only town, Carloforte.

We park nearby and check into Hotel Riviera. Our junior suite has two balconies. The front one faces the sea, albeit with a parking lot— there's our rented gray Fiat 500—between us and the water. Never mind, we disregard cars and look out at sailboats and choppy water. The airy room has a round table perfect for writing, a contemporary four-poster king bed, and a sofa. With terrace doors open, the sheer curtains lift and I am suddenly aware of being on an isolated island with three days to love every inch.

THE MAIN STREET stretches along the marina crowded with fishing and sailboats. Shaded by trees and almost uninterrupted café umbrellas, via Roma pulses with life and tropical atmosphere. All the buildings along this pedestrian boulevard are pastel watercolor shades with iron balconies and pale shutters.

This doesn't look Sardinian at all and there's a strange reason why. In 1541, a group of Ligurians from Pegli, near Genova, were resettled by a powerful Genoese family on Tabarka, an island off the coast of Tunisia, to fish and harvest coral. They remained until 1738, when the Savoy king of Sardegna Carlo Emanuele III moved them to uninhabited San Pietro. They brought their *tabarchino* dialect, a heritage from Genova, their skills in fishing and trading, and their love of couscous. They named the town they built Carloforte, strong Carl, in honor of the king who'd saved them from pirates, servitude, and degraded opportunities.

In 1798, a thousand of them were kidnapped *back* to Tunisia by pirates, but, thanks to Carlo Emanuele IV paying a ransom, within five years their captivity was reversed and they returned to live ever after on the island, bequeathing to their descendants light hair, a genetic tendency to be myopic, skills of bread- and focaccia-making, and a love they never lost for Liguria's sea-foam-green, persimmon, rose, and biscuit-colored houses.

Near the center, I look up at a statue of strong Carlo with one arm broken off and the other cracked. Wigged and benevolent, he's shown in a metaphorical act of freeing the people from slavery. Two grateful subjects sit beneath him.

The broken arm happened when the local people were trying to hide the statue from the invading French. Supposedly, they've left him like this in memory of that violence. The other injury came from soccer fans.

Lunch at a café under trees full of singing birds, surrounded by the island's youth hanging out together, high-fiving and drinking Cokes and beer. What a lot of kissing as people jump on and off bikes, come and go. A couple of older tattooed dudes roar up from the side street on massive motorcycles. We order big salads and eavesdrop on their conversation. Some are speaking the Genovese dialect, others standard Italian, sometimes a mix. Fascinating that the archaic form of dialect spoken in Genova has endured these many centuries and across cultures. The man in the map store tells us that around 87 percent of citizens know *tabarchino*.

Normally, the hotel staff can arrange sail or motorboat trips around the island. Because the mistral is blowing, we're left high and dry on land. We don't see much wind on this side of the island but it's whipping about on the other side. Also, we're told, it's mid-September; some of the services already are shutting down.

Meanwhile, the day feels blissfully warm as we drive around the island, stopping constantly to look down from rocky heights into clear lime-green waters, coves where spray hits, sending up slow-motion white spume; inaccessible, inviting coves with crescents of beach give rise to fantasies of lying under the mellow sun and letting the water wash away all troubles. Roads are few. Cuboid white houses have about them a whiff of North Africa. With four-wheel drive, we could have explored more of the inland, but I am happy turning in whenever there's a beach sign—there are many—and walking in the warm sand. The water is bracing but not impossible even for a wimp like me. A few souls are in up to their waists. Some beaches are rocky. At the hotel, they gave us a good map, circling the sand ones. I like both. The main attraction: the blues of the water shading into the dark green of malachite. The clarity!

At most beaches, we must park in a lot and walk. We pass small farms, hippie beach shacks transformed by invasive magenta bougainvillea, craggy holm oaks, defunct restaurants, and scrubby landscape of *lentisco,* white blooming cistus, and juniper. Often no one is on the beach at all.

Far on the other side of the island, which is only fifty-one square kilometers, a tower-lighthouse stands guard. Now an astronomical observatory, the structure occupies a wide vantage point. Paved trails snake along the dramatic coast. South of town, my favorite walk is above the water that leads to two dramatic chimney-like rock formations, Le Colonne, rising tall from the sea.

ISLAND TIME. WE do the same thing every day. Strike out in the car. Get out and walk. Wade. Pick up pretty rocks. Breathe in the scents of Aleppo pine in wooded areas. Keep an eye out for flamingos and for the sparrow hawks that have nested here for centuries. Myrtle and heather, wild orchids, scrubby bushes—a Mediterranean *paradiso* and shockingly undeveloped considering how idyllic it is. Only about sixty-five hundred people live here. Hotels are few. How long will this seclusion last?

Resting in the afternoons, I look online at houses for rent. It would be heaven to come here with the whole family. We would have to have a boat at our disposal. Snorkeling, scuba diving, sailing, finding secret coves and grottos—such pleasures to share, easy here, would be unforgettable.

In the twilight hours, we cover every narrow street branching off via Roma, all the small shops, the *panificio* with its array of farro, oat, semolina breads, tender *focacce;* a bookstore, ceramic studios, and gelato stands, where the preferred flavors are lemon and pistachio. In an antique shop, I find an *ex voto* for my collection. The subject, no surprise, the miraculous rescue of a ship at sea. The owner tells us about her daughter studying in Cagliari. She is about to close her shop for the winter and return to the mainland. When Ed asks about winter, she says, "It's lovely but many things are shut. No tourists at all." And in August? She shakes her head. "Oh, yes, tourists. But there are so many beaches it never feels crowded. Only the restaurants and cafés at night."

What an enchanted island! Carloforte—deliciously pretty but still a real place. Piazza Repubblica is the beating heart of the town. Four venerable ficus trees are ringed by benches. If you live here, you must come to the piazza every day: Your friends and relatives are here, your nasty cousin, too. Boys obliviously kick a soccer ball into groups of women with their shopping bags, girls on phones, and men playing cards. An antique market of only three tables sells little junk by the church. A man in a wheelchair rolls himself from group to group, chatting and moving on, dodging a boy doing wheelies on his bike. The trees simmer with birds. Maybe the sun is harsh in summer but now it's tamed and the light filtered through the giant trees gives everyone a vivid presence, as though we see each other underwater. We stop every time we pass this way for the vivid life, for the momentary feel of joining a community.

I HAVEN'T MENTIONED food. Or tuna. Turns out they're the same. We've seen the abandoned tuna processing plant on one edge of the island. Tuna was king. After all, Saint Peter, namesake of the island, is thought to have come here in A.D. 46 and stood in the waves teaching the natives how to fish. Tuna still reigns, but not as completely. Fishermen still practice the *mattanza* here, that spring ritual when scores of tuna are herded into a netted trap and bludgeoned to death, turning the sea red. This I can skip.

• • •

IN THE NARROW streets, restaurants set up outdoor dining under white umbrellas. To walk, we thread through tables covered with bright cloths and rustic chairs painted green, orange, yellow. We want to sit down and eat at each one. Tuna is on every menu, along with big red grilled shrimp and couscous with vegetables. We're having marvelous food and don't care at all that there's little to no "experimental" cooking going on. Fish and more fish. Grilled, raw, roasted, baked. Garden vegetables. Mint, rosemary, basil, fennel. Everything *sui generis*.

Da Nicolo on the esplanade is in a glass box called *jardin d'hiver* in French. (They don't seem to have a name in Italian or English. They're all along the via Veneto in Rome.) Perched outside a restaurant or just the kitchen, they're warmed with heat lamps in winter. Da Nicolo gets a mention in the Michelin guide. The food is fresh and prepared with, as Nicolo tells us, passion. Carbonara with swordfish, smoked bass, shrimp, and mussels. Linguine with tuna, capers, olives, *pecorino*, and lemon peel. Spaghetti and bottarga. Ed is infatuated with bottarga. I love the ravioli filled with purple potato and mint, served with a shrimp ragù and slivers of mozzarella. A grand fritto misto. We try Korem Bovale Isola dei Nuraghi made by Argiolas. A hearty glass. For dessert, perhaps the last taste of summer: lemon gelato with strawberry sauce. Tart and sweet.

At Ristorante Alle Due Palme, a casual place next to the hotel, they grill delicious shrimp served on a salad of greens and tomatoes. And crispy, skinny fries. Something simple and perfect. Outside, two giant palms guard the door. One has lost its top, which is covered with a tarp. The waiter tells us they're having a problem with palm blight on the island. This venerable one has had treatment and a transplant, and they're hoping it will recover.

One object reaches back to the burdensome days of Tunisian captivity. I stepped inside the Oratorio della Madonna dello Schiavo, Our Lady of the Slave, on one of the side streets, XX Settembre. The small chapel all blue and cake-frosting white displays a wooden Madonna found, some say, on a Tunisian beach between a date and a lemon tree, by one of the captives. It probably was a figurehead from a ship. He took the gift as a sign and when he was freed, he brought it to San

Pietro, where she is revered and celebrated with her own festival. How amazing in a small town to have an open chapel, right among all the shops. You can pop in for a quiet moment, then go on with your day. One of the miracles of Italy: Spiritual life, artistic life remain open to the everyday.

Iglesias and Piscinas

Off the ferry and turning north up the southwest coast
of Sardegna, we are entering old mining country—silver,
sulphur, copper, barium, zinc, lead. Elisabetta in Teulada
told us not to miss **Iglesias** while we're on our way to
Piscinas. The landscape is dotted with defunct buildings,
rusted machinery, wooden chutes, and roads leading off
into nowhere.

This former boomtown looks like a stage set. Elegant
façades, iron balconies, streets made for strolling. Although
mining activity is traced back to the Phoenicians, it
peaked in the Middle Ages and finally wound down in the
1970s. In the glory days, Iglesias was a locus for culture,
trade, entertainment. I imagine the wives from grim,
outlying mining settlements brought to town for bright
lights, a chance to mingle, shop for fabric and trims, see
a performance. Mining is not near the top of my travel
interests; going into dangerous underground tunnels seems
like as bad as work gets, but I am interested in the lives led
in this far outpost. Iglesias gives a glimpse.

We park near the piazza of the handsome church of Santa Clara. Inside, two astonishing things to admire: a painted, dressed wooden saint (or Madonna) holding a white feather plume. A marble holy water bowl held by an angel, so exquisitely carved that the folds of its robe look real. In the next piazza, we stop for a cappuccino at Antico Caffè Lamarmora, a colorfully decorated art deco building with a bar on the lower floor. Adorning the façade are faded paintings of bottles of vermouth, Marsala, Fernet-Branca. We then stroll on into via Matteotti, the scene of a playful installation. Hundreds of open umbrellas in bright colors hang over the street, shading it and casting shadows.

This main street opens to a park, where the mining wives must have strolled with their own umbrellas to protect them from torrid sun. We buy a hunk of *pecorino* and avoid the cheese that our favorite waiter at Vigilius in Alto Adige highly recommended. A Sardinian, he was full of enthusiasm for *casu marzu*. The name means "rotten cheese." As part of the process of making this *pecorino,* a core is drilled in the cheese and maggots are placed inside. They're given a little milk to make themselves at home, then gradually they lay eggs that hatch and they all work their way around the whole cheese, munching and breaking down fats with their digestive outpourings. Both worms and *pecorino* are then spread on bread with the maggots still alive. And the maggots can jump. We aren't interested.

"Want to see the mining museum?" Ed pinpoints it on the map.

"I think we should move on and get to Piscinas for lunch."

"Seems a shame not to explore every nook here."

'I can't wait to see those dunes."

"Can't see everything. *Andiamo*."

SARDEGNA IS ALL about beaches. If you have no interest in marvelous coasts, blissful clear waters, soft amber sand, food pulled out of the sea this morning, you'd be happier vacationing elsewhere. I love these secluded beaches. I like to walk, take deep breaths, feel silky sand between my toes, take out my book and read a paragraph. Put it down. Remember other times I've been beside clear seas, read another page, pick up a rock, let the water chill my legs.

. . .

ON THE WAY, we see more industrial archeology. After the turn for Piscinas, we're on an unpaved road. Soon we arrive at an abandoned mine.

The ruins seem to emerge from the bottom of a hill. A doorway, an arch, an oculus, rows of square columns. Blast furnace chimneys. The scene looks bombed. Looks ancient, too, the colors blending into the hillside. The sign says from 1900 to 1970 it was a washery, a place where the minerals were separated from "barren material."

Nineteen seventy! Impossible that the site has gone into ancient history so quickly. A great novel could emerge from these bricks. *The Hollow Earth* . . . A few intact houses exist; others have one side missing, showing interiors with scraps of plaster and sagging beams.

I SAW PISCINAS in a twenty-year-old guidebook. It mentioned a hotel, Le Dune, which I hadn't seen listed in my research. What luck. We have landed in a unique place on the planet. At the end of the nine-kilometer corduroy road that must become dicey when rain torrents flow, we come to a low, almost Spanish Mission—style building smack on an impossibly wide golden beach backed by rolling, gigantic sand dunes. These are not just any old dunes, these are the tallest dunes in Europe. Formed by the mistral winds, they rise to thirty or more meters. Arid as they look, plants still grow, especially wind-formed olives and juniper. The dunes undulate down the coast. You can almost hallucinate and see a camel cresting over the top.

After a quick salad lunch, we settle into our room. We booked late and are in a small room. Not a problem. We change into our suits and walk the long path across the beach to occupy our chaise longues. The sea is flat today, utterly transparent. On the wide expanse, there are only six people. The German couple near us sprawls in the sun as though they've waited their whole lives for this. We walk as far as we can see and back, then walk again. I finish *Sea and Sardinia*. Too bad old grumpy Lawrence didn't come here. He'd have to have waxed ecstatic. The sand is so soft I sink to my ankles with each step. The water feels too chilly for me but a couple of young boys chase a ball into the surf, throwing it back and forth.

At sunset, everyone staying here gathers in the courtyard for spritzes and sunset. Some are poised with cameras, hoping to catch the green flash. If you're ever going to see it, that would be now.

WHEN IT IS dark and the stars are burning holes in the sky, we go inside to dinner. The restaurant is green and eco-conscious, which must not be easy in this remote locale. We will always order cardoon when we see it. With a glass of prosecco, we have a salad of the tender stalks cooked in green tea and served with edible flowers. As our *secondi* arrive, Ed orders a wine made of a grape new to us: Nieddera Rosso, 2015 (*nieddu,* black in dialect), native of the island. Dark it is, rich, too, with a sensuous wild cherry flavor. Tannins, but not enough to worry me. The waiter recommends crisp red mullet with Jerusalem artichokes, salted lemon, and chicory. For me, pork belly with apple and ginger chutney and potato croquettes. All that, plus stars over the sea.

IN THE MORNING, we're back on the beach. It's cooler today but still no bite of winter.

The desk clerk tells us this place used to be an outdoor camp for miners' children. Another possible novel: *The Lead Miners' Children.* We drive away, imagining their fun and laughter on the beach.

Cagliari

Only eight days since we flew into Cagliari from Rome. We've traversed the southwest coast, dipped down to Isola di San Pietro and up to Piscinas. The sea, the sea! The constant and vivid presence of the sea. Even inland in the adamant, rocky landscape with scrubby vegetation, you sense the nearness, and soon you come upon a sudden sweet beach where you could pull over and run down for a dip in transparent water. My dreams of travel usually feature wild beaches and here they are, empty and pristine.

MY PRIMAL ATTRACTION to beaches goes back to earliest memories: digging in the sand and—*marvelous*—the ocean filling the hole, walking out with my father at Fernandina Beach to watch the sunrise, dripping sand castles over my feet, riding back to the water's edge on the rough back of a giant turtle who'd laid her eggs in warm sand under the moon, reading in bed, eating damp saltine crackers, and listening to the shush-shush of waves not far from the window. Belonging to all that, I see now, was the relief of escape from ordinary life, which in my childhood had a background beat of chaos. I'd recite John Masefield dramatically to myself as I ran along picking up shells. *I must go down to the sea again, to the lonely sea and the sky/and all I ask is a tall ship and a star to steer her by.*

"You had your beach time, Franny."

"I did." *Must go down to the sea again . . .*

"We have one more night—make the most of it. The hotel I booked is on Poetto, Cagliari's best beach."

We turn in the car at the airport. A half-hour drive and the taxi turns into a pedestrian road running in front of pretty houses and small inns. How smart to close off traffic along the sea. People are out jogging, pushing the stroller, power walking. Palm trees, bougainvillea, pink hibiscus flowers as large as a baby's face. Ah, the ferny jacaranda trees with lavender plumes! La Villa del Mare must have once been a home, then something else, then an inn. Our room faces a garden. Airy white and on the sea, touches of turquoise, a desk—thank you—and a crisp duvet. We drop our bags and ask for a taxi to town.

"No need for that. The bus stops a block away." The desk clerk, Michele, walks us up a little lane and gives us passes. We're dropped off on the harbor and turn up the street into town. Fantastic jacarandas line Largo Carlo Felice, a shaded boulevard of small shops and cafés as well as computer stores and Max Mara, always a tempting stop. Still, there's a nineteenth-century feel: iron balconies, flower stalls, kiosks, a fruit seller, women arm-in-arm going out for afternoon coffee, a drift of pale petals.

We've already scoped out Fork for lunch. Under tall trees, we contemplate an intriguing menu. Sardinian ingredients but tweaked and played with and served forth with élan. We love the classic *culurgiones,* an agnolotti- or ravioli-type filled pasta. A circle of dough is wrapped around potatoes and mint, then pinched closed in such a way that it resembles a plump tassel of wheat. They're poached, then served with tomato and basil or sometimes a nut sauce. Different areas have other preferences. The one we're served, listed as in the style of Jerzu, a *cannonau* wine center, has butter and sage with olives. This pasta takes a light hand; imagine how that potato filling could sink if not fluffy and freshly made.

When I see quail on a menu, I usually order it. Theirs is a salad of quail confit—never had that—with figs, and cucumber salad. Ed is a bit jealous, though his *merluzzo,* cod with mussels, squash flowers, cherry tomatoes, and bottarga, couldn't be better.

Dessert? We choose goat's-milk gelato with crunchy almonds and pineapple syrup. In Sardegna and Sicilia, the foreign conquerors' influence is often tasted in the cold desserts: cinnamon, jasmine, cardamom, rose water, almond, saffron. *Limone* comes from Arabic *Laymun. Arancia* comes from *al-naranja.* Fork's menu offers licorice gelato with almonds, surely a whiff of some invader.

Cagliari is a great walking town. Baroque houses, *palazzi,* sunny narrow streets of balconies dripping with flowers, streets branching and climbing up, up, characteristic weathered doors. People. People living their lives outside—with such sun, why stay in? Why not go to venerable Antico Caffè (1855) for an iced orange granita?

We walk—climb straight up—to the Museo Archeologico Nazionale in the old Royal Arsenal. An escalator is supposed to take you up the steepest part but, as is often the case with outdoor *scala mobile* all over Italy, it's out of service. The exercise circle on my watch starts spinning.

Worth the climb! Here's where, at the end of our trip, the artifacts from various parts of Sardegna bring history together. There are finds from Neolithic people. One powerful female, Cycladic Mother Earth–type figure is especially moving. She's crouched, her hands on her breasts, all volume and abstract features.

Within the mysterious Nuraghi heaps of rubble we saw around Teulada, archeologists found troves of small bronzes, some the size of toy soldiers. The detail is exacting and precise. An enigmatic priest in a cape holds up—what—a loaf of bread? Archers, so graceful, warriors who mean business with their shields. A bowl as small as my cupped hand turns at the end into the head of a stag. A highly developed aesthetic inside those mounds.

The Phoenicians moved in, pushed the Nuraghi aside, colonized and inhabited the region for centuries. At first, in the late ninth century B.C., they were traders with the Nuragic people. By 780 to 750 B.C., they'd settled on Sant'Antioco, the island next to San Pietro. Other settlements came quickly. There are funerary and domestic objects from these ancient sites, red jugs called mushroom jugs, small containers and dishes. The Romans, too; especially precious to see are their artifacts found at Nora. In the excavations, a shield with Phoenician writing helped date their occupations of the site.

I imagine being the one to discover a cache of dozens of lifelike clay hands at the bottom of a lake, or the life-size recumbent male with a snake entwined around his body—some religious ecstasy? Ah! Picking up a pearl necklace out of the dust, the beads around it carved in the shapes of heads.

The museum is choice.

NOT WANTING TO take the time to walk all the way back downhill, we call a taxi and it promptly arrives. We're back at La Poetto in time for a good hour on the fourteen-kilometer beach. Few others are out. Golfo degli Angeli, the stretch of water is called. The archangel Michele and his angelic troops fought the devil Lucifer and friends here until defeat. The saddle of the devil's horse fell into the water, turning into a stony gray hill rising at the end of the beach.

WHEN THE SUBJECT of dinner arises, I say, "Let's call Edo." Edo Perugini is a food-freak Cortona friend who often summers with his family in Sardegna.

Suddenly he's shouting at the other end, rattling off places we must go. *Shall I call friends to pick you up, there's a place in the harbor, you have to meet my buddies. They will take care of you.* Always in Italy, the crucial personal connection.

"No," Ed says, "another time that would be fantastic. But a quiet place for our last night. *Romantico!*"

"*Va bene.*" He tells us he will call and reserve at Da Marino al St. Remy.

A SLICE OF a street, a discreet entrance down some steps. We're welcomed like old friends by Marino, a slim man in super-fitted jacket and pants, gleaming shaved head, and a nice gap between his front teeth.

We're seated in a whitewashed grotto room with three tables. Several amuses-bouches and prosecco appear. Some enchanted evening! He selects the wine for us: Is Solinas Isola dei Nuraghi, Argiolas. Another, there've been many now, of these rich and drinkable Sardinian wines.

Spider crab salad. Zucchini soufflé with pine nuts, lobster tagliolini, sirloin with juniper berries—so much to love. Some pristine fruit for dessert, but then Marino brings an almond parfait with strawberry sauce.

At the end, he brings over a bottle of Mirto Dulcore from Villacidro, the myrtle-based after-dinner *digestivo*. It tastes essential, a juice straight from those scrubby hillsides with the rough bushes. An old taste— bandits and shepherds, farmhouse harvest feasts. We walk out into the last evening in Sardegna.

S icilia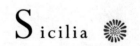

Marzamemi

"What's it like here in summer?" Ed asks the waiter who sets down two brimful glasses of prosecco.

"*Pieno, pieno,*" he says. Full, full.

This evening is anything but. In the vast piazza of Marzamemi, a few souls stroll about then settle, as we have, into one of the bars and restaurants with brightly colored chairs that ring the glorious space. A pretty church sits in one corner, but the main business of the place seems to be eating and drinking. Perhaps in another season, a place to see, be seen. A Facebook friend told me *we all go to Marzamemi.* I'm not sure who *we* is, but I imagine an artistic, international boho crowd of fashionista hipsters. (Are *they* on Facebook?) Maybe summer is like that—tie up your sailboat in the harbor and swan into town for bowls of mussels straight from the sea and cold wine.

But I'm loving this wan October twilight, still warm enough to sit outside, with the paving stones gleaming like wet soap from the lights on surrounding buildings. For such a tiny town, the piazza is huge. I imagine the summer film festival. Children running wild and fireworks, moon rising from the water. A thousand glasses of Aperol spritz circulating on trays. Tonight, no party yachts anchor in the harbor, just well-used fishing boats and piles of nets. Traditionally the main business was tuna, thousands caught in a series of entangling nets then killed, the ritual called *mattanza,* essentially massacre. *Tonnara* (tuna processing and canning) buildings still stand, ruins waiting for condo transformation. To the north stretches a long crescent of sand beach and a colony of small houses. Marzamemi, way south in Sicily—ideal low-key, picturesque Italian beach town. Colorful and crumbly, its evocative beauty makes me want to stay.

All quiet. We walk until dark.

WE CHECKED IN earlier at Scilla Maris, a small inn down a dirt road. Ah, the sleek room with mezzanine bed has a distant view of the Vendicari nature reserve with its wild beaches, and of the sea, with *nero d'Avola* vineyards, blackening into autumn, between us and the coast. More *nero d'Avola* vines in back. From our patio, we are already steeping in the idea of these wines.

ON LANDING IN Catania this morning, we walked into the arrival area and were hit with an array of delicious smells. This has to be a first! An airport permeated with aromas of warm focaccia, dark concentrated espresso, an array of fruit and cream pastries, and best of all— *arancini,* those delectable balls of rice stuffed with cheese or ragù and fried to crunchy greatness. A long bank of cafés introduced us to Sicily, one of the world's best places to feast. We have come here to eat. And drink. Anything we see along the way is a bonus. This is our fifth trip to Sicily. Although we've explored Palermo, Erice, Agrigento, Siracusa, Taormina, Cefalù, the Greek ruins, and the grand, intricate Baroque cities of Noto, Ragusa, and Modica, we've never made it to the southern towns. We're so far south, we could water-ski to Tunis.

WE FOUND SCILLA Maris by chance—a lucky choice. The landscaping keeps close to the native terrain: low stone walls, borders of lavender, santolina, and rosemary-lined pebble walkways. Relaxing with a prosecco by the pool, we have a chance to watch the antics of eight kittens. Will there soon be exponential population growth with a lot of recessive genes? Meanwhile, they are crazy fun.

THE CANDLELIT DINING room overlooks the courtyard. The cats come to the glass wall by our table, hoping for what? Surely not a bite of our shared *tempura di gamberi, scampi, e ortaggi con riduzione al limone,* tempura of shrimp, scampi, and vegetables with a tangy sauce of lemon, honey, and apple cider vinegar. (I'll be reproducing this at home.) Perfect antipasti, so very light. Or do they want a sip of Ed's chickpea soup with crispy onions, or our beauteous tomato and beef stew with potatoes roasted with oregano? Soon they leave for the evening and we linger at the table over an inexpensive bottle of Note Nere Syrah from Marzamemi. Ed gives it a hurrah, this easy syrah.

After dinner at home, usually Ed has an Averna, a Sicilian *digestivo* made from thirty-two herbs, while I'm content with the last of the wine, but tonight we both try the orange *digestivo* Amara, made on the slopes of Mount Etna. Distilled from Tarocco blood-orange peels and herbs, this rich, essential orange elixir appeals to me much more than its kissing cousin limoncello.

DEEP SLEEP. SUBMERGED dreams. Is it the ancient farmland? The lagoons of the nature reserve where pink flamingos stand in marshes full of birds, where there are paths to wander as in a dream? Ed wakes me early. "Look out," he says, sitting up in bed. The sun is wobbling up from the sea, a blood orange, a spilling of silvered gold light across the water. No better place to wake up in this world or the next.

WE ARE BIG fans of the Tuscan Tenuta Sette Ponti wines. How many celebrations have commenced with Ed opening bottles of their Oreno or Crognolo? As everyone knows, Sicilian wines have been on the rise for a couple of decades and now many of Italy's best come from the island. Antonio Moretti Cuseri, owner of Sette Ponti, bought vineyards here a dozen years ago. We love his grand Mahâris. And Corposo— big-bodied wine we pour at holidays and birthdays. When he learned that we were coming to Sicily, he invited us to stop by his Feudo Maccari. Three minutes from our hotel, we're there.

Alessandra, a young woman from Palermo with a passion for wine, comes out to take us around the property. The enormous storage room vaults upward like a cathedral. What a fabulous venue for a wedding on a scalding August afternoon. In the modern tasting room, she's prepared seven bottles: two whites, a rosé, and four reds. A stellar lineup, as we find out during an easy, contemplative chance to experience each wine. (I'm not really good at this. After a few, I'm lost. I keep wanting to go back to the second one, or the first.) We discuss and toast. Our old friend Mahâris (the name means sentinel tower in Arabic), and, oh my, Saia, whose name is from the canal system for collecting water used by the Arabs centuries ago. Dark, bursting fruit, but with a ray of Sicilian sun in each bottle. That must be, as one swallow makes you think good thoughts. I'd take a glass of this by fire late at night and read Neruda.

Maybe the soul in these wines comes from growing the vines in the ancient Greek *alberello,* little tree, form. Instead of espaliering vines, each one is grown separately on its own stake, not touching the next, for maximum exposure to light all day. The vine is kept low, more protected from the sun, and the leaves also protect the maturing grapes. So much of the ancient world still lives in this vineyard. I double back to the white Grillo (cricket); a crisp and mineral fragrance makes it as pleasant to smell as to drink. Fragrance, the hint of pleasure to come. I would love to sip Rosé di Nero d'Avola on a late summer afternoon under the rose arbor in the piazza of Marzamemi and watch the petals fall as our faces brighten.

THE FAMOUS PACHINO tomato grows in the eponymous town a few kilometers south. At first I thought I saw lakes in the distance. Closer, afraid not. Growing that acidic-sweet red bauble we love in salads has blotted the landscape with acres and acres of plastic greenhouses as far as you can see and much farther than you would imagine. Economy dupes aesthetics.

We reach Portopalo, near the bottom of Sicily, and stop for lunch on the harbor. Eerie to think of Allied troops landing near here in 1943, swarming and spreading into the area on their way to winning Sicily. One or two of the old people dining here might remember.

Slow service but the view of blue and white boats is lively. I order a simple pasta with tomato and basil. It tastes like a tin can smells. Ed has an enormous antipasto, chef's choice, and chef has chosen about fifteen of his favorites. One plump little fish stares at the ceiling. The *arancini* stuffed with mozzarella look very tasty. Then I feel sick. Something orange and squishy on his platter looks lurid. My mound of pasta, no. I feel really sick.

I'm doubled up in the car, cursing and sipping water. We omit the trip to see the beach of the tiny offshore Isola delle Correnti, the very southernmost point of Sicily. I wish we had another night with the eight kittens, a chance to spot a flamingo, and a dinner at Cortile Arabo, the Arab Courtyard, a white terrace overlooking the sea at Marzamemi.

Our destination: Scicli. We've got to stop saying Chee clee. It's SHE-clee.

NOTE:

By appointment, you can arrange a tour and tasting at Feudo Maccari. www.feudomaccari.it

Polpo Croccante su Vellutata di Ceci, Finocchietto Selvatico, e Zeste di Limone

CRISPY OCTOPUS WITH VELVETY CHICKPEAS, WILD FENNEL, AND LEMON ZEST,
SERVES 4 TO 6

Executive chef Ilaria Navilli combines four of the great tastes of Sicily in one dish. The missing ingredient? The salt-lashed breeze coming in from the sea.

2 pounds octopus, cleaned

1 onion, chopped

1 carrot, chopped

1 stalk celery, chopped

Salt and pepper, *QB*

Extra-virgin olive oil, *QB*

2 cups chickpeas, previously soaked overnight

A few fennel fronds

1 lemon, zested and thinly sliced

Boil the octopus and half the vegetables for about 50 minutes in a a large pot with water to cover. Season with salt and pepper. Let the octopus cool in its water.

Separately, in a medium saucepan, sauté the rest of the onion, carrot, and celery in olive oil for 3 minutes. Add the chickpeas and enough water to cover them. Season with salt and pepper, cover and simmer for 20 to 30 minutes, or until the chickpeas are just done. Drain, reserving the liquid. When the chickpeas are cool, add 4 tablespoons of oil and blend with an immersion blender until you've reached a creamy (not too thin) mixture. Use a little of the chickpea water if needed for a smooth texture.

Remove the octopus from its water. Cut into pieces and pat dry. To crisp the octopus, quickly fry the pieces in a hot skillet with a little oil. Test for seasoning.

Spread some of the chickpea mixture on the plate and put the sautéed octopus on top. Add a few drops of oil, sprigs of fennel, lemon slices, and lemon zest.

Scilla Maris, Marzamemi, Sicilia

Scicli

A first trip must include at least one of the great Baroque towns of southern Sicily: Noto, Modica, and Ragusa. Why the burst of Baroque in the rural south? On January 11, 1693, at nine P.M., lower Sicily was shaken apart by an earthquake. Seventy towns were reduced to rubble and more than sixty thousand people—some quote ninety-three thousand—killed. Now estimated at 7.4, the tremor lasted four minutes. Aftershocks lasted three years. Little remained of the medieval architecture and no one chose to repeat an old style. The three towns rebuilt in the exuberant Baroque. Bring on the new. Not usually mentioned in the story is our destination, the small town of Scicli, near the coast.

WE'VE RESERVED AT Eremo della Giubiliana, south of Ragusa and only a short drive from Scicli. Feeling a bit iffy, I fall asleep on the way, but hitting sudden potholes jars me awake, plus Ed is exclaiming frequently over the landscape.

Finally, I pay attention. Jungles of *fichi d'india,* prickly pear, line the narrow roads. Well-made bone-white stone walls cross and recross and divide and subdivide the land. Cribs for animals, border markings, bracing for hillside terraces, field separators—back-breaking labor. The stacked irregular stones are topped with a line of tight-fitting cut stones designed to stabilize and keep excess water off the lower wall. These are called *coltelli,* knives, in Tuscany and are very pleasing to my eye. (We learn later that here they're simply called *traversa,* across stones, and that the cut surface is called *pietra viva,* living stone.) Half-collapsed houses and agricultural buildings add to the hallucination that we are crossing a vast archeological site.

EREMO, HERMITAGE. OUT in the expanse of farmland, you come upon Eremo della Giubiliana as you do the lonely haciendas in Spain or the great ranches in Mexico. *"Benvenuti,"* welcome. A young man rushes out to help with our bags. "L'Eremo," he gestures with a sweep of his arm around the limestone complex surrounded by giant twisted olive and almond trees, and the ubiquitous prickly pear. He's Marco, immediately warm and ready to show us around. The structure somehow escaped the 1693 earthquake. Occupied for millennia, it was an Arab home and fortress against marauding Turks, later a stronghold of the Knights Templar (Malta is visible from nearby Punta Secca on a clear day), then held by the Benedictines. In the 1700s, the convent was bought by the Nifosì family, who still owns it. The venerable heir, Signora Vincenza Jolanda Nifosì, Marco tells us, sits all day in a strategic position between reception and the dining room door, benignly overseeing comings and goings. She gives me her frail, cold hand to shake and nods.

While Marco checks us in, Stefano—love it that they introduce themselves right away—brings cold glasses of almond milk to the lofty stone lobby made cozy by a low, cinnamon-red sofa and fringed chairs, books, and lamplight. The signora sits across the room, upright in her chair, a little mutt curled at her feet. She looks at us now and then and resumes her stare into the distance. We pretend we are distant American cousins, upstarts who've come back to the family roots to make trouble.

Marco takes us on a tour. We stop in the original kitchen, a tiny museum of antique cookware, where we taste the just-harvested olive oil. It's rich and fruity, but without, as Ed says loyally, the piquant hit that Tuscans prize in their oil. I like the mildness. It will marry well with a squeeze of lemon juice for a salad.

On the grounds, we find the remains of a cemetery, five stone graves cut into stone outcrops. Fifth-century B.C. children used to romp here. A brindled cat curls in one and looks up at us with his one good eye. Also on the grounds, black pigs, who have their own swimming place and mud baths. They are fed organic fava beans, acorns, barley, wheat, and chickpeas, all raised here.

The peace of the Benedictines who once chanted in these halls permeates the monastic corridors. (Wear white and drink almond milk.) Preserved are early Arab water channels spilling down two levels, creating music. A grass-surrounded swimming pool. All the layers of history in one place.

Terra-cotta pots are treasured in Italy. Around the courtyard, still prolific with roses in mid-October, are several fine old *orci* planted with flowers and held together with wire, earth showing through the cracks. That's it: The pot kept.

Our room is small, with an ornate iron bed; some monk used to snore here. We booked late and probably have the last-choice room, but with one of the musical Arab fountains right outside the window, I'm content.

THE RESTAURANT IS named for Don Eusebio, an ancestor whose photo shows a corpulent man almost muzzled by his unruly mustache. He ate well, as will we. Before dinner, an antipasto feast is served with prosecco by the fire. Nuts and big olives, crisp chickpea sticks, *caponata*, bite-size *arancini*, squares of ricotta crusted and fried. Dinner?

The signora disappears at dusk. We're alone but the silence is suddenly interrupted by an American group just in from a day of touring. Two of them have fallen and one has lost his computer. They look exhausted. We overhear Lorenzo telling them about tomorrow.

"What's in Modica?" a man asks.

A woman responds, "Chocolate."

Lorenzo slyly adds, "And the Baroque." Doubtless I've made a fool of myself in Greece or Peru. And probably in Italy, too.

They only light briefly. Quiet returns once the bus has carted off the group to a restaurant in Ragusa. Ed reminds me, "He travels fastest who travels alone."

THE TABLE IS laid with white linens, the china and silverware embellished with a coat of arms. Candlelight and gliding waiters—that enticing moment of the day, the anticipation of dinner.

Back to the black pig. We order the roasted tournedos. First, the best onion soup ever, oregano scented and served with a dollop of fondue on top. Not the crusty cheese-covered French onion soup I know, but a rich broth and a creamy topping. The basket of homemade breads that taste of wheat and rain. My favorite is the one made with *capuliato,* the sun-dried tomato sauce. A pitcher of beef broth comes with Ed's tortelloni pasta filled with onions, mint, and a cream of almonds. "Extra primo good," he says. I have a taste. Yes. A swirl of three flavors, each sparking off the other. Stefano, our waiter, tells us that the onions come from Giarratana, famous for the delicacy of its onions.

The pork! We take the first bite simultaneously and Ed looks at me wide-eyed. "*Dio!* This is *al di là.*" Beyond the beyond. Texture like the tenderest beef filet but the taste soars beyond that—a deep and amazing flavor, juicy and succulent. A stack of thin-skin potatoes topped with a sprinkle of crushed almonds. Simple but not easy to achieve; you must have the best of everything. The pork's sauce is its own pan juices with olive oil from Tonda Iblea (a well-known region for excellent oil) and field herbs. We want to thank the chef but he is away. He can be proud of his staff.

I remember from past trips to Sicily that the food was the best. The sun-warmed soil, the sea, the assumption of freshness—even a simple ragù, roasted vegetable, or grilled fish is somehow uplifted. The pork deserves a generous and open-hearted wine. We order close to home, Gulfi Nerojbleo, 2011, a *nero d'Avola* from Chiaramonte Gulfi. So much character and variation in these *nero d'Avola* wines. This one tastes as dark as the black pig, with a nice spice behind the fruit.

. . .

BREAKFAST IN THE dining room filled with golden October sunlight. The tour group gathers at a large table. The leader is cracking the whip for them to hurry and board the bus. They want to enjoy the cappuccino, the Turk's hat pastries, the *caciocavallo* cheese, and the morning— but she has plans. We sit at a side table mapping our day. We could linger over our omelets and the homemade jams but, like the tour guide, we have places to see. This is the day for Scicli!

WE ROUND A long hillside and the town sprawls below, set in a bowl with surrounding steep hills. What an odd choice—so indefensible. The ancient town used to be higher, I read, but migrated down over the centuries. On the hilltop above, a church and a castle ruin loom.

Unlike some towns that unfold gradually, Scicli gives itself to you immediately. The exhilaration starts in Piazza Italia, irregularly shaped and dominated by Baroque *palazzi*. Palazzo Fava is decorated with outlandish Moorish heads and animals that never were. Chiesa Madre, 1751, a sunny color with comparatively restrained ornamentation, is home to a fabulous piece of religious folk art—La Madonna delle Milizie, a life-size processional figure of a sword-waving Virgin Mary on a rearing horse. I've seen her on a donkey but have I ever seen her on a horse? Or with a battle in mind? She's papier-mâché, not as heavy as most statues that get dragged through the streets for festivals. Her black hair is human, said to have been donated by local women, and her steed is about to crush the twisted bodies and heads of two Moors. This is how the Virgin appeared to troops of Norman soldiers in battle at nearby Milizie with the Saracens in 1091. A large painting by Francesco Pascucci portrays her again, barefoot, red tresses flowing, in full battle on a white horse. Not your usual demure Madonna.

At the end of the street of Sant'Bartolomeo off the piazza stands his church, a tall three-tiered wedding-cake church that backs up against hills studded with caves where the poor used to live. Finished in 1752— one year after Chiesa Madre—and later given a more neoclassical look, Bartolomeo must have made quite a splash. Inside, all rich elegance and light. Gold-embellished white plaster frames with angels and swags around paintings on the ceiling, intricately carved choir stalls, an eighteenth-century *presepio* (nativity) scene of twenty-nine little figures and animals, the tiny infant with his foot raised, and delicate angels, all cunningly carved (1773–1776) from linden wood. I wish I could pick these up and look at them closely.

Around the elaborate ceiling frames and on some of the wall panels, old Arab-influenced tile designs have been re-created. I ask the caretaker if they are real ceramic or trompe l'oeil. She says they are painted. Marvelous! So much to see in this church. Sorry, Sant'Apollonia—patron saint of dentists—your martyrdom must have been awful but the painting of you getting your teeth yanked out with long pliers feels almost cartoonish. My favorite: an anonymous wood-panel painting of the Virgin and Baby. So curious. She's willowy and thin, poised on a crescent moon like her earlier prototype Diana, and she holds a chain attached to a sea creature. Object of wonder.

COLD DRINKS AT the kiosk in Piazza Italia: mint, barley water, mandarin, wild cherry, *chinotto* (with sour oranges), lemon, tamarind, almond milk, lemon salt soda. The chairs are emblazoned with Coca-Cola. At a lone vendor's table with sparse offerings of tiles, keys, and bits of pottery, I buy two rough ceramic jelly molds, one with grapes and one with a lizard. They have these in the kitchen at the Eremo. Eight euros.

IS MORMINO PENNA the prettiest street in Sicily? In one of my guidebooks, the novelist Elio Vittorini is quoted as saying that Scicli is the most beautiful town in the world. Walking along this street, I think maybe he's right. The buildings are a soft, monochromatic palette: buttercream, sand, ivory, limestone white. When I was little, I was taught that the streets of heaven were paved with gold. But this street must be as splendid because the smooth-worn stones gleam like pearls. Pink oleander trees and pale, human-scale *palazzi* line either side. How destructive that 1693 earthquake—but what a fervor for beauty it inspired. We stop at a bar just to catch up with our senses. Men are reading the paper, a woman pulling a sweater over the head of her baby, the waiter wiping the counter. Just as if they didn't know they must be angels because this is heaven, gold streets or not.

Palazzo Veneziano-Sgarlata's iron window balconies bulge at the bottom, a concession to the puffy skirts of women's dresses. It's a house you could dream of living in. The Baroque is tame; the symmetry of neoclassicism by then—mid-eighteenth century—moved into the local scene. In one handsome building, the Municipio, the hero Salvo Montalbano (of the popular TV version of the Andrea Camilleri detective series) came to town when he had to meet the commissioner. (There's a handout sheet listing all the places filmed in the area.)

WE PLANNED TO have lunch at Satra. We won't get to try their smoked macaroni with baked ricotta, lemon zest, and tuna, or the spaghetti with toasted almond cream and tuna bottarga. It's closed. We stop instead at an outdoor café and sit on a balcony overlooking this amazing street. It's the worst lunch I can remember. The house wine makes my tongue feel like an emery board. Even Ed, so easy to please, leaves half his pasta untouched. I surreptitiously drop bits of stony bread and leathery salami to the cat waiting in the bushes below. Poor cat. We don't even care about lunch; we want to wander. Lucky that the churches stay open in the afternoon.

Even this time of year, the sun feels very strong. I remember Lampedusa says in *The Leopard,* "appalling sun," "tyrannous sun," "monarchic sun." Sun defines Sicily. I'd like to come back in July when it really rages.

I count sixteen major churches on my map. Each one riveting! Jewel-box interiors, white stucco whipped into creamy decorative swirls, monster face carvings, and every square inch of surface adorned. A strict minimalist would collapse in a heap. Shall we revive her with a tamarind granita and take her by the elbow to:

San Giovanni, with a sweet ellipse inside, and a strange painting— Christ on the cross in a glowing white skirt. The only known painting of its type except for one in Burgos, Spain, it probably was brought over during a time Sicily was ruled by Spain.

Santa Teresa, so airy with pale aqua and white stucco ornamentation, plus a wild black-and-white floor (1756) that looks contemporary, the bold angular, geometric design at such odds with the feminine columns entwined with vines and the primitive ceiling painting of the nativity.

On to Piazza Busacca and the grand church, cloister, and monastery of the Carmelites. It's closed and we only photograph its massive doors and the piazza full of cafés, benches, and umbrellas.

Other stops:

Antica Farmacia Cartia's balancing scales, vials, mortars, amphorae, and containers—another scene used in the Montalbano series.

Costume Museum, closed.

The super-Baroque Palazzo Beneventano, now an antique shop. This is one of the several local UNESCO World Heritage Sites, selected for its pure late Baroque style. At the corner of the building, where one street meets another, the architect's genius shines. A wrap-around band of geometric medallions merges the two sides of the building with the angle of the streets. Balconies are supported by outrageous gorgon heads with big tongues and nostrils that probably breathe fire. Awful, really, but impressive and delightful.

Side streets. Underpass with an Arab arch. Spillway over the once navigable and important but now submerged Modica river. Neighborhoods. An impressive datura, dangling its golden trumpets in profusion. The city goes up the hillsides and beyond; there are more churches (why does such a small town have so many?) but that's enough for now.

A last stop for coffee and Ed starts a conversation with the barista, who's bandaged from a carpal tunnel operation, caused, she thinks, from pulling the lever on the espresso machine a few times too many. She's managing left-handed. "Can we go?" I whisper. He talks to everyone. She's telling him what good Italian he speaks. She can tell he's from Tuscany.

"*Magari,*" he says. Would that I were.

SCICLI LIES NEAR the coast. That, along with its position, where two valleys meet, and the important Modica river and its tributaries made the town a commanding spot. Now, it just seems idyllic, nestled down into the hills with the sea close by.

. . .

WE STOP AT the beach town, **Sampieri**. At a small rise down the coast, ancient ruins rise against the sky. Is this a Romanesque abbey? We drive over to find, instead, recent ruins, a stone brick-making factory with its furnace chimney as stark as a steeple, and empty stone arches tricking the eye. An arresting sight, it endures only from 1912 to 1924, when it was torched by arsonists, a worthy crime for Inspector Montalbano, it would seem, and, indeed, scenes from the television series were shot here. During its brief life, the factory produced bricks for constructing buildings in Tripoli after Italy conquered Libya in 1911. Scattered nearby are stone houses where workers lived. They look prime for beachside renovations but remain in decaying condition.

A few upscale hotels and a lot of simple houses line the long, long golden beach. The water, clear and chilly, is still inviting, even in October. We wade along the shallows. The towns along the coast are agricultural and fishing villages, not high on any tourist list; they don't even appear in most guidebooks.

Down the coast, we drive through **Donnalucata,** another fishing town with a sweeping stretch of beach, then we stop in **Punta Secca,** the distant sea view that is visible from our hotel grounds. This is a charming, low-key spot with a lighthouse. A walk along the harbor and seafront, and along a pretty beach, and Ed is saying, "This could be the next Marzamemi." Why not?

Inspector Montalbano haunts us again. His house in the books was located on a beach in a fictional town but was filmed at Punta Secca. One book opens as he takes a swim in front of his house, about where we stand, and meets a dead body in the water. A memorable beginning. As we start down the beach, Ed checks his watch; we've walked almost sixteen kilometers today. "Let's go. It's almost *aperitivo* time."

LAST NIGHT AT Eremo. Another superb dinner. Ed tries the chickpea and wild chard soup, and I choose pappardelle, a wide pasta, with red chicory, caper flowers, and a cream of Piacentinu Ennese, a sheep cheese from inland Enna, made with saffron (hence golden) and black peppercorns. We both have chops from milk-fed lambs, with a wild vegetable sauté with mint. Impeccable. A shame to miss all the desserts but there's only so much a body can do. Letizia, our waiter, knows a thing or two about wines. She recommends Milla e una Notte, thousand and one nights, a soft and strong blend of *nero d'Avola, petit verdot,* syrah, and other grapes. Some enologist's heady mixture, it works. "One of those quick bottles," Ed says. Gone before we are really through. But there's always Amara, a bittersweet close to the evening.

WHAT CAREFUL SERVICE at this hotel. We've seen Lorenzo conferring with guests, handing out sheets of travel suggestions as they set forth. The hotel even has its own airstrip and can arrange day trips to Malta, along with other enticing short tours on land. Because we'd wanted to have a cooking lesson with their chef and he isn't available this week, Lorenzo surprised us by arranging a morning at the professional Scuola Mediterranea di Enogastronomia at Hotel Antico Convento in **Ragusa Ibla**. He has also recommended restaurants at our next stop, and wines. Sad to say *arriverderci.*

JUST OUTSIDE RAGUSA Ibla, honey-colored houses climb the hill like steep stair steps. Soon we're in tight lanes, not sure where we are. A few loops and there it is, the Hotel Antico Convento. Oh, dio, no parking. Ed lets me out and I meet Barbara, who will introduce us to the chef. Gone a long time, Ed finally bursts in smiling but I can tell he's stressed. As we walk through the convent, he tells me he took a wrong turn and found himself driving in the *centro storico,* ouch, the historic center, pedestrians only, inching along hoping that the police didn't notice. It happens. And it's highly uncomfortable. How many impossibly narrow streets have we backed out of? Twenty minutes later he was able to exit and hopes he has parked legally.

We're given aprons in the large professional kitchen outfitted with stations for each student. We meet Giovanni Galesi, a young Sicilian with those dark eyes that seem to look out from Greek history. Confident and friendly, he's the director here of the seven-month courses that train chefs in every aspect of Sicilian cuisine. "We have forty-seven kinds of flour," he tells us. "You must know all about each." There are also short focused courses, three days, or even special arrangements such as we have, for a morning of cooking and lunch. He's from

Donnalucata, where we were yesterday, and we understand from him what *fresh* means. "The fishermen come in two, three times a day. That's where we get our fish."

We make caponata, what we called eggplant caviar in California. Giovanni lets us understand what caponata is in the culture. A million recipes for it. Everyone has a favorite. Essential. Used on crackers, bread, or vegetables, on meat, on fish. By itself. He has us prepare each vegetable separately then mix them, just as Simone Beck taught me to make ratatouille. Why is it so good? Because everything in it is so good?

We make ravioli out of a local hard wheat flour. As Giovanni mixes, I see that he's wearing two wedding rings. "Do you have two wives?" I ask.

He laughs. "One for the engagement and one for the wedding. Sicilian women are fierce."

The dough is firm and yellow, but rolls out thin as paper. We dot the filling, an herb-scented ricotta, onto the sheet with a pastry tube. The sauce, pork cheeks in red wine, I would have thought too heavy but, no, it's rich in just the right way, with the ravioli cooked al dente.

What we've created is served to us in the hotel's Ristorante Cenobio, the convent refectory, which is an aesthetic experience in itself. White and contemplative, the room's arches meet at the faded frescoes of saints. The staff is well trained and cordial. We must return for a three-day class and a stay.

We would love to check in and enjoy fabulous Ragusa but we have a short drive slightly north, to the vineyard of Occhipinti at Vittoria.

NOTES:

Large terra-cotta urns are called *orci,* plural, and *orcio,* singular. If used for olive oil, they were glazed or waxed inside and called *ziri,* plural, and *ziro,* singular.

Strattù is sun-dried tomato paste.

Chinotto, a carbonated drink made from the juices of *citrus myrtifolia,* a small orange tree with bitter fruit.

Filetto di Maiale Nero con Salsa Nero d'Avola, Patatine Porri e Verdure Selvatiche

BLACK PIG TENDERLOIN WITH NERO D'AVOLA SAUCE, LEEK CHIPS, AND WILD VEGETABLES, SERVES 4 TO 6

The characteristic black pig of the area won't be available to us, as it is to Chef Sebastiano Sallemi, but pork tenderloin works well. *Nero d'Avola* wines are easy to find. The chef calls for wild greens such as chicory and dandelion, but I've used more readily available ones with an earthy touch.

2 pork tenderloins

1 bunch wild vegetables (or improvise with fennel, carrots, chard)

Salt and pepper, *QB*

1¼ cups *nero d'Avola* wine

Zest of 1 orange

5 whole cloves

3 tablespoons sugar

1 tablespoon cornstarch dissolved in water

8 thin slices guanciale (pork cheek)

Sprigs of rosemary

Extra-virgin olive oil, *QB*

1 leek, sliced thickly and floured

2 cloves minced garlic

Preheat the oven to 350°F.

Cut the tenderloins crosswise into pieces of about 4 ounces and set aside. Prepare the vegetables separately and season.

In the meantime, put the wine in a saucepan with the orange zest and cloves and bring to a boil for about 10 minutes. Leave the orange zest and the cloves in the wine to simmer, covered, for at least 30 minutes. Bring back to a boil and stir in the sugar and cornstarch dissolved in a little water, then continue to boil until the liquid is somewhat reduced. Set aside.

Take the guanciale slices and roll them around the pieces of pork. In a non-stick pan on medium heat, sauté the pork until golden brown on both sides, about

3 minutes on each side. Add rosemary for perfume. Season and complete baking in the oven, 6 to 7 minutes.

Fry the floured leek slices in a dash of oil for 3 minutes, turning once to brown both sides. Add the garlic for a few moments. Taste for seasoning.

Serve the pork in the middle of each plate, spoon on the sauce, and surround with the vegetables, garlic, and the leek chips.

Ristorante Don Eusebio,
Hotel Eremo della Giubiliana, Ragusa, Sicilia

Conigghiu a' Portuisa (Coniglio alla portoghese)
PORTUGUESE RABBIT, SERVES 4

This is an old Sicilian recipe, popular in particular in Ragusa. The name "Portuguese" refers to the Portuguese port wine that was originally used for its preparation, wine that was later (1770) replaced by Sicilian Marsala.

1 rabbit, cut into pieces and rinsed

1 cup Marsala

Extra-virgin olive oil, *QB*

1 onion, finely chopped

2 cloves garlic, minced

2 stalks celery

2 red bell peppers, cut in strips

1 tablespoon tomato paste, dissolved in a little hot water

Salt and pepper, *QB*

5 tablespoons capers, rinsed and drained

12 green olives, pitted

2 to 3 tablespoons parsley, snipped

Dry the rabbit pieces and place them in a suitable container, then sprinkle with half of the Marsala. Let them marinate, refrigerated, for at least 4 hours but better all night long, turning them from time to time so that they always remain a little impregnated with wine.

Add olive oil to a skillet on medium heat and sauté the onion, garlic, celery, and peppers for about 7 minutes. Remove the vegetables to a bowl. Add the rabbit to the skillet and brown on both sides, then pour in the remaining Marsala and make it fade—almost evaporate. Add the tomato paste. Season with salt and pepper. Return the vegetables to the skillet, cover, and cook over medium heat. After about 15 minutes, add the capers and olives, and more olive oil, and continue cooking on medium low for an hour. The Portuguese rabbit is ready to be served with parsley sprinkled on top.

Ristorante Don Eusebio, Eremo della Giubiliana,
Ragusa, Sicilia

Caponata

SERVES 6

Sicilian soul food, as prepared by Giovanni Galesi, the chef at Nosco cooking school at the atmospheric Hotel Antico Convento. Use caponata with everything—fish, bread, meat, crackers, or just a dollop on its own. Cutting the vegetables into similar-size small cubes assures a balance of flavors. This southern version has no raisins or olives, the way it's made in the north. I slip in two cloves of garlic. Giovanni says that in winter, spinach, pumpkin, or chicory is often added.

Extra-virgin olive oil, *QB*

1 onion, cubed

1 red bell pepper, diced

2 carrots, diced

2 stalks celery, diced

2 tablespoons apple cider vinegar

1 tablespoon honey

2 to 3 capers, rinsed

¼ cup tomato sauce

Salt and pepper, *QB*

3 zucchini, diced

2 eggplants, diced

A few basil leaves

Add olive oil to a medium-size skillet and sauté the onion and pepper. Meanwhile, plunge the carrots and celery into boiling water for 3 to 4 minutes. Drain and mix with the onion and red pepper in the skillet. Bring up the heat and add to the pan the vinegar, honey, capers, tomato sauce, salt, and pepper. Mix well. Set aside. In another skillet, add more oil and on medium-high heat, fry the zucchini and then the eggplant until barely tender, about 2 minutes for the zucchini and 4 for the eggplant. Turn off the heat, mix everything, and add the basil. Best after a few hours for the flavors to blend.

Nosco, Scuola Mediterranea di Enogastronomia,
Hotel Antico Convento, Ragusa Ibla, Sicilia

Vittoria

A chance e-mail from our friend Todd sent us to stay in the
countryside at the six-room inn Baglio Occhipinti, a project
of Fausta Occhipinti, right down the ancient wine road
from her sister Arianna's vineyard. "Love, love, loved it," he
wrote. Anything he loves, we know we will, too.

All across Sicily, we've seen tumbled stone farms. This
one, low and spread out, is from 1860. Arabic *Baglio* means
courtyard. There are several walled spaces with tables and
chairs for relaxing outside, and a tall stone wall surrounds
the long pool.

The winemaking room retains huge sunken vats with
stone chutes where wine flowed in. Now they're a feature
of the inn's gathering room, a sophisticated design of
white sofas flanking an old fireplace, and antique chests
with arrangements of flowers, photos, tureens, silver
candlesticks, tea sets, and leaning prints on top. A guitar
stands by the hearth. The way-tall ceiling suggests that
the room might also have been a granary. What I love:
the capacious coffee table stacked high with books. As we
arrive, Sebastiano, the chef, asks if we want to have dinner

tonight. Yes! He's setting six tables with candles and white tablecloths. Only guests dine here.

He takes us in the kitchen for a glass of water and we stay for a few minutes. He's chopping pumpkin. I'm totally charmed, and he's amused that I find his kitchen so special. Any designer interested in efficiency would faint. Totally deconstructed, it seems to work for him. Two unmatched tables pushed together form the "island," antique china cabinets hold dishes and equipment. A cake is cooling by the sink. "For breakfast tomorrow," he says. A few rustic chairs. There's a normal stove, a couple of small corner tables jammed with trays and flowers and containers. In the corner, a wood oven. This kitchen goes against every rule. Rough cobbles. Baskets of potatoes, grapes, oranges, vegetables stand on the floor near the door. Wouldn't you think the space for one table against the wall could be a work station? Instead, it is covered with a collection of old silver: covered butter and cheese dishes, teapots, and wine coasters.

OUR ROOM, THE Botanica Suite, has clay tile floors, stone walls, sloping beamed ceiling. Otherwise, all white. Everything. The art consists of framed herbs and dried meadow flowers that look like a project one might do with a child on a summer afternoon.

Travel, for us, equals motion. We go. We keep going. Today, I'm claiming the rest of the afternoon to sit in one of those grassy enclosures that once held some donkey captive. I'm reading *Sicily: A Short History from the Ancient Greeks to Cosa Nostra* by John Julius Norwich, a thorough and readable historian. Fifty pages and dizziness sets in. Sicily . . . everyone attacked—Greeks, Byzantines, Phoenicians, Arabs, French, Spanish, Goths, Normans, their own internal power mongers, and last, the Germans. The invasions, beheadings, battles, expulsions, feudal semi-slavery, epidemics, and earthquakes are simply staggering. Numbing. How could such chaos have continued nonstop for so many centuries? But—who would *not* want this blessed isle right in the middle of the Mediterranean? Strategic and idyllic.

Norwich begins: " 'Sicily,' said Goethe, 'is the key to everything.' It is, first of all, the largest island in the Mediterranean. It has also proved, over the centuries, to be the most unhappy."

"History," he continues, "has endowed Sicily with some dark, brooding quality—some underlying sorrow of which poverty, the Church, the Mafia and all the other popular modern scapegoats may be manifestations but are certainly not the cause." That, and also that Sicily and the south in general have constantly been short-changed when the national goodies are handed around. Sicily, to the rest of Italy, is still *other.*

In the north, I've heard many times, "Below Rome begins Africa." I once asked a neighbor if a small, darker-skinned worker was Italian. "No," he answered, "he's Sicilian."

While Norwich's history broadens my understanding of the island, two other writers do the same. In Giuseppe di Lampedusa's *The Leopard,* the Prince of Salina bears the whole burden of his country's history. The novel takes place at a charged time, the Risorgimento under Garibaldi. Sicily, for the first time since the Roman Empire, is about to be unified. Change is coming and the prince, progenitor of all Sicilian history, must fold himself into the heavy past and die. The symbolism feels heavy but the novel is a sensuous marvel. That sensuousness—who could ever forget the lush description of desserts at the formal ball?—provides the reader a direct visceral route into the heart of Sicily. The novel imprints permanently the dark vortex of the island's history, and also the cunning, humor, and passion of those who lived it.

Another revelatory writer, and I am traveling with three of his books, is the droll and sharp Leonardo Sciascia. A literary writer, he chose subjects of crime and the Mafia. His characters often have, as Robert Frost wrote, "a lover's quarrel with the world," but there's a fierce strain of love for Sicily in his work. Even its foibles. In one story set earlier in the century, a group of Sicilians pays for passage to America. They sail for days, fantasizing about the new life, and finally are let off in the dark. They start out with their belongings on foot toward an American city. Suddenly they hear a snatch of song, recognize a road marker. They've disembarked near where they embarked. Duped again.

They wrote of different eras, Giuseppe di Lampedusa (1896–1957) and Leonardo Sciascia (1921–1989). Although they overlapped in life by thirty-six years, their styles differ drastically—one, lavish and Baroque, the other, lean and understated. What's common to both, a quick, often funny, irony and a metabolic-level love for Sicily.

• • •

AS A CURIOUS person on holiday, I don't experience the complexities. From a casual perspective, Sicilians don't have the upfront immediate and boisterous personalities that you encounter constantly in Tuscany. But then neither do the Piemontese, the Fruiliani, and others. The Sicilians I've met over several trips do not seem dark. They have been cordial, extremely polite, and present. Unless you've lived here, I suppose you're not able to comment on the national character, but I wonder if there is in the past decades a lifting of this darkness on this blessèd isle.

ED HAS BEEN off for a visit with Fausta's sister, Arianna, the winemaker at the restored Occhipinti vineyard. And now we have Sebastiano's dinner to savor, along with the wine of the house. We're visiting someone's home, it seems, only we don't dine with the other ten guests. Each couple has a private table and the room is hushed until everyone has had a bit of wine. Now, laughter. We end up talking to two young women next to us. Lawyers from New York, they're tearing up the roads all over Sicily. How lucky, to feel independent that young. And knowledgeable. Like travelers everywhere, we exchange names of places and restaurants. Sebastiano serves the dinner he made for us. Risotto with pumpkin, not too sweet, followed by a homey beef stew. Their Occhipinti Il Frappato 2015, from *frappato* grapes, is easy to love and tastes lighter than our usual *nero d'Avola* choices. Cannoli, signature dessert of Sicily, he serves deconstructed: Instead of the curl of deep-fried pastry stuffed with the sweet ricotta and sprinkled with pistachios, his ricotta comes in a bowl with the nuts and cracked pastry on top.

DEEP NIGHT IN the countryside of Sicily, Ed off to dreamland. I'm reading *The Day of the Owl* by Sciascia when I hear one calling from the fields.

A woman from the village serves our breakfast under the olive trees. Fresh cakes and fruit and cappuccino made with the Moka pot. Our two friends from last night are off to the ruins at Agrigento. We plan a leisurely day seeing some of the small towns in the area. Fausta appears, an immediate strong presence. She's forthright and smiles with her whole face, obviously a people person. Painted eyes, the name Occhipinti means. Hers are not but they are deep-set, fringed with thick lashes. Her genes must go back to the Byzantines. We learn more about how she and her sister restored the tumbled farms and built their secluded inn and a vineyard that is getting big notice in all the competitions. "We're dreamers in my family, artists, winemakers, landscape designers, architects. I'm a landscape person. I worked for years in Paris, but I love my island and came home to do something here." Her uncle nearby owns COS, another fine vineyard that is aging wine in clay amphorae, the way it was done eons ago. Fausta gives us advice about the day and we're off, though it would be great fun to spend the morning with her.

WE PARK EASILY in **Vittoria,** a good-size market town built around a shady piazza. I'd say three hundred teenagers are hanging out, talking in groups, huddled around café tables, and speeding about on motorcycles. On Friday, why are they not at school? We check out the Palazzo Carfí Muscolino, Palazzo Giudice-Santapá, Palazzo Traina, and other Liberty (Art Nouveau) buildings the town is known for, another piazza with palm trees and Chiesa Madre, Mother Church, a handsome pinkish-yellow façade topped by matching domes. On the altar floor, two inlaid marble *ex votos* commemorate John the Baptist saving the winemakers. On the left, a black marble urn, dated 1798, holds dead grapevines; on the right, dated 1801, the urn holds healthy grapes, hanging in abundant bunches. There's a fabulous painting, *Deposition of Christ,* attributed to Antonio Scalogna, 1725. Who is he? A quick Internet check reveals nothing. What draws me is the style. Scalogna is onto something here. He's finding planes and angles, chiseled edges to his figures. A knowledge of Caravaggio shows.

When we stop for coffee, Ed strikes up a conversation with an ancient man in a tweed cap and ascot. The students milling about? "They're on strike," he says.

"High school students on strike? Against what? Grades, teachers?" Ed asks.

"Oh, everything," the man answers.

Caltagirone

Before we left this morning, I asked Fausta where she found the old tiles she used above the sinks in the bathrooms. "Go to Caltagirone. It's one of the big ceramics centers of Sicily." Well, that's saying something, as decorative tiles define Sicily.

We cross a bridge decorated with tiles, a good intro to the ceramics-mad town. There are ceramics shops everywhere in the old *centro*. We're both stunned when the street ends in a wide sweep of 142 steps up to the church—steps with tile risers of blue, yellow, and white designs of waves, horses, acanthus leaves, birds, arabesques. Small shops line the way. In several, women are painting designs on the formed clay. I buy a tile clock in one, a spoon rest in another, a small bowl. That's it. We have carry-on luggage. These I can slide between my clothes but if there's more, we have a problem. We'd have to check, a practice Ed forbids. *No checked luggage,* he wants carved on his tombstone.

We don't find anything old that we could ship back for

the bathroom we are planning to add at Bramasole. Fausta must have bought them all. But I do see a great sun-yellow and blue tile to put under a pot that might ooze moisture onto a table. "I'll put it in my handbag. Really, promise."

We dutifully visit the ceramics museum and the Duomo, but I admit, my mind is singularly focused on the old tile. We have a quick vegetable crepe lunch in a bar and keep walking. Although the *centro* is mono-themed, a few Baroque buildings catch our eyes. Quite a few others look dreary and neglected. All the color goes into the ceramics. Gilda will like her spoon rest, and my daughter the little bowl. I'll think of Sicily when the tile clock ticks in the kitchen. The steps were amazing to see. Wonder if, as I've seen in Portugal in such places, anyone does penance by walking up to the top on their knees.

BY MID-AFTERNOON, WE are back at Baglio Occhipinti. We both are craving a calm few hours to read and rest in our quiet haven. Then dinner again, under the good care of Sebastiano. Tonight, the first fire of fall in the big room. Suddenly, the season is turning. We have a glass of prosecco and look through the books on the coffee table. One is on Mafia cooking. Can only imagine that it's quite good. Design books from London. Travel guides left by guests.

We're only three tables tonight and we keep to ourselves. Little bites of eggplant parmigiana, big plates of pasta with ragù, then lamb and chicory. Proud to drink SP68, Arianna's awarded wine (*tre bicchiere,* three glasses, the top distinction in *Gambero Rosso*), a mix of *frappato* and *nero d'Avola*. The wine, named for the road the vineyard is on, tastes quite at home with Sebastiano's refined and simple food. At this place, everything fits everything else.

The two young New York lawyers are dining somewhere up the coast. We toast them and all adventurous travelers. It would be lovely to sprawl on the sofas and read by the fire. The place is not quite *that* informal, so we sit upright and enjoy a thumb-size glass of Marsala.

· · ·

THIS WEEK WE'VE stayed in three places. We didn't really need to, as the distances we've covered are not extensive. If you check Marzamemi, Scicli, and Vittoria on a map, one base works if you're willing to drive a bit. I loved all the places we stayed. Now, after one more stop, we get to see Catania.

Chiaramonte Gulfi

A brief stop in a special town, a hill town with intimate medieval streets. Chiaramonte Gulfi has been lolling under the Sicilian sun since first established by Greeks in the seventh century B.C. The pleasant town today belies its rugged history. Seized and destroyed by the Arabs in 827, it retains the name they bestowed: Gulfi, meaning pleasant land. Added later, Chiaramonte was the name of the man who rebuilt the town after it was leveled in 1296.

Like everywhere else around here, it was hit by the harrowing 1693 quake. Unlike other villages, the citizens rebuilt on the old plan, winding and narrow and climbing, giving onto broad views of the valley below.

The rectangular Piazza Duomo, with palms, cafés, and small shops, is dominated by Santa Maria La Nova. Its weathered doors carved with saints in panels are exquisite and in need of care. A few people out, walking dogs, chatting with neighbors, having a coffee. No cars to dodge, an almost strange quiet.

We read about several museums inside Palazzo Montesano: embroidery, Liberty objects, ethnic musical instruments, and olive oil. Closed. One of the frustrations of travel! Often museums and churches are closed when you think they might be open. (Shops, too. Most of Italy outside the cities is closed on Monday.)

We walk under the arch of stone that used to be the gateway to the old town, the Arco dell'Annunziata, a rare medieval survivor of the earthquake. The street climbs up to the top of town where a church anchors a broad view over the plains.

WE'RE WAITING FOR *pranzo.*

Fausta, at Baglio Occhipinti, and our friend Todd both told us not to miss a meal at Majore. "I warn you," Todd wrote, "it's all pork." We find it on a street the width of a good sidewalk, stop in, and reserve, happily wandering until they open. This town reminds us of Tuscan hill towns with its lanes and townhouses abutting the street. How clean the steps and cared-for the potted plants on either side. One woman methodically polishes her doorknob, which is already gleaming—but, really, she's checking out what's going on in the neighborhood. It's only us for excitement. She gives a nod and a *buongiorno.*

MAJORE'S KITCHEN STANDS just inside the entrance, a vast stove and a chef with raven wing eyebrows, a long nose, the better to smell when the roast is done, and a grizzly mustache and beard. He's glowering at his pot of ragù—a pot large enough to bathe two babies—and at me asking about what's in the giant frying pan. When I start complimenting his stove, he warms and smiles. Molteni. French. A workhorse of a stove. How does he manage in such a minute space? He gestures with his arms and seems to say that the kitchen is an extension of himself. Actually, there's another prep kitchen. In the pan, he is sautéing about twenty stuffed pork chops. That's what I'm having. There's a large dining room, but we're seated in a smaller one whimsically painted with a trompe-l'oeil window, a shelf of grapes and platters, a niche of wine bottles, all in faded colors.

In solidarity with Ed, who has to drive, I forgo wine. The waiter seems to think that is a shame, and it is. We have risotto, then the hearty pork, which lives up to Fausta and Todd's raving. We were told not to miss the wine cellar, but we forget to ask in our rapture over the pork and the banter of the waiter who insists we have a glass of wine. Finally, we do.

Costata Ripiena

STUFFED PORK CHOP, SERVES 2

To match this super-hearty chop, Salvatore Laterra recommends Cerasuolo di Vittoria DOCG, 50 to 70 percent *nero d'Avola,* and the rest *frapatto,* a local varietal. When browning, turn the chops carefully to keep the stuffing inside. Secure with toothpicks if necessary. Serve with oven-roasted rosemary potatoes.

2 two-finger-high pork chops

3 tablespoons chopped raw pork tenderloin

2 tablespoons diced *ragusano* (or other cow's-milk cheese)

1 hard-boiled egg, diced

1–2 tablespoons Sicilian salami, diced

2 tablespoons extra-virgin olive oil

1 onion, thinly sliced

1 cup chicken stock

Salt, *QB*

Make a big pocket in each chop and fill with the chopped loin, the *ragusano,* egg, and local salami. Brown the chops in the oil. When you turn the chops to brown the other side, add the onion and complete the browning. Add the broth and salt. Cover and cook over medium-low heat for about 30 minutes, adding a little water if necessary.

Ristorante Majore,
Chiaramonte Gulfi, Sicilia

Catania

Fishermen in rubber boots and pants shout and call
out their catch. A hawker in a red hoodie with no shirt
underneath throws back his head in praise of a sparkling
gray-mottled fish. His register reaches so high he sounds
like a castrato. His neighbor, with wild hair feathering
around his head like some exotic chicken, displays a tray of
gleaming *spatola,* each one looped into a ring the diameter
of a basketball. I've never seen this elegant flat, eel-like
creature, a sabre fish in English. They have no scales, only
lean, silver skin that looks like mercury glass. Each stares
with a gold-rimmed black eye. Spooky. My shoes are wet
with fish juices and blood. When an octopus tries to escape
his bin, it's smacked back into place. The shrimp wiggle,
still alive. Just caught, the seafood smells salty and good,
not fishy. One burly, black-bearded seller of hunky tuna in
tubs of watery blood has plucked his eyebrows into delicate
wings. The hub of the market: a rowdy pit loud with the
hacking—knife like a guillotine—of enormous swordfish
into steaks, crowded women shrieking back at vendors, big

talk among friends. The daily Catania fish market makes Venice's Rialto market look like Whole Foods. The faces of the men are even more compelling than what's for sale. Crinkled from wind, sunburned too many times, crusty hands, pale lips that look hard as cockle shells, they have the look of everything the sea has done to them.

A boy pushes through the crowd. He's carrying an armful of parsley. Fifty cents for enough to garnish fifty grilled fish. On the periphery, plucked and skinned chickens and rabbits hang from racks. Stalls display all the glorious produce grown in the magic soil around Mount Etna. Walnuts the size of a baby's fist, purple cauliflower, waxy gold persimmons, pistachios for cannoli, cut prickly pear, lemons, lemons, lemons. There's the artichoke master, roasting them almost black. The vegetable fryer scooping up singed red and yellow peppers and spreading them across his racks. Behind mounds of green grapes stands the most talented hawker of all. An unusually tall man swaying in a gray hoodie, he could be a priest intoning mass or a muezzin calling us to prayer, except that he's louder. *Uve, uve, uve,* he ululates. Grapes. Even the prosaic *un a-ur-o (un euro)* turns to music. The words ring out like the first words ever spoken. We buy grapes.

The market trails off into a park where Africans sell cigarette lighters and tissue packs. Twelve or so groups of old men hover around tables where intense card games are in progress. Are they retired fishermen who must come down to market out of habit? The sky is as blue as it has ever been in the thousands of years of Catania Saturday mornings.

MY TRAVEL LIST for the south of Sicily did not include Catania. After the flight from Rome, we planned to pick up the rental car at the airport and drive straight to the south of Sicilia. Return the car after a week, then fly back to Rome.

One of the pleasures of travel is deviating from the best-laid plans.

DURING THE WEEK of exploring Scicli, cooking in Ragusa Ibla, wine tasting around Marzamemi and Vittoria, shopping for ceramics in Caltagirone, stopping into villages bypassed by time, I was also reading about other parts of Sicily. I kept turning down the pages on Catania.

A church with a thousand *ex votos,* a library of ancient texts, a street of coffin makers, the enormous fish market, a history as old as time. We decided to add on two nights to the end of our Sicily explorations.

WE DROPPED THE car at the airport and took a taxi into the city. The entry, not auspicious. Run-down buildings covered with graffiti, scattered trash, chaos of cars. Neither of us is saying *what have we done.* I'm still clutching the sheet given to us at the airport telling all the ways to protect ourselves by not wearing jewelry, leaving valuables in the hotel safe, stowing handbags under the car seat when driving, etc. "Don't go that way," the driver points, as he pulls up in front of our five-star hotel. "Dangerous. Go that way," he points in the opposite direction. "Best fish you will ever eat."

BY THE TIME we arrive late in the day on Friday, we are both worn down from travel. Never have we felt reinvigorated so quickly.

QUICK RESEARCH IN *Gambero Rosso* lands us at Trattoria di De Fiore, a short walk from the Romano House, where we are lucky to find a room. Walking here, some streets are dark but as soon as it feels dicey, we suddenly come upon outdoor cafés and restaurants with boisterous life streaming around the tables.

When we reach our trattoria, I have doubts, as we're seated on the sidewalk with motorcycles and cars a hand span away, my shoulder brushed by scraggly plants separating us from the street. We're handed menus with cracked plastic-covered pages. Not good. No one has changed the menu in eons. Turns out, there's no need to. Totally traditional fare it is, and everything is delicious. We scarf up the mixed antipasti, especially the *arancini,* caponata, huge olives, fried eggplant. Little sardines stuffed with bread crumbs and pine nuts. Homemade pasta (similar to cavatelli) with artichokes, finely grated ricotta salata, and basil. Everything purely simple and happy. Happy, too, is the inexpensive house wine from Etna. A half-liter. Then another half-liter.

After the dinner hour is well under way, traffic lessens. We begin to see elegantly dressed people walking by. "The opera," the waiter says. "*Don Giovanni* tonight. Three hours and twenty minutes. They'll be getting out after midnight." Men are in suits, some in black tie. No one is slouching along in jeans. The women have upswept hair, dark. They have not gotten the message: They're tastefully bedecked in gold jewelry. They are wearing heels and good dresses with silk jackets or pretty shawls. "1960," Ed observes. Many of the men with clipped mustaches and slick hair look as though they've stepped out of daguerreotypes from the 1890s. *Ah, Catania, this also is who you are.*

EARLY, WE'RE OUT. A few turns and we emerge onto the three-kilometer-long via Etnea, which leads from one piazza to another. At the end, Mount Etna looms, distant and eerie. In the first piazza we encounter, the university and *liceo* buildings on either side of a dignified square full of students and music. Then we enter the handsome Piazza del Duomo, with the surprise statue of an elephant topped with an obelisk. The surrounding upright, Baroque but rather severe buildings are charcoal gray, trimmed with white marble. Even the street pavers are dark volcanic rock. This sounds dreary but isn't. (Gray and white, after all, are quite trendy now.) The dark color on the façades comes from volcanic ash mixed into plaster. The handsome town layout and buildings make you visualize the new Catania rising after the 1693 earthquake. The earlier city, like many, was destroyed and the rebirth not medieval but Baroque. What an ideal city it must have been—the grand scale, all new and gleaming. Straight as an arrow, via Etnea provides a long and leisurely *passeggiata*. Trees shade the numerous cafés. Like Rome, Catania lives outside. It's exhilarating. I photograph street shrines, an old habit. We stop frequently to admire the extensive pastry selections—cannoli, baba au rhum, Turk's hats, almond tarts, endless other tasty confections with cream and candied fruits. "Leave the gun; take the cannoli," Ed quotes. I agree.

EVERYONE IS MINGLING on this warm October morning. We've visited the fish market and now, in front of the Carmine church where I see the *ex voto* collection, a vast market spreads for blocks. So many babies taking the air in their strollers. Lovers embracing every few steps. The *ex votos* are mainly from the 1920s to the 1950s, a new era for them in my experience. Most are of surgeries. The patient on the operating table miraculously saved by a saint, no credit to the doctor. A few show the saintly rescue from ships in storms, from falls from balconies, and spills from collapsing scaffolding. My favorite is of a woman at home in bed, her daughter praying at the foot as her mother throws up a long spurt of blood that lands in a bucket. The Virgin Mary rises in the upper right, and the panel to the left shows the woman resting in a hospital bed. Cured. I admire the simultaneous narrative.

We wander in a park dedicated to native son Vincenzo Bellini and photograph his bluish marble bust. I love the palms and the flowering tree that my plant app doesn't identify. The blossoms look like small pink lilies. A man is singing Italian torch songs and we hear him work his way around high notes. We browse in Libreria Vicolo Stretto, the Narrow Street Bookstore, which is tiny and literary.

Restaurant row is via Santa Filomena, a narrow street lined with tempting places to eat. We have lunch outside at Blanc à Manger. Bowls of *paccheri* (huge tubular pasta) with mussels on a bed of roasted tomatoes. Good bread.

Then we walk. For miles. We come to a neighborhood we turn back from. Abandoned ornate buildings, empty, not menacing but somehow we won't go there. In the afternoons, almost everything shuts up tight in these far south cities, even in October when the heat has abated and the climate seems made for the gods. Back at the hotel, we repack. Tomorrow we go. Can't think now of all we missed seeing on this quick stop. The library was closed. I didn't see the street of coffin makers. Or the opera.

FOR DINNER ON our last night, we're back on via Santa Filomena. At Il Sale Art Café, we again sit at a table on the street but this time no cars, only the lovely stream of life passing our table as we get to feast one last time on the marvelous Sicilian food. The olive oil, Cutrera, from Chiaramonte Gulfi, where we visited, tastes spicy and fresh. Oh, the antipasto plate we've loved all over Sicily: caponata, this time with pine nuts and raisins; divine cracked olives; *arancini* stuffed with ragù; sweet

sun-dried tomatoes to spread on the great breads. And we couldn't resist the mound of grilled vegetables covered with melted *caciocavallo*, a
cheese I could live on. Ed goes for the *baccalà* (salt cod) with a crust of
shredded fried potatoes, and by now I hardly can face my stuffed pork
filet with fried chickpea sticks.

We try Vivera, 2012, Etna Rosso Martinella. I wish I could say we
tasted the molten lava of the volcano, but really it was a soft and fruity
red, with a wash of mineral backtaste.

Best, we have another chance to witness the passing vibrant faces. A
gypsy accordion player with sad eyes, a couple puffing on e-cigarettes,
a woman with a shopping bag bulging with fennel, strolling studs in
threes who surprise with their confident smallness and sexiness.

At the next table, so close I could spear a bite of swordfish, a couple
with a baby are dining with friends. They are all young and polished,
glowing under the low lights. The baby is lying in her carriage, waving
her arms and legs constantly, rapt in an excess of joy. Intermittently, she
smiles. Her parents are enjoying their evening in the warm air. She is,
too, as she will innumerable times as she grows up in this city so abundant with life.

EPILOGUE: *Cortona*

Back at Bramasole. For now, the luggage rack is folded and put away. My desk has space to put down a book without it vanishing into piles of notes and maps. We've traveled from the Brenner Pass in the North to Capo Spartivento, the bottom tip of Sicily, and dozens of fascinating places in between. Surely I could fly through PhD orals in Italian history, art, architecture, culinary and oenological history. The greatest gift of travel: the steep learning curve. Second best: how your vision refreshes and you see with infant eyes. Third: memory. How the places seen will layer into life as time moves on.

OUR FRIEND, THE terrific chef Silvia Baracchi, welcomed us home with one of our favorites at her restaurant, delicious steaks coated in dried olives with a tang of green tomatoes. Long into the night we sipped Baracchi wines and talked.

• • •

THE NEXT DAY we started to build a new pergola, inspired by our travels. Grapevines covered our old one made of tree limbs, but for the new, we wanted a roof; the linden trees drop ants and pollen constantly. Black ants on ravioli are not appetizing. The iron pergola is topped with a slightly peaked metal roof the color of rust. The view sweeps over the dips and pleats of hills up to green mountains in the distance, and shadows of clouds. Blond light sifts across the valley to the mysterious villa built for a pope's visit. He stayed there only a single night (or so the story goes).

Everything seems renewed. I feel natural writing in my notebook outside rather than in my study. I relive the immense dunes at Piscinas in Sardegna, the emerald lakes of the Dolomiti, the watercolor harbor of Monopoli in Puglia, my grandson's delight in taking the dangling cable car to the remote hotel Vigilius, where he found, perhaps for the first time, that undeniable metabolic connection to a new place. Troves of vivid memories. The series of waterfalls at Campo Tures: The higher we climbed, the more plangent the cascades. At the top, we were drenched by mist. We will always remember.

I'VE BEEN UNFAITHFUL to Cortona. I've imagined preferring to live in other places—Trento, Scicli, Monopoli, Parma, Massa Marittima, Cividale del Friuli. If I were looking for home now, I might choose one of them. But how would I? My aunt Hazel claimed her thirteen beaux sat on the front steps the afternoon she announced the one she would marry. Although I'm certain that's apocryphal, I enjoy imagining such a dilemma.

THE FAMOUS QUOTE by T. S. Eliot, is it true?

We shall not cease from exploration,
And the end of all our exploring
Will be to arrive where we started
And know the place for the first time.

But I *don't* find myself awash in discovery. Cortona remains the place I know best, where the compass needle points anytime I'm adrift. Still,

Cortona *is* moved into a new light. Now I understand this town as a jagged little piece in the complex jigsaw of places forming the astounding country of Italy. We never finished the 1,000-piece puzzle in Puglia and I will never finish exploring this country.

T. S. Eliot again:

And to make an end is to make a beginning
The end is where we start from.

Hopeful and true, these words. I'm again relishing walks on the Roman road, coffee in the piazza every morning, cooking from my garden, Wednesday night dinners at the Cardinalis' house. I know there are amazing people in other places—and some cranks, too—but the friends I've known for many years are not replicable. Plus, I'm in love with my rooms full of books and collections, my blue stove, lemon pots and kitchen herbs, the lion's-head fountain spilling music. This is memory's crucible: family and friends who blossom here, six-hour feasts under the stars, all the books I've written in my third-floor study, even the mysterious hurts that visit now and then.

Trento is gorgeous and refined, Asolo, a fairy-tale setting, Carloforte, knock-out beach town, Campodimele, where everyone lives to be ninety-five, oh, many other contenders. But it turns out that Cortona already has imprinted as home, the perfect place to start from when Ed hauls the luggage from the storeroom, I stuff the book bag, and it's time again to go.

NOTE:

"Little Gidding," from *The Four Quartets,* T. S. Eliot.

Vitello Scottato con Pomodoro Verde in Olio Extravergine d'Oliva ed Erbette Aromatiche

STEAK WITH OLIVES, HERBED GREEN TOMATOES, AND PICKLED RED ONIONS, SERVES 4

Silvia Baracchi, starred Michelin chef, has a genius for using local ingredients in stunning new ways. I have made this with veal chops and with filet mignon. All good.

4 cups kalamata olives, pitted and coarsely chopped

4 boneless rib steaks, cut 1 ½ inches thick

Extra-virgin olive oil, *QB*

Sea salt and freshly ground pepper, *QB*

3 green tomatoes, cut into 1-inch wedges

3 cloves garlic, slivered

2 to 3 tablespoons freshly chopped herbs of your choice: parsley, basil, rosemary, thyme, oregano

Pickled red onions (recipe follows)

Preheat the oven to 175°F.

Spread the olives on a baking sheet lined with parchment paper. Bake them for at least 4 hours or overnight, until they are dried out but not burned. Let cool, then transfer to a blender or food processor and pulse until coarsely ground.

Trim excess fat from around the steaks. Brush lightly with olive oil. Season the meat lightly with salt and generously with pepper. Press the ground olives onto both sides of the steak to coat completely. Wrap in waxed paper and refrigerate for 2 to 8 hours. Let stand at room temperature for 1 to 2 hours before cooking.

In a bowl, toss the green tomato wedges with ¼ teaspoon salt and a generous grind of pepper, the garlic, herbs, and 2 tablespoons olive oil.

Preheat the oven to 450°F.

Line a heavy skillet (preferably cast iron) with parchment paper. Pour in 3 tablespoons olive oil and set over medium-high heat until hot. Add the steaks and sauté for 1¼ to 2 minutes on each side until nicely browned. Transfer to the oven. Roast for 5 to 8 minutes, until the meat is rare to medium-rare. Remove to a cutting board and let rest for 5 minutes. Do not tent.

While the steak roasts, heat 2 tablespoons olive oil in a medium skillet. Add the green tomatoes, their juices, the garlic, and the herbs. Sauté over medium-high heat until they are softened but still hold their shape, 3 to 5 minutes.

To serve, cut the steak against the grain into thick slices. Arrange on plates with alternating layers of the sautéed green tomatoes and pickled red onions.

PICKLED RED ONIONS

¼ cup white wine vinegar

2 tablespoons sugar

2 teaspoons coarse salt

1 teaspoon black peppercorns

3 whole cloves

1 bay leaf

2 medium-size red onions, thickly sliced

In a medium-size saucepan, combine 4 cups water with the vinegar, sugar, and salt. Bring to a boil, stirring to dissolve the sugar. Add the peppercorns, cloves, and bay leaf. Reduce the heat and simmer for 5 minutes.

Add the red onion slices and simmer for about 3 minutes, until the onions are just softened but still hold their shape. Transfer the onions to a glass container. Let the brine cool slightly, then pour over the onions. Marinate for at least 30 minutes before using. If you have extra, let cool. Refrigerate for up to 5 days.

Il Falconiere, Cortona, Toscana

ACKNOWLEDGMENTS

This book belongs to Edward Mayes, my husband, as much as it belongs to me. A great Italian driver, he took us on many journeys into the heart of Italy, always with a sense of adventure. Extensive wine research, endless reservations, early trains, translations of obscure texts, and so much more—he was on it. He's the consummate traveler; I'm in luck to take to the road with him. We were also lucky to have on some of our most fun trips grandson William Mayes King, age fifteen, then sixteen. Expert at directions and playlists and full of curiosity about every stop, he added sunlight and joy. Thanks to my daughter Ashley King and Peter Leousis, his parents, for allowing us to take him away for so long, and thanks also for the grand welcome home dinners.

I met hundreds of people along the way, too many to list, but they endure in my memory of each place. I'd like to thank especially the chefs who shared recipes so generously. Their names are in the book. Two kitchen geniuses, Susan Wyler in the USA and Gilda Di Vizio in Cortona, helped enormously with the testing. All fun! Charlie Conrad, Todd Alden, Sheryl Turping, Kip Keenan, Ondine Cohane, Steven Rothfeld, Robert Draper, Fulvio Di Rosa, and Aurora Patrito gave me great tips, and Coco and Jim Pante and Susie and Rowan Russell tasted and commented. It's a privilege to be able to share the innovative recipes from some of our favorite restaurants. As always, Silvia and Riccardo Barrachi, owners of Il Falconiere, cooked, poured, and cheered this project along. And *mille grazie* to Giorgio Zappini.

And speaking of luck, Peter Ginsberg has been my superb agent since *Under the Tuscan Sun*. I depend on his humor as much as his sound advice.

I'm fortunate to work with the brilliant team at the Crown Publishing Group, especially Rachel Rokicki, director of publicity. Elina Nudelman and Elena Giavaldi, thank you both for the design, and Melissa Esner for good outreach ideas and tech help. Copyediting this book must have been tough, with all the facts to verify, variant spellings, italics, on and on. This person is anonymous but a big thanks goes out to you; thank you to Cindy Berman for keeping everything on track. I'm grateful to Maya Mavjee and Molly Stern for their continuing support of my work. *Sopratutto,* above all, my gratitude to Claire Potter, my editor. She lavished attention on every page, with astute queries and perceptive comments. She is a delight to work with start to finish. I'm glad this book sent her off traveling to Italy.

RECIPE INDEX

Index

Under the Tuscan Sun was Frances Mayes's first book about Italy. Previously, she published six books of poetry and a popular college textbook on reading and writing poetry. Her Italian memoirs *Bella Tuscany* and *Every Day in Tuscany* followed *Under the Tuscan Sun*, along with *In Tuscany, Bringing Tuscany Home,* and *The Tuscan Sun Cookbook.* She has also written the travel narrative *A Year in the World,* the novel *Swan,* and a southern memoir, *Under Magnolia.* Her most recent novel, *Women in Sunlight,* takes place in Italy.

Frances and her poet husband, Edward Mayes, live at Bramasole in Cortona, Tuscany, where it all began, and on a farm outside Hillsborough, North Carolina.